PARISH CHURCHES OF LONDON

Parish Churches of London

Basil F L Clarke

B T BATSFORD LTD   LONDON

First Published 1966

© Basil F L Clarke 1966

Made and printed in Great Britain by
William Clowes and Sons Ltd London and Beccles
for the Publishers B T BATSFORD LTD
4 Fitzhardinge Street London W1

PREFACE

This book about the churches of London is primarily intended to be a work of reference. I have tried to mention every church, and this inevitably has meant including a good deal that is of no particular interest; at times I have been tempted to leave out less interesting churches, but as I wanted to give a complete picture I have resisted the temptation. Some churches are clearly worthy of praise, and some are, by any standards, unremarkable. Of the rest, I would hesitate to say which are worth visiting. I have always visited everything that I could, and have found interest everywhere. At one time I had a guilty conscience—some churches, I thought, *ought* not to be enjoyed: but since then taste has widened, and if one takes an interest in churches of any date, one is not regarded as odd or precious. Though not everything is admirable, anything *may* be, and it is unwise to assume beforehand that a church will be good or bad because of its date or type.

And so I have put in everything: people who visit churches must decide for themselves what they think about them. I could have included a great deal more about the atmosphere if I had the courage or the room. For example, I wrote of one church in my notebook: 'It is stuffed with pews, very low, silent, and rather sad. It does not give the impression of being much of a place of pilgrimage. We were very surprised that we got in at all—and we should not have done, if the man who does the garden had not had a day off from work, and been there; and introduced us to the cleaner, who happened to be in the hall.' There is a great deal of that kind of thing; and it could be supplemented with recollections of encounters with clergymen, and of attendances at Mattins in some of the more forbidding South London churches in the 1920s. It might make the book more readable—but it would also make it much too long. Perhaps those (if there are any) who are inspired to follow my footsteps may have similar experiences themselves: but perhaps by then everything will have altered and they will get an entirely different impression of the churches.

It is always important to know what was said about churches at the time when they were built. They ought not to be judged—though they often are—by standards that were not the standards of the people who built them. To know what was in their minds, it is necessary to read what they wrote, and I have tried to remember this without giving too many quotations. I have, however, allowed myself to quote occasionally from the *Ecclesiologist*. The Ecclesiological Society in its London period had a distinguished membership, and was neither mediaevalist nor romantic in its ideas about church-building. The ecclesiologists naturally enough had their own views about how a church ought to be built and arranged, but they were both flexible and surprisingly sensible. If some of them did begin in a Puginesque dream, they soon wakened out of it. They talked and wrote about all the problems which we in the twentieth century discuss as though no one had ever before thought about them; and they were, in general, very severe critics of the churches being built at the time. It is always interesting to see the churches as they looked when new, through the eyes of those who saw them first: and the *Ecclesiologist* helps us to do this for the exciting period between the middle '40s and the middle '60s of the nineteenth century.

Historical associations deserve to be mentioned, though there is room only for a very few: there are so many in the City that most have had to be omitted; details about them may be found in many other books.

I have always been interested in the clerical personalities of the nineteenth century, and would like to have said more about them, but have only mentioned them when they had a direct connection with the building or character of a particular church.

I have dealt only with parish churches: this has meant excluding, at one end of the scale, St Paul's, Southwark Cathedral and the Temple Church; and, at the other, the mission churches and dual-purpose buildings. But it would not be possible to exclude those of the City churches that once had parishes, but have them no longer. And there are a few others that have lost their parishes, and have become chapels of ease. I have also, rather unreasonably, included a few buildings of parish-church size that have been chapels of ease from the beginning. Demolished churches are not included, but churches that are used for worship no longer are mentioned, though not at length.

'London' is taken to mean those parts of the dioceses of London and Southwark which lie within the old London boroughs. But I have classified the churches—with one or two exceptions—not by boroughs, but by the pre-eighteenth-century parishes. This often comes to the same thing; but in some cases several old parishes were included in one borough.

I have been into very nearly every church: I can only think of about four or five into which I have never penetrated. But I admit that in some cases the visit has not been as recent as I would have liked. Fewer churches are kept open now than 40 years ago, when I was first visiting them. The story is usually the same—all-too-probable vandalism and no verger in attendance. This makes a visit to the vicarage necessary; but if no one is in, or if the vicar has taken the keys away in his pocket, what can be done? Some vicars—and this is no doubt to their credit—seem always to be out; so I may have missed some alterations made in the last few years.

My thanks are due to E. P. Hyslop, with whom I have visited about 1,250 churches, including a considerable number in London: he has constantly supplied me with books, and has shared many discoveries with me. Also to R. H. Harrison and G. Cobb, who know all about the City, for reading my notes, correcting some mistakes, and suggesting additions; and to G. L. Barnes, who can answer most questions on London churches in general, for answering many of mine, and for telling me a great many things that I did not know. Also for giving very generous help with the illustrations: he has made available his unique collection of London photographs, and has taken many more for the purposes of the book. Many assistants at libraries and record offices, whose names I do not know, have been patient and helpful.

I say again, a great deal has been left out: the book would become intolerably long if everything were to be included. If anything that has been put in is wrong—as I am sure it must be—I should be glad to know about it.

BASIL F L CLARKE

CONTENTS

THE ILLUSTRATIONS

ACKNOWLEDGMENT

The Author and Publishers would particularly like to thank G. L. Barnes for the majority of the photographs which appear in this book. Other photographs were taken by:

A. F. Kersting, F.R.P.S., figures 1, 4, 14, 18, 20, 24, 29–31, 33, 95–6, 99, 103, 106, 121–2, 135–42, 146, 148, 155–6, 161, 165, 186, 189, and 190.

The National Buildings Record (photographer G. L. Barnes), figure 22.

Figure 6 is from the Publisher's collection.

INTRODUCTION

T. Francis Bumpus began his book on *Ancient London Churches* with the words: 'No ecclesiologist needs repine whose lot is cast in London. To the student, or to him who takes it up as a pleasant relaxation, the ecclesiastical architecture of the Metropolis, whether it be looked at from its Mediaeval, Revived Classical or Modern Gothic side, affords a field for research as fascinating as it is well-nigh inexhaustible in interest.'

That is undoubtedly true, and there must be many who are grateful to Bumpus for pointing it out. His own two volumes—*Ancient* and *Modern*—are gossipy, and not very well written: many of his better passages are borrowed from other people's works without acknowledgment. But he is full of enthusiasm, and the fact that he was old enough to have met some of the Great Victorians makes him very interesting to the twentieth-century ecclesiologist. How pleasant it would have been to meet Mr Bumpus.

He must have gone everywhere. 'There are districts and suburbs in London', wrote C. L. Eastlake in the *History of the Gothic Revival* (1872), 'in which if a new building is raised it stands no more chance of being visited by people of taste than if it had been erected in Kamschatka. What amateur or *dilettante* would even think of exploring such neighbourhoods as Shoreditch, Hoxton, and Plaistow in search of architectural beauty?' However, Eastlake himself did so: at any rate he braved the terrors of the slums to visit the East End churches of James Brooks. But Bumpus did more: without calling attention to his own heroism, he penetrated into every poor district, and into every shabby-genteel area, and enjoyed every moment of it. To find a church was enough compensation for any inconveniences—and after all he probably had very few: by his time, the poor had lost the habit of throwing bricks, or dead cats, at strangers, and he would have come back with nothing worse than muddy boots. There must have been many church-hunters who were inspired by Bumpus to go out and follow in his steps. I was one of them; and it has been most rewarding.

Outside the City, there are the eighteenth-century churches, solid and serene, in tidied-up churchyards, where old men doze on the benches.

And there are the thin, cheap, brick churches of the 1830s and early '40s, grimy outside, but usually brightened up within. Their interiors are a palimpsest of changing taste: the oak choirstalls and carved reredos of the '80s: the Mary-blue side altar of the 1920s: and then the redecoration—already suffering from damp—of the 1950s, and the new glass in the east window paid for by 'War damage'.

And the Middle-Pointed churches of the '50s, with ragstone walls and Bath stone dressings, standing, surrounded by laurels, in the middle of squares: rather stuffy inside, with shiny seats, and a large quantity of glass by various firms.

I

And the big, red brick churches in what were once slums, with a long, unbroken line of slated roof. A low, windowless passage-aisle rises from the pavement, and there is a clerestory of tall lancets, with a few panes of glass broken. Here are Noyes Lewis stations of the cross, and the high altar is baroque, of the period of the first Anglo-Catholic Congress.

And the frankly ugly French Gothic churches by, say, Newman and Billing, or Habershon and Brock, which may be either very High or very Low.

The churches in certain districts have a character of their own. Islington is Evangelical. The key has always to be sought, and entrance effected through the vestry: the main doors do not look as though they open very easily.

Most of the Kensington churches have an atmosphere of gentility, and visitors are obviously expected. South London churches have made a determined effort to brighten themselves up, and tend towards Parish Communion.

In all directions, there are the outer suburbs, which are always interesting to explore. How pleasant they must have been to live in when they were first built. Even Mr Pooter, who lived at Holloway, could go for a Sunday afternoon walk through the cornfields; and Eliza's husband, who lived further out, had the countryside at his door. Many of the late Victorian or Edwardian streets are still attractive; but they must have been more so when the dusty road, which has now been flattened down, covered with tarmac, and joined up with hundreds of miles of other roads, petered out at the end of the houses and became a field path.

There were, of course, less attractive suburbs, with a poorer kind of house; but they too had the advantage of being near the country.

In the middle of these new developments a church was always built. It might have to be, to begin with, an iron building; but before long the chancel, vestries, and a bay or two of the nave of a large permanent church, usually of brick, began to arise. The west end was often left incomplete, and patched up with wood or corrugated iron: it was always assumed that, before many years, enough money would have been collected to complete the nave and aisles, and to build the front. The fittings were generally not of a permanent kind: the seats and pulpit were temporary, and there were only hangings behind the altar in the place where the large carved and gilded reredos would one day stand. The font was often a present from another church.

But how often the hopes of the builders remained unfulfilled. The west end was never built, the unworthy pulpit and font remain, and only one or two of the aisle windows have been filled with stained glass—not according to the scheme which Kempe planned for the whole church, but at random, with glass by some unheard-of firm.

If it happens that the church has been completed—except for the tower—we know what we shall find: nave and aisles, and a baptistery at the west end, flanked by porches, one of which is never used. There will also be a doorway towards the east of one of the aisles, which is more likely to be unlocked on a weekday than those at the west. The chancel has vestries on one side, and an organ chamber, arranged transeptally, on the other. Here, too, are several unused doors. The east end often faces a rather untidy piece of ground, enclosed by a privet hedge: it is worth exploring, as the foundation stone is usually there, with the date, and the names of the architect and contractor.

Certainly no ecclesiologist, unless he is one of the dwindling number who can find no interest in anything but Early English, Decorated and Perpendicular, will repine in London. There are not many ancient churches, and the proportion of fine Victorian buildings may be smaller than it is in some parts of the North. But there is always variety, and there are very few districts in which it is not possible to find a church that is interesting, or odd, or satisfying.

*   *   *

Some of these churches were built by the generosity of individuals—but not very many. London was not without its benefactors: the City produced many of them, and the City churches profited from their gifts. But most of the churches had to be built for new districts which had grown up out of nothing, in which there was no one who could help much. So they were usually provided by a succession of concerted efforts. Some were national, others were diocesan. Some might be called parochial—but this needs to be explained. The old system of raising money by rates, levied by the vestry, was adequate for keeping a parish church in repair—always provided that the rate could be collected. But it was difficult to make it work in the new, poor districts; and it could not be stretched to make it cover the building of the new churches that were required. The only thing that could be done was to form a voluntary local association for raising funds, apart from the church rate. Church rates, anyhow, were abolished in 1868, and after that, all parochial efforts at raising money had to be voluntary.

As these efforts will often have to be referred to, it will be as well to give, at this point, a short account of some of them.

The Fifty New Churches Act

The first large-scale attempt to provide churches for the people of London was the Act of 1711, for the building of Fifty New Churches in the Cities of London and Westminster, or the Suburbs thereof. The committee appointed by the House of Commons to consider the matter had calculated that, if 50 could be provided, the average population of the suburban parishes would be reduced to 4,750.

In the event, the number of churches built was very much less than 50. St Alphege, Greenwich, and St Mary Woolnoth in the City, were rebuilt. The tower of St Michael's, Cornhill, was added. And ten new churches were built: St George's, Hanover Square,

Christchurch, Spitalfields, St George's in the East, St Anne's, Limehouse, St Mary le Strand, St John's, Westminster, St George's, Bloomsbury, St Paul's, Deptford, St John's, Horsleydown, and St Luke's, Old Street. Later, the churches of Woolwich and Gravesend were rebuilt.

Three of these were bombed. St George's in the East has been repaired, though not as it was. St John's, Westminster, is to be kept, but not used for worship. St John's, Horsleydown, is a fragmentary ruin. St Luke's, Old Street, has been stated to be dangerous, and has been dismantled.

The rest of the churches remain, and most of them (not Woolwich and Gravesend, which are ordinary) are at last appreciated as they deserve to be.

The Church Building Act, 1818

This Act authorised the grant of a million pounds for church building in England and Wales. The needs of London figure largely in the lists that were made at the time of people for whom there was no room in the existing churches.

The commissioners who were appointed under the Act are sometimes referred to as the Church Commissioners. This would not originally have been liable to misunderstanding, but since the Ecclesiastical Commissioners adopted the title for themselves, it has become misleading.

Their activities have, until recently, been found fault with by most of the writers on the subject. They have written from the Victorian point of view, regarding church building as something to be done to the glory of God, and involving personal self-denial: the Commissioners have been represented as cheese-paring and hard-hearted men, whose aim was simply to provide as many sittings as they could for as small a sum as possible. In fact, they were keen Churchmen, and did their work conscientiously. To act as agents of Parliament did not seem discreditable to them, as it did to later nineteenth-century churchmen, irritated by controversies about doctrine and ritual, in which Parliament always took the wrong side. To the older type of High Churchman, it would seem the obvious thing.

Anyhow, they did what they were appointed to do, and the results of their work were more satisfactory than those of the 1711 Act—as regards the quantity of their churches, if not their quality. In the next ten years, 38 churches were consecrated in the Diocese of London.

A second grant, of half a million, was made in 1824. During the second stage, which lasted for many years, smaller grants were made to a larger number of churches, and the Commission became less of an agency for building churches, and more of an organisation for helping to build them. The term Commissioners' Churches is used for the churches originally built under the Act.

Bishop Blomfield and the Metropolis Churches Fund

The parliamentary grants had helped the Church to catch up with its church building. But it was realised that there would be no more help from the nation, and that in the future the money would have to be raised by the Church people themselves. 'Accordingly in London itself, our prelates are now obliged, in a nobler cause than Peter the Hermit's, to raise the banner of the cross—the cross of personal self-denial.' So wrote the *British Critic*. The reference is to Charles James Blomfield, who was appointed Bishop of London in 1828.

He soon took in hand the provision of new churches. In his charge of 1834 he mentioned ten parishes which together contained a population of 353,460. In these parishes there were 18 churches and chapels, served by 24 incumbents and curates: the average was not quite one church or chapel for every 19,000 souls, and one clergyman for every 14,000.

In 1836 he proposed the formation of the Metropolis New Churches Fund, for the building of 50 new churches. It was 'a work of prudence no less than charity', and its object was to 'reclaim hundreds of thousands of the poor from practical heathenism, and to give increased efficiency and therefore stability to the Church'. A meeting was called, and the cause was urged on property-owners, the City companies, merchants, bankers, and tradesmen. The bishop was disappointed at the result of the appeal; but by the end of the year £100,000 had been subscribed, and further sums had been promised.

In the eight years from the opening of the appeal, arrangements had been made for the erection of all the proposed new churches. But although the committee was able to give help for some time longer, and the total of churches built, or helped, was 78, the contributions fell off. In 1848 the committee said that their resources were exhausted. In 1853 they said that they had received only £18,000 in four years, of which £14,500 was from four individuals. There were only three annual subscribers.

In that year a pamphlet was issued—*Remarks on the Present State of the Metropolis Churches Fund*, by a Layman. It proposed the formation of a diocesan society—which was inaugurated in May 1854 as the London Church Building Society. Once again, the subscriptions were disappointing, but the society 'laboured honestly, heartily, and effectually to fulfil its appointed task'. Its final report was issued in 1864.

Bishop Tait and the Bishop of London's Fund

When Blomfield resigned in 1856, he had consecrated nearly 200 churches. He was succeeded by A. C. Tait, who continued his predecessor's efforts.

In 1858 the Committee of the House of Lords on Spiritual Destitution published a report, entitled *Report from the Select Committee of the House of Lords appointed to enquire into the Deficiency of Means of Spiritual Instruction and Places of Divine Worship in the Metropolis* (etc.) *and to report thereon to the House, together with the proceedings of the Committee, Minutes of Evidence and Appendix*. It said that 'Middlesex, the county which may be considered as the central seat of the civilisation, the enterprise, the wealth and power, as well as the government of this great empire, is actually the very lowest of all the counties of England in the provision made for divine worship by all denominations'. Examples were given—e.g., Shoreditch, Stepney, Clerkenwell, and Haggerston.

In his charge of November 1862 Tait referred to the difficulty of keeping pace with the growing population.

Canon Girdlestone wrote to the bishop saying that a great proportion of the property in London was held by non-resident landlords, and that a list should be made of such men, and application made to them. If this were done, the amount raised by Blomfield for church building might be doubled in a year. Tait referred the letter to a committee of the Diocesan Church Building Society, who resolved that the appeal should be made. On 29 April 1863 a meeting was held at London House, at the bishop's invitation. He proposed to raise a Bishop of London's Fund of half a million pounds: the meeting, carried away with enthusiasm, amended this to a million, to be collected in ten years. Tait himself subscribed £2,000.

By 1864 over £100,000 had been promised, including £3,000 from the Queen. Before the end of 1867, 28 churches helped by the fund had been consecrated; and of 13 more, four had been consecrated, and nine were in process of erection. The Fund did not itself undertake building, but acted as an auxiliary, providing grants which seldom exceeded one-quarter of the estimated cost. As much as possible had to be subscribed locally.

The report of 1868 mentioned three points: the large number of laymen who had taken part; the help given by the clergy by appeals from the pulpit; and the help given by local associations in various parts of the Diocese.

Local Church Building Associations

The St Pancras Church Extension Fund

A Church Trustees Act was passed in 1816, appointing a board with power to raise rates for building a new parish church and a chapel of ease. In 1842, as there was opposition to church rates, the trustees invited the parishioners to co-operate, and began the St Pancras Church Building Fund for the collection of voluntary contributions. The response was not very encouraging. In 1846 the vicar, Dr Moore, died, and was succeeded by Canon Dale, afterwards Dean of Rochester. He revived the scheme, enlarged its scope, and changed its name to the St Pancras Church Extension Fund. Many churches were built during his incumbency. He was succeeded by Canon Champneys. By 1863 money was running short, and in 1865 the St Pancras Fund was amalgamated with the Bishop of London's Fund.

The Haggerston Church Scheme

The schemes so far mentioned were the result of revived life in the Church of England. Even the Church Building Act, in spite of its official character, was carried out by keen churchmen. But what was missing so far was a definite inspiration by the ideals of the Oxford Movement, and of the Cambridge ecclesiologists. Blomfield's churchmanship was of an old-fashioned kind, and he had no sympathy with the new movements. In 1842 he directed his clergy to wear the surplice in the pulpit, but then changed his mind. And in 1850 he sternly rebuked the clergymen who 'thought themselves at liberty to imitate, as nearly as it is possible, the forms and ceremonies of the Church of Rome'. Tait spent a great deal of his time in trying to put down Ritualism. Both these bishops had a sincere desire to get people to come to church: but the kind of services to which they wanted to attract the people—and especially the working people—cannot have been very interesting.

But the Haggerston scheme was an attempt to do something different. There had been quite enough churches built to contain as many sittings as possible, in which two Sunday services were conducted in a harmless but dull way. What was wanted was churches obviously built for Catholic worship, correctly arranged according to the rubrics, with room for kneeling rather than sitting: grand and solemn churches, in which the altar would be the most important thing.

The scheme was begun by the Rev Thomas Simpson Evans, vicar of Shoreditch, with the help of the Rev John Ross, vicar of St Mary's, Haggerston. Richard Foster and Robert Brett, of Stoke Newington, were drawn into it; and Brett was particularly active. He had already been the chief promoter of St Matthias', Stoke Newington, and had helped to save St Augustine's, Canterbury, for the Church. There were two conditions on which he would support a church building scheme: a new church must be free and open, and the Prayer Book system of worship must be completely carried out in it. The Haggerston scheme was most satisfactory. Brett gave the profits from the sale of his devotional books, and also contributions sent by his readers as thank-offerings. He had several friends among the wealthy London merchants, whom he persuaded to give subscriptions.

The new churches were St Saviour's, Hoxton, St Michael's, Shoreditch, St Augustine's, Haggerston, St Columba's, Haggerston, St Chad's, Haggerston, and St Stephen's, Haggerston. He lived to see them all built, and given parishes of their own. The patronage was vested in trustees for 40 years: after that, it would revert to the bishop. There were some good churchmen who thought this rather risky: but Brett said that, by then, the Catholic movement should have made such progress in the Church of England that bishops could be trusted to appoint sound High Churchmen. If it had not, it would not be worth while, by that time, to try to further it.

Other local efforts were the *Westminster Spiritual Aid Fund*, founded in 1846 to provide additional clergy and schools in the parishes of St Margaret and St John: and the *Islington Church Extension Society*, begun about 1855.

South London: The Southwark Fund

London south of the Thames was formerly in the Diocese of Winchester. It was transferred to Rochester in 1877, and the new Diocese of Southwark was formed in 1905.

It was a great problem to Bishop Sumner of Winchester, in whose time the spaces between the old villages were being rapidly filled up, mostly with poor property. On 7 June 1845 a meeting of clergy and laity was held at Winchester House, and the bishop gave some statistics. The Southwark Fund for Schools and Churches was begun, and after two years its committee reported the formation of five new districts in the parishes of Lambeth and Bermondsey, towards which—except for one church built immediately before the formation of the Society—grants had been made. Sites had been obtained for three other churches.

In the next 20 years, 25 new churches were built, some proprietary chapels were consecrated and given districts, and schools and parsonages were also built.

The South London Church Extension Fund

This was begun in 1865: its name was afterwards changed to The Bishop of Winchester's South London Fund. £20,000 was raised under Sumner's presidency.

The Ten Churches Fund

This was opened early in 1882, by Bishop Thorold. A wealthy layman, Francis Peek, of Peek, Frean and Co, had offered to build a church at his own cost if others would first build nine. Another layman then offered £2,000, and 'the Bishop marked the rising tide and at once floated upon it his Ten Churches Fund'. By Advent 1883, 11 churches had been either completed or begun. Peek's own church was St Clement's, East Dulwich.

The motive of all this was excellent, and the zeal of the church builders was most commendable. But was the result really satisfactory? The answer No was very soon given, with some emphasis, by thoughtful people.

In 1861 there were strong criticisms in the *Christian Remembrancer* (December 1861, vol xlii, pp 472f). Bishop Blomfield had tried to solve the problem by what he thought was common sense. If a church holds 1,000, and there are so many thousand people in London without church accommodation, how many churches will be wanted? But this was too simple. It was impossible to get either the men, or the churches, or the money. The bishop had lived to discover this. But if he could not do everything, he would do something, and so the Bethnal Green churches were built, and other cheap churches were put up in the suburbs. At first there had been some success. The first incumbents had often been men of energy, and sometimes of means. But they could not keep things going for long.

'And so the great scheme of Church extension in London languished, and before the death of the late Bishop, it may be said to have passed out of official hands into those of private energy. Here and there a splendid church has been erected by private munificence, but the Metropolis Churches' Fund died of absolute inanition before its exemplary and excellent founder. Bishop Blomfield lived to see the rise and extinction of parochial sub-division on the old scale, and according to the old idea.'

The same thing was said by many others. Sir Robert Peel's Act had made it too easy to form new parishes, and far too many had been formed. Even if the churches had been completed, there was often a debt; and single-handed and poorly paid incumbents were struggling to keep things going. It would have been far wiser to have built a few churches, each with a staff of four or five.

A writer in the *Church Quarterly Review* (No xxxviii, January 1885, pp 336–356) reviewed the history of church building in East London. He wrote of the 'dangerous fascination of bricks and mortar'. Churches had been built, but in most cases parsonages had only followed after a long interval; and then they were often built in inconvenient places. Some had not been built yet. He concluded that 'in many districts in East London, taking the average attendance on Sunday, one church would suffice where there are now six'.

Even if all the new churches had been properly equipped and adequately staffed, they could not have been successful unless a certain number of people had been willing to go to them, and unless there had been people in the neighbourhood to go. But in fact the church building movement has been more disappointing in London than anywhere else. The reason has been that the population has been constantly on the move. Densely populated areas have become almost empty within a few years: one or two parishes, for instance, were practically obliterated by the railways. Neighbourhoods, sometimes for no obvious reason, have gone down, or have become inhabited almost entirely by Jews, or by foreigners who have had no desire to conform to the Church of England. Slums have been cleared, and the people moved to new areas further out, so that churches have become useless, and the building programme has had to be begun all over again.

No one could foresee what would happen: there seemed, in the early nineteenth century, no reason why the people in the newly built streets should not settle down to become stable, church-going communities. And if the one thing that was needed to make them so was a church for them to go to, then let the church be built. But many of them were not, and never could be stable.

By the end of the century, the population of some of the London boroughs was beginning to fall. Finsbury, for instance, which had 153,000 inhabitants in 1861, had 124,000 in 1891. And some of the Blomfield churches were becoming really useless. They can never have been attractive. They had not the solid decencies of the normal Georgian church, nor the cheerful appearance of a Gothick one. And they had none of the scholarly devoutness of the ecclesiological churches. No one has ever been enthusiastic about a brick Norman church by Blore, and it is not likely that there will ever be a craze for such things. They were grim enough when they were first built: after 60 years the smoky atmosphere of Victorian London has made them really dirty; and they were becoming dilapidated as well. Some of them were ripe for demolition by the beginning of this century, and several more were not destined to reach their centenaries. (It is worth noting that the population of Finsbury, a typical dim and declining district, fell to 70,000 in 1931, and to 35,000 in 1951.)

Bethnal Green reached 130,000 in 1891, so that, though it was absurdly over-churched, there were still plenty of people to go to the churches that had been so generously provided. But by 1951 the population had fallen to 58,000.

One or two churches disappeared in the early years of the twentieth century. In the 1920s and '30s new estates were built on the edge of London, and people were removed from the inner boroughs. In 1923 the present code for parochial reorganisation was established by the Union of Benefices Measure, followed by the Union of Benefices (Amendment) Measure in 1936. The evacuation at the beginning of the 1939–45 War hastened the process of the dispersion of Londoners: some never came back. The bombing damaged indiscriminately both the wanted and the unwanted churches, those that were architecturally good, and those that were worthless.

After the War came the Pastoral Reorganisation Measure, in 1949, and the Union of Benefices (Disused Churches) Measure in the same year. The Reorganisation Areas Measures, between 1944 and 1954, dealt with the War-damaged districts.

Some churches have been rebuilt. But the opportunity has been taken of having a general reorganisation, with a weeding out of such churches as are thought to be unnecessary. This weeding out is still going on, and is done in what seems to be a very arbitrary manner. Churches may disappear almost overnight—certainly in the course of a week or two. Where—if anywhere—the fittings have been taken, no one seems to know. And memories are so short that it is possible to enquire about a recently demolished church, and to be answered only with, 'I can't say, I'm sure.'

No map of London can keep up to date in this matter, and all street plans are peppered with crosses or *Ch*'s which now lead the ecclesiologist to nothing but a gap, or to a new garage, or a block of flats.

It is quite certain that some of those that are mentioned in any book will have disappeared by the time the book is published.

CHURCHES NORTH OF THE RIVER

The City: Pre-Fire Churches

There were 109 parish churches in the City before the Great Fire of 1666. Most of them were destroyed: and of those that remained, several were rebuilt at a later date. Seven survive that are recognisably mediaeval. Two—St Sepulchre's and St Bartholomew the Less—have substantial ancient remains, though their general appearance inside hardly suggests it. One—St Catherine Cree—was rebuilt in the seventeenth century, some years before the Fire.

All Hallows by the Tower, Great Tower Street (11)

Underneath the church are the pavement of a Roman house, and three sides of the lower part of the walls of a room.

The church was probably founded by Erkenwald, Bishop of London from 675 to 678, and it was attached to the Abbey at Barking which he had founded and of which his sister Ethelburga was the first abbess. After the bombing a Saxon arch of Roman brick was discovered, and so were parts of the walls: the Saxon church was about 70 feet by 24, and was without aisles. There are also parts of two pre-Conquest crosses: one, found after the War damage, is dated about 1030–60, and the other, found under the floor in 1951, about 1000.

The church was enlarged in the late twelfth century: three bays of the arcades were of this date. The crypt, with its ribbed barrel vault, is fourteenth-century, and there was some fourteenth-century work in the chancel: the north-east respond remains. Otherwise, it was rebuilt in the middle of the fifteenth century.

The new tower was built in 1658–9 by Samuel Twyne, bricklayer: the interior was adorned after the Restoration, and during the eighteenth century, e.g., the altar piece, 1685, new pewing (faculty given November 1704), and the fine brass rails, 1750. In 1813 there was a repair by D. A. Alexander. The later nineteenth century treated the church kindly, and allowed it to keep its quiet, old-fashioned atmosphere. Three faculties were given: 3 June 1886: to remove the pews from the chancel, and substitute choir stalls; and to remove the royal arms from above the holy table and place them on the gallery; 12 December 1888: to alter the seating; and 6 September 1892: to alter and improve the parapets and roofs, and to rebuild the roof of the vestry room; to cut back the gallery; and to restore the end of the north aisle. The porch, and the room above, were built in 1884–95.

The Rev P. B. Clayton, the founder of Toc H, was appointed vicar in 1922, and he made the church the centre of his movement: the casket and the burning lamp are kept here.

In 1925 the undercroft was constructed: the altar came from the crusaders' church in the Castle of Athlit in the Holy Land.

The church was damaged on 8 December 1940, and on 29 December was largely destroyed, only the crypt and undercroft, the porch, and the walls of the tower and the aisles remaining. When the debris was cleared up much of the old material was taken away. The rebuilding—which was helped by gifts from all over the world—was designed by Seely and Paget, with pillars of Painswick stone, and reinforced concrete roofs. It does not attempt to be a restoration of the church as it was—nor is it in a particularly modern style. The foundation stone was laid on 19 July 1948, the north aisle was reopened on 14 July 1949, and the rededication was on 23 July 1957. A graceful, Scandinavian-looking spire has been added to the tower. The painting on the east wall is by Brian Thomas, and the glass in the north aisle by Reginald Bell. The font, of Gibraltar limestone, was made by a Sicilian prisoner of war.

Very little remains of the furnishing. The lectern has ironwork of 1613. The brass altar rails are a reconstruction, with a little of the original work. The beautiful font cover is of 1682, and there are three eighteenth-century sword rests. The pulpit came from St Swithin's, London Stone, which was pulled down after being damaged by bombs.

Monuments   Alderman John Croke, 1477, and his family—damaged in 1940, and restored by Cecil Thomas. Hieronymus Benalius, 1583. John Winder, 1699. Sarah, wife of Giles Lytcott, 1713, and Giles.

Several brasses, the most noteworthy being the Flemish brass of Andrew Evyngar, *c.* 1535, and his wife. Another, also early sixteenth-century, has a representation of the Resurrection.

Effigy of Alfred Henry Forster, a memorial of the First World War, by Cecil Thomas, 1926.

St Andrew Undershaft, Leadenhall Street (5)

The base of the tower and the staircase are fifteenth-century. The rest of the church was rebuilt from 1520 at the cost of Sir Stephen Jennings (Lord Mayor in 1508, died 1524) and of the parish: it was finished in 1532; the arms of those who contributed were placed in the aisle windows. The church is of the usual late Perpendicular plan: a rectangle, divided by arcades into nave and aisles, with no chancel arch, and a shallow sanctuary. The steeple was out of repair in 1669, but the parish was 'about repairing of it'. In 1704 Edward Strong junior, mason, Richard Jennings, carpenter, and John Smallwell, joiner, gave an estimate of £1,151, and a rate was levied to raise the money.

Although the pre-Reformation fittings had a very short life, the church was well cared for in the seventeenth and eighteenth centuries—as most of the City churches were. The font was made by Nicholas Stone in 1631; the pulpit is late seventeenth-century; the organ, by Renatus Harris, was put up in 1696. The rails, by Tijou, were installed in 1704 (they were removed in 1876, and replaced in this century). In the same year the church was newly wainscoted, pewed, and paved: there was another repair in 1723; in 1724 the East India Company gave 20 guineas towards beautifying the altar piece. In 1725–6 Henry Tombes, a parishioner, who had subscribed to the organ and altar piece, gilded the organ, and gave a picture to stand over the altar; the chancel roof was painted with a heavenly choir, and the walls with a rustic basement, Corinthian columns, and 'landscapes and architecture in the intercolumniations'. The Apostles were painted between the clerestory windows, and the miracles of Christ in the spandrels of the arcade. The east end also had 'a rich crimson curtain, fringed with gold, painted in grand folds, and with hovering angels, &c'. Altogether, the church was adorned in the grandest style of the late seventeenth and early eighteenth centuries.

In 1830 there was a repair. The tower was given pinnacles and an octagonal lantern; the clerestory windows, which had lost their mullions, were restored; the altar piece was removed, and a new Gothic reredos was erected.

A. W. Blomfield and Ewan Christian restored the church in 1875–6, and the eighteenth-century paintings were removed, except for those in the spandrels. The glass in the east window was removed to the west; it dates from the late seventeenth century, though nothing seems to be known about it: the figures are of Edward VI, Elizabeth I, James I, Charles I, and William III: it has been much restored, and a great deal of it is nineteenth-century. The new glass in the east window is by Heaton, Butler and Bayne.

In 1883 the upper part of the tower was reconstructed by T. Chatfield Clarke: the present pinnacles were built, and the turret was added at the north-west. The whitewash was removed from the paintings in the spandrels which were restored in 1956. The flat panelled roof was repaired in 1949–50.

Monuments   Sir Thomas Offley, Lord Mayor in 1556 (died 1582), by Gerrard Johnson. John Stow, the historian of London, 1605, by Nicholas Johnson. Sir Hugh Hamersley, Lord Mayor, 1636. Sir Christopher Clitheroe, Lord Mayor, 1642. Peter Vansittart, 1705.

14

St Bartholomew the Great, West Smithfield (1, 4)

The Priory and Hospital of St Bartholomew were founded by Rahere in the reign of Henry I. Stow says that the date was 1102. The *Liber fundationis ecclesiae et prioratus S Bartholomaei* says 1123, but goes on to say 'about the third year of Henry's reign', which would agree with Stow. The year 1123 was probably the date of the consecration of the eastern parts. A royal charter was given in 1133. The transepts, and the east end of the nave, were built later in the century, and the nave was completed in the thirteenth century.

Roger de Walden, Bishop of London 1405–6, built a chantry to the north-east of the choir, and about this time the clerestory and the Lady chapel were rebuilt. The apse was taken down (Parker thought that it had never been completed), and a straight wall was built across the chord of the apse. In 1409 Alexander V gave an indulgence to all who contributed to the repairs, and said that he had heard that John Watford—prior from 1404—had rebuilt the cloisters and the chapter house.

After the dissolution in 1539, the nave was pulled down, and the buildings were afterwards sold by the King to Sir Richard Rich: the church was to be a parish church for ever, and the void ground to the west—where the nave had stood—was to be a churchyard. But it soon became dilapidated, and in 1563 Bishop Grindal proposed to remove the lead roof, and to convert the refectory into a church: 'I assure you, without partialitie, if it were roofed up, it were farre more beautiful and conveniente than the other.' This was not done, and the church was repaired in 1622–8, when a new tower, of brick, was built on the one remaining bay of the south aisle of the nave, 'and very richly and fairly finished'.

The unwanted parts of the church were let off for various purposes, and by the end of the eighteenth century it was in a strange state of encroachment and debasement, though it was not completely neglected. In 1789 there was a repair under George Dance junior, and in 1791 another under Thomas Hardwick. In 1815 Hardwick again superintended work, and in 1836 the vestry decided on further repairs: the surveyor was John Blyth of Aldersgate Street. It was Blyth who took away the enormous classical altar piece and substituted a reredos of Norman arcading.

In 1855 it was suggested that the church be restored, and William Slater made plans, which were discussed in the following year. He proposed to remove the soil from the walls, lower the floor, repair the roof, and rebuild the apse. The fringe factory of Messrs Stanborough and Graves projected over the upper part, but their lease had expired, and it was hoped that it could be disposed of. A faculty was given on 23 August 1864, to lower the floor, open out the south transept, remove and reconstruct the west gallery, remove the earth from the walls, repair the stonework generally, and complete the apse with triforium, clerestory, and roofs. Work was begun under Slater and T. Hayter Lewis, and the church was reopened in 1866. The lower part of the apse was rebuilt, but the floor of the factory still extended over it, supported on two iron columns. Work was resumed under

Sir Aston Webb in 1884, and in the next two years the factory, with the land adjoining, including the Lady chapel, was bought, and the apse completely restored, at the cost of the Rev F. P. Phillips. The freehold of the blacksmith's forge in the ruined north transept was secured, and the church reroofed. Afterwards, when a new building was opened in 1889, the school was removed from the triforium. The consent of the Charity Commissioners was obtained for selling the house on the site of the north transept, next to the forge. A shallow south transept was built to take the place of the transept destroyed by fire in 1830.

In 1891 an appeal was made for funds to complete the restoration, by the building of a north transept with a room over, the repair of the west end and tower, the building of a west porch, the restoration of the vaulting to the south aisles and the building of vaulting in the north aisle, the repair of the north triforium, the building of a new vestry, and the restoration of the Lady chapel. This was all accomplished, the Lady chapel being completed in 1896. Restoration of the cloister was undertaken later. In the new work Bath stone was used internally and flints and Portland stone externally.

The interior is very impressive: big, dark, and solemn. There was, of course, no such gloom in the priory church—nor, indeed, in the truncated fragment of pre-restoration days, which was lit by two large windows at the east end, and one at the west, and no doubt adorned with whitewash. Rahere's work in the choir is simple Norman: circular pillars with scalloped capitals and an outer ring of billet moulding. The triforium openings are filled with four small arches and a solid tympanum. In one of the bays on the south is Prior Bolton's window—an oriel projecting into the church. Bolton was prior from 1506 to 1532.

Naturally, there are no old fittings in the church, although the fifteenth-century font has survived. A new high altar by Seely and Paget was erected in 1950, with cross and candlesticks by Omar Ramsden.

Monuments   The most important is that of Rahere, to the north of the sanctuary, *c.* 1500: a recumbent effigy under a canopy, with a shield-bearing angel at the east; at the back are three small openings to the ambulatory. Others are of Percival Smalpace, 1568, and Agnes, 1588. Sir Walter Mildmay (the founder of Emmanuel College, Cambridge), 1589, and Mary, 1576. Sir Robert Chamberlayne, 1615. Elizabeth Freshwater, 1617. Francis Anthony, 1623.

St Bartholomew the Less

The Chapel of St Bartholomew's Hospital, which also became a parish church after the dissolution. The old work is fifteenth-century. The church became dilapidated in the eighteenth century, and in 1789 George Dance junior removed the inside and constructed an octagon of wood within the walls. In 1823–5 Thomas Hardwick rebuilt the octagon in stone and iron, and it was later restored by P. C. Hardwick, who put tracery into the upper windows, and built a sanctuary 'in the style of the Lady Chapels in Normandy'. The church was reopened on 11 January 1951, after repair by Seely and Paget. The new windows are by Hugh Easton.

Monuments   William Markeby, 1439, and Alice (a brass). Sixteenth-century tomb, with a tablet to Elizabeth Freke, 1741, and John, 1756. Elizabeth wife of Sir Thomas Bodley. Mary Darken, 1773, and John Darken, 1784, both by J. Bingley.

St Ethelburga's, Bishopsgate (3)

This small, early fifteenth-century church is sandwiched between business premises, and until 1932 there were two shops in front of it. The west end is now fully revealed—not that there is much to see. It is of ragstone, finished horizontally with brick, and has an eighteenth-century turret. In 1724 the vestry ordered that the front of the church should be beautified, and the steeple weather-boarded. In 1775 the steeple was to be 'taken down as low as it is found necessary and rebuilt in such a manner as Mr Shirley the Surveyor and the Committee shall think proper'.

The church consists only of nave and chancel under one roof, and south aisle. In 1796 Joseph Patience and Bowman Brown, surveyors, recommended that a new roof should be erected, 'Which by being properly constructed will admit of the range of Gothic Columns and Arches in the body of the Church being taken away', but the work was not done. The roof was rebuilt by William Grellier about 1835, the columns and arches being spared. The picture of the interior in George Godwin's *Churches of London*, 1839, shows the south gallery, erected in 1629 'only for the daughters and maid servants of this parish to sit in': the altar piece of 1705, and the large, plain east window with seventeenth-century armorial glass.

There was a restoration by R. J. Withers in 1862 when the post-Reformation fittings were removed. The screen and organ gallery are by J. N. Comper, 1912. The font cover and sword rest came from St Swithin's, Cannon Street: the sixteenth-century Flemish painting of the healing of Bartimaeus came from St Dionis Backchurch. Windows, 1928, 1929, and 1930, by Leonard Walker, are in memory of Henry Hudson, who, with his companions, received Communion here before setting out on his travels. The window to the memory of W. F. Geikie Cobb, rector 1900–41, is also by Walker. Three panels of late seventeenth-century glass, with the arms of the City and the Mercers' Company, the Saddlers, and the Vintners, were restored to their place in 1951.

The mural at the east is by Hans Feibusch, 1962.

St Giles's, Cripplegate (8)

This was once the church of a very populous parish. The Commissioners for the Fifty New Churches Act proposed to build three churches in the parish. Only one was built—St Luke's, Old Street; but when St Bartholomew by the Exchange was pulled down, parts of it were used in the new church of St Bartholomew, Moor Lane, which was consecrated in 1840. By the end of the century, the population had almost disappeared, and St Bartholomew's was demolished.

Bomb-damage was particularly extensive in this area. The church suffered, though the tower, the walls, and the arcades remained: most of the surrounding buildings were destroyed, and for years there was very little around the church except for broken walls and cellars. Now the enormous blocks of the Barbican development are going up. The church was restored by W. Godfrey Allen.

It was rebuilt in 1390, burned in 1545, and restored afterwards. The top of the tower was raised, and cased in brick, in 1682–4 by John Bridges. The eighteenth century, as usual, did its share of repairing and beautifying—e.g. new pulpit, font, pews, altar piece, Communion table, and organ 1704–5; repairs 1764; in 1790–1 the roof was raised, and two additional bays added to the clerestory (which resulted in the curtailed appearance of the east end): east window glass by James Pearson.

A restoration was carried out in 1868–9: new roof and clerestory, new sanctuary arch, seats cut down, etc. In 1885–6 the south side was refaced. On 12 September 1888, a faculty was given to raise the chancel floor, enlarge the choir stalls, and erect new clergy desks and Communion table. In 1903 buildings against the south side were taken down, and the wall was repaired by F. S. Hammond.

Most of the eighteenth-century woodwork was allowed to remain, and the altar and altar piece, doorcases and some panelling, from St Bartholomew by the Exchange, were brought here when the church in Moor Lane was taken down. They perished, with the rest of the woodwork, in the raids.

John Milton was buried here in 1674: his bust was made by John Bacon in 1793.

The church has been used since the beginning of 1960 by the congregation of St Luke's, Old Street.

St Helen's, Bishopsgate (7)

This most interesting building is a double church, with two parallel parts—conventual on the north, and parochial on the south. A priory of Benedictine nuns was founded between 1204 and 1216 by William, son of William the goldsmith, and its church was built against the north side of St Helen's, which was reconstructed and enlarged rather later in the century. If Norman work remains in the south wall, it is not obvious. The south transept was added, and the nave was probably lengthened westward.

The chapels to the east of the transept—the Holy Ghost and Our Lady—were built according to the will of Adam Francis, Mayor in 1352–3 and 1353–4: the date is about 1374. Sir John Crosby, who died in 1475, left 500 marks for 'renewing and reforming' the church: the arcade between the two parts is of this date, except for one earlier arch, and the roofs were rebuilt. Some windows were inserted, but most of the present windows are later. There were repairs in 1631–3, when the south doorway was inserted. The turret was built in the early eighteenth century, and there were further repairs in 1710, 1722, 1786, and 1807: for the last, which cost £973, the surveyor was Chapman.

Restorations in the nineteenth century were done under J. F. Wadmore and A. Baker (1865–8), Edward I'anson (1874), and J. L. Pearson (1892–3). The faculty for the latter (5 December 1891) specified the following work: the repair of the walls; removing the outer modern roofs of the nave and north aisle, restoring the old roofs and covering them with lead, and rebuilding the parapets; providing new oak roofs on the chantry and eastern chapels; building new vestries on the south; lowering the floors of the nave and north aisle to their original level; repairing the whole church; improving the choir stalls, and erecting a chancel screen, sedilia, and reredos; and removing the dark-coloured grounds of the painted glass, and substituting glass of a silvery tone.

When the church of St Martin Outwich was taken down in 1874, several monuments and the Communion table and font, were brought here.

It will be convenient to deal with each part of the church separately. There are more monuments than in any other parish church in London and there is no room here for detailed descriptions.

The Parochial Church

The west part of the nave was divided off by a screen, 1744, with the organ loft above. This was taken down in 1868, and the organ was rebuilt in its present position; the case, however, was retained. The two doorcases date from the seventeenth-century repair, and are extremely fine in their different ways: the one at the west is more correct than that on the south. The pulpit is magnificent seventeenth-century work. The glass is by Gibbs.

In the chancel the screens, pavement, sedilia, altar and reredos are by Pearson. The fifteenth-century stalls came from the Nuns' choir, and there is seventeenth-century woodwork in the other choir seats. The most uncommon wooden sword rest dates from 1665. East window glass by Heaton, Butler, and Bayne. Between the chancel and the chapel of the Holy Ghost is the tomb of Sir John Crosby and Agnes his wife, with the arms of Crosby, the Grocers' Company, and the Staple of Paris. Opposite, on the north, is the tomb of Sir William Pickering, 1574. The heraldic glass in the east window of the Chapel of the Holy Ghost is connected with Sir John Crosby. There are several brasses in the transept.

Monuments   The Nave—Alderman Richard Staper, 1608. Sir John Spencer, 1609, a very fine monument, recoloured in 1950. Abigail Lawrence, 1682. Robert Dingley, 1741.

Monuments   The Chancel—Sir John de Oteswich and wife, early fifteenth-century. Rachel Chamberlain, 1687. Gervash Reresby, 1704. Alderman Walter Bernard, 1746. The transept contains other tablets, which are placed too high and are too dirty to be read with ease.

The Nuns' Church

In the north wall is a night staircase, and Easter sepulchre and squint, 1525. The font is 1632. A little ancient glass in two windows, and nineteenth-century glass by Heaton, Butler, and Bayne (the lancet), Gibbs, and Powell (the east window).

Monuments   Alderman Hugh Pemberton, 1500, and Katherine. Sir Andrew Judd, Lord Mayor, Citizen and Skinner, 1558. Sir William Pickering, 1574. Alderman William Bond, 1576. Sir Thomas Gresham, founder of the Royal Exchange, 1579. William Kirwin, 1594, and Magdalen (he was a mason, and the inscription refers to the buildings with which he adorned London). Alderman John Robinson, 1599, and Christian, 1592. Sir Julius Adalmare, alias Caesar, Master of the Rolls, etc., 1636, by Nicholas Stone: a deed is represented on the top, declaring, in Latin, that he will 'cheerfully pay the debt that he owes to nature'. Valentine Mortoft, who lived comfortably with two wives, 1641. Martin Bond, 1643, shown in his tent, with sentries outside. Francis Bancroft, 1727, whose body was kept embalmed in a large monument buried under the floor in 1827.

St Olave's, Hart Street

There is a thirteenth-century crypt under the church, but the building itself was practically all rebuilt in the fifteenth century, the work being attributed to Richard and Robert Cely. Most of the smaller pre-Fire City churches must have looked something like this. The vestry on the south was added in 1661. The top of the tower needed to be rebuilt in 1731, and 'Mr Townsend Surveyor . . . reported the Estimate of the Mason's Charge' for rebuilding in Portland or Bath stone. In fact, the rebuilding was done in brick, under John Widdows, and completed in 1732. The altar rails are seventeenth-century: the pulpit came from St Benet, Gracechurch Street. The panelling in the vestry, and some monuments, were brought from St Katherine Coleman. The galleries were taken down in 1853, and a new reredos, by Thomas Little, took the place of the classical altar piece. There were

1 St Bartholomew the Great: the restored cloister and the
seventeenth-century tower

2 St Sepulchre's: the
fifteenth-century tower

, St Ethelburga's, Bishops-
;ate: the simple Perpendicu-
ır front and eighteenth-
entury turret

4 St Bartholomew the Great: the twelfth-century church. The tomb of
Rahere is on the left

5 St Andrew Undershaft, mostly sixteenth-century

6 St Catherine Cree, 1628–30, a church of the Laudian revival

7 St Helen's, Bishopsgate: the west end, with its eighteenth-century turret

8 St Giles's, Cripplegate, once the church of a populous parish, isolated by bombing. Early Perpendicular, restored with seventeenth-century top to tower

repairs in 1863, by Scott, and a restoration in 1871 by Blomfield. The faculty (21 December 1870) mentioned the relaying of the floors, and the moving back of the front of the west gallery. Scott's font was given to St Olave's, Toronto, in 1937.

The church received four direct hits during the War, but was rebuilt by Ernest B. Glanfield: the contractors were Dove Brothers. A stone was laid by King Haakon of Norway on 15 June 1951, and a fragment from Nidaros Cathedral, Trondheim, was placed beside it. The figure of St Olave is by a Norwegian sculptor, Carl Schou. New glass is by A. E. Buss, made by Goddard and Gibbs. The church was rehallowed on 9 April 1954.

Monuments   Peter Coppon, 1582. James Deane, 1608. Paul Bayninge, 1616, and Andrew, 1610. Elizabeth Pepys, 1669. Sir John Mennes, 1670. Sir Andrew Riccard, with large standing figure, 1672. Samuel Pepys, 1703, designed by Blomfield, and erected in 1883.

St Sepulchre's, Newgate Street (2)

The church was 'newly re-edified' in 1450: Sir John Popham was a benefactor. Repairs were done between 1624 and 1634, including the rebuilding of the battlements and pinnacles. It was damaged by the Fire, but was found not to be past repair. About 1670–4 the church was restored, probably under Wren: the mason was Joshua Marshall, the carpenter was Hodgkins, and the plasterer was Blount. The walls were refaced, the old arcades cleared away, and new arcades built, with Doric columns on tall plinths, and round-headed arches. It was, of course, all refurnished. The organ, by Renatus Harris, was put up in 1677. The top of the tower was rebuilt in 1711–14: mason, Samuel Fulkes; carpenter, Richard Jennings. There was a repair in 1738. In 1789 round-headed windows were substituted for the surviving fifteenth-century ones, and a straight parapet took the place of the battlements. Round-headed arches were built under the fifteenth-century arches of the tower. A new roof and ceiling were provided in 1834: the architect was Clark.

In 1873–8 the porch and tower were repaired by W. P. Griffith, an architect who was also a scholarly antiquary. In 1879–80 Arthur Billing cleared away the pews and galleries, removed the eighteenth-century tower arches, and restored the pointed windows on the south side and at the ends of the aisles. A number of fragments of the pre-Fire church were discovered.

The tower, of ragstone, with its four pinnacles, is of very imposing outline, though its details are restored. The south porch has been completely refaced, but the inside, with vaulting in the lower part, is more or less unaltered.

The interior of the church is, as Hughson said, spacious and handsome, but less interesting than it might be. There is some woodwork—particularly the organ case which was moved from the west end in 1878, and placed in its present position in 1932. The font cover from Christchurch, Newgate Street, was rescued in 1940, and eventually brought here.

The church is the headquarters of the Royal School of Church Music, and the north chapel—St Stephen's—is the Musicians' chapel.

There are several windows by the A. K. Nicholson Studios.

St Catherine Cree, Leadenhall Street (6)

Cree Church or Christchurch: St Catherine's was in the precinct of the Priory of Holy Trinity, or Christchurch, Aldgate.

A pier from the old church remains at the west of the south aisle, and the lower part of the tower is early sixteenth-century. Otherwise, the church was rebuilt in 1628–30, and consecrated by Laud on 16 January 1630–1. At his trial—on 11 June 1644—Laud was accused of 'coming in a pompous manner' to consecrate this church, and St Giles in the Fields. He denied that he had thrown dust into the air, or 'used divers Curses'. He maintained he had followed the order of Bishop Andrewes, and not the Roman Pontifical: there is no reason to doubt this (even if it had been true, it would not have been a just cause for putting the Archbishop to death).

The church is well known as an example of the hybrid Gothic-Classic of the early seventeenth century. It is divided into nave and aisles by Corinthian pillars and round-headed arches, but the windows are late Perpendicular of the kind that seventeenth-century masons sometimes used, with the central light somewhat taller than the others (e.g. the tower of Goudhurst, Kent, and Berwick on Tweed church, by John Young). The east end, with its rose, recalls the east end of old St Paul's, and there is a flat Gothic vault of plaster. The designer is unknown. The organ, by Father Smith, was erected in 1686. A faculty was given on 26 October 1732 for replacing the seats, pulpit, and desk. In 1776 it was agreed to rebuild the 'turret': the top of the tower and the cupola date from this time. Later in the year, it was resolved that James Pearson should repair the glass in the 'great painted window'. There was a repair and beautification in 1805.

The obscure church of St James, Duke Place, was taken down in 1874, and some glass and monuments were removed here: in 1880 new glass took the place of the royal arms in the lower part of the east window: the lights are now blocked.

The post-War repair was undertaken by Marshall Sisson, and the church was rehallowed on 6 July 1962.

Monuments   Sir Nicholas Throkmorton, 1570. Samuel Thorp, 1794, by John Bacon.

The City: The Churches of Sir Christopher Wren

The first Act for the Rebuilding of London, passed in 1667 after the Great Fire, levied a tax on coals coming into the Port of London, to be used for certain purposes; but it made no provision for the rebuilding of St Paul's or of the City churches. A further Act of 1670 increased the tax, and made a proportion of it available for Church purposes. The Act provided for the rebuilding of 51 churches, and for the uniting of many parishes. Wren was the surveyor, with Robert Hooke, John Oliver, and Edward Woodroffe as colleagues.

The money from the coal was used only for the fabrics of the churches: the fittings, in almost every case, were supplied by the parishes. Wren was responsible for the designs (with one possible exception); but in the execution of them he must often have left a good deal to the craftsmen who built them. (I have followed the example of H. M. Colvin in naming them as fully as possible.) The fittings were not designed by Wren himself, but were left to the artificers whom the parishes employed. It is curious that in the nineteenth century the plasterwork, and the fat cherubim, were considered to be the peculiar characteristics of Wren's work, and if a new building had them, it was said to be in the Wren style. In fact Wren was responsible for the planning and the general design of the churches, and not for their adornment.

A start was made fairly quickly, and parishes able to find some money paid it into the fund. However, the income from the Coal Tax could not accumulate at once, and it was many years before some of the churches were begun: the parishes had to be content with their temporary tabernacles. Wren, in any case, was extremely busy, and the parishes had to attract his notice if they wanted attention.

For one reason or another several of the churches took some little time to complete: the steeples took longer still, not being necessary, as the churches were. When they did come the parishes must have been glad to get them: it was the steeples that gave each particular church its individuality, and it is of the steeple that we generally think, first of all, when we try to visualise a Wren church. They were certainly the work of Wren, or of his staff, and were designed with great care, being meant to be seen above the low roofs of the surrounding buildings. All Wren's towers obviously rise from the ground, even if they are embedded in one of the angles of the main building. But they do not begin to do much until they have risen above the roofs. A few of the less ambitious towers were, it is true, content to be simply square. Others had an outline given to them by a noteworthy parapet, or by pinnacles. But in most cases the tower is modulated into a turret or spire, or it has a picturesque and ingenious steeple placed on top of it. These were not designed to be seen from too close: it is difficult, in London, to stop and gaze up at anything immediately above you. But they could—and, to some extent, still can—be glimpsed, at an angle, either from further down the street or through openings between the buildings. And they all took their place in the more distant view of the City—from one of the hills, or from the other side of the river.

The steeples were designed in relation to the churches' positions in the City: and so were the churches themselves. Almost all the sites were constricted, and, more or less, surrounded by buildings: there were no island sites. (It has always been possible to walk round St Andrew's, Holborn, St Bride's, St Andrew by the Wardrobe, St Benet's, Paul's Wharf, and St Lawrence Jewry, but the passages are so narrow that it is not possible to stand back, and get a good view.) So Wren did not design the churches to be seen from all sides: there was no need to spend money on what could not be seen, and the architectural display was placed where it would be visible. St Mary at Hill, and St Peter's, Cornhill, have an east front that ranges with the street, and which has some adornment: the side walls are quite plain.

The sites also account for Wren's plans. A good deal has been written about the planning of the City churches, of Wren's initiative in working out something suitable for Anglican worship, and of his resource in devising ingenious shapes. The Liturgical Movement enthusiasts have commended him for designing churches without chancels, in which the people are near the altar, and there is no separation between them and the celebrant. There is something in all this: but the reason for it is that most of the pre-Fire churches were very small, and built on constricted sites, often of irregular shape. Wren had to use the old sites, and make the best of them. Usually they were, approximately, a rectangle—which was sometimes accepted simply as that, but often made the basis of something more interesting: Wren could think of many things to do with a rectangle. Sometimes it was so irregular that it suggested a geometrical figure of some kind: St Benet Fink, for instance, was ten-sided.

But when Wren had plenty of room, or when he designed an entirely new building— as St James's, Piccadilly, and St Anne's, Soho—he used an ordinary basilican plan—though the space was certainly used in a way that would not have occurred to the builders of the middle Ages, and which can be claimed as an original contribution to the solution of the problem of how to accommodate an Anglican congregation.

When the churches were rebuilt, there was a vigorous parish life in the City, and the churches were well used: at the end of the seventeenth century, and well into the eighteenth, a large number of them had two daily services. But in the second half of the eighteenth century the trek from the City began. Merchants and business men built themselves houses in such places as Islington or Camberwell, and the City began to be a place to work in, and not to live in. The parish life began to decline, and by the 1830s and '40s many of the churches were empty. Dickens's description, in *The Uncommercial Traveller*, of his church-going experiences in the City—the emptiness, the cold, the dust, and the smells—is exaggerated; but it is a good piece of reporting, and there must have been many churches in which the worship had declined to something like that.

The first comprehensive scheme for weeding out a number of churches was made in 1833, but was turned down by the Archbishop of Canterbury and the Bishop of London. In 1854 the Church Building Acts Amendment Bill—which applied to the whole country, not only to London—would have involved the demolition of several City churches. It was not passed: but in 1860 the Union of Benefices Act became law. This resulted in the demolition of a number of churches, and the use of the money made by the sale of the sites for the building of new churches in the suburbs. Nineteenth-century churchmen were practical in their outlook, and saw no point in maintaining churches often only a few yards from their neighbours. The rectors might live at Tunbridge Wells: the churches were locked all through the week: and on Sunday only about half a dozen people would go to them. But the endowments were large, and the sites were extremely valuable: would any-one respond to appeals for funds to build churches in the suburbs if the Church continued to maintain the useless and expensive City churches?

The obvious answer was, 'No: pull them down'. But it was not given by everyone.

The ecclesiologists replied that it was sacrilege to destroy anything that had been con-secrated to God. New churches must be built by self-denying gifts from churchmen, not by selling what our ancestors built, and making a profit on it. Certainly, they said, the City churches, as they are at present, are useless: but there is no need for them to be so. Let them rid themselves of their Bumble-ish atmosphere: take away their pews, brighten them up, and open their doors for services on weekdays—and no one will be able to find fault.

So some of the churches underwent 'restoration'. There was obviously an untrue suggestion about the word: the justification for restorations was that they did restore. Could it be called restoring when something that had been in the church from the begin-ning was taken away, and something substituted that never had been there? Obviously not. But there was this much to be said for it: that Sir Christopher Wren had expressed a dislike of pews, and wished that he had not had to provide them. It was possible to say that, by removing pews and substituting low benches, you were fulfilling Wren's real inten-tions. And he was thought of as a Christian architect. Living when he did, he had had to design in the Renaissance style as a general rule: but he did attempt Gothic at times. It was well known that he came of a High Church family. Was it not possible to alter his churches into what he would have designed if he had lived in the more enlightened nineteenth cen-tury?

The answer was thought to be Yes, and the attempt was made not only to remodel the churches, but also to use them for special services. In 1867 St Lawrence Jewry, for in-stance, was reseated, rearranged, and redecorated. And in the same year a series of services was held in connection with the Lambeth Conference, which aroused a quite extraordinary interest. But the keenest of churchmen realised that they would have to resign themselves to losing some of the churches: even with open seats, encaustic tiles, and glass by Clayton and Bell, they would not all be able to justify their existence.

In 1899 a commission appointed by the bishop suggested the removal of ten further churches: three were in fact destroyed. In 1919 another commission was appointed, which suggested that 19 should be demolished. There was much opposition, chiefly on architectural grounds, and the measure—which had been passed by the Church Assembly—was finally defeated in the Lords in 1926.

Most of the churches were in some degree injured by bombing in the second World War, and one or two of the worst damaged were allowed to disappear afterwards. The reorganisation scheme drastically reduced the number of parishes, and created a new kind of church—the Guild Church—the incumbents of which would have no parochial responsibilities, but would be free to do the work for which they were fitted. The Church of England has never had many posts for men with special gifts who are not particularly interested in general parish work: this scheme provided several. It is now in working order, and the churches that remain are safe for the future.

St Benet's, Paul's Wharf (15)

Built in 1667–83. The mason was Edward Strong, carpenter Israel Knowles, joiner William Cleer, plasterers Henry Doogood and John Grove. The exterior is of brick, with stone quoins, and some stone panels carved with festoons: the roof is hipped: the tower has a lead dome and a short lead spire.

The plan is more or less a square, plus a north aisle of three bays, and a west aisle of two, to the south of the tower. These aisles keep their galleries. The opposite walls, south and east, echo the columns with pilasters. The order is Corinthian. The east wall has two windows: the central compartment, somewhat narrower than the others, is windowless, and filled with the very fine altar piece. All the fittings remain—though the pews have been cut down—and the interior is highly satisfactory. It was repaired and beautified in 1836, and the organ was erected in 1837. There is a noble royal arms over the doorway. The church is used by a Welsh congregation.

Monuments   Sir Robert Wyseman, 1684, with a bust in relief. Stephen Brice, L.L.D., 1688. Mark and Alice Cottle, no date.

St Michael's, Cornhill (14)

The old tower was taken down in 1421, and the foundation stone of the new one laid on 25 September; it was completed about 1430. This tower survived the Fire. The church was rebuilt by Wren in 1670–2: mason, Nicholas Young; bricklayer, Antony Tanner;

carpenters, Thomas Gammon and — Miller; joiner, William Cleer; plasterer, John Grove. The plan is uncomplicated—a nave and aisles, and a slightly projecting sanctuary; Tuscan columns, round-headed arches, a clerestory of circular windows, and a groined vault.

In 1704 the Archbishop ordered that the tower be rebuilt out of the Coal fund, but it was not until 1715 that the churchwardens reported that they had been able to get the money and begin work. By 1717 the tower was half completed, but the money was exhausted: the parish was successful in getting a grant from the Fifty New Churches fund, and work was resumed. Wren had made the plan, but the completion, in 1718–22, was from Hawksmoor's designs, the mason being Edward Strong junior; the tower is on the lines of its fifteenth-century predecessor, with angle turrets: but Hawksmoor's top is more elaborate, with the turrets panelled, and King's Chapel terminations to the pinnacles. There were repairs in 1751, 1775, and 1790, the last two under George Wyatt, surveyor. In the last, the south aisle windows, and the east window, were made circular, and there was a good deal of refitting: new pulpit, desk, and altar rail, new east window glass, and 12 new brass branches.

In 1858–60 there was a recasting by Gilbert Scott. A house that stood against the tower was taken down, and a porch was built in 'Franco-Italian Gothic'. This was completed in 1859. The problem with the church was, as the *Ecclesiologist* said, to convert the Italian forms of Wren into something of an ecclesiological and mediaeval character, which would produce harmony between the church and its steeple, and satisfy the purer religious sentiment of the nineteenth century. To this end, it was said, Scott 'proposes to brighten all the roof with colour . . . and he fuses the vaulting into something transitional between Pointed and Italian. And he inserts tracery in all the round-headed windows, and the great ugly stable-like circles of the clerestory become roses under his plastic hand.' A choir was formed, and a marble reredos erected—Italian, but with some French details.

This recasting is better than others in two respects: the wood carving, by W. Gibbs Rogers, is very good: and the glass, by Clayton and Bell, is excellent—why, though, have the windows in the south aisle been deprived of their backgrounds? The interior has been redecorated, and the polychrome has been removed: the clerestory windows are no longer roses. Scott's marble reredos includes paintings of Moses and Aaron by Robert Streater. The seventeenth-century altar piece and rails are now at Great Waldingfield, Suffolk—the altar piece at the vicarage, and the rails in the church.

St Mary le Bow, Cheapside (13)

The church was rebuilt in 1670–3 by Thomas Cartwright, mason, Antony Tanner, bricklayer, Matthew Bankes, carpenter, William Cleer and Thomas Whiting, joiners, John

Grove and Henry Doogood, plasterers. The steeple was completed in 1680: the masons were Thomas Cartwright and John Thompson.

When Wren was preparing the foundations of the church, he found what he called a temple or church of Roman workmanship. This was the late eleventh-century crypt: it was used for burials in the eighteenth century, and opened out by George Gwilt junior in 1822. It has been reconstructed, and was rededicated on 24 February 1960: it is in three parts—the Chapel of the Holy Spirit, the Court of Arches, and the Common Room.

The tower, which stands out on Cheapside, joined to the church by a vestibule, is one of the best known of Wren's works. The Doric doorways from the street are recessed in rusticated niches. The belfry stage has pairs of Ionic pilasters: above the cornice is a balustrade, and at the angles are groups of scrolls in a pyramid form supporting urns. The circular base of the spire is surrounded first by a circular Corinthian temple, from the balustrade of which rise curved flying buttresses, which 'elevate and magically support' a smaller, square temple with four little porticoes of two columns. Then come little consoles, and an obelisk spire. The beauty, of course, is in its proportions: later architects sometimes tried to reproduce the steeple, but they never got it quite right. It was repaired by Sir William Staines in 1764, by George Gwilt junior in 1818–20, and by Laurence King in 1956–61: in the last repair, the steeple had to be taken down, until the tower had been strengthened, and it was then rebuilt stone by stone.

The church itself, of red brick, lies back from the road, and is now far more conspicuous than it used to be. It was modelled on the *Templum Pacis*, or Basilica of Maxentius, at Rome: a nave and aisles, with three arches on piers with Corinthian columns attached; the nave covered with an elliptical arched ceiling.

A faculty was given on 5 April 1867 to reseat, take down the north and south galleries and the gallery over the west door, re-erect the organ, and remodel the pulpit and desk.

The church was completely wrecked in 1941, and reconstructed, at prodigious expense, by King in 1956–62: the contractors were Dove Brothers. The church was reconsecrated on 11 June 1964.

The structure reproduces Wren, but the interior has been arranged 'on contemporary liturgical lines', with a free-standing altar, and a bishop's throne at the east end. The glass is by John Hayward.

The custom of erecting a bishop's throne in parish churches seems to have begun in the later nineteenth century: it was always a carved chair, placed on the north of the sanctuary. Now the throne is put at the east end, behind the altar. This was the position in primitive times, when there was a bishop for every small town: it is not so suitable now, when a bishop has several hundred churches under his care. However much dioceses may be sub-divided, he is not likely to occupy his throne, in any particular church, very often.

9 St Lawrence Jewry, 1671–7 by Sir Christopher Wren

10 St Andrew's, Holborn, 1684–7
by Wren: top of tower 1704

11 All Hallows by the
Tower, the seventeenth-
century tower, with
twentieth-century spire

12 St Margaret's, Lothbury, 1686–90 by Wren: screen from All Hallows',
Thames Street

13 St Mary le Bow, Wren's best-known steeple, finished in 1680

14 St Michael's, Cornhill, 1670–2 by Wren, tower completed by Hawksmoor 1718–22

15 St Benet's, Paul's Wharf, 1667–83 by Wren

16 St Peter's, Cornhill, 1677–81 by Wren

St Edmund's, Lombard Street

Sir John Summerson has pointed out that the drawing of the elevation of the front of this church seems to be the work of Robert Hooke, Wren's fellow surveyor—who was, like Wren, an ingenious man, but was, unlike Wren, rather disagreeable, and not a very good architect. It is true that Wren's initials also appear; but signatures on drawings can be ambiguous: they may simply mean approval by the person who signs. This, then, may be the one church that Wren did not design.

The mason was Abraham Storey, and the other workmen were Maurice Emmett, bricklayer; George Choby and Henry Wilkins, carpenters; Thomas Whiting and Thomas Creecher, joiners; Daniel Morrice and John Sherwood, plasterers. Work was begun in 1670, and the church was finished in 1676: there was a cupola over the sanctuary, which has disappeared. The spire was not completed until 1705: for it there were payments to William Kempster, mason, John Roberts, plumber, and Richard Jennings, carpenter.

The church was repaired at the same time, and again in 1727, 1745, 1755–6, and 1832–3. Butterfield rearranged it in 1864 and 'in great measure preserved the old character of the church by judicious re-use of the carved woodwork and other ornaments'. The pews were converted into open seats, and choir stalls were constructed. In 1917 a bomb fell on the roof. In May 1941 there was some damage by incendiaries, and the glass was destroyed: the worst loss was the arms of Queen Anne, which were set up in the altar window in 1708, and afterwards removed to the other end.

The tower is in the middle of the front (which, in this case, faces south), very slightly projecting: it has an octagonal lantern, and spire, of lead. The organ is in the base of the tower, and the bays on each side have galleries.

The church is not very interesting: a rectangle, with arched niches in the walls, some containing windows; and a projecting sanctuary. But the woodwork is good, particularly the pulpit. The font in enclosed within semi-circular rails against the left-hand wall: the cover had figures of Apostles, four of which remain.

Monument   By Bacon, to Jeremiah Milles, 1784, Dean of Exeter, and rector of the parish.

St Mary at Hill

The rebuilding of this church began in 1670, and in 1672 the vestry agreed to borrow £500 or £600 to help complete it: it was not finished until 1676, the old tower, and some of the old walls, being kept. Joshua Marshall was mason; Thomas Lock, carpenter; William Cleer, joiner. In 1695 payments were made, for building a new spire and additional work, to Christopher Kempster, mason; Henry Doogood, plasterer; William

Thompson, painter; Abraham Wilkins, carpenter, etc. When in 1787 George Gwilt was appointed surveyor for repairs he specified 'the Steeple to be rebuilt with proper Stone Work, the West Front likewise to be rebuilt ... Part of the Southern Front to be rebuilt'; and considerable repairs to be done to the galleries, pews, etc. The work was completed the following year. Thomas Piper was the mason, and John Harrison the bricklayer. The tower is, in fact, of brick.

In 1827–8 the church was repaired, partly rebuilt and refitted by James Savage, and the last traces of the mediaeval church were cleared away. In 1848–9 he repaired it again. The lantern of the dome was filled with stained glass, and a great deal of woodwork was introduced, carved by William Gibbs Rogers—which could be original: a wonderful achievement for a craftsman of the period. The plan of the church is a Greek cross within a square: the dome in the centre is supported by four Corinthian columns. The details, and the plaster work, are obviously not by Wren.

The church has a rich and impressive interior, with a particularly fine altar piece (original) and pulpit (by Rogers). There are two sword rests. One commemorates the two terms of office of Lord Mayor Beckford, the other, which came from St George's, Botolph Lane (as did the carved royal arms), serves as a memorial to him. The box pews remain, so that the seating is, for once, in proportion to the rest of the church.

Wilson Carlile, the founder of the Church Army, was rector from 1892 to 1926.

Monuments John Woods, 1658. Thomas Davell, 1700. Henrietta Vickars, 1712–13. The Rev W. J. Rodber, secretary of I.C.B.S., 1843.

St Magnus the Martyr, Lower Thames Street (19)

The church was rebuilt in 1671–6: John Thompson, mason; Robert Brown, bricklayer; Matthew Banckes, carpenter; William Cleer, William Gray, and — Massey, joiners; John Grove and Henry Doogood, plasterers. The steeple was completed in 1705: Samuel Fulkes, mason; Thomas Robinson, smith; Abraham Jordan, carpenter; William Thompson, painter; Henry Doogood, plasterer.

There was a fire in 1760, and the church was repaired afterwards by Peter Biggs. Later the same year Strickland Holden was appointed surveyor to examine the church with a view to the alterations suggested by the London Bridge committee: it was proposed to widen the Bridge and to make a footpath under the tower. George Dance made a plan in 1762, the year in which the Act was passed. The vestry rooms on each side of the tower were taken away and another vestry was built on the south of the church in 1768. In 1782 John Tricker was chosen as surveyor, and a repair was carried out: at this time, the windows on the north side were made circular.

Samuel Robinson, Tricker's successor, made a report on the church in 1802, and in the next year an order was made to take down the south wall as far as the windows, and rebuild it. Alterations were made by E. I'anson in 1893.

The church lost its commanding position when the new London Bridge was built, and is now hidden by Adelaide House, built in 1924–5. The tower is surmounted by an octagonal lantern, with Ionic pilasters and arched openings, with a lead dome and small spire. The projecting clock was set up in 1709: it had some gilded figures, which have been removed.

The church is divided into nave and aisles by tall Ionic columns: an arched roof is cut into by the clerestory windows. Hughson says that the interior is 'elegant, without appearing gaudy; and has all the requisites proper for a place of serious worship'. The requisites have been considerably added to in this century.

Work was done in 1924–5 under Martin Travers, who restored the altar piece. This is one of the finest in the City, of great size, with Moses and Aaron on either side of the altar, a pelican above the Commandments, and a glory in the upper part. The reredoses to the side altars have been made out of doorcases. The iron Communion rails, and the font and cover, were given in 1683. A very fine pulpit, with tester, and a sumptuous west gallery, with churchwardens' pews below, and organ of 1712. Sword rest 1708.

Recent glass in the north aisle is by Alfred L. Wilkinson, and in the south aisle, by Lawrence Lee.

St Lawrence Jewry, Gresham Street (9)

This is the church of the Lord Mayor and Corporation. It was rebuilt in 1671–7: Edward Pierce, mason; Thomas Newman, bricklayer; John Longland, carpenter; William Cleer and Richard Kedge, joiners; Thomas Mead, plasterer; Edward Pierce, wood-carver.

The church forms a rectangle, with a north aisle which ends one bay before the east end: at the west is a tower, with pinnacles and a lead-covered spire (a restoration): there are vestibules on either side. The frontispiece is the east end, which is based on the east end of Wren's Model Design for St Paul's, with attached Corinthian pillars, a pediment, and attic.

The interior was sumptuously fitted up, and the organ case was particularly fine. It was not improved by Blomfield in 1866–7, and there was too much stained glass; but apart from the pews, and the north gallery (an addition of 1706), the furniture was allowed to remain.

The church was bombed on 29 December 1940, and almost everything in it was destroyed. The rebuilding was done in 1954–7, very well, by Cecil Brown. The ceiling reproduces what was there before and the new fittings have the dignity that should accompany the Lord Mayor. The architect painted the picture on the altar piece: the glass is by Christopher Webb. The font, *c.* 1620, came from Holy Trinity, Minories; the seats were brought from Holy Trinity, Marylebone. In the north vestibule there is a chapel, with paving and seats from Christchurch, Westminster.

Monument   John Tillotson, Archbishop of Canterbury, 1694 (his sermons were extemely popular at one time, but then acquired the reputation of being dull: they are, as a matter of fact, very readable). Some other monuments, which survived the bombing, are in the vestibule at the west end.

St Nicholas Cole Abbey, Queen Victoria Street

The church was built in 1671–7: Thomas Wise, mason; Henry Blowes, carpenter; William Cleer and Richard Kedge, joiners; John Sherwood and Edward Martin, plasterers.

It is a very simple little church: the body is a rectangle, with Corinthian pilasters and a flat ceiling: at the west are three arches, leading to the base of the tower, at the north-west, and the organ gallery and vestry. The concave lead spire, with a balcony, was destroyed in the War, but has been restored. The interior was rearranged in 1873, and partly restored in 1928–31.

The church was burned out in 1941, and was restored by Arthur Bailey, F.R.I.B.A.: it was reconsecrated on 10 May 1962. The glass in the east windows is by Keith New.

St Bride's, Fleet Street (18)

The rebuilding of the church was begun in 1671, by Joshua Marshall: Samuel Fulkes also worked as a mason. The masons' work of the church was finished by 1674, and the first service was held in December 1675, though the furniture was not finished by the time of the reopening and the tower was not completed until 1678. Other workmen were John Longland, carpenter; John Grove, plasterer; William Cleer and William Grey, joiners; William Emmett, woodcarver; and Robert Streeter and Edward Bird, painters. The total cost of the church was £11,430.

The steeple was built in 1701–3, though the design was probably made a good deal earlier; it recalls the erection that stood on top of the dome in the Warrant Design for St Paul's, 1675, for which Wren may have imagined that there was some classical precedent. It consists of four diminishing octagonal stages, with pilasters, and openings—round-headed in the first three, and square-headed in the fourth—with an obelisk spire above. This could easily be mechanical, but the careful adjustment of the proportions makes it a thing of beauty. It was struck by lightning in 1764, and mostly rebuilt by Sir William Staines, who is said to have lowered it slightly.

St Bride's did not suffer too much from nineteenth-century alterations: it kept its box pews and galleries. The sanctuary was decorated by Basil Champneys, and new glass was put into the east window. On 26 March 1885 a faculty was given for making a choir vestry out of a building on the south that had formerly been the entrance to the vaults.

The church was bombed, restored by Godfrey Allen, and reopened on 19 December 1957. Extensive excavations were made under the church. A Roman building, with its pavement, was found, together with coins, pottery, and tiles. Also a Saxon church, with an apse, remodelled at the east end by the Normans; the foundation of the Norman tower, and traces of the subsequent mediaeval enlargements. Many vaults were opened, and thousands of skeletons were discovered. It has been reconstructed as it was originally, except for the galleries and the seating, and is now arranged as a college chapel.

It is divided into nave and aisles by coupled Doric columns and coffered arches: there is a tunnel vault, with the clerestory windows cutting into it. The painting on the east wall, by Glyn Jones, gives the appearance of an apse. The font came from St Helen's, Bishopsgate.

St Stephen's, Walbrook (20)

This well-known church was rebuilt by Wren in 1672–9: Edward Strong and Christopher Kempster, masons; John Longland, carpenter; Roger Davis, Stephen Colledge, and Thomas Creecher, joiners; Jonathan Maine and William Newman, carvers; Henry Doogood and John Grove, plasterers.

The exterior is plain, but with a very pleasant steeple surmounting the tower: a square stage, with three projecting columns at the angles: a smaller square stage: and then a little lantern. The steeple was begun in 1713, and payments were made to Edward Strong junior, mason; Richard Jennings, carpenter; Thomas Robinson, smith; Andrew Niblett, coppersmith; Joseph Thompson, painter; and Joseph Roberts, plumber. The last payment to Strong, for 'additional Worke on Vauses and Ornam^ts about the Spire and Parrapett Wall upon the Tower', was made on 22 June 1717. The entrance is in the middle of the west end: up a flight of steps (where the bank of the Walbrook was), and through a western apse into the church.

Elmes says of the church: 'a halo of dazzling light flashes at once upon the eye; and a lovely band of Corinthian columns, of beauteous proportions, appear in magic mazes before you ... On a second look, the columns slide into complete order, like a band of young and elegant dancers, at the close of a quadrille.' There are sixteen of these columns, so disposed as to work wonders with what is, in fact, simply a rectangular space. First comes the nave, with double aisles for two bays: at the next bay, the inner aisle is eliminated, and the entablatures turn outward, and then eastward. At the next, slightly wider, bay, they turn outward again, and meet the wall, so that there is the effect of transepts. After this, the process is repeated in reverse—except that there is only one double-aisled bay at the east.

The dome is in the—more or less—central space, supported on eight arches which spring from the points at which the entablatures make their right-angle turns: pendentives turn it into a circle. The dome—which is, of course, constructed of wood and plaster—ends in a lantern.

In 1779 the painting by Benjamin West, now on the north wall, was given, and put in front of the east window. In 1850 it was moved, and the pediment of the altar piece, which had been removed to make room for it, was restored by W. G. Rogers. The east window was filled with glass by Willement, destroyed in the War. In 1887–8 F. C. Penrose removed the pews (which has not improved the appearance of the church), and altered the bases of the columns. One faculty (8 March 1886) mentions the taking down of the pews, and altering and refixing them: another, soon after (22 April 1887), adds further minor work, and the restoration of the bases. The dome was mostly destroyed in 1941, and was reconstructed in 1951–2: the church was re-hallowed on 29 March 1954.

The woodwork, apart from the pews, all remains: an altar piece; a small, semi-circular table, and rails; panelling; a magnificent pulpit, with canopy; font cover; and a splendid organ gallery, and organ case (about 100 years later than the rest of the woodwork).

Monuments   There are a good many, placed high up, and not too clean or easy to read. They include John Lilburne, 1678. Dr Nathaniel Hodges, 1688. Robert Marriott, S.T.P., 1689. Deschamp family, 1726 onwards, by S. Oliver, 1776. Mary Wilson, 1772, and Thomas, D.D., 1784, by J. Moore.

St James Garlickhythe, Garlick Hill (23)

The rebuilding was begun in 1676; the church was reopened on 10 December 1682, and completed in the next year. Christopher Kempster was mason; Thomas Warren, bricklayer; Israel Knowles, carpenter; William Cleer and J. Fuller, joiners; William Newman, carver; John Grove and Henry Doogood, plasterers.

The church has a very pretty steeple, which stands on a dome supported by piers in the angles of the belfry; the piers transfer the weight to the thicker lower walls. It is in three diminishing square stages, the lower with projecting Ionic columns at the angles, carrying an entablature and urns; the next with scrolls at the angles, and urns above the cornice; and the third, very small, which carries a tiny cupola and vane. It was built in 1714–17, at a cost of £1,559:19:11; the mason was Edward Strong junior, and the other craftsmen were the same as at St Stephen's, Walbrook. A projecting clock, with a figure of St James, was erected in 1682: it is not there at present, but will be restored.

A faculty was given on 1 December 1815 for rebuilding the chancel—which was done. There were repairs in 1838, 1854 (steeple), and 1866. In 1878 fittings were brought here from St Michael's, Queenhithe. Further repairs were undertaken in 1883–5, and decoration by Basil Champneys in 1886. The plaster was removed from the tower in 1897 after damage by a fire in neighbouring buildings. The nave has aisles with Ionic columns carrying an entablature: in the central bay, this turns outward, to give the effect of transepts. There is a small projecting sanctuary.

There is a good deal of woodwork: a rather plain altar piece—not the original, and probably dating from 1815; a carved Communion table, rails with spiral balusters, a pulpit (from St Michael's, Queenhithe), doorcases (also from St Michael's) now forming screens behind the choir stalls; seats (cut down), churchwardens' pews, gallery, screen, and organ case. Font, sword-rests, and hat-stands.

The church suffered somewhat from bomb damage, and also from the death-watch beetle. It was repaired in 1954–63, by Lockhart Smith and Alexander Gale. The roof, and the upper parts of the walls, were rebuilt, and the tower was refaced. The nineteenth-century glass was removed, and the altar piece was deprived of its Victorian paintings.

The mummified body of a man, found under the chancel, is kept in a cupboard at the west end; but he is not usually visible.

The painting of the Ascension, by Andrew Geddes, was given in 1815.

Monument   Peter Jones, 1694.

SS Anne and Agnes', Gresham Street

The church was built in 1677–80 though the cupola was not completed until the beginning of the eighteenth century. R. Walters and William Hammond, masons; John Fitch, bricklayer; John Hayward, carpenter; Ralph Cadman, and Messrs Cheltenham, Fuller and Page, joiners; John Sherwood, plasterer.

This was a very elegant little church, square in plan, with a Greek cross interior and four Corinthian columns, with their entablatures forming the cross: the middle bays raised, with larger windows. The centre had a groined vault, the arms of the cross were barrel-vaulted, and the squares at the angles flat roofed, with a circle of plasterwork.

The outside was covered with cement by Charles Tyrell in 1820–1, and the interior was altered by W. M. Brooks in 1838–9, and by Ewan Christian in 1888–9. The faculty (19 June 1888) gave leave to clean and colour the walls and ceiling, reglaze, reseat, remove the gallery, and move the organ.

The church suffered badly from bombing, and from subsequent neglect. Plans were made in 1954 for reconstruction, by Braddock and Martin Smith. In 1963 a considerable part of the east and south walls, and part of the north wall, were taken down, and the church was subsequently rebuilt. The result is a careful reproduction of the church as it was before 1820–1. The brickwork of the walls is now exposed.

St Peters', Cornhill (16)

Rebuilt in 1677–81 by Joshua Marshall and Abraham Story, masons; Thomas Warren, bricklayer; Thomas Woodstock, carpenter; William Cleer, Thomas Poultney and Thomas Athew, joiners; Edward Freeman and Richard Howes, carvers; Henry Doogood and John Grove, plasterers.

The east front, towards Gracechurch Street, is quite grand: the rest of the exterior is more homely. A pleasant small churchyard lies to the south, with plane trees, above which rises the red brick tower, with copper covered dome and spire, and the plain, stuccoed south wall.

The inside is divided into nave and aisles by square piers, with round-headed arches, and pilasters, from which spring the ribs of the barrel vault. The east end has a row of five windows—three in the sanctuary, and two at the ends of the aisles: and, above, one more arched window and two round ones. This is one of the two Wren churches that were given a screen: the rector, Dr William Beveridge, afterwards Bishop of St Asaph, insisted on it, and when the church was consecrated, on 27 November 1681, preached on *The excellency and usefulness of the Common Prayer*, and explained why screens are desirable.

The organ gallery, with curved ends to the front, keeps its organ—originally by Father Smith—in its case: the font is of 1681, and the panelling, doorcases, altar piece, and pulpit remain. But the pulpit was lowered and moved in 1872, when J. D. Wyatt restored the church, repaved, and reseated it. The east windows were filled with rather crude glass by Gibbs. There are two recent windows in the north aisle by Hugh Easton.

St Martin Ludgate, Ludgate Hill

Built in 1677–84 by Nicholas Young, mason; Allan Garway and Thomas Horn, bricklayers; Henry Blowes, Robert Day and Matthew Banckes, carpenters; Messrs Poulden and Athey and William Gray, joiners; William Emmett, carver; Henry Doogood and John Grove, plasterers.

The front is to the south, with the tower in the middle projecting slightly, and with scrolls to connect it with the other bays. It turns adroitly into an octagon, and then has an ogee dome, balcony, lantern, and spire, covered with lead. The spire appears in the fore-

17 St Vedast's, Foster Lane, a late Wren church, 1695–1701, restored after the War

18 St Bride's, Fleet Street, the post-War reconstruction of Wren's interior; the church was first opened in 1675

19 St Magnus the Martyr: the gallery and organ case in Wren's church of 1671–6

20 St Stephen's, Walbrook, 1672–9, Wren's best-known interior

21 St Mary Abchurch, 1681–6, by Wren

22 St Margaret Pattens, by Wren 1684–7; spire finished 1703

23 St James, Garlickhythe, by Wren, the steeple completed 1714–17

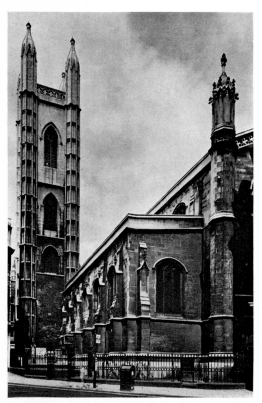

24 St Mary Aldermary, Wren's Gothic reconstruction of 1681–2: tower somewhat later

25 St Michael Paternoster Royal, 1686–94, by Wren steeple finished 1715

ground, and on the left, of all the photographs of St Paul's as seen from Ludgate Hill, and it is easy to see how right it is in that position.

The bays to the left and right are similar: one a vestibule, the other a vestry: they, and the base of the tower, open into the church by coffered arches, filled with screens and galleries. Without these parts, the area of the church is a square, inside which Wren has inscribed a Greek cross: four tall Composite columns form the central square, with entablatures reaching out to pilasters on the walls. The arms of the cross are barrel vaulted: the squares in the corners have flat ceilings.

The altar piece is 'ornamental and spacious': of the usual type, though less exuberant than some. The pulpit, and other woodwork, remains. Some pieces of furniture from St Mary Magdalene, Old Fish Street, were brought here in 1890. The organ was erected in 1684; the picture of the Ascension is by Benjamin West. There is a large chandelier. A faculty for rearranging the interior was given in 1894.

The church was very conservatively dealt with and has a solemn and impressive appearance. Bumpus thinks that, if Wren could come to life, he would approve of the lowering of the seats. So he might: he is known to have disliked box pews. But he designed his churches to include them, and their absence makes the plinths of the columns look rather too tall.

Christchurch, Newgate Street

The church was built in 1677–87. The workmen were John Shorthose and John Crooke, masons; Edward Elder and John Horn, bricklayers; John Longland, carpenter; Matthew Williams, joiner; and Henry Doogood, plasterer.

This church is not to be used for worship and has remained unrestored since the War: only the outer walls survive, though the tower still stands: this is a very impressive composition: the top has segmental pediments, and above are diminishing square stages, the first with a surrounding colonnade.

The steeple was completed in 1701–4: Edward Strong, junior, was the mason; John Longland, carpenter; Thomas Robinson, smith; Matthew and John Roberts, plumbers.

St Mary Aldermary, Queen Victoria Street (24)

The rebuilding of this church was begun in 1510 by Sir Henry Keble, Lord Mayor, who died in 1518. The tower was left incomplete, and in 1626 William Rodoway and Richard Pierson gave money to complete it: the work was finished in 1629.

The church was burned in the Fire, but the tower was not much damaged. Henry Rogers offered £5,000 for rebuilding—before the money from the coal tax was allotted to the City churches: he made the condition that the new church should be a copy of the old. His intentions were carried out by his widow, and the church was rebuilt by Wren in 1681–2. The mason was Edward Strong, the carpenter John Longland, and the joiner Thomas Creecher. The foundations and parts of the walls were used. The altar piece, rails, and the frame of the Communion table were the gift of Dame Jane Smith; Dutton Seaman gave the font. The pewing and wainscoting were done at the cost of the two parishes of St Mary Aldermary and St Thomas Apostle.

The restoration of the tower—of which the lower part remained—was begun in 1701: the mason was John Clarke. The design is thought to have been made by William Dickinson, Wren's assistant, who was interested in Gothic. The pinnacles were damaged in the great storm of 1703: the cost of repair was met from the public fund. At the same time, money was granted for the painting of the blank north wall of the north aisle with five large windows, with trees, sky, and clouds seen through them: the work was done by William Thompson.

An organ, with a Gothic case, was erected in 1781. In 1823 Samuel Ainger repaired the church.

In 1876 there was a restoration by Richard Tress and Charles Innes, who refaced part of the walls and ravaged the interior. The altar piece—with the royal arms in the pediment, and a glory above the Commandments, between two cherubim—was already thought to be a 'blemish' when James Elmes published his life of Wren in 1823. It was removed, together with the pews, desk, altar rails, panelling, organ screen, gallery front and staircases, and the marble paving and steps in the sanctuary. The pulpit was left, without its tester: and so were the font and sword rest.

Repairs to stonework 1909: new reredos 1914.

The church is straightforward late Perpendicular in style, except for the plasterwork in the spandrels of the arcades. The plaster fan vault, with saucer domes, is not at all likely to be a reproduction of anything that was there in the sixteenth century: Pevsner suggests that a similar vault may have been put up in the early seventeenth century.

The church was restored after War damage by Arthur George Nisbet. The nineteenth-century glass had been destroyed: the new east window, 1952, and the east window of the south aisle, 1955, are by Lawrence Lee and the west window, 1952, is by John Crawford.

Monument Margaret Bearsley, 1802, by Bacon, junior.

St Mary Abchurch, Abchurch Lane (21)

This attractive church, with its walls of dark red brick (formerly covered with stucco), hipped roof, and tower with lead dome and spire, was built in 1681–6. Christopher

Kempster was the mason, and Thomas Woodstock the carpenter: the bricklayers were John Evans and John Bridges, and the plasterers Henry Doogood and John Grove. The plan is a rectangle plus the area of the tower, which is in the north-west corner, and the space filled by the gallery. The square is covered by a dome above an enriched cornice: it rests on eight arches, with pendentives springing from corbels in the form of Corinthian capitals and a column and pilaster at the west.

The church was repaired and beautified in 1708, and it was probably then that the dome was painted. The work is ascribed to Sir James Thornhill, though payments were made to Mr Snow in 1708-9. William Snow was a painter, who lived in the parish, and he may have been the artist. There is a painted cornice above the porthole windows: below are eight female figures, representing Christian virtues: in the centre is the tetragrammaton in a glory, and a choir of angels, some playing instruments.

The altar piece is by Grinling Gibbons—the only one in the City that is known to be his work: his signed receipt still exists. There are two pairs of Corinthian columns, supporting an entablature, and a broken elliptical pediment: above is an attic with urns. A pelican is above the Commandments, and there is a profusion of Gibbons's delicate carving of flowers and fruit. The rest of the carving in the church is mostly by William Emmett: the fine pulpit, with tester, is by William Grey. The font, by William Kempster—who also did the paving—has a cover with figures of the four Evangelists in niches. The carved front of the organ case came from All Hallows', Bread Street, demolished in 1877, via All Hallows', East India Dock Road. The walls are panelled, and there are carved doorcases.

New seating was installed in 1878-9, and new rails were provided, but the other fittings were untouched.

The church was damaged by bombs in 1940 and after, and from 1948 onwards Godfrey Allen did repairs to the fabric of the church while Professor Tristram in 1946 and Walter Hoyle in 1953 restored the painting.

There is a small mediaeval crypt under the churchyard.

Monuments   Sir Patience Ward, Lord Mayor in 1681, 1696: 'the decorations are in a very correct style'. Anthony Tournay, 1726. Eaton family, signed by Oliver. Alderman Matthew Perchard, 1777, also by Oliver. Martha Perchard, 1787.

St Clement's, Clement's Lane, Eastcheap

The church was built in 1683-7 by Edward Strong, mason; Israel Knowles and William Gray, carpenters; Thomas Poultney, joiner; Jonathan Maine, carver; John Grove and Henry Doogood, plasterers.

A rather dim exterior is covered with stucco: the church is well hidden away. It is not large, but tall in proportion: the south aisle has Corinthian columns, and there is a clerestory north and south. There was a rearrangement in 1872 by Butterfield: the faculty (16 August 1871) mentioned the demolition of the galleries in the south and west aisles, the the moving of the organ, the rearrangement of the pews, and the moving of font and pulpit.

In 1936 there was a repair, in which the mistakes of 1872 were put right: the organ, by Renatus Harris, was replaced in the gallery, and the walls were redecorated. There is a good deal of woodwork; an altar piece (not improved by Sir J. N. Comper), and a very fine pulpit with a large canopy.

St Margaret Pattens, Rood Lane (22)

The church was built in 1684–7. Samuel Fulkes, mason; John Evans, bricklayer; Thomas Woodstock, carpenter; William Cleer, joiner; John Grove and Henry Doogood, plasterers.

The tower is very striking; it is tall and thin, with a balustrade and pinnacles, and a lead-covered, Gothic-looking spire. This was built in 1699–1703. Samuel Fulkes was the mason, and Abraham Jordan the carpenter. Matthew Roberts, plumber, was paid 'for worke done at the Spire being 88f high with all the ornaments and gutters round the same'.

The church is a rectangle of five bays, with a north aisle, at the west of which is the tower. The Corinthian pilasters on the walls become columns where the aisle opens. A clerestory of round windows is carried all round the church. The west bay of the nave is mostly taken up with the organ gallery: at the east end is a small altar recess.

There is plenty of woodwork: gallery, and rather plain organ case, screen beneath the gallery, canopied pews—one dated 1686; royal arms, a plain pulpit, altar piece, and a doorcase, now used as a reredos, in the north aisle. The church was reseated in 1879–80, and woodwork from the pews was used for the choir stalls. The font has an eighteenth-century cover. The sword rest is dated 1723. The altar painting is ascribed to Carlo Maratti.

Monuments Susannah Batson, 1727. Peter Delmé, 1738, by Rysbrack. There is a Della Robbia plaque in memory of Thomas Wagstaffe, appointed rector in 1684, who was deprived as a Nonjuror in 1689. He was one of the two chosen by James II as bishops, and was consecrated Bishop of Ipswich in 1694. He died in 1712. The Rev J. L. Fish, who was rector at the end of the nineteenth century, was a strong supporter of the Jacobite and Nonjuring cause.

St Andrew's, Holborn (10)

Though this church escaped the Fire, it was in bad repair, and was rebuilt by Wren in 1684–7: Edward Pierce and William Stanton, masons; John Longland, carpenter; Valentine Houseman, joiner; Edward Pierce, wood-carver; Robert Dyer, plasterer. The fifteenth-century tower was newly faced and heightened in 1704.

It was a very noble interior—Elmes called it 'one of the finest and most appropriate protestant churches in Europe'—of the same general type as St James's, Piccadilly, but with a roof of somewhat different construction. The glass in the two-tiered east window, of the Last Supper and the Resurrection, was by Joshua Price, 1718.

The interior was altered by J. H. Good in 1818. S. S. Teulon in 1871–2, reseated it, removed the organ gallery and case, altered the sanctuary, and put the pulpit on a crude stone base.

The church was badly bombed, and nothing remained but the tower and the walls: all the contents were destroyed. It was rebuilt by Seely and Paget, and reopened in 1960. The font, pulpit, and organ came from the Chapel of the Foundling Hospital, and the altar piece, and other fittings, from St Luke's, Old Street. The body of Thomas Coram, the founder of the Foundling Hospital, is now buried at the west end.

St Andrew by the Wardrobe, Queen Victoria Street (26)

This church gained its prominent position when Queen Victoria Street was made. It was begun in 1685, and finished in 1693. Nicholas Young, mason; Thomas Horn, bricklayer; John Longland and Israel Knowles, carpenters; Roger Davis, William Cleer, and William Smith, joiners; Henry Doogood, plasterer. Hawksmoor was concerned with the design of the altar piece. The west gallery is dated 1774.

The interior was very gently dealt with by Thomas Garner, and kept its box pews. It was a small-scale version of such churches as St Andrew's, Holborn, with galleries, and columns below and above: in this case, very simple Doric piers.

The church was badly damaged by bombing, and was restored by Marshall Sisson: it was rehallowed on 14 July 1961. The nineteenth-century embellishments of the south front were removed during the restoration. The font and pulpit are from St Matthew's, Friday Street, and the royal arms from St Olave's, Old Jewry. The organ—1769, by Snetzler—was made for Lord Hatherton of Teddesley Hall, Stafford. The north aisle is enclosed, and is used by the British and Foreign Bible Society.

St Margaret's, Lothbury (12)

Built in 1686–90. Samuel Fulkes, mason; John Longland, carpenter; William Cleer, joiner; Henry Doogood, plasterer. 'It faces Mr Soane's new front of the Bank of England, and is not disgraced by its modern neighbour.' (Elmes). The tower, at the south-west, has an elegant doorcase, and a slim leaden spire on a domed base, and was built in 1698–1700: Samuel Fulkes, mason; John Longland, carpenter; Thomas Robinson, smith; William Knight, plumber.

The church is similar to St Margaret Pattens, but with the aisle on the south instead of the north. There is a great wealth of furnishings: the altar piece was made for the church, and so were the pulpit, and the font—which is carved with the Fall, the Ark, the Baptism of Christ, and the Baptism of the Ethiopian. Other fittings came from the demolished churches of All Hallows', Thames Street, and St Olave's, Old Jewry, and were arranged by G. F. Bodley.

From All Hallows' came the screen, the gift of Theodore Jacobsen: this is a splendid piece of carving, with open, twisted balusters. The centre has open pilasters, and an entablature, and a broken pediment: below is an eagle, and in the pediment are the royal arms. The tester of the pulpit, and branches, also came from All Hallows'. St Olave's, Old Jewry, supplied the Communion table and altar piece, now in the south aisle, the altar rails and gallery. The large paintings of Moses and Aaron, which fill what were once windows in the east wall, came from St Christopher le Stocks. One of the sword rests is from St Olave's.

Monuments   Bust of Sir Peter Le Maire, 1631, from St Christopher's, perhaps by Le Sueur. Alderman Boydell, 1791, by Banks, carved by F. Smith: from St Olave's. Mrs Simpson, 1795, by Nollekens. There are some in the aisle, high up and hard to read, but they are not very important.

St Michael Paternoster Royal, College Hill (25)

The old church was rebuilt by Sir Richard Whittington, Lord Mayor, who died in 1423, and was buried here. The rebuilding after the Fire was begun in 1686, and completed in 1694, but the steeple was not finished until 1715. This is similar to that of St James's, Garlickhythe, except that the stages are octagonal, not square, and that the projecting columns are placed singly, at the angles. The craftsmen were Edward Strong, mason; Thomas Denning, carpenter; William Cleer, joiner; Henry Doogood, plasterer. For the steeple, Edward Strong, junior, mason; Richard Jennings, carpenter; Thomas Robinson, smith; Andrew Niblett, coppersmith; Joseph Roberts, plumber.

The tower stands at the south-west of the church, which is a simple rectangle. The interior was rearranged by Butterfield in 1866. There was fine woodwork, and in 1894 several items were brought from All Hallows', Thames Street—e.g., west screen, organ (1749), Moses and Aaron, and a figure of Charity, which was placed in front of the lectern.

The building, and much of the furnishing, was damaged during the war.

The church is being repaired (1965), but has not yet been reopened.

St Vedast's, Foster Lane (17)

The old church and tower were repaired by the parish after the Fire, for about £1,300. But in 1694 a petition was made to the Bishop: the church, in spite of the repairs, was decayed and tottering, and would have to be rebuilt: they asked for help from the public funds. The church was rebuilt in 1695–1701 by Edward Strong, mason; Richard Hows and Thomas Colbourn, smiths; John Longland and Philip Rogerson, carpenters; John Smallwell, joiner; Matthew Roberts, plasterer; William Thompson, painter.

The tower was completed in 1709–12: William Dickinson seems to have superintended the work. The craftsmen were, Edmund Strong, junior, mason; Richard Jennings, carpenter; Joseph Roberts, plumber; Thomas Robinson, smith. The stonework of the spire was worked at Greenwich, and brought up the Thames to the City. The design is a change from Wren's earlier work, and shows some influence from Borromini, in whose baroque style 'undulating flexibility supplanted all regularity of form'. The steeple of St Vedast's has first a concave stage, with grouped diagonal pilasters: then a convex stage, and then an obelisk spire. It is very restrained baroque, and very attractive.

The body of the church is a simple rectangle, with a south aisle and an arcade of Doric columns and arches. It was wrecked by bombing in 1940, reconstructed by S. E. Dykes Bower, and reopened in 1963.

The reconstruction has been very carefully done, and the church is adorned with a collection of furniture from other churches. The altar piece came from St Christopher le Stocks, and was for many years in Great Burstead church, Essex. The altar table came from St Matthew's, Friday Street. The pulpit was in All Hallows', Bread Street, and there are carvings from the Communion table of All Hallows' in the side altar. The font came from SS Anne and Agnes', Gresham Street. The organ, by Renatus Harris, 1731, was made for St Bartholomew by the Exchange, and was transferred to St Bartholomew's, Moor Lane: in 1904, when the second St Bartholomew's was demolished, it was sold to St Alban's, Fulham. The three new east windows are by Brian Thomas.

Monuments   A bust to the Rev G. A. Hatch, 1837, and other monuments, were in St Matthew's, Friday Street.

The City: Post-Wren Rebuildings

St Mary Woolnoth (29)

The north side of the church was rebuilt, and a new roof erected, by Wren after the Fire, the work being finished in 1677. This work was, however, unsatisfactory, and in 1711 the parish presented a petition to the Commons—that the church was so ruinous and weak that the inhabitants did not dare to go to it. Another petition, in 1715, asked that the church should be included among the Fifty New Churches. Many parishes asked in vain, but in this case the request was granted. The church was rebuilt in 1716–27, by Nicholas Hawksmoor, one of the surveyors to the Commissioners. The mason was Thomas Dunn, plasterer Chrysostom Wilkins, joiner Gabriel Appleby; and the carpenters were William Seager, Thomas Denning, James Grove and John Meard.

Hawksmoor was devoted to everything that was Roman, but his taste, and temperament, led him to eschew what was elegant and modish, and to admire what was solemn, massive, and monumental. All these adjectives could be used of the exterior of this small church, as well as the others that have been applied to his work—sombre, awe-inspiring, august, unsmiling, etc. The west end has a projecting centre, with rustication that is continued round the Tuscan columns at the corners. The tower above this—which is unlike any other tower anywhere—is far broader than it is long, and its columns are so disposed as to suggest a kind of Siamese-twin union of two towers: there are, in fact, two separate turrets at the top. The masterly north wall has recessed niches, heavily rusticated, containing Ionic columns which support an entablature curved inwards.

The interior is built on the model of a Roman *atrium*: nearly square, with three Corinthian columns in each angle, supporting an entablature with semicircular windows above. There is an imposing altar piece, with twisted Corinthian columns, and an inlaid, bulging pulpit with a canopy supported on two square columns. The organ was built by Father Smith in 1681.

In 1875–6 William Butterfield formed a choir, laid the floor with encaustic tiles, raised the altar, substituted low benches for pews, and took down the galleries, the fronts of which were arranged round the walls. The church was saved from destruction in 1863, 1892, and 1897–1900. The City and South London Railway wanted it, but in the event the station was built underneath it. While it was being constructed, the church was redecorated by Heaton, Butler and Bayne under A. R. Stenning. The bishop of London's Commission in 1921 included it among the churches to be demolished. But it was preserved, and is now one of the Guild Churches.

Monument   There is a tablet to the Rev John Newton, the Evangelical, author of well-known hymns, who died in 1807 aged 82. He was rector of this church for 28 years, and was buried in the vaults underneath, but his body was taken to Olney, Bucks., in 1893.

St Botolph's, Bishopsgate (27)

In 1718 the parish applied unsuccessfully to Parliament to include their church among the Fifty New Churches. In 1723 they made a further petition: the church had been surveyed, and there was no doubt that it needed to be rebuilt. A bill was passed to enable the money to be raised.

The new church was begun in 1725, and consecrated in 1728. There is nothing in the parish records about the rebuilding, and it is not known who the architect was. Malcolm, *Londinium Redivivum*, says James Gold (? Gould), and this is repeated in George Godwin's *Churches of London*. But Langley, *London Prices*, 1750, says John James; and a print of 1803 says G. Dance (i.e., Giles, the father of George Dance I).

The tower and the frontispiece are towards the east, and the east window, in the base of the tower, is enclosed between twin Doric pilasters, with a pediment above. The stone tower, of a good height, is surmounted by a circular stage with an ogee top. The body of the church is of brick. It is divided into nave and aisles by large composite columns supporting, without an entablature, a barrel vault with plasterwork. The galleries remain.

A faculty of 1 February 1755 confirmed alterations that had been made: the church had been beautified, the pulpit had been moved, and an alteration had been made in the window at the west end. The organ was erected in 1764. In 1821, as buildings on the north side obscured the light, the glass dome in the roof of the nave was erected, from designs by Michael Meredith.

C. J. Blomfield, afterwards Bishop of London, and founder of the Metropolis Churches Fund, was rector here from 1819 to 1828. It was not considered remarkable at the time that he should also have been rector of Great and Little Chesterford, archdeacon of Colchester, 1822, and Bishop of Chester from 1824. But he also managed, somehow, to be a zealous parish priest. The population of St Botolph's was so large that an additional church had to be built—All Saints', Skinner Street, designed by Michael Meredith. But the inhabitants soon began to drift away, and the church was pulled down in the '60s.

The chancel was remodelled in 1878 by A. T. Carter. The pulpit, 'in a grand stile, richly ornamented and inlaid', is original. In 1947–8, redecoration was done by Campbell, Smith and Co. under N. F. Cachemaille Day, and the sanctuary was altered.

Monuments Sir Paul Pindar, 1650: the front of his house is now in the Victoria and Albert Museum. John Tutchin, 1658. Andrew Willaw, 1700. The Rev William Rogers (Hang Theology Rogers), 1896, by J. F. Bentley.

St Botolph's Aldgate

In 1727 the churchwardens reported that all was well: 'Our Parish Church & Steeple hath been lately well and sufficiently Repair'd, the floors, Pews & Seats in good Order.' Four years later, they erected a new altar piece. But in 1740 Benjamin Glanville, surveyor, gave evidence to the Commons that he had surveyed the church, and found that it was in danger of falling down. In 1741 an Act was obtained for rebuilding, and a new church was built on the old site, but facing north and south, by George Dance, clerk of the City Works: it was finished in 1744. Some monuments were replaced, and so was the organ—'ye Gift of Mr Thomas Whiting to the hole Parrish 1676'. Dance's church is plain and solid, of brick, with stone quoins: there are Venetian windows in the middle bay. The tower has an obelisk spire. The altar window, by Clutterbuck, was put up in 1857.

A faculty was given on 5 September 1860 to reseat and rearrange the ground floor. In 1884 (15 October) permission was given to remove the side galleries, and build a chancel: the pillars of the nave were to be altered, and arches placed upon them. The plans had been made by George Sparks, 'an eminent architect'. Fortunately, the parish had second thoughts about this scheme, and in 1887 a more reasonable restoration was proposed, J. F. Bentley making the plans. The faculty was given on 20 August 1888: the work took several years, and the church was not reopened until January 1891. Bentley lowered the pews and formed a choir: he kept the galleries, but gave them an open balustrade in the front. The undersides, and the ceiling of the church, were adorned with plasterwork. This is very different from anything that Dance would have designed, but it succeeds very well: the cove of the ceiling has a row of standing angels, between shields with coats of arms. Bentley also designed the reredos. The eighteenth-century font, pulpit, and wrought iron altar rails remain. In the gallery are also royal arms, and a seventeenth-century carving of David, and musical instruments, from St Mary's, Whitechapel.

Monuments In the gallery: Thomas, Lord Darcy of the North, and Sir Nicholas Carew, both executed by Henry VIII in 1538, and others of their families—represented by the figure of a corpse. A coloured bust of Robert Dow, merchant tailor, a benefactor of the parish, 1612.

All Hallows', London Wall (28)

A petition for rebuilding was presented to the Commons on 7 February 1765: Strickland Holden had surveyed the church, and reported that it must be rebuilt. The faculty was given on 9 February. The minutes of the committee for rebuilding were very carefully kept. Plans were sent in by five architects, and the committee showed some enterprise in choosing those of George Dance junior, a young man (born in 1741), just returned from Italy. The contractor was Joseph Taylor.

The new church was consecrated on 8 September 1767. It is a single compartment, built over vaults, with a low west tower and cupola, and an eastern apse. The exterior is very plain (inevitably compared to a riding-school): the interior is extremely elegant. It is lit entirely from above, by large lunette windows which penetrate the barrel vault. Attached Ionic columns support the vault. Dance dispensed with a complete entablature, and provided only a frieze, with Adam-like ornament, which is continued round the apse. The incorrectness, from a Palladian point of view, of the detail of this church was found fault with by critics; but Sir John Soane, who was Dance's pupil, came to see it as a step in the right direction: it was the beginning of the simplification which he himself carried to a further stage.

The pulpit, against the north wall, is entered by a staircase from the vestry room. The apse is simply panelled: the picture of St Paul receiving his sight, by Nathaniel Dance, George's brother, serves as an altar piece. This is one of the most restrained and delicate of eighteenth-century interiors.

There was a restoration under Blomfield in 1891. The church was badly damaged in 1941, but was carefully restored, by David Nye, as the headquarters of the Council for the Care of Churches, and rededicated on 10 July 1962.

Monument   Joseph Patience, architect, 1797, by Thomas Patience.

St Botolph's, Aldersgate (31)

This parish kept the Commons busy with petitions. One of 1711 said that the church could not be repaired, and must be pulled down. To rebuild it would cost £5,760, and £2,750 for the steeple. In 1718 a petition asked whether the church could be counted as one of the Fifty (the answer, as usual, was 'No'). In 1753 a petition said that the church needed repair, and money had to be raised: a bill was passed. A faculty for rebuilding had been given in 1751, but the church had been only repaired. Another, for repairing and improving, was given in 1787: this time, the church was rebuilt. It was demolished in 1789, but the old east wall was preserved. The new church, 1789–91, was built under the direction of Nathaniel Wright, district surveyor for the North district of the City of London.

The east façade, of Roman cement, dates from 1831: the builders were John Ward and Son, of Jewin Street. John William Griffith, of Clerkenwell, was surveyor to this parish, and is said to have enlarged and decorated the church, so that it may be assumed that the design was his. Otherwise, the exterior is of the plainest possible brickwork.

The interior is extremely elegant: 'taste seems to predominate', as one writer said. There are eastern and western apses (constructed inside the walls). The galleries rest on square columns, with a frieze: there are Corinthian columns above. The ceiling is arched, with delicate plasterwork, cut into by semi-circular windows, as at George Dance's All Hallows', London Wall.

The pulpit is original. The organ gallery is on Ionic pillars and the organ case of inlaid mahogany. The glass in the eastern apse is by James Pearson, from designs by Nathaniel Clarkson. J. Blyth refitted and redecorated the church in 1874, and new seats were installed.

Monuments Anne Packington, 1563. Lady Elizabeth Richardson, 1639. Elizabeth Ashton, 1662. Sir John Michlethwaite, 1682. Elizabeth Smith, 1750, by Roubiliac. Zacharia Foxall, 1758, by John Annis. Daniel Wray, 1782. Catherine Mary Meade, 1790.

St Dunstan in the West, Fleet Street (30)

The old church escaped the Fire, and was repaired in 1701. George Dance senior made a plan for rebuilding in 1752, but it was repaired instead, and again repaired in 1774, and as the result was 'mostly now of the Tuscan order, though some part is of the modern Gothic'. The inside was almost entirely eighteenth-century work. It was well known for its clock, set up in 1671, with figures of wild men to strike the quarters, which were 'more admired by many of the gaping populace than the most elegant preacher from the pulpit within the building'. Sweeny Todd advised Tobias to go and look at them. They were banished to Regent's Park, but have been replaced. The statue of Queen Elizabeth I was moved here when Ludgate was demolished in 1760.

An Act was passed in 1829 for taking down the old church and building a new one. The foundation stone was laid on 31 July 1831, and the consecration was on 31 January 1833. The architect was John Shaw, who died on 30 July 1832, the twelfth day after the external completion of the church, his son John Shaw II finishing the work. The new church was built farther to the north than the old one, with the altar at the north end, and the street was widened and straightened.

The chief feature is the tower, of Ketton stone, with an open lantern on the top on the model of All Saints', Pavement, York. The body of the church, which is of brick, is an octagon with a clerestory, vaulted with plaster: there are recesses on all eight sides, straight-sided on the north, south, east and west, and three-sided on the diagonals. Galleries at the sides have been taken down.

The original glass in the altar window was by Willement: the clerestory windows had the letters of John Shaw, one in each. The present glass in the northern window is by Gerald Smith (A. K. Nicholson Studios), 1950.

Monuments These are haphazardly arranged in the recesses, and include Henry Dacres (a brass) and Elizabeth (his date is not filled in, hers is 1530). Elizabeth North, 1612. Cuthbert Fetherston, 1615. Margaret Talbott, 1620. Richard Hutton, 1638. William Morecroft, 1657. Elizabeth Moore, 1668. Edward Marshall, master mason to Charles II, 1675, and Joshua his son, who succeeded him. Henry Jones, 1695. Sir Richard Hoare, 1718, by Thomas Stayner. Richard Pearson, 1718. Sir Richard Hoare, Lord Mayor, 1745.

Chelsea

Chelsea was well supplied with churches in the first half of the nineteenth century. The splendid St Luke's was built in 1820–4 with the help of the Parliamentary Commissioners; and there followed Holy Trinity, 1828–30, another Commissioners' church; and Christchurch, St Saviour's and St Jude's, consecrated respectively in 1839, 1840 and 1844. Not many were added in the latter part of the century. The eighteenth-century Park Chapel, and St Jude's, have been demolished. Holy Trinity has been replaced. The old church was most skilfully reconstructed after bombing: St John's was bombed, and has not been rebuilt.

All Saints', Cheyne Walk (32)

The church was bombed in 1941, and destroyed, except for the More Chapel on the south. But everything that could be saved was retrieved from the ruins and stored in the crypt of St Luke's, and preservation work was done on the chapel. The diocesan scheme did not include this as one of the churches to be rebuilt, but its friends fought for it, and eventually won the battle. Work was begun in 1949: in 1950 the More Chapel was opened for services: in 1954 the chancel and north chapel (Lawrence) were rededicated: and in 1958 the whole church was reconsecrated. The architect was W. H. Godfrey, who did a wonderful piece of reconstruction: the church looks as it did before it was bombed. There was every justification for such a careful reinstatement of the church, both for historical and for visual reasons.

The chancel was probably thirteenth-century, and the chapels were added in the fourteenth. In 1528 the capitals of the arch to the More Chapel were carved in Renaissance style. The design is similar to work in France, and was probably done by French masons: there is no reason for attributing the design to Holbein. At the same time Sir Thomas More reconstructed the chapel.

In 1667–74 the nave and tower were rebuilt in brick, and the walls of the More Chapel and the east end of the chancel were refaced. Mr Burt, bricklayer, was paid £792:16:4, Mr Wilcox, carpenter, £119:2:7, and Mr Lilley, plumber, £248:11:8.

Two attempts were made in the eighteenth century to get a larger church. In 1718 the parish made a petition to the Commons to include Chelsea among the Fifty New Churches: nothing came of this. In 1775 the Hon and Rev W. B. Cadogan was appointed vicar. He made 'a very advantageous proposal for rebuilding it. . . . He could not, however, awaken the same zeal in his parish, and accordingly his proposal was rejected'. There were the usual eighteenth-century repairs, and additions to the seating, and the arch from the chancel to the Lawrence Chapel was taken down and rebuilt. Work was done in 1832, and in 1857–8 there was a restoration by H. H. Burnell, a local architect. But no attempt was made to alter its character, or to gothicise the seventeenth-century work, and it remained a pleasant, old-fashioned parish church. Sir Gilbert Scott once said, 'I have built a great many new churches, and restored many old ones, but for worship I like the old church at Chelsea.'

The altar, rails, pulpit and font are seventeenth-century. The font cover is a reproduction of the one destroyed in the bombing.

Monuments   These are numerous and interesting, and include the following:

In the chancel   Sir Thomas More, 1532, with an inscription composed by himself. He was beheaded in 1535. Sir Edmund, first Lord Bray, 1539. Thomas Hungerford, 1581. Lucy Smith, 1781, and Anne Wilton 1787 (by J. Wilton).

Lawrence Chapel   Richard Jervoise, 1563. Sir Thomas Lawrence, 1593. Sara Colvile, 1631: she is shown rising from the tomb in her shroud. The seventeenth century had a firm faith in the resurrection of the body, and expressed it realistically. Sir Robert Stanley, 1632: his bust is on the front of the base of a large urn, and there are two more urns with figures of his children on their pedestals. This monument is probably by Edward Marshall. Sir John Lawrence, 1638.

More Chapel   Jane Guildford, Duchess of Northumberland, 1555.

Nave   Gregory Fiennes, Lord Dacre of the South, 1594, and his wife Ann Sackville, 1595, and one child. This is ascribed to Nicholas Johnson. Lady Jane Cheyne, 1669, a benefactress of the parish: the inscription records that a little while before her death she ordered that the church should be roofed over with rows of beams. This was made in 1672 by Pietro Bernini, and the figure was carved by Antonio Raggi from 'a draught of the face'.

Churchyard   Sir Hans Sloane, 1753, by Joseph Wilton.

St Luke's, Sydney Street (33)

The Chelsea vestry decided in 1818 to build a new parish church, and an Act of Parliament was passed in 1819. The rector was the Hon and Rev Gerald Valerian Wellesley, brother of the Duke of Wellington: he laid the foundation stone on 12 October 1820. The consecration was in 1824. The architect was James Savage, who did his best to produce a really good Gothic church. No expense was spared—the church cost £40,000—and there is a genuine vault, built of stone, and not a plaster imitation. The builder was John Wilson.

The church consists of a lofty nave with aisles, tall enough to hold galleries, though the windows are not brought down to light the passages below: and a tower with octagonal angle turrets and open pinnacles. There was to have been a spire like that of St Dunstan in the East. On each side of the tower is an open porch of two bays, and at the east there is a vestry.

Charles L. Eastlake, whose book on the Gothic Revival was published in 1872, well expresses the questions that this church raises. It has every necessary feature: it is of a good size, and its workmanship is sound. Why is it a failure from an artistic point of view? His answer is, first, that there is an unfortunate lack of proportion. This can be seen in the division of the buttresses into two long and equal heights; in the windows, which are identical, in general outline, throughout the church; in the turrets of the tower, with their nine string courses at regular intervals; and in the walls, which are of large blocks of stone of the same size. All these defects deprive the building of scale, and give it a cold, machine-made look. Then the details are clumsy: the stone carving is poor and lifeless. And there is a 'foolish, overstrained balance of parts': everything is balanced by something exactly similar—as it was in all the churches of the time.

It is, in fact, a church of 1820 adorned with carefully copied fifteenth-century features, not one built in the spirit of the Gothic builders. The same can be said, of course, of all the Gothic churches of the time. But St Luke's is so much nearer to the real thing, in its outward features, that it has always been taken more seriously, and judged more severely, than its contemporaries, which, to the Victorians, did not seem to be worthy of their attention.

The inside is very imposing, in an early nineteenth-century way. The east end has a large seven-light window, a reredos of stone panelling, now covered with curtains, and two large niches over the doorways to the vestry. The west end has stone panelling, and organ gallery with royal arms on the front.

On 31 October 1893 a faculty was given to raise the floor of the chancel, and extend it westward, and to raise the altar. The flooring of the chancel and sanctuary was to be of black and white marble, the new super-altar of stone and marble, and the pulpit, and the screen wall, of Aubigny stone. The pulpit is renaissance in design. A new altar, with marble mosaics, was erected by a faculty of 18 April 1904. The glass in the east window by Willement, 1850, was broken during the War: the new glass, by Hugh Easton, dates from 1959.

Monuments　These are not very interesting, except for the one to Luke Thomas Flood, which has a relief of an angel summoning him to heaven. The sculptor was Pepper of Brighton: the date is 1860, but it looks much older. Savage, who died on 7 May 1852, is buried in the churchyard.

Christchurch, Christchurch Street

Founded by Catherine Elizabeth Hyndman in 1838: the architect was Edward Blore. (I cannot resist the temptation to add the quite unimportant fact that, although Blore was born in 1787, I have met someone who remembered meeting him.) It is of brick, in a plain Early English style, with a south-west turret. A faculty was given on 1 December 1890 to demolish part of the gallery at the east of the south aisle, and to move the organ. A further faculty, of 28 May 1898, gave permission to extend the chancel, and build vestry and organ chamber; make the west porch into part of the church, build new porches, and extend the front further to the west, altering the galleries; also to build a church room at the north-east. The work was done in 1900–1: the architect was W. D. Caröe. The iron columns have been cased, so that they now appear as tall, capital-less circular pillars.

　　The pulpit was brought here in 1876 from St James's, Garlick Hill—to which the pulpit of St Michael Queenhithe was taken. The organ came from St Michael's. The west window is by A. K. Nicholson.

St Saviour's, Walton Street

The architect was George Basevi: the church was begun in 1839, and consecrated on 27 May 1840. It is very simple, tall and thin, with a rather appealing interior. An additional north aisle, designed by E. P. Loftus Brock, was built in 1878. A faculty was given on 24 December 1889 to do extensive work, of which the chief items were, to build a new chancel and morning chapel; demolish the east walls of the nave and of the south and inner north aisles, with the turrets on each side; and also remove the clergy vestry. Small detached columns of Bath stone, with capitals and bases, were to be fixed to the nave columns, with statues and canopies, in oak, above them. This was not done.

　　The new work was designed by the Rev Ernest Geldart—one of the remarkable nine-

St Andrew by the Wardrobe, 1685–93: a Wren church, constructed after War damage

27 St Botolph's, Bishopsgate, rebuilt in 1725–8

28 All Hallows', London Wall, rebuilt in 1765–7 by George Dance junior

9 St Mary Woolnoth, by Nicholas Hawksmoor 1716–27: the west front

30 St Dunstan in the West, the tower of John Shaw's church completed 1832

31 St Botolph's, Aldersgate, 1789–91 by Nathaniel Wright

32 All Saints'; the reconstruction of the old church, and of its monuments, after almost total destruction in the War

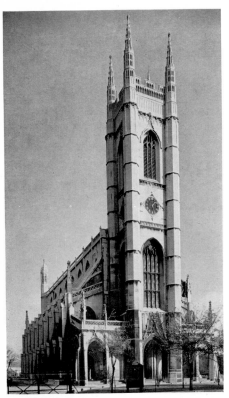

33 St Luke's, 1820–24 by James Savage: the first stone-vaulted church of the Gothic Revival

34 St Simon Zelotes, 1858 by Joseph Peacock

teenth century all-rounders: priest, architect, artist, and musician. J. N. R. Vining was associated with him. The chancel—really only a sanctuary—and chapel were built in 1890. The pulpit was erected in 1893.

St Simon Zelotes, Milner Street (34)

The church and vicarage were built in 1858 'as one among similar means of appropriating a legacy from William Coles'. The sites were bought by the parishioners of Upper Chelsea, and others. Joseph Peacock was the architect: the builder was White, who built both church and vicarage for less than £7,000. The church was consecrated on 21 March 1859.

The plan is determinedly original: quite a short nave, with low aisles, and a gallery in the west bay: then an arch, and two more bays, with taller aisles, which once contained galleries: they were removed in 1896. This is the eastern end of the nave, not a chancel. The altar is in a small sanctuary.

'Peacock was determined', wrote H. S. Goodhart-Rendel, 'that no visitor should be dull for a single moment.' He mentions the east window, which is richly traceried—but all the upper part is blocked with carved foliage, except for a small opening at the top. 'Few would have thought of the shape of the clerestory window, and none, except Peacock, could have conceived such a stone screen as divides aisles and chapels.'

The *Illustrated London News* called St Simon's, 'One of the most original and beautiful of the many churches which have been built of late years in the metropolis.' But the *Ecclesiologist* was not amused. 'Altogether we fear that this building will be no gain to art.' There was a certain skill in the management of the details; the good stone construction and the internal polychrome brick walling, were praised. 'But here our praise must stop.' The church has been very little altered, except for oak panelling of the 1920s in the sanctuary. The glass in the east window is by Lavers and Barraud.

Holy Trinity, Sloane Street

The original building was a Commissioners' church. George Godwin (I) made a design, which was not accepted, and James Savage was appointed as architect. The church was begun in May 1828, and finished in December 1831. It was fifteenth-century in style, with two large turrets at the west end. This church continued in use until July 1888, when it was closed and demolished. J. D. Sedding had prepared designs for a large new church, the fabric of which would be paid for by the patron, the Earl of Cadogan. The builders were Higgs and Hill. Work proceeded steadily, and after the foundation stone had been laid on 30 May 1889, 'the company dispersed about the building, where the stone columns and the red brick pillars, and even the tracery of the great windows, are beginning to rise above the confusion of scaffolding and crude materials' (*West London Press*). The church was consecrated on 13 May 1890.

It consists of a wide nave, with a vault, and chancel of the same width and height; with aisles, narrow on the south, and wider on the north. The front, which is Perpendicular, of brick and stone, embattled, with four turrets, is made symmetrical by the projection of the right-hand porch beyond the aisle. The walls, apart from the front, are of the plainest brickwork. The east and west windows are very large, as the fashion was at the time.

The style is Sedding's own invention. He used fourteenth- and fifteenth-century features, but he did not mean to be bound by any precedent: a church ought to be 'a design *by* living men *for* living men'. It can only be called Free Gothic, or Arts and Crafts Gothic, and there are Renaissance features.

Peter Anson points out that the consecration coincided, more or less, with the publication of Oscar Wilde's *The Picture of Dorian Gray*, and suggests that the church is something like the book: both were extolled by their admirers as wonderful works of art, and attacked as dangerous by their enemies. He describes the church as '*fin-de-siècle*'. That is fair enough, provided there is no suggestion that Sedding himself was either precious or decadent. He was romantic and sensitive, but deeply religious, a keen Churchman, and impeccable in his life.

The church is remarkable as a building: but Sedding was not content to design a church, and leave its fittings to chance. Many fine churches of the late nineteenth century are spoiled by their fittings, which were obviously chosen from the catalogues of the church furnishers. Sedding had been taught by Ruskin that he must always have pencil or chisel in hand; and he had tried to form a school of masons and modellers and carvers from nature. He was a member of the Art Workers Guild, and on the committee of the Arts and Crafts Society. He believed that a church should be 'wrought and painted over with everything that has life and beauty—in frank and fearless naturalism covered with men and beasts and flowers'. In Holy Trinity he tried to carry out his ideal. He died in 1891, before much work had been done; but he was succeeded by his disciple Henry Wilson, who had worked with him.

Sedding wanted to employ the leading artists of the day, and Sir Edward Burne-Jones came to see the church. He approved of it, and said that a complete scheme of decoration should be made at once: no haphazard idea, however enchanting, should be carried out until this had been done. He designed the glass for the east window, with William Morris, who designed the foliage and the surroundings: the figures are by Burne-Jones. He also made drawings for sculptures in the frieze above the arcades, but these were not carried out.

There were other schemes that were never realised, such as the carving of the medallions in the spandrels of the arcades, by Armstead: only one was executed. And the piers were to have had figures of the Apostles by Hamo Thornycroft.

But a great deal was done. The ironwork at the west of the chancel was designed by Sedding: the additional hammered work is thought to be Wilson's design. Wilson also designed the altar rails, the grille behind the side altar (carried out by Nelson Dawson), and the rails outside the church at the west. The figures on the choir stalls were modelled by F. W. Pomeroy. The cherubim round the shaft of the font were worked by F. Boucher, under Onslow Ford. The painting in front of the side altar is by W. Reynolds-Stephens.

Three windows in the chapel were designed by Sir W. B. Richmond, and executed by Powell: other glass is by Whall. A large reredos was designed by Sedding, but never carried out: the faculty for the present reredos was given on 31 January 1901: it was designed by John Tweed.

F. C. Eden succeeded Wilson as architect. He thought that the additions to the furniture and decorations made since Sedding's time were 'clever but style-less', and were already dated. So, of course, they were: they recall back numbers of the *Studio*, and the brown reproductions in the *Builder*. But we do not find them tiresome, as Eden said that he did. A certain amount of cleaning and whitening was done under Eden.

In 1941 the roof was destroyed in an air raid. Repairs were done in 1950–1, under Verner O. Rees, and a lower roof was substituted for the vault. This was taken down in 1959, and Michael Farey replaced it by a new one similar to the original, of Carlite plaster, on expanded metal, with precast moulded plaster ribs. The cost was £5,000.

St Andrew's, Park Walk

This church took the place of Park Chapel, built in 1718, and mainly rebuilt about 1810. It was demolished about 1910.

The new church is very ordinary. It was designed by Sir A. W. Blomfield and Sons, and built in 1912–13: of red brick, with a south-west tower and spire.

Clerkenwell

This parish, close to the borders of the City, soon became built up. The choir of the church of the Knights of St John, which had been a chapel—Anglican and Presbyterian—was bought in 1721 by Simon Michel, who enlarged and repaired it. In 1723 he sold it to the Commissioners for the Fifty New Churches, and it was consecrated as a parish church. In 1931 the parish was added to that of St James's, and the church was assigned entirely to the Order of St John of Jerusalem. This was a sign of the usual fall in population: in the early and mid-nineteenth century it was growing (and included 'some of the best paid and best informed artisans in London'): by the end of the century it was falling. So that it was a place first for building churches, and then for pulling them down.

St James's, Clerkenwell Green (36)

On the site of the church of the Benedictine Nunnery of St Mary, which came to the parishioners after the dissolution.

The church needed rebuilding at the beginning of the eighteenth century, and an attempt was made in 1718 to get it included among the Fifty New Churches. But it was not until much later that anything was done. In 1787 a petition was made to the Commons: it was reported on 2 May, when James Carr and Joseph Carter gave evidence that the church was dangerous, and would have to be rebuilt. An Act was passed enabling trustees to raise the money. The new church was consecrated on 10 July 1792: the architect was James Carr. It cost over £11,000.

The church is plain, of brick, with the end bays on the south marked by stone quoins and a balustraded parapet. The stone steeple—which looks rather lonely in Clerkenwell, as though it had strayed from the City—has an open octagonal stage, then a smaller concave one, and an obelisk spire. It was rebuilt, without alteration, by W. P. Griffith in 1849.

The plain interior keeps its galleries, Doric altar piece, and wrought iron rails. It was restored and redecorated in 1882 by Blomfield and Roland Paul, and the usual choir stalls have been inserted; but it keeps its eighteenth-century atmosphere. There is bright glass in the east window by Heaton, Butler and Bayne, 1863.

Monuments　Sir William Weston, Prior of St John's, 1540: an effigy in a shroud. Thomas Crosse, J.P., a benefactor of the parish, 1712. Henry Penton, 1714. Gilbert Burnet, bishop of Salisbury, died 17 March 1714/15: a marble slab by Robert Hartshorne, carrying out Edward Stanton's design. Thomas Crosse, 1729, by Roubiliac.

St James's, Pentonville Road (35)

The chapel was built in 1777–8: the architect was Aaron Henry Hurst, who died in 1799, and is buried here. In 1790 an Act was passed for rebuilding St James's, Clerkenwell, and for purchasing Pentonville Chapel, and making it a chapel of ease to the parish church. It was consecrated on 8 June 1791.

The front has Ionic pilasters, and a pediment, with a cupola over. A plain interior. The painting of the raising of Jairus' daughter was painted by James Frearson, an amateur.

There was a repair in 1816: 'the nakedness of the ceiling was relieved by a handsome circular ornament in the centre, so contrived as, at the same time, to ventilate the building by a connected aperture in the roof'. In 1933 there was a remodelling by T. Murray Ashford. The side walls above the galleries were taken down, and the roof was cut back to the width of the nave: the walls were rebuilt at the same width as the front of the galleries. The children's galleries, on each side of the organ, still remain.

St Mark's, Myddleton Square (37)

The New River Company developed some of its property, and the streets were laid out, from 1819, by the Company's engineer and surveyor, William Chadwell Mylne. A site was given for a church, to be built by the Commissioners, and the Company asked that Mylne should be employed as the architect: the Commissioners agreed that he might submit designs 'of a plain Gothic character'. This he did, and the church was begun in 1825, finished in 1827, and consecrated on the first day of 1828. The builder was Robert Streather, the cost was about £16,000.

It is of brick, in the usual thin Commissioners' Gothic, but with an unusually solid west tower. The vestibules, on either side, have pinnacles and open parapets, like the tower. The rest of the church is less ambitious. A chancel was arranged in 1873 by W. Slater. A faculty 11 June 1879 to reseat, move the organ, and open out the vestry to receive it; and remove the super-gallery. The church was damaged in the War, and only partly restored. The interior is very bare.

Holy Redeemer, Exmouth Market (38)

On the site of Spa Fields Chapel, a nonconformist place of worship; the congregation moved elsewhere. Begun in 1887, and consecrated on 13 October 1888. The design was by J. D. Sedding: it was shown at the Royal Academy in 1888. The church was completed— e.g. the tower and the east end—by H. Wilson. It is of Italian design, and reminded Walter Pater of the Renaissance churches at Venice, and of Wren's London churches— as they must have looked when they were fresh and clean.

It is constructed of steel stanchions and girders enclosed with concrete columns and entablature: there is a groined vault. The light comes from the large circular windows of the clerestory.

The altar stands under a massive ciborium. The organ belonged to the Prince Consort.

Fulham

Fulham in the early nineteenth century consisted of the old village, down by the river, dominated by the palace of the Bishop of London; Walham Green; a cluster of good houses at Parson's Green; and North End. Church accommodation was duly provided: a proprietary chapel, soon to be given a district, was built at North End in 1813–14; and St John's, Walham Green, a Commissioners' church, was built in 1827–8.

James Thorne's *Environs of London*, 1876, says that Fulham had by then become a portion of the outer fringe of London, though the village itself kept 'something of its ancient local and independent aspect'. Parson's Green had fallen from its high estate: North End was losing its mansions, and new and smaller houses were rising. There were nurseries and market gardens, but they were continually being eaten up by building.

By the end of the century, the borough was almost all built up. The development was completely undistinguished: small middle and working class houses—for the inhabitants of which, churches were supplied in the usual proportions. Casualties have been few: three were bombed, of which two have new and different churches on the site, and one is not being rebuilt; and one damaged, no longer to be used as a church.

All Saints', Fulham High Street

The tall fifteenth-century tower was restored by George Godwin in 1845. The church was one of those picturesque, much patched buildings that were to be found in most places near London. A faculty was given in 1768 to repew, take away the south arcade to make room for a gallery, alter the windows, etc. In 1840 there was an enlargement by Edward Lapidge. A proposal to rebuild was made in 1869, and Scott made plans; but there was, for the moment, not enough money. Then Blomfield made designs for a large new Perpendicular church. A faculty was given in 1879, the old church was closed in 1880, and the new one was consecrated on 9 July 1881. The font dates from 1622, the reredos, by Heaton, Butler and Bayne, from 1885. The window of the Evangelists, by Wailes, was given by Bishop Blomfield: it used to be the east window.

Monuments Altar tomb, with inscription gone. Another to Sir William Butts, 1545. Margaret Hornebolt (a brass), 1529. William Plumbe, 1593. Thomas Bonde, 1600. Lady Margaret Legh, 1603. Katharine Hart, 1605. Sir Thomas Smith, 1609. William Payne, 1626, and Jane, 1610. Thomas Carlos, 1665. William Rumbold, 1667. John Mordaunt, Viscount Mourdaunt of Avalon, 1675, by John Bushnell: a standing figure, in a toga, with a baton in his hand, as Constable of Windsor Castle. Elizabeth Limpany, 1694. Dorothy Clarke, 1695, by Grinling Gibbons. Bishop Gibson, 1748. Elizabeth Hatsell, 1805, by P. M. van Gelder. Sir John Beckett, 1847, by Bedford. Bishop Blomfield, 1857, by Sir George Richmond.

In the churchyard are several tombs of bishops of London: that of Sherlock, 1761, is signed by John Vardy.

St John's, Walham Green (40)

Designed by George Ledwell Taylor, and built in 1827–8: the cost was £9,539, towards which the Church Building Commissioners gave £6,957. The builders were Samuel Baker and Sons. There was a restoration by E. P. Warren in 1893. The work, as specified by the faculty (4 February 1893) involved reseating, shortening the galleries, providing oak stalls, screen, pulpit, and new altar; and reglazing. It is of white brick. The tower has triplets filled with pierced stonework, and the west window is two-light Decorated. Otherwise the windows are large, bare lancets: a triplet at the east.

A plain panelled west gallery has a pleasant Gothic organ case: the aisle galleries have been taken away. It is not a very exciting interior.

St James's, Moore Park Road (41)

The building of this church was due to Baroness Burdett Coutts. The foundation stone was laid 20 June 1867, and the church consecrated on 19 December of the same year. The cost was only £4,500. The architect was H. A. Darbishire, who was employed by the Baroness in her philanthropic schemes—flats in Bethnal Green, the Columbia Market, Holly Village, St Pancras, and the fountain in Victoria Park. He produced a most original church. There are very low walls on the north and the south, above which is a large expanse of slated roof, with a clerestory of dormers. The inside is divided into nave and aisles by thin pillars supporting light wooden arches, with large quatrefoiled circles in the spandrels, and the arch braces of the roof. There are painted screens to the transepts.

The apsidal chancel, in a more normal style, was added by Ewan Christian: the faculty was given on 28 January 1874, and on 28 August 1906 another to replace the dormers by larger ones.

St Andrew's, May Street, West Kensington (39)

Designed 1873–4 by Newman and Billing, the builders being Dove Brothers, the church is of banded brick, in French thirteenth-century style, with an effective French-looking spire. The clerestory is of circular, crudely-traceried windows. Most of the capitals have been left uncarved. A new vestry was added in 1895–6, by Aston Webb, and the former vestry was converted into a chapel. In 1896–7 the nave was extended one bay westward, by the same architect: the cost was £1,560.

The interior is very dark. The reredos and sedilia date from 1900. An inscription says that the roodscreen was erected in 1897: there is a rood on a beam of dark oak and difficult to see; but no screen. The bell, dated 1623, came from the City church of St Martin Outwich.

St Peter's Reporton Road

Newman and Newman were the architects, and Gibbs and Flew the builders of this church, built 1882–3. The foundation stone was laid on 8 November 1882. A large, rather dull brick church in Early English style: the apsidal chancel is vaulted, with stone ribs and brick filling. The west end was severely damaged in 1940, and rebuilt after the War. The pulpit came from Wren's church of St Matthew, Friday Street. In 1965 it was taken to the restored church of St Andrew by the Wardrobe, and a new pulpit by Faithcraft took its place.

St Dionis', Parson's Green

An Order in Council in 1876 authorised the demolition of Wren's St Dionis Backchurch, and the Ecclesiastical Commissioners proposed that, of the money obtained by the sale of the church and the site, £7,000 should be used for the building of a new church at Parson's Green, and £3,000 for its endowment. The foundation stone was laid on 15 July 1884, and the church was consecrated on 19 June 1885. The architect was Ewan Christian, and the builders were W. H. Brass and Son. The tower was completed in 1895–6. The style is fifteenth-century—which is most unusual for Ewan Christian, and rather successful. Nave and aisles, with a tower at the east of the north aisle, and a western narthex opening into the nave. Waggon roofs, and aisle windows of East Anglian type.

The font came from the City church: it was the gift of Sir Henry Tulse, master of the Grocers Company, and Lord Mayor in 1684: the cover, in the shape of the tower of the old St Dionis', was designed by Martin Travers. The pulpit also came from the City church. A screen was erected in 1919: the base remains, but on it there is a screen, with loft and rood, by Martin Travers, who also designed the altar, 1932–3, and the memorial to the Rev J. S. Sinclair, under whom the church was built. The glass in the east window, by Christopher Webb, takes the place of glass broken in the War.

Ten bells from St Dionis' went to All Hallows', Lombard Street. When All Hallows' was taken down, two of them were allotted to the new St Dionis', but were given by mistake to St Paul's, Westminster Bridge Road. St Dionis' was presented, as a compensation, with a bell that had been in St Michael Bassishaw. (St Paul's was bombed, and its two bells have disappeared.)

60

35 St James's, Pentonville Road, 1777–8 by Aaron Hurst; saved from demolition and reduced in size in 1933

36 St James's, Clerkenwell Green: the steeple of James Carr's church, built in 1788–92

37 St Mark's, Myddleton Square, 1825–7 by W. C. Mylne

38 Holy Redeemer, Exmouth Market, 1887–1888 by J. D. Sedding, completed by his disciple H. Wilson

39 St Andrew's, West Kensington, 1873–4
by Newman and Billing

40 St John's, Walham Green, 1827–8
by G. L. Taylor

41 St James's, Moore Park: nave and aisles by
H. A. Darbishire, 1867; chancel by
Ewan Christian, 1874

42 St Etheldreda's, Fulham Palace Road: Guy Biscoe's
more modest replacement of a large Late Victorian
church destroyed by bombing

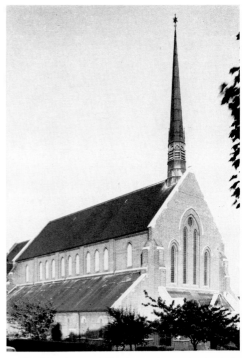

43 St Matthew's, Wandsworth Bridge Road,
1893–5 by Sir A. W. Blomfield and Sons. Typical of large churches built in the suburbs at a
time when a church had only to be built and it
was filled

St Clement's, Fulham Palace Road

Designed by A. W. Blomfield: the date is 1885–6, but it looks earlier. It consists of nave and aisles, with apsidal west baptistery, and a lofty chancel with north organ chamber and south chapel. There is a tall flèche over the eastern gable of the nave. The nave has, in places, a distinctly Butterfieldian look: the chancel, with its quintuplet, is more normal later Blomfield. The chapel has, rather unusually, a dwarf wall and ironwork before the sanctuary. Nearly all the glass is by Jones and Willis, and is not good. The font came from Wren's St Matthew's, Friday Street.

(Since this was written, the church has been closed. The font was taken (1965) to St Andrew by the Wardrobe.)

St Matthew's Wandsworth Bridge Road (43)

The church was built in 1893–5: the architects were Sir A. W. Blomfield and Sons. Very large and rather ugly, [it is] of brown stock brick, relieved with red, in the lancet style: a tall and thin lead-covered flèche. The pillars are of red brick, with stone bases, capitals, and springers. The glass by Clayton and Bell was put here in 1925: it came from St Mary's, Vincent Square, Westminster, and was given in 1866–96 by Sir James Knowles in memory of his wife. The three paintings on the east wall are by H. E. Webster, 1928. The bishop's chair is made from bits of the altar piece of St George's, Botolph Lane. At the north-west are the panels with the usual writings, from the same altar piece, re-used as War memorial tablets. The lettering can just be seen under the new black paint.

St Alban's, Margravine Road

The original plans were made by Robert Willey, and the foundation stone was laid on 17 June 1895. But owing to a misunderstanding with the architect the work was held up until the autumn. New plans were made by Aston Webb and E. Ingress Bell, and the nave and aisles were opened in 1897. The chancel has not yet been built. The church is Perpendicular in style, of red brick externally, and yellow and red inside. The organ from St Bartholomew by the Exchange, which came here in 1904 via St Bartholomew's, Moor Lane, has been taken to St Vedast's, Foster Lane. St Alban's now has, in its place, the organ of St Philip's, Bethnal Green.

St Oswald's, Anselm Road

The church, built in 1898–9, by Alfred J. Hopkins and W. Valentyne Aspen, is of red brick, Perpendicular, over a basement, with no structural chancel. The nave and aisles have five bays on the north, and four on the south side: the east bay on the south is the vestry, with an organ loft above, and steps down to the basement. The three middle bays on the north have not been completed, and have a lean-to roof. A reredos was proposed by Michael Tapper, but has not been carried out. In fact, very little has been done to the church since it was built.

Christchurch, Studdridge Street

A red brick church in fifteenth-century style, by J. E. K. and J. P. Cutts; the foundation stone was laid on 18 October 1902, and the consecration was on 19 May 1903. The chancel was built in 1908, and consecrated on 24 January 1909. 'Everything of ordinary kind, but a little better than usual.' (Goodhart-Rendel.) The font cover came from St Benet's, Gracechurch Street, after being in the crypt of St Paul's for over 30 years; and the pulpit and altar rails came from St George's, Botolph Lane.

St Etheldreda's, Fulham Palace Road (42)

This is now a post-War church, which bears no resemblance to its predecessor, and is not a reconstruction of it. The mission was begun in November 1894 and Dr Temple laid the foundation stone of the church that was expected to be permanent on 16 June 1896; on 2 April 1897 Dr Creighton consecrated the first portion of it.

A. H. Skipworth was the architect: there was a broad and lofty nave, with passage aisles, and a narrow chancel raised above a crypt.

The church was destroyed by bombing, and it was at first proposed to build flats on the site. However, a smaller church was built, and consecrated in 1958. The architect was Guy Biscoe. It is of reinforced concrete and brick: the font, of copper, is in a semi-circular baptistery, which has glass by Carter Shapland. The crucifix on the east wall was carved by Rita Lang: the oak came from Brighton pier.

St Mary's, Hammersmith Road

This was a chapel built in 1813–14 by Richard Hunt, of the Cedars: the architect was H. J. Wyatt. Hunt assigned it to the churchwardens of Fulham and received it back from them at a nominal rent, for 999 years. On these conditions it was consecrated on 6 May 1814 as a chapel for the parish of Fulham. In 1835 it was given a district: but it was regarded as a proprietary chapel, and was offered for sale by auction as such on 23 June 1837.

The auctioneer, Mr Hoggart, described it in glowing terms. 'This elegant CHAPEL comprises a building of the most substantial character, and of chaste elevation, constructed by an exceedingly clever artist, at an expense of upwards of 10,000 l exclusive of the valuable ground upon which it stands; the whole of the interior has been fitted up in the best possible taste, the galleries are of solid oak, the window over the altar is of beautiful stained glass, and hot air stoves have been placed at every convenient part of the chapel...', etc. It was bought, with money advanced on mortgage, by the Rev J. S. Byers, who found that he was, in fact, not the owner at all. It became a parish church—and, though he was the patron, he could not make the church the source of profit that he had hoped, and reimburse himself.

There was enlargement and alteration in 1883–4 by E. P. Loftus Brock.

It was destroyed by bombing in the War and Viscount Brentford laid the foundation stone of the new church on 2 April 1960: the consecration was on 21 January 1961. The architects were Seely and Paget, the east window is by Hugh Easton. The pews are of African mahogany: the pulpit and lectern of reconstructed Cotswold stone. The contractors were G. E. Wallis and Co.

Hackney

The eighteenth and early nineteenth centuries did their duty in providing church accommodation in Hackney. The old church was rebuilt, and consecrated on 15 July 1797. The Chapel of Ease at South Hackney was consecrated on 13 May 1810. West Hackney, a Commissioners' church with a very large accommodation, was consecrated in 1824. Homerton had Ram's Chapel; and at Clapton the eighteenth-century Stamford Hill Chapel was enlarged in 1827, and consecrated on 22 October of the same year. St Philip's, Dalston, and St Peter's, De Beauvoir Town, were consecrated in 1841, and St James's, Clapton, in 1842. St Barnabas', Homerton, owes its existence to Joshua Watson: it was consecrated in 1847. St John of Jerusalem, South Hackney, which took the place of the former Chapel of Ease, was consecrated in 1848.

Church building in the district was undertaken by an unusually keen set of churchmen. The spirit in which they worked is shown by the rules of the Stoke Newington and Hackney Church Association (1854): the second rule states: 'That the object of the Association be the Glory of God in the extension of His church by all lawful means, the promotion of the increase and efficient performance of all the offices of the church, the diffusion of Christian knowledge, the exercise of Works of Charity, and the Mutual Improvement of the Members of the Association.'

Some rather mediocre churches were added later, and some that were more satisfactory—those, for instance, designed by Francis Dollman. The church building programme ended with the erection of two outstanding churches: Bodley's St Mary of Eton, Hackney Wick, begun in 1890, and Professor Reilly's St Barnabas', Shacklewell, 1909.

Ram's Chapel, an elegant eighteenth-century building, became unsafe, and was taken down in 1934. Smirke's enormous West Hackney Church was bombed: every trace of it has been removed, and a small church has taken its place. The four other churches that have been demolished were less interesting.

St John-at-Hackney, Mare Street (48)

The early sixteenth-century tower is all that remains of the old church which, as usual, had become by the eighteenth century too small for the parish. It was surveyed in 1779 by William Jupp and in 1789 by William Blackburn, who proposed to build a new church to hold 3,000 on a different site. He was appointed surveyor for the work, but died in 1790. James Spiller was appointed in his place. He made three plans, one 'upon the Principle of an Octagon': the present plans, 'in the plainest manner of brick', were accepted in April, and early in 1792 the bishop approved the specifications, estimates, and contracts. Hobson was to do the bricklayers' work, Peter Banner the carpenters' work, and John Spiller the masons' work. Banner afterwards became bankrupt, and the roof was completed by Edward Colebatch, who also did the pewing. The new church was consecrated on 15 July 1797. In 1812 Robert Streather's estimate for building the steeple was accepted: the porches were built at the same time.

The plan is a Greek cross, practically a square, with the slightest of projections. There were pediments on the four sides, and projecting eaves. The walls are of brown brick (but they were to have been mostly covered with stucco by Bernasconi): the steeple on the north is of stone. It adds a touch of fantasy to the sombre exterior—which is, otherwise, obviously the work of an architect with a temperament, who had something to do with Soane.

Inside, there is a large central area, with a shallow vault, which began to give way, and was secured by Beresford Pite in 1929. The pews were reduced in height by Blomfield in 1883.

The church was badly damaged by fire on 18 May 1955 and restored by N. F. Cachemaille-Day and William C. Lock: it was rededicated on 24 June 1958. The pediments on the north and south were removed. Some changes were made in the arrangement of the interior. The eighteenth-century organ, which was burned, was replaced by the organ from All Saints', Ennismore Gardens, Westminster.

Monuments Brasses of John Lymsey, 1545, and Arthur Dericote, and four wives, 1562. Christopher Urswyck, Dean of Windsor and Rector of Hackney, 1521–2. Lucye, wife of John Nevill, Lord Latimer, 1582–3. Richard Hallily, 1605–6, and Margaret. Henry Banister, 1628, and Anne, 1632–3. David Doulven, Bishop of Bangor, 1633. Thomas Wood, 1649, and Susan, 1650. Benjamin Dod, 1706. Richard de Beauvoir, 1708, and Mary, 1722. Captain Henry Newcombe, 1797, by Charles Regnart. Lieutenant Harry Bingley Sedgwick, 1811, also by Regnart.

St Thomas's, Stamford Hill

This was a proprietary chapel, built in about 1774 by John Devall for his tenants. It was bought by the Rev George Richards, who was appointed vicar of St Martin in the Fields in 1824: in 1827 he sold it to Joshua Watson, and three other gentlemen. The chapel was enlarged, and given a tower, from designs by Joseph Gwilt, and it was consecrated on 22 October 1827.

In 1873 a faculty was obtained for a reconstruction. The work was done under William Burges: the galleries were removed, the two rows of windows were reduced to one, a new wooden roof was erected, a choir was formed, and the church was painted and decorated, and given much stained glass. For the chancel Burges 'endeavoured to adopt the time-honoured arrangement existing at St Clemente at Rome, adapting it to our own ritual'.

The body of the church was destroyed in the War and rebuilt by N. F. Cachemaille-Day. Glass by Goddard and Gibbs.

St James', Lower Clapton

Built in 1840–1 by E. C. Hakewill; it was consecrated on 14 October 1841. The style is Early English: a wide nave, transepts with galleries, and turret on the south side. The kind of church that might well be called 'barn-like'. But Bumpus says that the chancel was 'a by no means unpleasing specimen of revived Early English'. The reredos is now at the west end.

The foundation stone of the present chancel—with organ gallery over a narrow north aisle, and south chapel—was laid on 21 July 1902. The architect was W. D. Caröe. The rest of the church was reseated at the same time. The east window is by Burlison and Grylls.

St Peter's, De Beauvoir Town (44)

Built in 1840-1, of stock brick, in rather starved Gothic; the architect was William C. Lockner. It has the usual pre-ecclesiological plan: the tower is flanked by vestibules containing the gallery stairs the tops of which, open to the church, have pleasingly shabby plaster vaults. There are catacombs beneath the church, now used as a parish hall, etc. The galleries remain: the nave has been reroofed.

The chancel, with north aisle and south organ chamber, was added in 1884: it is Romanesque, and looks like the work of Blomfield, but was designed by H. R. Gough. The faculty also mentions reseating, and moving the pulpit.

St John of Jerusalem, Lauriston Road, South Hackney (49)

This church was built by Henry Handley Norris, who became perpetual curate of the Chapel of Ease in Well Street, which was built in 1806, and consecrated in 1810. It became a rectory in 1831. Norris was a High churchman, and one of the Hackney Phalanx which included J. J. Watson, rector of Hackney, Joshua Watson, his brother, and Edward Churton.

The new church was built to supersede the chapel. E. C. Hakewill made the designs, the foundation stone was laid on 15 May 1845 and the consecration was on 20 July 1848. The church is in Early English style, with walls of Kentish rag with Speldhurst stone dressings. Tower with spire (now removed), suggested by St Mary's, Stamford: a broad, aisled nave, transepts, and chancel with an apse.

The *Ecclesiologist* naturally took a great interest in it. There were faults, but there was also much to be thankful for. It was one of the largest churches built since the revival of Christian architecture, and 'a striking monument, reared by one of a generation now passing away, of how soon and to what an extent the Church of England has already begun in her religious structures to assert her unity with the Catholic Church of ancient times'.

There was glass by Wailes, Powell, and Castell: this was lost in the War. The repair after War damage was done by N. F. Cachemaille-Day, who put a slender new spire on the tower.

St Barnabas', Homerton High Street (47)

This church owes its existence to Joshua Watson, who obtained grants amounting to £3,000 from the Church Building Commissioners, I.C.B.S., and the Metropolis Churches

Fund. He also gave the endowment, and half the cost of the vicarage. The architect was Arthur Ashpitel. The building committee, suspicious of High Church tendencies, made him substitute an arrow for a weather-cock, and Portland stone paving in the chancel for the encaustic tiles which he had promised to give. Building was begun in 1845, and the church was consecrated on St Barnabas day, 1847: the north aisle was added in 1851.

The *Ecclesiologist* was very critical: all that it could praise was the material—Kentish rag and Bath stone. The chancel was too short; the sacristy was in the wrong place; the style was Third-pointed, with a poor attempt at Middle-pointed tracery; the mouldings were inaccurate; the tower was too small.

This was unkind: it is really quite a good church, though certainly the style is on the late side. But the foliage, on the capitals and corbels, is not very attractive. The chancel was rearranged by R. J. Withers in 1874. The church suffered severe damage in 1944, but was restored by William C. Lock, and rededicated on 13 September 1958. What remains of the chancel has been converted into vestries. The nave has been fitted with furniture from the demolished church of St Andrew, Bethnal Green. This looks very well, particularly the large triptych. All the windows have, of course, been reglazed. The church makes a pleasant group with the vicarage and the school, also designed by Ashpitel.

St Mark's, Dalston (51, 52)

Chester Cheston junior made plans in 1862, and a contract was made with Dove Brothers. The Earl of Shaftesbury laid the foundation stone on 20 June 1864. Building proceeded rather slowly, and there were several disputes and set-backs. The church was opened in 1866, but not consecrated, because of the debt, until 6 August 1870. The completion of the tower was begun in 1877: Cheston had designed a spire, but the completion was done to a new design by E. L. Blackburne. About 1880 the chancel roof was raised, new windows were inserted, and a mosaic reredos was erected.

The church is difficult to describe: it needs to be seen. The interior, which has walls of coloured brickwork, and slender iron columns, glows with glass (by Lavers and Barraud). An unusual feature is the provision of two glazed openings in the roof, at the points where the roofs of the transepts join it: they are filled with figures of angels.

St Matthew's, Warwick Grove, Clapton (50)

Begun in 1867, and consecrated on 5 April 1869. The architect was Francis Dollman, the contractors were Myers and Son, and there was a cooperation of several Victorian craftsmen: James Forsyth, sculptor, Skidmore, metal-worker, Godwin, tile-maker, and Powell, glass-painter. The walls are of brick, faced with Kentish rag outside, and Bath stone ashlar within: the columns are of Mansfield stone. The church has a nave and aisles, a chancel with apsidal sanctuary, a north chapel, and south tower: the lofty spire was, unfortunately, taken down in 1962. The church stands well, and the views from the east are impressive. The approach from the north along an avenue of trees is also pleasant. The whole thing reminds one of Gilbert Scott, and Skidmore's metal screen and gates contribute to the Scott-ish effect. The sanctuary, which has a painted roof, is elaborately adorned with arcading filled with mosaics by Salviati, and a reredos with a relief of the Last Supper. The church was damaged by bombing, and restored in 1953: only scraps remain of the original glass.

All Saints', Blurton Road, Clapton (46)

A. J. Beresford Hope laid the foundation stone on 29 October 1870, and the church was consecrated on 2 November 1871. The architect was Francis Dollman, and the church is of red and black brick, faced with Kentish rag, with dressings and arcades of Bath stone. The aisles are rather low, with buttresses carried across them: the clerestory is tall, with windows of a French type. The outside has a satisfactory cliff-like appearance. The tower was never built: Bumpus meditates on what it might have been.

There is a good Victorian interior. The alabaster reredos is a Crucifixion group by Earp. There has been some clearing up in the chancel: the standard lights, and the choir-stalls, have been removed, and so has the iron screen—which is rather a pity. The glass in the east window is of the Ascension, but the central light has deteriorated, and now looks something like a drawing of a bombed church by John Piper. The west window is by Mayer, 1883. No one has, so far, touched the dado of chocolate and yellow glazed tiles in the aisles.

St Luke's, Chatham Road

Built in 1871–2 by Dove Brothers, and designed by Newman and Billing, this is a quiet, very Victorian church, in a rather out-of-the-way position. The style is square-abacus thirteenth-century, with a tall tower and spire at the south-west, completed in 1882. The interior is rather sombre. The east window, 1950, by H. Vernon Spreadbury.

Holy Trinity, Mayfield Road, Dalston

Built in 1878–9, by Ewan Christian, from the proceeds of the demolition of St Martin Outwich, in the City. It is of red brick (now whitened inside), in the lancet style, cruci-

St Peter's, De Beauvoir
wn, 1840–1 by
C. Lockner

45 St Mary of Eton, Hackney Wick, begun by G. G. Bodley 1890 and completed
by C. G. Hare 1912. The interior after the moving of the screen

6 All Saints', Clapton, 1870–1
y F. T. Dollman

47 St Barnabas', Shacklewell, 1909–10
by Professor C. H. Reilly

48 St John at Hackney: James Spiller's church, consecrated in 1797, with the steeple added in 1812

49 St John of Jerusalem: the tower of this church by E. C. Hakewill 1845–8 has lost its stone broach spire

50 St Matthew's, Clapton, 1867–9 by F. T. Dollman

51 St Mark's, Dalston, by Chester Cheston, begun in 1864

52 St Mark's: the tower completed by E. L. Blackburne 1877

form, with the chancel beneath the central tower, and a sanctuary, the east wall of which rises, in a satisfactory town-church way, above the pavement. The south transept was damaged by fire, and has been reduced in height. The east window glass is by A. F. Erridge.

All Soul's, Overbury Road, Clapton

The foundation stone was laid 2 December 1882 and the church consecrated 1 December 1883. Designed by Francis Dollman, but less remarkable than his other churches. A brick church, with nothing unusual in its design or plan. The reredos, with a carving of Christ bearing the Cross, has a rather Butterfieldian look.

St Paul's, Glyn Road, Homerton

Built 1890–1 and designed by Henry Cowell Boys, architect to the Grocers Company. A large red brick church, lit by rather bald lancets: it is cruciform, with a small tiled belfry, with timber top and slated spire, at the crossing. The chancel has aisles, continued round the east end as a vestry. It has a rather striking interior. The north aisle is cut off with a partition of wood and glass. The chancel was decorated early in this century: a dado of tiles, and a reredos. An amusing window in the south aisle shows two soldiers confronted by a crucifix to their evident embarrassment.

St Mary of Eton, Hackney Wick (45)

The site was given by Richard Foster, and the foundation stone was laid by Princess Christian on 7 June 1890. The tower forms a gateway to the Eton mission buildings. G. F. Bodley was the architect: the two western bays were built in 1911–12 by Cecil Hare.

The exterior is of red brick with Bath stone dressings: the east end rises well from the pavement; there is a continuous nave and chancel, with aisles of eight bays, and a small bay at the east; a west bay and porches, and a south chapel; tall rectangular piers, with plain pointed arches on corbels; painted cornice, and white painted cradle roof. The aisle windows are placed high up in the walls. There is a painted and gilded screen.

The altar and reredos, 1930, were designed by W. Ellery Anderson, and executed by R. L. Boulton and Sons, of Cheltenham. There is a new east window by Francis H. Spear, 1953: the previous one was by Comper.

The church is of the same type as Bodley's All Souls', Leicester, though some might like it less: the delicacy and refinement, which look well on a small scale, seem rather thin and spectral when enlarged. It might look better if the screen were completed with cove, loft, rood, tympanum, and celure. (These notes were written some years ago: since then, the screen has been removed to the west.)

St Barnabas', Shacklewell

This is a good church, designed by Professor C. H. Reilly. The foundation stone was laid on 3 July 1909, but it was not consecrated until 1929. The vestry was added in 1937. It is of concrete and stock brick: a nave with passage aisles, which are carried round the west end as a baptistery: there is a concrete tunnel vault on brick arches. Chancel and apse, with the aisles carried round as an ambulatory, and a small south-east chapel. The stone screen wall has ambones, and a tall wooden screen is adorned with figures added in 1934. The cross and candlesticks on the high altar, of hammered pewter, were designed by the architect. The Gothic stone pulpit came from Christchurch, Rendlesham Road—a church, now demolished, designed by William Wigginton.

St Paul's, West Hackney

West Hackney church—which had no dedication at first, but was afterwards known as St James's—was begun in 1821, and consecrated in April 1824. The Commissioners paid the whole of the cost—£17,910. It was one of Sir Robert Smirke's unemotional churches: very large, with a Greek Doric portico and his favourite circular tower.

The church was bombed on 18 September 1940 and almost completely destroyed, though the portico and tower stood undisturbed. It was hoped that the portico could have been preserved, but it has not been. St Barnabas' was made the parish church, but it was decided to build a small church here. The foundation stone of St Paul's was laid on 29 November 1958, and it was consecrated on 17 March 1960. The architect was N. F. Cachemaille-Day, and the builders were W. J. Marston and Son.

The church has a hall at right angles to it, which can be opened into it. It is built on a concrete frame, with brick outside walls: facing the road are four long windows, with small square ones below them, filled with glass set in concrete, designed by A. E. Buss and executed by Goddard and Gibbs. The altar is free standing, in circular rails. Paintings on the east and north walls by Christopher Webb, in cooperation with Campbell, Smith and Co.

St Michael's, London Fields

Nothing remains of the previous church, by J. H. Hakewill: it was bombed, and the remains have been cleared away. The new church, on a different site, was designed by N. F. Cachemaille-Day: the foundation stone is dated 7 November 1959. A square church under a central concrete dome: a west gallery over a vestibule. There is a hall at the back which can, if necessary, be opened into the church. The altar is not in the middle, though there is a passage behind, and the rails go all round. The windows beneath the dome on all sides have glass designed by the architect and executed by Goddard and Gibbs. The painting in the baptistery by John Hayward was the first to be executed: the other murals were done later. Hayward also designed the aluminium sculpture of St Michael on the outside west wall.

Hammersmith

Hammersmith was a chapelry of Fulham, and did not become a separate parish until 1834. It suffered the usual fate of outlying villages in the nineteenth century. 'Now the builder has very nearly supplanted the gardener and farmer; the mansions are for the most part pulled down, occupied as schools or institutions, been subdivided, or given place to factories, and nobility and wealthy citizens seek more distant and romantic regions for their summer or autumn retreats' (Thorne). One church was pulled down before the War: the only wartime casualty was St Katherine Coleman (which has now dropped the 'Coleman'), the successor to the City church.

St Paul's, Queen Caroline Street

The foundation stone of the original Chapel was laid on 11 March 1629, and it was consecrated by Laud in 1631. The inhabitants were responsible for keeping it in repair and paying a curate; but they were still liable to be assessed for the repair of Fulham church and had to go there on Easter Day. It was simple Gothic survival with a tower: there was glass with the arms of Sir Nicholas Crispe and other benefactors. It was repaired in 1825, and reseated and enlarged in 1864, by G. Saunders, architect. The faculty (16 August 1864) authorised the extension of the aisles to the east end of the chancel, reseating, the inclusion of the vestry in the church, and forming a new vestry in the south chancel aisle; and the removal of the organ from the gallery.

Early in 1880 the proposal was made to build a new church. Plans were made by H. R. Gough and J. P. Seddon: the foundation stone was laid on 1 July 1882, and the nave and aisles were consecrated on 30 September 1883, after the last service had been held in the old church. The chancel and tower followed, being consecrated on 2 July 1887. The church is now isolated in the midst of non-stop traffic, and has to be approached by a subway: the fly-over is just south of the churchyard. It is large and dignified, in a rather frigid Early English style: the walls are faced with red Mansfield stone. The tower, with its tall pinnacles, gives something to look at in the middle of Hammersmith—where there is nothing else: but it does not greatly improve the church.

Inside, the walls are of brown Ancaster stone, and the clustered columns of black Belgian marble. There are painted barrel roofs, with ribs, in the nave and chancel. The glass is not very noteworthy—e.g. by Clayton and Bell in the south aisle, Lavers and Westlake in the baptistery, and Heaton, Butler and Bayne in the south chapel. The font is a seventeenth-century bowl, set on a ring of marble renaissance columns. The pulpit came from Wren's church of All Hallows the Great, and was placed here in 1900.

Monuments There are many from the old church, but only two that are worth noting: the bronze bust of Charles I, probably the work of Le Sueur, was erected by Sir Nicholas Crispe to commemorate the 'Glorious Martyr King Charles the First of Blessed Memory'. Beneath it is an urn in which was placed the heart of Sir Nicholas, who was 'a loyal sharer in the sufferings of his late and present Majesty'. North of the sanctuary, James Smith, citizen and salter, 1667, and Sarah, 1680, restored by the Salters' Company in 1917. He had 20 children.

St Peter's, Black Lion Lane (53)

A Commissioners' church, built under the second grant: £9,099 was given towards the total of £12,099. The architect was Edward Lapidge, and the builder G. Bird, of Hammersmith. The foundation stone is dated 16 May 1827 and the church was consecrated on 15 October 1829. It stands just away from the very attractive St Peter's Square, completed in 1831, with a garden planned by Loudon. The front has an attached Ionic portico: above is an attic. The tower has an octagonal base, a circular stage—with antae attached, which give it an octagonal appearance; and a cupola and cross. The body of the church is a plain rectangle of Suffolk brick and Bath stone, with one row of round-headed windows. The vestries are underneath the galleries, which stand on Tuscan columns: there is no upper order. The church has been reseated, and a choir has been formed. The east window is by Clayton and Bell; decorations round it by Sir William Richmond, and murals on the east wall of 1928 and 1930. The reredos, 1906, is by G. C. Horsley. A statue of the Virgin and Child by Alan Howes.

Monuments Reuben T. W. Sayers, 1873, who painted a picture of Christ before Caiaphas, which was taken to Hever church in 1902.

St Stephen's, Uxbridge Road, Shepherds Bush

Built in 1849–50; by Anthony Salvin: the builder was Bird. 'A structure in which the distinctive features of a Christian church are developed through the medium of the Second-Pointed style' (*Ecclesiologist*). The church was a gift from Bishop Blomfield, and the *Ecclesiologist* thought that it had a peculiar value in showing how far the Bishop would go in the direction of ecclesiology—which was clearly further than they would have expected. It is is of Kentish rag and Bath stone: nave and aisles, with a tower to the west of the north aisle: the spire has been taken down. There is a chancel of one bay, a north aisle, and a south vestry, also a later iron screen and wooden reredos recently gilded and painted. There was glass by Wailes, but most of it was blown out in the War: the church was repaired by D. G. Martin, and the new east window is by Goddard and Gibbs, 1951.

St John's, Glenthorne Road (55)

By William Butterfield. The foundation stone was laid on 23 April 1858, and the church was consecrated in 1859. It is tall and severe, of brown and red brick, with Bath stone window-heads, and has a western narthex, between the buttresses, and an almost-detached south-west tower, 1881–2, completed with a saddle-back top, but designed for pinnacles and a spire. The clerestory is lofty and dignified, and the roof high-pitched, with heavy cusped arch-braces. 'As is always the case in Mr Butterfield's churches, the organic structure of the plan, so to say—i.e. the relation of the several parts to each other—is clearly defined by the architecture' (*Ecclesiologist*).

The chancel has been toned down in recent years. The boarded sanctuary roof was painted, but is so no longer. Pevsner, 1952, describes the east wall as tiled and gilt: it ought to be so still. The nave has been allowed to remain as Butterfield meant it to be. The glass was by Lavers and Barraud, under the direction of Butterfield—who kept finding fault with it and annoying the makers. All that remains is windows in the north aisle, of Old Testament worthies: the contrast between these and the recent east window is instructive. The beautiful organ case was designed by Bentley, and so was the south chapel, which has a painted altar and reredos: the window above is by Kempe.

St Matthew's, Sinclair Road, West Kensington (54)

The church was built in 1870–1 by Blomfield in his earlier style, and consecrated on 25 July 1871. It is of the usual brown brick, relieved with red; unclerestoried nave and aisles, with a bellcote over the east gable; chancel with transept and vestry. It has a slate roof of two colours.

Faculties were given on 25 November 1893 for a new porch on the north and vestry adjoining it; on 7 September 1897 for taking down the Caen stone and marble reredos, increasing its height, and providing a painting in the centre; and for oak panelling on the chancel walls; on 23 May 1914 for rearranging the seats and forming a south chapel. The church was restored in 1956.

St Luke's, Uxbridge Road

The church was built in 1871–2, and consecrated on 20 January 1872. The architects were A. Evers and C. H. M. Mileham. It is a brick church, some features of which suggest a late, and minor, design by Butterfield. There was to have been a tower, with an octagonal top and a spire. The screen, by Maurice B. Adams, was a War memorial. The reredos is painted and panelled and there is a carved altar of 1947. There is some very poor glass.

St Simon's, Rockley Road, Shepherds Bush

This is a large church by Blomfield. The nave was built first (foundation stone 6 March 1879; consecration 28 February 1880). The chancel followed (foundation stone 6 August 1885, consecration 25 January 1886). The spire was completed in June 1886. The church is of brick with Bath stone dressings; nave and aisles, with an octagonal tower and spire at the north-west. The two western bays of the south aisle have outward gables: then the aisle curves inwards, and the other bays have smaller windows, and dormers over wooden posts. The chancel has a north vestry and a south organ chamber; the arcades are square-abacus, with stiff-leaf foliage; the aisle windows are foiled lancets under square lintels—un-thirteenth-century in effect. There are similar, though taller, lancets in the two western bays on the south, and in the clerestory. The east window has glass by Jones and Willis, 1903: the only glass in the church.

St Thomas's, Godolphin Road, Shepherds Bush

The church was built in 1882 and the nave and aisles consecrated on 28 December; in 1887 the chancel was added. The design is by Blomfield in his earlier, vigorous, style. It is very simple—indeed rather crude—of brick, with no ornament whatever. It was repaired in

1928 and the enormous baroque altar was erected in 1932. The pulpit and rails came from Belgium. There are various objects of devotion, which it is unnecessary to list.

St Mary's, Stamford Brook

The Duchess of Teck laid the foundation stone on 23 August 1886, and the nave and aisles were consecrated on 31 December: the chancel was built afterwards. The architect was Charles J. Gladman, 'R.I.B.A., etc.' (for what does 'etc.' stand?). It is of red brick in the lancet style, with a slated roof. It is said to have been designed 'on strictly Evangelical principles', and therefore has a wide nave, wide transepts, and a very small apsidal chancel.

Holy Innocents', Paddenswick Road (56)

A very large church by James Brooks, begun in 1887, and consecrated on 7 March 1891. It was built in two pieces by Messrs Faulkner and Son, and is of red brick, with a wide nave, with large buttresses pierced by passage aisles; a gallery is at the west. It has double transepts, a chancel with rather a low arch, south chapel, north vestries, and sanctuary. Bumpus calls it 'bold and vigorous Early Pointed, recalling such Burgundian examples as Auxerre and Potigny'. He also remarks that like other late Brooks churches it is admirably adapted to present-day requirements. (Would he say that now?) It is 'a fine example of simple and solid work, producing its effect by massive construction and picturesque outline and grouping, without any adventitious aid from decorative detail'. With this we agree. A beginning was made of a screen by the Rev. E. Geldart, but the present screen is by Charles Spooner. The lectern is 1894, the pulpit 1896. The triptych in the chapel was designed by Geldart in 1902.

St Saviour's, Cobbold Road, Shepherds Bush

Begun in 1888: the nave and aisles were consecrated on 4 March 1889, the rest on 26 May 1894. The architects were C. N. Tudor and J. S. Alder. It was the gift of Christchurch, Lancaster Gate. All of red brick, except for the pillars. Marble steps to the chancel, 1910: the pulpit is of stone, with alabaster panels by Wippell: a similar screen wall is a War memorial.

The church is not very cheerful: it does not look as though Lancaster Gate's gift was much appreciated.

St Katherine's, Westway

The City church of St Katherine Coleman was rebuilt by James Horne, who was chosen as surveyor in 1739: the church was finished in 1740. David Hughson, early in the nineteenth century, called it 'obscure'—and so it remained. It was closed in 1921, and demolished in 1925.

The Hammersmith church, designed by Robert Atkinson, and built by J. McManus, was consecrated on 24 February 1923: it was of concrete and brick, on a steel framework, Romanesque—'plain early Christian'—in style, with an apse, and cost £17,000. The pulpit, font, organ gallery, rails, two bells, and some monuments, were moved from the City church. It was bombed on 14 September 1940. The foundation stone of the rebuilding was not laid until 25 October 1958: the consecration was on 12 September 1959. The design was made by the son of the original architect, J. R. Atkinson: this time the cost was £52,000. The foundations of the previous church were used, but the apse was omitted—though, even so, for these days, the church is a good size. It has walls in the form of piers supporting the roof principals, with brick panels between: on the road side are figures by A. W. Banks. The heating is in the roof, and all the lighting comes from it. The contractors were Messrs Pitchers. The fittings were executed by Mowbray's, from designs by Colin Shewring. The cross behind the altar, with the risen Christ, is by Michael Clark.

All that now remains of the original church is the rails, which are in the Blessed Sacrament chapel. The pulpit and organ gallery, which survived the bombing, were allowed to perish through neglect.

Hampstead

Hampstead is a place of pilgrimage for those who like to trace the footsteps of nineteenth-century architects. Sir Gilbert Scott lived there for a time, and it was the home of Ewan Christian, whose house was decorated with texts. Sir T. G. Jackson spent his boyhood here. When Canon Anthony Deane came to the parish in 1913, he found that his congregation included Basil Champneys, Norman Shaw, Temple Moore, and Reginald Blomfield. (But in spite of this he only stayed for three years.)

Well Walk Chapel ceased to be used over a century ago. Otherwise all but one of the churches are still there—even St John's, Downshire Hill, which Ewan Christian used to attend, though its architecture must have given him pain: which has outlasted almost all other proprietary chapels. The exception is St Paul's, Avenue Road, S. S. Teulon's rather sinister church, which had a small parish and was not considered to be worth keeping.

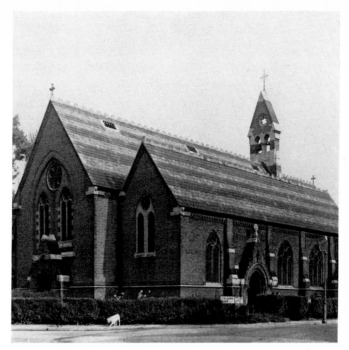

53 St Peter's, 1827–9 by E. Lapidge

54 St Matthew's, West Kensington, 1870–1 by A. W. Blomfield

St John's, by William Butterfield 1858–9 and 81–2. The tower was to have had a spire

56 Holy Innocents', 1887–91 by James Brooks

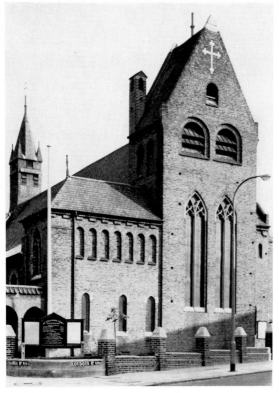

57 All Souls': additions by Nicholson and Corlette 1904 to the church by Wadmore and Baker 1864–5

58 St Mary's, Kilburn, by F. and H. Fra 1856–7 and 1861

59 St Stephen's, Rosslyn Hill, 1869 by S. S. Teulon

60 St Mary's, Primrose Hill, by M. P. Manning 1871–2 and 1890–2

St John's, Church Row

The old church was out of repair at the beginning of the eighteenth century. In 1744 Henry Flitcroft offered to design and build a new church free of charge, provided there was no competition. The vestry did not accept the offer, and appointed another parishoner, John Sanderson. The faculty was given on 15 March: the new building was begun in 1745. It was being fitted up in 1746, and was consecrated in 1747. In 1759 part of the steeple had to be rebuilt, 'owing to the knavery of the mason, in using Purbeck, instead of Portland stone'. The copper spire was added in 1784.

The church is of plain brickwork, with an unusual embattled tower at the east end: the inside is on the St Martin in the Fields model, but of the Ionic order. In 1843–4 transepts and a western extension were built from designs by Robert Hesketh, and the church was reseated: the contractor was Henry Burton of Aldersgate.

Between 1874 and 1875 there was a controversy about proposed alterations to the church. There was an outcry against the proposal to pull down the tower, and add a chancel at the east end. A petition was signed by W. Butterfield, J. P. Seddon, and Alfred Waterhouse, among others: they said that the houses of Church Row, and the church, were all of a piece. 'Such a group of English architecture of its period is almost unique in or about London, and the proposal to destroy or transform its principle ornament will be condemned by every man of taste.'

The matter was dropped for the time being, and when the church was enlarged in 1878, by F. P. Cockerell, it was turned round, and the chancel was built at the west. The architect 'accepted the main lines of the nave', but used more Portland stone dressings, and gave the sanctuary a balustraded parapet. New open fronts were given to the galleries. The builders were Jackson and Shaw.

Alfred Bell, who lived in the parish, designed the decoration of the nave, and the firm of Clayton and Bell executed most of the glass. The window at the west, and the painting of the Baptism of Christ, were designed by Professor Ellis Wooldridge, who also decorated the chancel (faculty 23 May 1883). The stalls, organ case and reredos were designed by T. G. Jackson.

In 1911 Temple Moore, yet another parishioner, designed the vestries, and arranged the chapel. The pulpit is eighteenth-century and the iron gates to the churchyard came in 1747 from Canons, in Middlesex, the house of the Duke of Chandos.

Christchurch, New End

The church was built in 1851–2 by S. W. Daukes. It is an ordinary Middle-Pointed church with nave and aisles, chancel and north tower and spire. Gilbert Scott, a member of the congregation, designed the west gallery. The *Illustrated London News*, 14 January 1860, remarked that it was one of the few galleries that improve, rather than mar, a church.

A faculty was given on 31 August 1881 for the erection of a new north aisle; the extension of the north porch; reseating; the removal of the organ to the south chancel aisle, the conversion of the basement of the tower into a vestry; the placing of new glass in the east window, and the removal of the former glass into the east window of the new north aisle. The architect was Ewan Christian. The new font was installed in 1902: the Powell mosaic reredos is 1912. The church was restored after the first World War, and the new work was dedicated in 1920.

St Saviour's, Eton Road

This church had rather a complicated origin. The plans of H. E. Kendall junior, district surveyor for Hampstead, were chosen in March 1847. The foundations were laid by Samuel Cuming but there was not enough money available: work stopped, and a temporary church was erected instead. Kendall's design was exhibited at the Academy in 1848. It was in the Middle Pointed style, cruciform, with a central tower and spire: the *Ecclesiologist* thought it pretentious.

Efforts were made again in 1850, and on 30 December 1852 R. P. Pope, who worked with Kendall, was asked to draw out the quantities: the builder was to be Glen of Islington. But the committee quarrelled with Pope, and he resigned in 1855. E. M. Barry was then engaged as architect, and made a new design: a contract was made with Lucas Bros of Lambeth, the foundation stone was laid on 18 July, and the church was consecrated on 7 July 1856. The design was shown at the Academy in that year. The *Ecclesiologist* called it 'First-Pointed of a meagre character', with nothing but couplets and triplets: it was redeemed by the length of its chancel, and by satisfactory fittings.

The tower and spire were added in 1864. In 1872 the west end was repaired, and the wall of the north aisle rebuilt: the choir vestry was added in 1883. Ewan Christian was the architect.

The reredos is 1885, the screen 1890, and the extension of the chancel 1906.

There is not much else to be said about the church, which is very old-fashioned for 1855. The glass is by Clayton and Bell: north transept window by Ward and Hughes.

St Mary's, Priory Road, Kilburn (58)

The church is built on the site of the nunnery of Kilburn, and part of a fifteenth-century brass was discovered—the head of a prioress.

It is a Middle-Pointed design by F. and H. Francis; the foundation stone was laid on 31 May 1856, and the nave and aisles were opened in 1857. The chancel and transepts were finished in 1862, and the church was consecrated on 26 February. The contractors were Messrs Holland. The design was slightly simplified in building, and some ornamental parts were left out: only in the clerestory have the architects allowed themselves any licence.

There have not been many alterations. The reredos is 1885, and seven new panels were inserted in 1902. The chancel walls have been painted, and there is glass by Clayton and Bell and Westlake. The vestry was enlarged in 1889. In the '60s this was 'one of the leading ritualistic churches in London', but it ceased to be so in 1867 (see St Augustine's, Kilburn, Paddington).

St Peter's, Belsize Park

The church was built 1858–9 and consecrated on 11 November 1859. The Rev F. W. Tremlett paid for the nave, aisles, and transepts, and the parishioners for the chancel. The architect was W. Mumford, but the tower and chancel were erected under J. P. St Aubyn. The nave has tall pillars with foliated capitals, rather like Scott: the aisles are gabled outwards, also like Scott, but the gables are over-acute, and the windows have a nonconformist look. The tower, though embattled, has belfry windows with square abaci. The west bay of the nave, aisleless, but flanked by the tower, has a gallery. North and south galleries were taken down in 1927.

The east and west windows have bright and striking glass by O'Connor: the chancel was decorated in 1880 by W. J. Taylor, O'Connor's successor, by whom there are three very poor windows in the south aisle. The alabaster wall of the chancel is by George Ernest Nield. A new reredos has recently been erected.

All Souls', Loudoun Road (57)

The church was founded and endowed by the Rev Henry Robinson Wadmore, who was the first vicar; he died in 1897; the architects were J. F. Wadmore and A. Baker. Nave, north aisle, and apsidal chancel were built in 1864–5, of yellow London brick, with bands of red, and tracery of Bath stone. The organ chamber and vestry were added soon after. The arcade has square abaci, stiff-leaf capitals and voussoirs of red brick and stone.

A repair by Spencer W. Grant in 1903 was followed by an enlargement by Sir Charles Nicholson and H. C. Corlette: they added a south aisle (in which the older windows were re-used), a saddle-back tower, porches, and a choir vestry. The new work was consecrated on 31 January 1905. The conjunction of 1865 and 1904 makes this an unusual and interesting church.

The east end has been sumptuously refitted. The lower part of the screen—an alabaster balustrade, a 'modified copy' of a screen in S Maria dei Miracoli, Venice—was executed by John Underwood and Son in 1902. The rest, of oak, is mostly Gothic, but has a cornice of cherubs' heads: this was the work of Bacon Bros. The chancel has a marble floor, and the sanctuary mosaic: the apse is panelled and filled with a large carved triptych designed by C. G. Hare, 1909. Marble font, with copper cover, 1905.

St Stephen's, Rosslyn Hill (59)

The church was designed by S. S. Teulon and the foundation stone laid 12 May 1869. The consecration was on 31 December of the same year. This great, ponderous church looks very impressive from all directions. From the north, from up the hill, it seems to be chiefly tower; the west end, with its vaulted open porch and wheel window, is muscular French thirteenth-century: it is imposing, but it gives no idea of the real size of the church. The ground slopes away to the east, and as one walks eastwards, down the hill along the south side, the church grows, as it were, downwards. The east end is built above an undercroft and to those who stand at the base of the buttresses of the apse, and look upward, it appears enormous.

The walls are built of brick from Luton, 'of a curious mottled pink-red colour': Eastlake remarks that it ranges 'from pale gray to Indian red'. The dressings are of stone and granite. Teulon's architecture is never refined or reticent, and St Stephen's has many of the aggressive early French features that were in fashion at the time. But as Eastlake says, it would be unfair to suggest too much Continental influence: 'in many respects it retains a national character, while certain details—as, for instance, the ornamental brickwork of its interior—can scarcely be referred to any precedent but that of modern fashion'. It is, in fact, an original mid-Victorian design, and it could only be by Teulon.

The arcades have foliated capitals, and Moorish-looking arches, with the brickwork notched and billet-moulded. The tower arches rest on blocks carved with the story of St Stephen, the Nativity and the Crucifixion: the apse is vaulted.

The alabaster roundels were carved in 1880: Ewan Christian gave Latimer, as a protest against romanising practices in the Church of England. The stalls and screen, 1912, are by Temple Moore: chapel in south transept 1905: the pulpit tester 1913.

The glass is by Lavers and Westlake and Clayton and Bell. Two windows were given in memory of Teulon, one by the family, and one by the congregation.

St Mary's, Primrose Hill Road (60)

A boys' home founded in Euston Road in 1859 was afterwards moved to Regent's Park Road. Services held in the schoolroom were attended by some local people, and in 1867 the chaplain put up an iron church in Ainger Road. In 1870 the site for the permanent church was given by Eton College. The architect was Michael P. Manning, of the firm of Manning and Simpson; the builders were Dove Bros. The foundation stone was laid on 25 November 1871, and the nave, chancel, north aisle and transept were opened on 2 July 1872. Bishop Jackson refused to consecrate the church, and it remained unconsecrated until 1885 (2 May: the first consecration by Frederick Temple after he became Bishop of London). The choir vestry was added in 1890, and in 1891–2 the south aisle and chapel were built. Additions were constantly being made to the furnishings—e.g. a small window by Comper (by the font), 1893; pulpit, by Bodley and Garner, 1893; stalls 1893–4, and chapel reredos 1894: tripytch, by Bodley, 1895; west windows, by Kempe, 1896.

This red brick church, in the style of James Brooks—a well-designed example, by a little known architect—became well known in the early part of this century as the scene of the liturgical reforms of Percy Dearmer, who was vicar from 1901 to 1915. For some years a High church had been expected to have an altar raised on many steps, with a row of six candles—reinforced by three-branched or seven-branched candlesticks—arranged on shelves. There would also be a row of brass flower vases. This kind of altar was not particularly Roman: it can only be called Victorian High Church. Dearmer had no difficulty in proving that there was no authority for it, and that the English mediaeval altar was low, and had almost nothing on it—two candlesticks at the most, and certainly no flowers: and that its ends were enclosed by curtains.

The usual 'advanced' nineteenth-century ceremonial, as set forth in *Ritual Notes*, and such like books, was fussy, and based largely on Roman Counter-Reformation practice. The true English ceremonial was simple, un-fussy, and beautiful. Church music would be plainsong or folksong: not *Hymns Ancient and Modern*, and some Victorian composer in E♭.

It was at St Mary's that he showed how things ought to be done. And, as a setting for it all, he whitewashed the brick walls. Dearmer began a fashion, and during the 1920s and 30s English altars were put up almost everywhere, and far too many walls were whitened. But he had said something that needed to be said, and there is no doubt that his writings, and his practice, produced a great improvement in Anglican worship.

There were many more additions to the furniture of St Mary's in Dearmer's time, including the rood beam and figures, by Gilbert Bayes, 1914. Bayes also remodelled and lowered the reredos in 1915. The altar ornaments and sanctuary lamp are by Frank Knight of Wellingborough, 1960. The Communion benches are by W. H. Randoll Blacking.

Beside the windows already mentioned, there are others by Clayton and Bell (apse, chapel, and north aisle), and H. V. Milner (south aisle).

Holy Trinity, Finchley Road

The Earl of Shaftesbury laid the foundation stone on 1 August 1871, and the church was consecrated on 9 August 1872. The cost was about £17,000. The architect was Henry S. Legg, and the builder Dove. The chancel was added in 1874. The tower and spire were never built. Holy Trinity is a rather dull church, in Victorian Gothic; Kentish rag and Bath stone outside, and patent pressed bricks, with red bands, inside. The pillars are of polished granite, and the capitals have naturalistic foliage. The chancel and apse are vaulted in brick. Ewan Christian gave the font. The arcading is by Hemming of Belsize Terrace.

St Cuthbert's, Fordwych Road

There was, as usual, an iron church to begin with, which was superseded by a brick mission church, by W. C. Street—now the parish hall—and then by the permanent church. This was also designed by W. C. Street, and built in two parts: the foundation stone of the nave and aisles 17 July 1886: consecration 11 November 1887; the proposed tower was not even begun. Foundation stone of the chancel 18 June 1903: it was consecrated on 23 January 1904.

The church's front faces the road, and the apse overlooks the railway. It is the usual brick suburban church, quite uninspired. The apse is lined with stone, with mosaic panels, and a mosaic reredos (faculty 10 September 1919). The choir stalls were carved by the vicar in the 1930s.

St James's, West End Lane

The site for this church was bought in 1882. A. W. Blomfield, who had already designed the mission hall, made plans for the permanent church, which was to have had a spire 'at once graceful and massive'. The designs were amended in 1885, and the foundation stone was laid on 25 May 1887. The builder was John Woodward. The church was finished early in 1888, and consecrated on 11 February. It is almost entirely of red brick, except for the pillars: the interior is spacious, simple and dignified. The glass in the east window, 1890, in the west, 1892, and in the north wall of the north chapel, 1893, is by Kempe: that in the apse of the chapel is by Westlake.

An eighteenth-century figure of St James, perhaps Spanish.

Emmanuel, Lyncroft Gardens

The first services were held in a school (1845). After that there was a mission church, built in 1874, and enlarged in 1884. The foundation stone of the permanent church, designed by Whitfield and Thomas, was laid on 19 June 1897. The builder was John Bentley of Waltham Abbey. Consecration 10 October 1898. This is another large brick church—red without, and white, banded with red, inside, in the Lancet style. A baptistery with porches at the west, and the base of a tower, forming a porch on the north side towards the east. The chancel is apsidal. The interior could qualify for the adjective 'handsome'. The carved oak reredos was installed in 1956. The glass in the apse is by Kempe and was patched after the War.

St Luke's, Kidderpore Avenue

The church is surrounded by an unusually varied collection of prosperous, architect-designed houses of about 1900. It forms a group, with the vicarage, etc., on the right. The architect was Basil Champneys: the foundation stone was laid on 18 June 1898, and the consecration was on 21 October 1899. St Luke's is a very pleasant, simple, sophisticated, end-of-the-century Perpendicular church of red brick. The front has two porches at the sides of a gallery-bay, and a projection for the staircase to the gallery. The aisles are rather low, with the usual octagonal pillars without capitals: the clerestory is tall, with two three-light windows to each bay. Aisleless chancel, with organ-loft and vestries. The windows are by Powell. The walls have been whitened.

Holborn

The arrangement by pre-eighteenth-century parishes breaks down here. That of St George the Martyr was not formed until 1723: but the original parish church was St Andrew's, Holborn, which is inside the City. But the parish extended beyond the City boundaries, and so the rest of Holborn has to be mentioned separately.

St George's was built for genteel new streets; but they were at the extremity of the parish. Some parishes on the edge of the City had a rather unsavoury area just outside its boundary: St Andrew's was one of these. In its crowded and poor districts, a Commissioners' church was built—St Peter's, Saffron Hill, now demolished. This was followed by the famous St Alban's, Brooke Street, which was bombed, but has been rebuilt.

Further out, there was St John's, Red Lion Square, one of Pearson's best churches.

It was badly bombed, and drastically restored afterwards. The vicar wrote, 'Rolls and rolls of lead from the roof were sent to a dump; beautiful wrought-iron grilles were torn from perfectly sound arches, ready for the scrap-heap; and if constant appeals had not been made to the diocesan surveyor, all would have gone.' The damaged walls were demolished, although they were so thick, and well built, that they were only pulled down with great difficulty. The remains of the church stood for some years, and were then cleared away.

St George the Martyr, Queen Square

Sir Streynsham Master and 14 other gentlemen including Robert Nelson, author of *Fasts and Festivals of the Church of England,* were appointed trustees for the building of a chapel: in 1705 they agreed with Arthur Tooley to give him £3,500 for building the chapel and two houses.

The Commissioners for the Fifty New Churches decided to make the chapel one of the new parish churches: they bought it, spent £2,000 in repairing and beautifying it, and it was consecrated on 26 September 1723. The first incumbent, John Marshall, D.D., planned a battlemented tower 97½ feet high: it remained on paper.

Nearly £1,000 was spent on repairs in 1772, and there were further alterations in 1813. In 1867 the church was recast by S. S. Teulon. A chancel was formed on the south side, the pews, and all but one of the galleries were removed, the windows were enlarged and given tracery, a new spire was built, and the inside was refitted. The old altar piece remains in its original position, now a side wall.

St Alban's, Brooke Street, Holborn (61)

The church was built in what was at the time an appalling slum: the site was bought by Lord Leigh, who could not obtain as much ground as he would have liked: and the church was built by J. G. Hubbard. Building was begun in 1861, and finished by the end of 1862: Bishop Tait consecrated the church on 21 February 1863.

'Mr Butterfield', said the *Ecclesiologist,* in another connection, 'always seems to build *con amore* when there are extraordinary difficulties; and he succeeds with bricks better, in proportion, than with any other material.' That might have been written about St Alban's. The site was cramped, though less so than at All Saints', Margaret Street; and the problem was, to design a town church, which would stand boldly up above the houses, and be both impressive and also easy to drop into: this was to be a free and open church, to bring the Faith to the very poor, and to teach them to worship.

61 St Alban's, Brooke Street, Holborn, 1861–2. Butterfield's west end and tower survived the bombing

62 Christchurch, Woburn Square, 1831–3 by Lewis Vulliamy

63 St Giles in the Fields, 1731–3 by Henry Flitcroft

64 St Mary Magdalene, Holloway, 1812–14
by William Wickings

65 St Peter's: the enlargement by Gough an
Roumieu, of Charles Barry's church of 1834–5

66 St Saviour's, Aberdeen Park, 1865–6
by William White

67 Christchurch, Highbury Grove, 1847–8
by Thomas Allom

Butterfield designed a very tall, and also wide church, with aisles, and a western saddle-back tower, opening into the nave by an enormous arch: on each side are transepts. It looks almost as though he wanted to revive a catechumenate, and keep the unbaptised separate at the end of the church. The chancel arch, lower than at the west, but of extremely fine proportions, opens into a rather short chancel, with aisles of one bay, and a sheer east wall, in which it was not possible to place a window.

The *Ecclesiologist* was appreciative, and showed that it understood what the architect was trying to do. He had gone beyond the repetition of mediaeval forms; a 'free eclectic manipulation of parts' had been 'grafted upon a system of polychromatic construction, having its basis in the fact that London is naturally a brick town'. The west end was 'a striking piece of street scenery in a city which is so much in need of salient points'. It noticed that the windows were thoroughly English, and that the arcades were such as Carpenter would have been delighted to produce: but that Butterfield had eschewed carving. There is none, except for the moulded capitals and corbels, and there are no representations of the human figure. Butterfield played down the features that other architects liked, and concentrated on details that they did not take much care of.

The walls were (and are) of yellow stock brick, banded with red, and the pillars and arches of Portland stone: the chancel walls were lined with alabaster, and the chancel was enclosed with light iron screens at the west and at the sides. The paintings on the east wall were designed by Styleman Le Strange, who designed most of the cartoons, and began the work; dying suddenly, he was succeeded by Frederick Preedy.

St Alban's became the most famous ritualistic church of the nineteenth century: its services were described again and again in the newspapers, and the names of A. H. Mackonochie, the vicar, and Arthur Stanton, the curate, were well known to all who took an interest in Church matters. There were prosecutions for illegal ceremonial; and certainly some things were done at St Alban's which it would be hard to defend on the basis of the ornaments rubric—e.g. 60 candles on and around the altar at Christmas 1863. But almost everyone agreed that there was evangelistic fervour as well.

Naturally the church received embellishments later in the century. The enormous altar piece was designed by Bodley and Garner, and executed by Farmer and Brindley. C. H. M. Mileham designed the hanging rood, 1893, the chapel at the west, to the memory of Mackonochie, 1890, and the Chapel of St Sepulchre—with reredos and glass by Kempe. Comper, in this century, designed the font cover and the statue of St Alban.

The church was badly bombed in 1941, but the London Diocesan Reorganisation Committee scheduled it for repair after the War. Sir J. N. Comper made a design, which was rejected. In 1945 Sir Giles Scott, and his brother Adrian, made two schemes: one for doing what was absolutely necessary, and the other for restoring the church to its original beauty. The rebuilding has been done, but the church has certainly not been restored to what it was: there is more of Scott about it than there is of Butterfield.

Islington

Islington in the early nineteenth century was a pleasant residential place, which had grown sufficiently by 1814 to need a second church—St Mary Magdalene's, Lower Holloway. Building continued through most of the century. There are many streets and squares of middle-class houses: some have declined in status, and now look seedy, but some are again becoming fashionable.

The church life of Islington takes its tone from Daniel Wilson, who was appointed vicar in 1824. He was an Evangelical, and ran the parish with great efficiency. In his time the three big new churches by Sir Charles Barry were built: St John's, Holloway, St Paul's, Balls Pond, and Holy Trinity, Cloudesley Square. Though a strong Evangelical, Wilson was a loyal churchman: he introduced early celebrations of the Holy Communion, the use of the Litany on Wednesdays and Fridays, and services on saints' days. He was appointed Bishop of Calcutta in 1832, and continued in the same way. He had no appreciation of the Tractarian movement, which he called an 'egregious drivelling fatuity'; but he dreamed of a magnificent cathedral in the 'Gothic, or rather, Christian style of architecture', and succeeded in building St Paul's Cathedral, in which things were done decently and in order.

The Evangelical tradition remained in Islington, and when in 1842 Bishop Blomfield charged the clergy of his diocese to preach in their surplices, the vicars of the Islington parishes, which by then numbered 13, refused to obey. Blomfield bowed to the storm, and withdrew his direction.

As in most London boroughs, too many churches were built, and though some have been weeded out, a good many still remain. One or two have interiors of almost unbelievable dreariness, but I have refrained from saying which they are.

St Mary's, Upper Street

The parishioners tried in 1718 to get this church included as one of the Fifty New Churches, but the attempt was, as usual, unsuccessful. On 28 February 1750 a further petition was made to the Commons for the rebuilding of the church. A bill was brought in, and passed; a faculty had been given on 27 February. The new church was begun in 1751, and opened in 1754. The architect was Launcelot Dowbiggin, 'citizen and joyner of London', who died in 1759, aged 70, and is buried here. The builder was Samuel Steemson.

Only the tower remains: it is surmounted by an octagonal balustrade, an open circular stage and an obelisk spire, in diminishing stages, with circular openings, and crockets.

Those who like to read of the vanished glories of the eighteenth-century churches may be interested to know that the altar piece was of mahogany, of the Doric order, with a painting above by Nathaniel Dance—the Annunciation, with the emblems of the Law and the Gospel in chiaroscuro.

The chancel was added in 1902–4, and the west porch in 1903, by Sir A. W. Blomfield and Sons: the porch remains.

The church was wrecked by a bomb on 9 September 1940. The rebuilding was designed by Seely and Paget, and the church rededicated on 17 December 1956. The plan of the eighteenth-century building was kept, except for the addition of transepts at the east end, within which the sanctuary is marked by slender pillars. To the west are desk and pulpit of similar design. It was at first proposed to put the eighteenth-century font, which survived the bombing, at the east end; but it was finally sited in the south side, somewhat towards the west. Choir and organ are at the west. The murals on the east and west walls are by Brian Thomas.

St Mary Magdalene, Holloway Road (64)

The first new church to be built in the parish of Islington; the Act for its building was passed in 1811 and the foundation stone was laid on 16 June 1812; it was consecrated on 17 August 1814. The architect was William Wickings, surveyor to the County of Middlesex, and the builder was Joseph Griffiths. The estimate was considerably exceeded, and there was a good deal of controversy about the additional expense.

It is a good, straightforward church in the plain eighteenth-century manner, with no Grecian innovations. A large stock brick body, and a tower at the east end, adorned with Ionic pilasters and urns, and flanked by the usual vestibules containing the gallery staircases. Under the church are vaults, in which some rather attractive coffins may still be seen.

The interior is plain and dignified: galleries on Tuscan columns, with the royal arms at the west, and the organ in its proper place; a ceiling with coves, and three roses. A handsome pulpit of mahogany. A very shallow recess at the east, with Ionic pilasters enclosing the usual writings, and a painting of *Noli me tangere* by Tibbets, a churchwarden.

Both the ground floor and the gallery have been reseated, but it has been decently done. A faculty was given on 31 July 1895 to demolish the upper galleries in the north-west and south-west corners, and open out windows at the ends of the north and south galleries, and similar windows at the west ends of the aisles; also to refloor and reseat.

There was a restoration in 1910 by J. R. Manning and W. Gillbee Scott: the builders were Thurman and White. At this time the Coade-ware vases on the tower were replaced by similar vases of stone. The interior was redecorated in 1959.

St John's, Upper Holloway

Sir Charles Barry had studied abroad, and had never paid much attention to Gothic. When he was asked to design churches in the Gothic style, he had to begin to study it, 'and he threw himself into the new study with characteristic diligence and perseverance. His first essays were not very successful, though certainly not below the average of the time; he used to think and speak of them afterwards with a humorous kind of indignation; he carefully destroyed every drawing relating to them, and would have still more gladly destroyed the originals.'

St John's is one of his first essays. The foundation stone was laid on 4 May 1826, and the church was consecrated on 2 July 1828. The cost was £12,658, towards which the Commissioners granted £9,958. It is plain Perpendicular, built of brick; with a rather slim pinnacled tower and small gallery-stair adjuncts. The nave and aisles are of six bays and there is a shallow sanctuary. There have been a certain number of alterations at the east end: the central pulpit has been removed, and a carved late nineteenth-century one substituted: choir stalls have been inserted (1900), and the altar and rails are post-Barry. But the general impression is of an unaltered church. Redecoration has been reasonable: the box pews—separated by a wide and dignified central passage—remain: and so do the seats round the walls, and the west gallery (though the organ was moved in 1895). The eastward view—towards the bright east window glass by W. Bacon—is soberly Evangelical.

Monuments   Two tablets by Sievier: Anne, daughter of Nicholas Sykes, 1835, with a relief of a female with a lamb: Flaxmanism turning into Victorian sentiment. And Martha, wife of the Rev Henry Venn, 1840, with a figure of Charity.

St Paul's, Balls Pond Road

George Basevi made plans for this church which were not approved, and the Commissioners told Barry to make the church a replica of St John's. He and the parish protested and as a compromise the tower was put at the east end. The foundation stone was laid on 15 September 1826, and the consecration was on 23 October 1828. The site was given by the Marquis of Northampton.

The basement of the tower has a groined ceiling, and the altar screen is in front of it with a gallery on top. The east window had the arms of George IV: the present glass is 1944 and is by John Hall and Sons. There have been the usual later alterations. Faculties: 8 September 1880, to reseat, alter the position of the pulpit, and form a choir; 20 December 1882, to erect a new pulpit and desk; and 27 June 1900, to build a new choir vestry, and move the organ.

Holy Trinity, Cloudesley Square (72)

In 1517 Richard Cloudesley left to the parish a parcel of ground called Stone Field, and this was used as the site for the church. James Savage made plans, but the Commissioners rejected them, and Barry's were adopted instead. The foundation stone was laid on 15 July 1826 and the consecration was on 19 March 1829. The cost was £11,900: the Commissioners granted £9,231. It is Perpendicular in style, of brick, with an aisled nave, turrets at the four corners, and a small sanctuary and north vestry. It was restored by Ewan Christian, who did the usual things: the organ was moved, and choir stalls were inserted. A faculty was given on 24 July 1900 to reseat, raise the east end, and take down the north and south galleries. Another 5 June 1915 for new choir vestry, new organ screen, etc. The church is not bad as Sir Charles, in his later days, liked to think: it is straightforward Commissioners' Perpendicular. But the alterations have not improved it much. The best thing in the interior is the glass in the east window, by Willement, 1828, with a kneeling figure of Richard Cloudesley.

St Peter's, St Peter Street (65)

Designed by Sir Charles Barry, begun in 1834, and consecrated on 14 July 1835. The cost was £3,407 and the builder was King. It deserves to be called a brick box, and the style is pitiably mean Early English. It was decided in 1842 to enlarge it, and A. D. Gough and R. L. Roumieu made plans of which Barry appproved; John Jay of London Wall was the builder. A new front was added, and a strange north-west tower and spire, with flying buttresses—very thin and spidery. 'Means of ingress and egress' were provided by separate entrances and lobbies to the galleries, as well as to the body of the church; and transepts, a short sanctuary, and a vestry were added. The interior was repaired and decorated.

The galleries, which were carried past the transepts, now stop short of them: the pulpit has been moved from the centre, and the body of the church has been reseated. This was done by a faculty of 22 August 1884, which also gave leave to demolish the north-east porch, and build a vestry instead, to arrange choir seats and to take down the upper gallery on each side. The estimate was £1,500. The church now has the Angel's throne from the Catholic Apostolic Church in Duncan Street.

All Saints', Caledonian Road

The Metropolis Churches Fund gave £3,500 for three new churches in Islington, on condition that one was built at Battle Bridge. The site was bought for £200 from George Thornhill, M.P. for Huntingdon. The church was designed by William Tress, begun in

1837, and consecrated on 5 July 1838. The cost was £4,412: the share of the Metropolis Churches Fund grant was £1,000. This is not a very interesting church—a brick rectangle with large lancet windows, and an east end, facing the road, with a debased Perpendicular window, a turret and pinnacles. In 1857 it was said to be out of repair and an appeal was made for funds to renew the windows on the north and south and to clean the inside.

The baptistery was dedicated on 8 December 1914, and the north-west porch dates from the same time. It was proposed to build a chancel at the west end, and to turn round the interior, but this was given up because of Ancient Lights. It is better inside than out: not too big, and there is quite a worshipful atmosphere. The galleries remain, except at the west. The nave has been reseated with chairs (1914), and there have been the usual alterations at the east end.

St James, Chillingworth Road

The church was built 1837–8, by H. W. Inwood and E. N. Clifton. In 1839 it was enlarged to the east by Hambley of Holloway. In 1850 there was an extension to the west, and the tower was built. In the enlargements, as Mackeson says, attention was paid rather to accommodation than architecture.

This enormous church—there was seating for 1,840—suffered from bombing in 1944 and was restored as a hall in 1952. The hall is, in fact, constructed within the church: above it are derelict galleries and the roof.

St Stephen's, Canonbury Road (71)

Begun in 1837, and consecrated on 18 June 1839. The architects were W. and H. W. Inwood and E. N. Clifton: the design was shown at the Royal Academy. It is an uninspiring piece of Gothic. The east front has an octagonal turret and spire, with small turrets at the sides, and flying buttresses. The spire was said to have been modelled on that of St Mary's, Oxford, but this claim was not taken seriously by the architectural critics. The rest of the church is a plain brick rectangle with two-light windows.

In 1850 two porches—now removed—were added at the east end; the side windows were altered and the church was lengthened: the architect was A. D. Gough. The building was considerably damaged by bombing, and reconstructed by A. Llewellyn Smith and A. W. Waters in 1957: the contractors were Douglas Grant and Partners. It was shortened by about 11 feet to make space for vestries and a chapel; and the interior was turned round the other way.

The wall behind the altar is decorated with a mural by Brian Thomas: the window at the other end is by Carl J. Edwards. The organ, with its console sunk in the floor, and the pipes hidden behind a screen at the east, incorporates the organ from A. D. Gough's vanished church of St Matthew, Essex Road.

Christchurch, Highbury Grove (67)

The site and £500 were given by Henry Dawes; the building committee resolved that 'the building must not be unsightly, nor the ground used for burials'. The design, by Thomas Allom, was exhibited at the Royal Academy in 1848; building was begun in August 1847, and the church was consecrated on 16 October 1848; the contractor was George J. Carter of Hornsey Road.

The plan is most peculiar: a large central octagon, and nave, transepts, and chancel, all with aisles and clerestories. There is an apsidal sanctuary, and a tower and spire on the (ritual) north. It is true that, as the *Illustrated London News* said, 'From whatever point it is viewed, the building presents a varied and striking form.'

The walls are of Kentish rag, with Bath stone dressings: the style is decidedly sub-ecclesiological Middle-Pointed. The *Ecclesiologist*'s reporter saw the church in an un-finished state. The pillars were of brick, and had not yet received their coating of plaster: he hoped that it would take the form of Middle-Pointed capitals and bases. He was, of course, scornful of Allom's planning, and his attempt at grandeur on such a scale; but he concluded by saying that there was something to be said for the church: at any rate 'preaching houses are being decked out in the trappings of real churches'. (These were curious remarks for an ecclesiologist to make. He must have believed that honest con-struction is the essence of Gothic, and ought not to have approved of plaster mouldings added to a brick core. And that correct planning is necessary: you could not really make a meeting house any more like a church by adding Gothic ornament. Who could the writer have been?)

There was an enlargement in 1872, by Williams and Crouch, who extended the nave, at a cost of £2,190. This has made the plan even more unusual, as the nave is now in two parts, divided by an arch.

A faculty was given on 14 October 1911 to enlarge the choir vestry: the builders were Dove Bros. Restoration and redecoration 1929 and 1948. Windows in the apse, 1954, and in the transepts, 1955, by Francis H. Spear.

St Andrew's, Thornhill Square

The site was given by George Thornhill and the church built in 1852–4 by Francis B. Newman and John Johnson. The design was exhibited at the Royal Academy in 1852: 'an ostentatious cruciform pile, all gables and transepts, with an exaggerated broach' (*Ecclesiologist*).

It is of Kentish rag and Bath stone, in Middle-Pointed style: money has been saved by eliminating ornament on the less visible north side. The plan is the Low Church version of the ecclesiological one: nave and aisles, wide transepts with galleries, and a short, aisled chancel. Tower and spire at the south-west.

The interior remains much as it was, except that the organ has recently been moved to the west. The east window is dated 1873 and of it the centenary handbook says, 'Some of the St Andrew's worshippers have remarked that it is the most beautiful window that they have seen.'

St Mark's, Tollington Park (69)

This is the oldest surviving of the Islington churches by Alexander Dick Gough, an architect who always infuriated the ecclesiologists. His Gothic was old-fashioned, and he had a curious way of making his details look sinister. His plans were far from being correct. He was in partnership with Robert Louis Roumieu: 'either singly or together, they seldom fail to be vulgar without being either funny or interesting' (H. S. Goodhart-Rendel). Two Gough churches have gone: St Matthew's, Essex Road, 1850–1, and St Philip's, Arlington Square, 1855–7. St Anne's, Poole's Park, 1869–70, a brick church quite unlike the others, was standing when this was written, but its days were numbered.

St Mark's was begun in 1853 and consecrated on 22 May 1854: the cost was £5,000. It is Early English in style, of Kentish rag and Bath stone. On the south is a very thin tower and spire. Wide transepts open into the nave, without any arch: there is a spirelet at the crossing, but nothing visible inside. (It can, indeed, hardly be called a crossing, as there are no arches at all.) Then comes a chancel, flanked by vestries.

There have been a good many alterations. In 1883 a faculty was given for new choir seats, and raising the floor of the chancel. In 1884 (13 February) there was a further faculty: to take down the vestry and W.C., and to build on the site a new church room, vestry and W.C., and to cut an opening in the north wall of the chancel. Soon after (13 July) a third gave permission for a more extensive alteration: to take down the walls of the nave and the galleries in the transepts, and build new aisles; to rearrange the seats in the transepts and move the pulpit; to build a new heating chamber; to move the stained glass windows from the nave into the transepts; and to move the font. The estimate was £1,280. The architect of the alterations was F. R. Farrow. The pulpit was carved by H. Hems.

At the jubilee in 1904 the Church was renovated: a new east window and vestry were installed at a cost of about £1,000. Most of the glass is by A. L. Moore, but the triplet in the south transept is by Ward and Hughes.

68 St Luke's, Holloway, 1859–60 by Charles Lee

69 St Mark's, Tollington Park: F. R. Farrow's enlargement of the church by A. D. Gough 1853–4

70 St Clement's, Barnsbury, 1864–5, a typical east end by Gilbert Scott

71 St Stephen's, Canonbury, 1837–9 by Inwood and Clifton, reconstructed after bombing

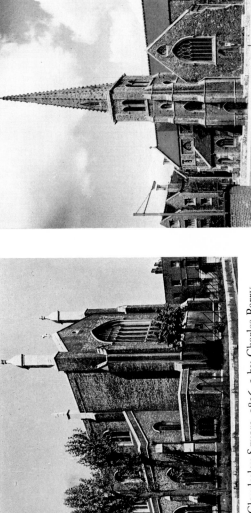

73 St Jude's, Mildmay Park, 1855–6 by A. D. Gough, enlarged
by Edwin Clare

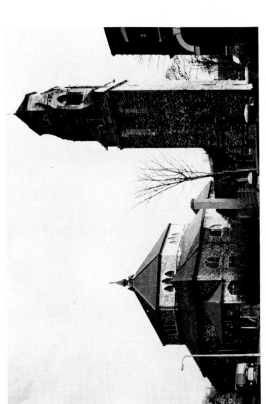

75 St Silas', Penton Street, begun 1860 by S. S. Teulon, completed 1863

72 Holy Trinity, Cloudesley Square, 1826–9 by Charles Barry

74 St George's, Tufnell Park, 1866–7 by George Truefitt

St Matthias', Caledonian Road

This was a Presbyterian chapel built about 1853: the architects were John Barnett and Birch. It did not succeed, and became Anglican about ten years later. The short chancel and the hall to the right were added in 1883 by William Smith of Basinghall Street. The church was consecrated on 14 January 1886, and was given a parish in 1888. It is now united to St Andrew's, Thornhill Square. It is sandwiched between shops, and shows only its ragstone-faced front, with its two porches. A wide and mean body the floor of which slopes towards the (ritual) east, with lancets where the neighbouring buildings allow. No one could call this an attractive church.

St Jude's, Mildmay Park (73)

By A. D. Gough: the foundation stone was laid on 1 July 1855. 'The edifice is in the Transition style from Decorated to Perpendicular, the early part of the fifteenth century' (*Illustrated London News*). It is cruciform, with the usual thin flanking-tower and spire (restored in 1911). There was an eastern apse with tiny aisles which had windows with crocketted canopies internally.

There was an enlargement by Edwin Clare in 1871: the foundation stone was laid on 25 June, and the church reopened on 12 December. A long chancel, aisles, and a clerestory were added. Clare's style is much the same as Gough's: the clerestory windows are large spherical triangles, with one large and two small foiled circles: the rest is Perpendicular, and the chancel windows duly have their ogee, crocketted canopies. The arcades have thirteenth-century foliage and square abaci, with Perpendicular bases. A faculty was given on 10 August 1906, for a new holy table, and for a choir vestry on the south of the chancel.

St Luke's, Hillmarton Road, Holloway (68)

A temporary church was built in 1857. The permanent church was begun in 1859, and consecrated on 9 February 1860. Thomas Poynder gave the site, Allen Poynder £500, and Alfred Batson, owner of the Copenhagen estate, £1,000. The architect was Charles Lee, the former partner of T. T. Bury, and the church is very like those that Lee and Bury produced: Middle-Pointed, of Kentish rag and Bath stone, with a north-west tower and spire: it was cruciform, but the north transept was destroyed in the War. The builder was George Myers.

Two faculties were given early in this century: 11 February 1903, to build a choir vestry and church room; 25 July 1914, to reglaze the windows, move the font, erect a dwarf chancel screen, raise the holy table, and panel the chancel in oak. The church was damaged on 19 March 1941 and rededicated after repair on St Luke's day, 1956: the walls are all whitened. New east window 1960, by Francis H. Spear. In 1961 a new building was erected on the site of the north transept: the architect was A. Llewellyn Smith.

St Mary's, Hornsey Rise

Another church by A. D. Gough: the foundation stone was laid on 29 June 1860, and the consecration was on 20 June 1861. George J. Carter of Hornsey Road was the contractor. The church has a nave and aisles, with tower and spire at the south-west, wide transepts, and small sanctuary. The style is Decorated as understood by Gough, who had not advanced much since the '40s. The windows have deep reveals: the spire as usual is very thin. The arch-braces of the roof rests on shafts, alternately long and short, on corbels with naturalistic foliage. Bishop Tait thought it all very fine. After the consecration, he had the privilege of being shown round by Gough, and two gentlemen of the committee: he was 'highly pleased with the construction and general appearance of the building'.

There was a major operation in 1883: a faculty was given to remove the stone pillars, and insert new ones of granite; build new aisles to the transepts, and north, south, and west porches; alter the chancel roof and insert two windows; lengthen the shafts of the chancel arch and provide and fix panels at the side of the piers; alter and refix the choir seating, pulpit, desk and font; and erect a west gallery.

1 June 1911: a faculty to raise the chancel floor, with new steps and a dwarf wall, and provide new stalls. There is a good deal of glass: the best is the west window, a tree of Jesse, by Westlake.

St Michael's, Bingfield Street

St Michael's is obscurely placed in a side street not far from St Pancras Station. Foundation stone 25 October 1863: consecration 5 August 1864. The architect was R. L. Roumieu. It is of the usual stock brick, relieved with red and black: slate roofs. Nave and aisles, with a large south porch, and chancel with a round apse. The inside is whitened, except for the arches, and round the clerestory windows. The glass in the apse is by Powell. The church was reopened in 1954 after the repairs by A. Llewellyn Smith.

St Silas, Penton Street (75)

The founder of this church was the Rev. A. L. Courtenay of St James's, Pentonville. The ground was bought and a temporary iron church was put up. S. S. Teulon made the design for the permanent church, and the foundation stone was laid on 19 July 1860. Courtenay, however, ran into trouble, having to pull down part of the newly built wall and set it further back. He brought an action against the architect and the builder for using bad materials. The church was completed by E. P. Loftus Brock, of Habershon, Brock and Webb, with considerable alterations and much simplified. It was opened in April 1863. The dedication was Christchurch: it was altered to St Silas at the consecration (16 July 1867).

The walls are faced with rag, with an odd admixture of brick. The nave is very large with passage aisles: the clerestory windows are under gables. It has a peculiar roof: two long wall-posts per pier, supporting twin tie-beams at a low level. A west gallery, and a square south-west turret with a slated cap. The chancel was added by William White in 1884, and a new altar and reredos were erected in 1931.

St Clement's, Barnsbury (70)

The church was built by Thomas Edmund Wilfred Cubitt, so that the inhabitants of Islington could have the chance of a less Evangelical kind of worship than was (and is) supplied by the other local churches. He laid the foundation stone on 11 July 1864, and the church was consecrated on the same date a year later. The builder was Dove.

Gilbert Scott was the architect, and he produced a good, sound brick church. The west end has four large buttresses, three porches, and a bellcote: the east end has three lancets and a vesica. The south side is scarcely visible, and the north side not visible at all. The nave has aisles of six bays: as Bumpus says, it might have looked better with fewer. The chancel is more effective, with its cradle roof and arcaded reredos, with commandments, Agnus Dei, and AΩ (which looks better than these ingredients might suggest). There is glass by Clayton and Bell at the east and west, and one lancet in the south aisle by Gibbs.

St Barnabas', Harvist Road

1864–6, T. K. Green, architect. This church remains, but is not used for worship.

St Saviour's, Aberdeen Park (66)

F. T. Mackreth of Canonbury Park offered to build a church in which daily service would be held: also a parsonage house, and, if necessary, a school. The vicar of Islington refused the offer: 'it emanates', he wrote, 'from one identified with the Romanizing movement in our Church'. Mackreth was vexed, and pointed out that the Prayer Book, after all, does order daily Mattins and Evensong. Anyhow, the church was built, with the approval of the bishop and the consent of the Ecclesiastical Commissioners: it was begun in 1865 and consecrated in 1866.

The architect was William White. It is all of brick, except for the heads of the windows, and the mullions of the windows of the clerestory. Nave and aisles, and a short additional bay at the west end; transepts, and a central tower with octagonal top; chancel, with north organ chamber and vestry, and a south aisle. The internal walls of the sanctuary are slightly splayed.

The piers in the nave are square, of brick: the influence of Butterfield is manifest in the brickwork of the clerestory, and of the wall above the chancel arch. The walls of the chancel and sanctuary are polychromed: the sanctuary and the tower are vaulted in brick. This is one of the best of White's churches.

St George's, Tufnell Park (74)

Built 1866–7, designed by George Truefitt, who was surveyor of the Tufnell Park estate. He had previously designed the temporary church, 1858, which was of wood, circular, 84 feet in diameter, and 64 in height.

The plan is most original. The body is octagonal, with a circular ambulatory round it: at the north-west and south-west are angular projections, and there is an additional porch at the south west. The tower is detached, joined by a passage. The chancel, apse-ended, projects rather far: its western part has aisles, which cut into the ambulatory of the body. East of the aisles, the chancel itself is surrounded by an ambulatory, leading to a circular lavatory with a pyramidal capping, and an eastern vestry.

The plan is well adapted to a large congregation of listeners to sermons: the pulpit however, is by no means centrally placed (though it is not original, and may have been moved). The long chancel is also irrelevant to the central plan. The tower, with its octagonal top, never completed, is rather an oddity.

Inside, the main colour scheme is grey of various shades: the columns are faced with terra cotta. This was done in 1883: the faculty (19 September) gave leave also to reglaze the clerestory with tinted geometric glass; to put a sunburner in the centre of the octagonal lantern; to erect the 'circular turret at the south-east for a closet'; to move the organ; and to place stone panelling behind the Communion table. The apse windows, 1949, are by H. Vernon Spreadbury.

St David's, Westbourne Road

Built in 1866–9; by E. L. Blackburne; it was burned down in 1935, rebuilt by T. F. Ford, and rededicated on 28 February 1936.

The arcades remain (whitened), and pieces of the walls: the rest is very plain, with a Perpendicular west end and a shallow eastern apse.

St Augustine's, Highbury New Park

Built 1869–70; by Habershon and Brock. This is a big church in a frankly ugly style, re-calling S. S. Teulon—particularly the west windows. Of stock brick banded with red. Very wide, with a flimsy-looking roof: banded pillars, ringed with dots, and square abaci. Incomplete south-west tower. The chancel has an enormous organ in chambers to the north and south: as the ground slopes away to the east, the vestries are underneath.

The choir vestry was enlarged in 1889. On 19 January 1905 a faculty was given for newly flooring the chancel and sanctuary, new choir stalls and painting on canvas in the panels of the reredos. The interior has been redecorated: the chancel is coloured blue. The glass in the aisles is a mixture: some of it is recent, none is noteworthy.

St John Baptist's, Cleveland Road

Built 1871–2: consecrated on 6 August 1872: it was designed by William Wigginton. The church is simple and cheap. It stands on a triangular site, at the junction of two roads, and diminishes somewhat towards the east, ending in a three-sided apse. The stock brick walls rise from the pavements, except in the enclosed point of the triangle at the east.

St James's, Prebend Street

The church was built to take place of Lamb's Chapel, Monkswell Street, in the City, which was demolished by Act of Parliament in 1872. It was begun in 1873, built at a cost of about £10,000, and consecrated on 4 May 1875. The architect was Frederick William Porter, architect to the Clothworkers' Company. It is of Kentish rag, thirteenth-century in style, with a tower and spire on the south. Rather ordinary, and might have been designed 20 years earlier: Porter was probably not much of a church builder. But it stands quite well on its more or less island site.

A coloured figure of William Lamb was brought from the old Chapel, and is in a niche over the door. The interior has been whitened. There is some glass by Lavers and West-lake. Four Flemish roundels, placed in 1857, were brought here in 1895.

St Peter's, Dartmouth Park, Upper Holloway

Designed by C. L. Luck, and built in 1879–80, St Peter's is a rather good town church, of the same plan as Luck's two churches in the Isle of Wight—at Sandown and Shanklin. A tall and wide aisled nave, with no division between it and the chancel: indeed, there is no structural chancel at all, only a short, unaisled sanctuary. Of brick, in late First-Pointed style, with—as so often—arcades of an earlier type. The east window of the north aisle is by Lavers and Westlake: others by Clayton and Bell. A vestry was added in 1955.

St Stephen's, Elthorne Road, Upper Holloway

Built in 1879–80: architect Ewan Christian. A routine production of his, but more likeable than some. Red brick Early English, the windows with plate and early bar tracery. An unclerestoried nave, with wide, separately gabled aisles, and a one-bay chancel without an arch.

St John's, Highbury Vale

Built 1880–1; by William Bassett Smith. This is not a very enterprising church: of stock brick, with red internally for the lower part of the aisle walls. An apsidal chancel, with a north chapel—firmly divided off, and used as a vestry. The middle window of the apse by Clayton and Bell: one on each side by Heaton, Butler and Bayne.

Emmanuel, Hornsey Road

Built in 1884, and designed by Frederic R. Farrow and E. Swinfen Harris. This is a very large red brick church of nave and chancel under one long slated roof with a curious turret at the junction, and a poor makeshift tower at the west of the south aisle. The only ornament is a wooden reredos with painted Evangelists, the usual writings, and diaper.

All Saints', Dalmeny Road

A mission church of St Matthew was opened on 18 January 1881. Five architects were invited to send designs for the permanent church: the cost was limited to £5,000. The plans of J. E. K. Cutts were accepted, and Dove Brothers' contract price was £4,975. The foundation stone was laid on 20 September 1884, and the church consecrated on 9 May 1885. It is of red brick in the Perpendicular style. After being bombed in April 1941 it was restored by A. Llewellyn Smith: the contractors were Douglas Grant and Partners. It was reopened on 14 January 1953.

St Saviour's, Harley Road

Designed by J. P. Cutts; the nave and aisles 1887–8, chancel and vestries 1890, west porches 1900. The proposed tower was never built. The east wall was decorated in memory of the first vicar (1902): the three arches were filled with painting. There is nothing noteworthy in the way of glass.

The church was repaired in 1961, and clear glass was put in the clerestory windows. It is of a more reasonable size than are most churches of this type.

St Thomas's, Finsbury Park

Built as a successor church to St Matthew's, Friday Street, in the City, which was demolished in 1888: it was consecrated in 1889. Ewan Christian was the architect. It is of red brick, in Christian's usual lancet style: nave, with separately gabled aisles, west baptistery and porches; chancel and apsidal south chapel, and a mixture of hall (added in 1901), passages and vestry on the south; waggon roofs; dormer windows in the chancel. The low iron screen was a Great War memorial. The east window is by Kempe and glass in the chapel and baptistery by Clayton and Bell.

St Andrew's, Whitehall Park

The latest suburban development on the very edge of Islington was given a temporary brick church in Archway Road, now used as the parish hall. The foundation stone of the permanent church was laid on 11 July 1894, and it was consecrated in 1895. The architect was Frederic Hammond, surveyor to various properties in and around the City, and later district surveyor of North-West Islington, and of Hampstead. This was his only church.

It is a very ordinary red brick church, with lancet windows, and one or two in Decorated style. It stands at the junction between two roads, so that it becomes narrower towards the west, and on the slope of a hill, so that the roads rise by the side of it; there are steps from the clergy vestry down into the church. The only things worth noting inside are the pulpit, and two sixteenth-century glass figures—St James and St Simon—from Ram's Chapel, Homerton, built in 1729, and demolished in 1935.

St Anne's, Poole's Park

St Anne's was consecrated on 16 April 1870; the architect was A. D. Gough, who at last produced a church that might be by anyone else. St Anne's was Romanesque, of brick, with large nave and aisles, a projecting tower at the south-west, with a short spire, and a very narrow chancel with north vestries; square abaci, foliated capitals; there was some glass by Gibbs. The tower and spire were added by H. R. Gough in 1877.

The church was closed and stood derelict for some years, mostly dismantled and with many windows broken. When I saw it in 1957, it was prepared for an enormous jumble sale: wares were displayed in heaps all down the nave, and on the chancel steps were many rows of pairs of shoes. It was all very dark, and the effect of the arches rising above the piles of merchandise was most peculiar.

It was proposed to construct a smaller church inside it; in the event, a small new church, by Romilly Craze, was built alongside it and was consecrated on 29 September 1960. The original church was taken down in 1965.

Kensington

The first place of worship to be built, beside St Mary Abbots, was the Chapel in Montpelier Road, Brompton, afterwards used as a school.

Holy Trinity, Brompton, and St Barnabas', Addison Road, were built by subscription among the inhabitants, and a grant from the Parliamentary Commissioners. John Sinclair, vicar of Kensington from 1842 to 1875, rebuilt St Mary Abbots. During his time, many new churches were built, of which most remain.

St Mary Abbots, High Street

The old church was adorned with various gifts in the course of the seventeenth century, and enlarged twice. It became unsafe, and in 1696 was taken down except for the tower, and rebuilt. The work was badly done, and the church was inspected by 'substantial workmen and artificers', who said that it would have to be partly rebuilt again. The faculty was given on 25 July 1704 and the north and south walls, and the roof, were reconstructed. At the visitation in 1715 the churchwardens reported that all was well, except for the steeple, which was much out of repair. It was patched up, but it soon became unsafe again. Estimates were obtained, but it was not rebuilt until 1770.

In 1801 the altar piece was 'new modelled in stucco'. There were various repairs in subsequent years, but the church fell into a bad state of decay. In 1866 Gordon Hills sur-

76 St Barnabas', Addison Road, 1827–9 by Lewis Vulliamy

77 All Saints', Notting Hill, 1852–5 by William White: the view across the transepts

78 St Jude's, Courtfield Gardens, 1867–9 by G. and H. Godwin

79 All Saints', Notting Hill, the tower

80 St John's, Ladbroke Grove, 1844–5 by Stevens and Alexander

81 St Mary's, The Boltons, 1849–
by G. Godwin

82 St Peter's, Kensington Park Road, 1855–7
by Thomas Allom

83 St Cuthbert's, Philbeach Gardens: the structure by H. R. Gou
1884–8; reredos by the Rev. Ernest Geldart; other fittings
by Bainbridge Reynolds

veyed it, and said that it might collapse completely in a few years' time: his opinion was confirmed by Professor Lewis. An appeal was made, and Gilbert Scott was appointed architect for the new church. The faculty for demolishing the old church was given on 2 September 1868 and the new building was finished in 1872 and consecrated on 14 May: the spire was completed in 1879. The contractors were Dove Bros.

The walls are of stock brick, faced externally with Kentish rag, and internally with Corsham stone. The columns in the chancel are of Irish marble.

It is a very large church in careful late thirteenth-century style, without any of Scott's peculiar features. The east and west ends recall Dunblane Cathedral. The tower and spire, at the north-east, are 278 feet high: it is hard to imagine Kensington without them. The vaulted cloister, by which the church is approached from the High Street, and the south porch, were completed in 1889–93, by Micklethwaite and Somers Clarke.

The altar and reredos were executed by Clayton and Bell, who did nearly all the glass in the church (from which too many borders and backgrounds have been removed). The window at the east of the Chapel of the Resurrection is by Powell. This chapel was furnished as a War memorial by Sir Giles Gilbert Scott, and dedicated in 1921. The pulpit, from the old church, is dated 1697.

Monuments   There is a very large number, of which the most noteworthy is that of the 7th Earl of Warwick, 1721, ascribed to J. B. Guelfi. Others that might be mentioned are, Thomas Henshaw, 1700. William Courten, 1702, by Grinling Gibbons: this was once a fine monument, but only a tiny portion of it survives. Colin Campbell, 1708. General Edmund Fenning, 1818, by John Bacon junior. Col Hutchins, 1823, by Chantrey. The Rev Thomas Rennell, D.D., 1824, also by Chantrey.

Holy Trinity, Brompton Road

Built with the help of the Commissioners: the cost was £10,407, towards which the Commissioners' grant was £7,407. The architect was T. L. Donaldson, and the builder was Archibald Ritchie. It was begun in 1826, and consecrated on 6 June 1829.

It is very plain Gothic in style, of stock brick, with a thin western tower. In 1845 the *Ecclesiologist* reported that the incumbent had put tracery into the windows, and fitted up the east end as a kind of chancel: there was glass by Willement in the east triplet, and there were double sedilia on the south.

A faculty was given on 6 August 1879, to build an extra chancel; convert the north vestry into an organ chamber; renew the ceiling of the nave, and alter the fronts of the galleries. The architect was Blomfield.

There have been several small twentieth-century additions. A faculty of 14 March 1904 specified the erection of a small west gallery and a small south-east chapel and porch; the improvement of the south-west porch; and the building of south-west and north-west vestibules. Certain parts of the walls of the church were to be covered with mosaic. The architect for the additions was R. W. K. Goddard.

A further faculty—21 April 1906—mentioned a large vestry, and a lobby and porch outside it, and a staircase between the parish room under the chancel and the proposed lobby. This was the work of the Blomfield firm. The memorial chapel and the north transept were completed in 1926. The glass in the nave is by Powell.

St Barnabas', Addison Road (76)

Built 1827–9, by Lewis Vulliamy: the builder was William Woods. The Commissioners gave £7,983 towards the cost. It is of stock brick in late Perpendicular style, with octagonal turrets at the corners and a western porch.

The church sets a good example by displaying a record, engraved on brass plates at the west end, of the subsequent alterations that have been made. The main items are as follows:

1860, chancel and vestry. (The faculty for these was given on 25 July). The architect was Thomas Johnson.

1878, organ moved to a new chamber on the south of the chancel.

1881, new west window.

1885, new seating on ground floor. (The faculty, 5 July 1883, also mentions alteration of the west porches, putting windows into the side walls, and altering the position of the pulpit.) The architect was Arthur Baker.

1887, choir stalls, and chancel floor extended.

1890, choir vestry enlarged (faculty 7 August).

1895, pulpit and dwarf screen, and the glass of the east and west windows transposed (faculty 17 July).

1904, nave redecorated.

1910 (23 January), new chancel consecrated, mosaic pavement in the sanctuary, and new glass in the sanctuary windows. (The faculty, 7 June 1909, also mentions the reconstruction of the arch, and new reredos and Communion table.) The architect was T. G. Jackson, and the new windows were by Morris.

The west window is by O'Connor, and the east by Clayton and Bell. The nave has an assortment of glass in the upper part of the windows, and a large number of monumental tablets, none of which deserve special mention.

St John's, Ladbroke Grove (80)

This church stands on the site of the Hippodrome, which was opened in 1837 'as a racing emporium more extensive and attractive than Ascot or Epsom'. It failed completely, after a very short time, and the ground was sold for building. The site of the grandstand was given for the church by Robert Roy, and building was begun in 1844. The architects were John Hargrave Stevens and George Alexander, and the builder was Hicks. The church was consecrated on 29 January 1845.

The *Ecclesiologist* thought that it looked too much like a cathedral, and criticised it in several respects; but it was the best church that the architects had so far designed, and it was hoped that they would continue to improve. It is Early English, cruciform, with deep transepts, and a central tower and spire rather like Witney on a small scale.

Faculties: 16 April 1873, for removing the organ from the west gallery: 22 August 1883, for a clergy vestry: 18 April 1890, for panelling behind the altar, to be continued later round the walls of the sanctuary.

The inside has been redecorated, and, having been cleared of unnecessary seats, looks extremely spacious. Nothing remains of the glass, except for the Kempe windows at the east, and a small panel in the south aisle with the name of George Alexander.

Monument The youngest son of Sir Aston Webb, Philip Edward Webb, architect, who was killed in France in 1916, aged 30, is commemorated by a tablet.

St James's, Norland Square

Designed by Vulliamy and Johnson, and built in 1844–5. It is Early English, of stock brick, and designed—in a very un-Gothic way—with a symmetrical south front with pinnacled tower in the middle, to close the view up Addison Avenue. The east end was extended by R. J. Withers in 1876.

A faculty was given on 1 September 1880 to erect a reredos, reseat the north and south galleries, and open an arch westward from the organ chamber. Another, 10 May 1894, gave leave to extend the chancel floor westward, enclose it with a screen wall and iron-work, erect new stalls and raise the walls of the organ chamber. There are high and thin arcades, with iron pillars: the galleries have been removed.

St Mary's, The Boltons (81)

Built 1849–50, designed by George Godwin, and restored by Joseph Peacock in 1872. It is rather an original design: cruciform, with an aisleless nave, and an octagonal central lantern tower and spire. The *Ecclesiologist* criticised the plan on the grounds that it was not suitable for common worship. The congregation would be divided into three, and for those in the transepts the pulpit and desk, in the crossing, would be the centre, and not the altar.

Changes were soon made. By a faculty of 31 January 1866 the organ was moved from the west gallery into a loft in the north transept, and the choir seats were moved to under the tower. A new pulpit was erected. The church was restored, after War damage, in 1952. An altar has been placed in the crossing. East window glass by Margaret Kaye.

The organ was too large for the church, and was sold after the War to St Nicholas', Great Yarmouth.

Christchurch, Victoria Road

This church is a chapel of ease to St Mary Abbots, but it might as well be included. It is one of Benjamin Ferrey's quiet, ordinary churches: the builder was Myers. Foundation stone 24 July 1850, consecration 23 July 1851. The windows were Powell's flowered quarries, and the tiles by Minton. The west porch was erected 1897, and font in the same year, from a design by Ferrey; chancel furnishings 1914; screen and stalls by Heaton, Butler and Bayne; altar rail and pavement designed by J. Arthur Reeve; Powell mosaics are in the reredos. The choir vestry was built in 1927.

Monuments   Charlotte Athanass, by Manning of London; she was the widow of Major Murray Stewart, 1860; there is a relief of her on her deathbed. The bust of Archdeacon John Sinclair, vicar of Kensington 1842–75, is by John Bell.

All Saints', Notting Hill (77, 79)

In 1852 the Rev Samuel Edward Walker, of St Columb Major, Cornwall, bought 51 acres of land and began to build a new town. It would, of course, include a church; and he had designs made by William White for a church, with a college of priests attached, which would be a memorial to his parents. The foundation stone was laid in 1852, and the structure of the church was finished by 1855. But Walker found himself in difficulties: many of his houses were incomplete, and money had run short. The church was left derelict, without furniture or glass in the windows: inevitably, it was known as Walker's Folly. It was finally completed and furnished under a civil engineer, and consecrated on 9 April 1861. The college, which was to have been on the north side of the church, never materialised: the position of the north aisle windows, high in the wall, shows where the cloister would have been. New vestries were added in 1898 by C. Hodgson Fowler.

All Saints' is a remarkable church, full of vigour and finely proportioned. Most of the accounts of it say that it was modelled on St Columb Major: but there is really no resemblance. It is an original design by White, who was only in his twenties at the time.

The tower is unlike any other of the Gothic Revival: rather thin, of four stages, with an octagonal top adorned with stones of different colours. It was to have been crowned by a very tall spire, but the tower settled, and the spire was not built: the base of it has been taken down.

The church has a straightforward plan of nave and aisles, transepts, and chancel with aisles; but the arcades are carried past the transepts, and there are open arcades above them, continuing the clerestory. The clerestory is also carried round the transepts.

The furniture, of course, was not what White intended. A reredos was erected later (1878), carved by Redfern, and there were wall paintings by Henry Holiday in the chancel. The present reredos is by Cecil Hare, 1933, carved by Bridgeman.

The church was damaged by bombing in 1940, reopened in 1944, and damaged again in that year. Repairs after the War were done by Milner and Craze, and completed in 1951. The high altar came from St Columb's, Lancaster Road, and so did the altar in the south transept (by Martin Travers, but the reredos is new). The altar in the north transept is by Comper, who also designed the altar and the glass in the south chapel, the font cover, and the painting on the east wall of the chancel. North chapel altar by Martin Travers—but the figure is by Dupont of Bruges. East window and windows in the north chapel and transepts by Gerald Smith (A. K. Nicholson Studios).

St Peter's, Kensington Park Road (82)

Built 1855–7, by Thomas Allom, surveyor to the Ladbroke Estate. The design for the church and for Stanley Gardens was exhibited at the Royal Academy in 1856. The architect boldly used the classical style: the *Ecclesiologist* called it 'a faint and debased imitation of the Wrennian style which was in vogue thirty years ago'. It is not, in fact, particularly debased, though there is a Victorian feeling about it. Other criticisms were kinder—e.g., 'an Italian basilica with a good colonnade of the Corinthian order'. There are galleries, and flat panelled ceilings.

In 1879 the chancel was extended by Edmeston and C. Barry; the alabaster pulpit dates from 1888, with reliefs by T. Nelson MacLean: it was rebuilt in 1905. The dwarf chancel screen and gates are of 1900. There have been many other adornments, about which it is not necessary to go into detail.

Dr C. M. Davies visited the church one Easter Sunday (*Orthodox London*, 1876), and looked round him during the Litany. Everything was refined, and nothing Roman. There were no candlesticks or vases, but all was rich in the extreme. This was the Church of England, pure and simple. Even the glass steered a middle course, between the grotesque and the commonplace.

St Philip's, Earls Court Road

This was planned as a simple brick church to hold 1,000 and cost about £5,000: it was built by the Rev J. D. Claxton, helped by contributions, and the architect was Thomas Johnson of Lichfield, who was Claxton's father in law. The foundation stone was laid on 6 May 1857, and Bishop Tait consecrated the church on 1 May 1858: the builder was W. Hill of Whitechapel, and the clerk of the works was John Cooper.

It is a very unpretentious church in simple fifteenth-century style. The south aisle was enlarged and a transept with a gallery added in 1863 (faculty 13 August).

'The church contains a most beautiful and costly reredos of carved stone and alabaster, and a very fine marble and alabaster altar-rail, (and) two windows of stained glass by Heaton and Butler, richly illuminated' (Mackeson). The glass was destroyed in 1940. The Lady chapel on the south, on the site of the original vestry, is by Francis Bacon.

St Paul's, Onslow Square

Charles James Freake, afterwards Sir Charles, who died in 1884 aged 70, was a building contractor who erected houses in Cromwell Road, Brompton Road, Onslow Square, and Cranley Gardens. Since every new building development needed places of worship, he planned two churches: it is said that he meant one to be High, and the other Low. St Paul's was the Low church, and for that reason it was built facing west. The architect was James Edmeston, though the design was published under the name of Freake. It was begun in 1859, and first used on Christmas Eve 1860. It is a very large galleried rectangle, with a small tower and spire and Perpendicular windows: the kind of church that was years out of date at the time. The galleries scarcely attempt to be Gothic, and there is even a clock at the west.

The best known vicar was H. Webb-Peploe, 1876–1919, who made it a famous Evangelical centre. In his time (1888–9) an extension of the sanctuary was built, with gallery staircases on each side: the architect was Wallace. The Countess of Seafield gave the stone reredos, with Mexican onyx panels, and a new pulpit was erected. The faculty also provided for the reglazing of all the windows. The glass is nearly all by Clayton and Bell, but there is one window by Arild Rosenkrantz, 1930. There is a memorial to Freake.

St Mark's, Notting Hill

Charles Henry Blake gave the site, which was then at the edge of the town. The foundation stone is dated 1 November 1862. On March 26 1863 E. Bassett Keeling was introduced to a meeting of the Ecclesiological Society. He produced designs for a church to be sent in for a competition, and also drawings for St Mark's, which was nearly completed. He was told that 'the style of these buildings was not such as the committee could sanction'. There is no evidence that he ever came again.

The committee's decision is not surprising. Bassett Keeling's designs were always ugly, and he broke most of the ecclesiological rules. St Mark's—which was consecrated on 27 November 1863—is of brick, as heavy and coarse as it could be. It has a dissenting-looking front, with windows to light the gallery staircases and the gallery; a low south-west tower and spire, and a spirelet at the north-west. Inside, there are high arcades, with arches of black and white brick and stone, with a tiny clerestory of circular windows above. There are wide transepts: the well-raised chancel has an apse. The removal of the galleries (1896) endangered the building, and the pillars have been encased in concrete, and concrete beams built out to the walls. The west gallery was taken down in 1905. New flooring, and a new pulpit and font, date from 1907.

The interior is not unimpressive, in a rather barbaric way: though it is easy to see why the ecclesiologists were not enthusiastic.

St George's, Campden Hill

Bassett Keeling's other Kensington church, in a similar style to St Mark's, is due for demolition. It was built in 1864 by John Bennett of Kensington, to provide a living for his son. The contractors were Myers and Son. The interior has been completely de-Keelingised by the alteration of the arcades (A. H. Ryan Tenison), the removal of the galleries, the whitewashing of the walls, etc.

St Stephen's, Gloucester Road (84)

The foundation stone was laid on 28 February 1866, and the church was consecrated on 10 January 1867. Joseph Peacock was the architect. It is faced with stone outside: the polychrome brick in the interior has been whitened over. Peacock is on the whole restrained in this church, though he has enjoyed himself in the design of the clerestory. The plan is not quite orthodox: nave and aisles, double transepts, a chancel with two-storied transeptal projections—that on the north with the organ: and sanctuary with vestries. The east wall has three lancets with a round window above.

A gallery was erected in 1868 by a local builder, against the advice of the architect, and without a faculty. In 1887 a petition was made for a faculty to take it down; also to build new vestries, to enlarge the present vestry and convert it into a side chapel; and to make a new entrance at the south-west. The faculty was granted on 24 November. The architect was H. R. Gough. The west gallery was removed by a faculty of 21 August 1896.

On 28 May 1903 a faculty was given for a new altar and reredos. This is by Bodley, and, as usual, very large. He also decorated the east wall, designed the altar hangings, etc. There have been various subsequent alterations. The glass is a mixture: that in the aisles is a series by Lavers and Westlake.

St Peter's, Cranley Gardens

This was Freake's High Church—though it has not, in fact, ever been strikingly High. It was built in 1866–7 from designs prepared in Freake's office and at his own cost: the clerk of the works was J. Brown. It is a large, rather rambling church, of brick faced with Kentish rag, with a low tower and spire at the north-west. At the east of the aisled nave is an arch, which does not lead to a chancel, but to the space between two large transepts, with galleries: there is an eastern apse.

The east end was adorned in the nineties, and on 29 January 1900 a faculty was given to erect new marble walls, with an iron screen, on the west and south. The clerestory windows were reconstructed in 1906. In 1909 the organ was rebuilt in a new chamber, the west gallery was rebuilt in stone, the north chapel was added, and the hall and vestries were built: the architect was W. D. Caröe. In 1922 the sanctuary was embellished as a War memorial.

The glass suffered in the bombing. The west window—with two panels missing—by Ward and Hughes: there is also glass by Clayton and Bell and Heaton, Butler and Bayne. Freake has a tablet here, as at St Paul's.

St Clement's, Treadgold Road

A cheap church—£4,000, to hold 900—by J. P. St Aubyn: it was consecrated in 1867. It is of brick, divided into nave and aisles by iron columns supporting the roof: there are double transepts, and a chancel with aisles. The south chancel aisle was rebuilt in 1908 as a chapel with a sanctuary, and a vestry was built across the east end of the chancel. The high altar, now enormously long, stands in front of a reredos of 1896: the chancel has been whitewashed. There is glass by Kempe in the south aisle, and a little more in the south chapel; two windows by Jones and Willis are in the sanctuary.

St Jude's, Courtfield Gardens (78)

Built 1867–9, consecrated in 1870, and completed in 1879; the architects were George and Henry Godwin. 'They have here successfully met the three demands of the day—moderation in cost, the use of iron in conjunction with wood and stone, with the utmost practical absence of obstruction to the seeing of the officiating clergyman by the whole congregation.'

The plan is entirely non-ecclesiological. The nave is wide: first comes a short stretch with narrow aisles: then come large transepts, double, each one the width of two bays, with porches at the west. A short chancel with vestries: then the sanctuary. The arcades have slender iron columns. At the west, a porch; tower and spire at the south-west, and an unnecessary little apsidal projection at the north-west. The walls are of ragstone outside, and brick within. The tower and spire are coarsely French: the rest of the church is Decorated. The whole thing has a strongly Nonconformist appearance.

The interior has been redecorated after War damage, and the polychrome brick has been covered up. The walls of the chancel and sanctuary have been allowed to keep their painting: the marble and mosaic reredos has been adapted to twentieth-century taste. The Rev C. M. Davies, when he visited the church, thought that the Evangelicals were going gay: all was as 'proper' as possible. The pew-openers were 'male attendants in white ties, bearded like Broad Churchmen, but smiling seraphically' (*Orthodox London*).

St Michael's, Ladbroke Grove

Begun in 1870, and consecrated in May 1871. The architects were J. and J. S. Edmeston, and the style was called 'Romanesque of the Rhine'. It has large windows of grey and other brick, with some terra cotta ornaments on the south, and none on the north. The large German-looking tower and spire at the south-west were never completed. The north transept was added in 1882. There are three apses, eastern, western, and southern.

The Rev H. P. Denison describes his ministry at this church in his *Seventy-Two Years' Church Recollections*, 1925, an interesting though tiresome book. Denison had served as curate to his uncle, the formidable Archdeacon Denison, and came to St Michael's in 1896: he lived on until the 30s. He says that the organ had been brought down by the second incumbent, and placed at the side of the choir at the east end. He, Denison, had it put back in the gallery, and altered what had been the choir into part of the sanctuary. He must have known: but a faculty had been given as long ago as 1880 for rebuilding the gallery, and moving the organ into it. The baroque altar piece was acquired in his time.

St Augustine's, Queen's Gate (86)

The nave was opened in 1871, and the chancel in 1876. The architect was William Butterfield, who showed his contempt for the street architecture of Kensington by designing one of his most violent fronts, with all kinds of Butterfieldian features, finished off with a straight parapet, turrets, and an aggressive bellcote.

Bumpus's description of the interior ought to be read. It has now been whitewashed all over, obliterating the red and white stone of the pillars, the paintings in the aisles, and the tile mosaic in the spandrels of the arches. The iron screen, put up 12 years after the consecration, has been removed. This was done by Martin Travers, 1928, who erected an enormous baroque altar piece, blocked most of the east window, and put some glass of his own design in the top. The Lady chapel altar is also his. Nothing can destroy Butterfield's proportions, but the colour which went with them has, of course, gone completely. There is a small iron gallery under the west window: the chancel arch is low, with openings above. The font, pulpit, and brass lectern have been allowed to remain.

St John the Baptist, Holland Road (85)

St John's is a large, vaulted stone church, designed by James Brooks. The apsidal chancel and Lady chapel were built first, in 1872, and the transepts and nave followed in 1889. The over-elaborate west front was built in 1909–11, from designs by J. S. Adkins who acquired the practice of Brooks and Sons: Brooks's west end would have been different, and he designed a tower and spire. The church has a dignified and solemn interior, not unlike Pearson. The stone screens to the chancel and chapel, and the parcloses, are overdone, and the tops are crowded with rows of figures. The massive stone reredos, with painting and gilding, is far more successful. Nearly all the glass is by Clayton and Bell: there is one window by Kempe.

St Luke's, Redcliffe Square

The architect was George Godwin in 1872–3, who also designed the Square: the builders were Corbett and McClymont. It has a more ordinary plan than St Jude's: nave and aisles, with a baptistery at the south-west, and tower and spire at the east of the north aisle. The chancel is apsidal.

Most of the interior carving was done by Boulton and Sons, of Cheltenham, in 1874. The arcades have statues of saints, and there are Protestant divines in the spandrels (1889). The roof has small hammer-beams and large arch-braces: it rests on corbels that are alternately above the apexes of the arches and above the heads of the divines: the effect is disturbing. A large organ at the west, with pipes rising restlessly in front of the west window. The organ screen is by W. Aumonier, 1919–20. Some Ward and Hughes glass below. Windows in the chancel and baptistery were painted by Mrs Handcock.

The chancel was restored in 1930 by A. B. Knapp-Fisher: it has been panelled, whitened (as also have the eastern two bays of the aisles), and reglazed.

St Helen's, St Quintin Avenue

This was a brick church, designed by Henry Currey, and consecrated on 15 January 1884. It was bombed in 1941, and there is nothing left of it.

The new church is by J. B. S. Comper: the foundation stone was laid on 4 December 1954. It is in the usual Comper late Gothic style, with a concrete vault. The altar is at the east end of the nave: an eastern chapel opens into the nave by three arches. The east windows of the nave and chapel are by Sir J. N. Comper. Hall and vicarage are attached to the church, and project north and south of the forecourt.

The parish now includes that of HOLY TRINITY, LATIMER ROAD, Norman Shaw's admirable church, which was built in 1887–8 and is now adapted for other purposes.

St Cuthbert's, Philbeach Gardens (83)

The Rev Henry Westall, curate of St Matthias', Earls Court—a church which has now been demolished, and its parish added to St Cuthbert's—undertook the building of a new church. A temporary building was opened early in 1883, and the foundation stone of the permanent church—a stone specially brought from Holy Island—was laid on 7 July 1884. The consecration was on 11 November 1887: the Lady chapel was completed in 1888.

The architect was H. Roumieu Gough, who designed a fine, large church, of the usual suburban type—which would be quite ordinary if it were not for its fittings. So many churches of this kind have been left more or less empty, and have never received even the furniture that the architects designed for them. St Cuthbert's has had a great deal more, and has been furnished with quite exceptional lavishness. The walls are covered with diaper work by the Guild of St Peter, under Mrs Dalton. Statues in the clerestory are by Boulton of Cheltenham.

William Bainbridge Reynolds, 1855–1935, a devoted craftsman, who hated mass-production, and took infinite care over all that he did, was a worshipper in this church. He designed the pulpit, and some of the glass, and made the lectern (of wrought iron and *repoussé* copper), the royal arms, the communion rails of the high altar and of the Lady chapel, the screens of the chapel, organ and baptistery, the clock, the sedilia and piscina, the door of the tabernacle, and the paschal candlestick.

The enormous reredos, 1914, was designed by the Rev Ernest Geldart (framework by Gilbert Boulton, and carving by Taylor and Clifton). The theme is 'the worship of the incarnate Son of God, with incense and lights', and it includes the scenes in holy scripture in which these are mentioned. The two shafts have figures of the four Latin Doctors and the four major Prophets, and 32 statues of saints: in the lower stage, above the altar, are the Apostles. There is no reredos quite like this in any other English church.

The font and cover are by H. Hems; the rood and loft were erected in 1893. Glass in the aisles—the life of St Cuthbert—by Tute, a pupil of Kempe. Stations of the Cross by Vinck, who painted the stations in Antwerp Cathedral. The canopy of the pulpit, 1907, and Lady chapel reredos, 1908, are by J. Harold Gibbons. A nave altar has recently been erected.

The church has relics of St Cuthbert: his tomb at Durham was opened in 1827.

St Columb's, Lancaster Road, Notting Hill

The original mission church was dedicated in 1889: the permanent church, a brick basilica designed by C. Hodgson Fowler, was begun in 1892, and completed and consecrated in 1901. The baldachino was erected in 1907.

The church flourished under the Rev George Lovelace, who was vicar from the beginning until 1928, but afterwards it began to decline. When All Saints' was damaged by bombing, the congregation migrated to St Columb's: but in 1951 the diocesan authorities decided to close it and to re-unite the parish with All Saints'. The church was lent to the Serbs.

Paddington

Paddington was still a village at the beginning of the nineteenth century. There was a good deal of handsome urban development, which was afterwards cut up and partly spoiled by the coming of the railway. A large number of churches was built in the nineteenth century, the majority of which are still there.

St Mary's, Paddington Green (87, 88)

A petition was presented to Parliament early in 1788: William Boyd, surveyor, gave evidence that the old church could not be effectually repaired, and must be rebuilt. The Bill passed the Commons on 14 March. Plans were made by John Plaw, whose *Rural Architecture* had been published three years before. The Bishop of London saw the design, and wrote on 21 July, saying that a very eminent architect had agreed with him in giving decided preference to it. But the elevation had not the form and air of a parish church: Plaw should be asked to 'remedy this Fault by making the Cupola more in the Manner of those to be found in Cathedrals, only avoiding what is Gothic'. On 30 September a contract was made with Thomas Wapshott of Tufton Street and the foundation stone was laid in October. After a year, the walls began to crack, and the vault fell in: Plaw attributed the disaster to the wet weather: Wapshott, to faulty design. The damage was made good, and the church consecrated on 28 April 1791.

The church is of brick, square, with four lower arms: there is a semi-circular Tuscan porch at the west. The interior is cleverly designed: a small congregation would not be lost in it; but, with the galleries, it could hold a considerable number. Four slender columns carry the shallow dome, and the arms have low, segmental vaults. There is restrained late eighteenth-century detail. A faculty for reseating and repaving was given on 15 August 1899. The chancel has been evacuated, and the altar moved forward.

Monuments   Frances Aust, 1794, by John Bacon. General Crosbie, 1807, by J. Bacon, junior. Lieut-Col Thomas Aubrey, 1814, by Rouw. Charlotte Cumberlatch, 1818, by Crampthorn. Joseph Nollekens, 1823, by Behnes.

In the churchyard are buried John Bushnell, 1701, Thomas Banks, 1805, Sarah Siddons, 1831, and Benjamin Haydon, 1846.

St John's, Hyde Park Crescent

Designed by Charles Fowler, the architect of several markets—Gravesend, Covent Garden, Hungerford (Charing Cross), Exeter and Tavistock; also of a few churches; the largest being Honiton, Devon, and the most attractive Teffont Ewyas, Wilts. St John's was begun in 1829, the foundation stone was laid on 23 March 1830, and it was consecrated on 26 January 1832. It is a brick church in the usual early Perpendicular style of the period: of seven bays, with tall clustered columns, and a plaster vault.

In 1888 Blomfield made a report on the church: he proposed to reseat it, move the organ, move the pulpit and desk to the sides, set back the galleries, take the lobbies into the church, and build a porch and staircases outside. The church was closed on 1 September and all this done: at the same time he designed new east and west windows.

The galleries were subsequently taken down. The screen and pulpit are 1910.

Monument   There is a tablet to Charles Theomartyr Crane, D.D., 1829 whose exertions in promoting the erection of the church are commemorated.

St James's, Sussex Gardens

It was decided to build a new parish church for Paddington in place of St Mary's, and an appeal was issued in 1840: a plan had been made, and the estimate was £10,000. The architects were John Goldicutt, a pupil of Henry Hakewill, and George Gutch, the surveyor to the Bishop of London's estate, and architect of Southwick Crescent, Gloucester Square, and Sussex Square. The Metropolis Churches Fund gave £3,000, and the Commissioners £2,000. Work was begun in 1841. The church was consecrated on 13 May 1843: by an Order in Council of 28 January 1845 it was made the parish church of Paddington. Goldicutt died on 2 October 1842.

It was a large galleried Gothic hall, with tower and spire, flanked by porches at the east, facing Sussex Gardens: the base of the tower was the sanctuary. A faculty was given on 16 August 1864 for additional entrances, a new vestry, and for moving the pulpit and desk. The space occupied by the present vestry was to be thrown into the chancel.

In 1881 the whole church was pulled down, except for the tower and porches, to be rebuilt from designs by G. E. Street, who died on 6 December. The foundation stone was laid by Princess Christian on 11 February 1882, and the consecration was on 22 December. The work was superintended by Blomfield.

The new church faces in the opposite direction, with the chancel at the west. It is large and handsome, in fourteenth century style: but Street's inspiration was running down towards the end of his life. The spandrels of the arcade, and the lower part of the aisle walls are faced with marble. The white marble Last Supper of the reredos is by Forsyth: the former reredos is now part of the organ case. The marble panels on the east wall, with plants of the Bible, are by Blackler, of St Marychurch. All the glass in the chancel and the south chapel and that at the end of the aisles is by Clayton and Bell: the later windows are by Heaton, Butler and Bayne. The old altar window was by Warrington: the present post-War glass is by A. E. Buss, executed by Goddard and Gibbs.

St John's, Kensal Green (93)

The architect was H. E. Kendall, junior. Foundation stone 2 November 1843: consecration 8 August 1844. The builder was Thorne, and the cost £3,435. It was described as being 'in the ancient Norman style': but it is said that Kendall spent a holiday in the Rhine valley, and derived his inspiration from there. The design was exhibited at the Royal Academy.

The *Ecclesiologist*'s critic had 'seldom seen a building with so much vulgar pretence and cheap attempt at effect'. It was a parallelogram with a shallow apse at one end, and at the other 'two cathedral-like towers crowned with stumpy spires, fringed by still more stumpy pinnacles, all of the "Norman style", and constructed of an elegant admixture of yellow brick and white brick, and cement, and black flint, and white mortar and black mortar, arranged in many a fantastic pattern'.

A faculty of 15 August 1894 gave leave to extend the nave one bay to the east by pulling down the apse and building the first bay of a proposed chancel. The chancel was completed in 1903: it is Gothic, vaulted in wood. The architect was A. Billing. The church was restored at great cost before the War, damaged in 1941, and repaired afterwards.

Holy Trinity, Bishop's Bridge Road (91)

The scheme for building this church was begun by the Rev John Miles, of Brompton, who offered £4,000 on condition that the church should not cost less than £10,000. The Church Building Commissioners gave £1,000, and the Ecclesiastical Commissioners £2,000 and the site. The cost was £13,221, exclusive of ornamental work; and nearly £20,000 altogether.

Thomas Cundy made the plans, and building was begun in 1844: the ground was very wet, and the floor was raised on a brick crypt. There was, and is, a reservoir under the tower. The foundation stone was laid in November, and the Bishop of London consecrated the church on 3 July 1846. The architect gave the reredos. The tower and spire were completed later.

The church is fifteenth-century in style. The proportions are rather like those of St Luke's, Chelsea: it was obviously designed for galleries. It made the *Ecclesiologist* very angry: 'It is externally a heap of misapplied ornament; battlements, finials, gurgoyles guiltless of gutters, panellings, &c., &c., all carved in good stone, figure in tasteless confusion.' Inside, there was a plaster groined roof; and there were galleries, seats with doors, and a prayer desk facing west. 'Such monsters are the inevitable birth of a transitional age like ours.' They must be borne, in the hope that an age of All Souls' (Langham Place, of course, not Oxford), and St Pancras, would change to one of Patringtons and Heckingtons.

The usual alterations were made afterwards. The east window, 1876, is by Ward and Hughes; a new pulpit and lectern were also installed the same year. The organ was moved to the north of the chancel: it was given a screen of Caen stone in 1879.

In 1881 the interior was cleaned and the chancel was coloured. A new reredos of Caen stone, carved by Earp and Hobbs, was erected: St Peter and St John at the sides were added in 1916. The font was moved in 1888. New seating, 1893: chancel paved with marble, and mosaics on the east wall, 1908. The new altar, 1914, was designed by G. H. Fellowes Prynne.

In 1926, under Sir Charles Nicholson, the galleries were taken down. The borough surveyor intervened, and said that the pillars would not be sufficient to support the roof. They were found to have a core of brick, not of iron, and had to be considerably strengthened. The vaulting and the ceilings of the aisles were coloured. The painting over the Lady chapel altar is by Miss B. E. Lithiby. The hanging rood came from the demolished church of St Paul, Harrow Road.

Christchurch, Lancaster Gate (92)

Built 1854–5: the consecration was on 5 September 1855: the cost was £14,500. F. and H. Francis were the architects, and the builder was Myers.

It is a large, rather showy, Middle-Pointed church, the walls faced with Kentish rag, in even courses, with Bath stone dressings; with nave, aisles, south porch, and north-west tower and spire (completed after the rest of the church); very large transepts, obviously designed for galleries, which were removed in 1881; and chancel with aisles and vestry. The arcades are very tall: there were originally galleries in the aisles. The stone west gallery remains.

The *Ecclesiologist* did not think much of it. '*Big* it is, and heavy outside—not in fact to be much praised, and manifesting to the full the ungracefulness attendant upon the cross form without so much as a central fleche. But inside there is really considerable grandeur despite a certain heaviness.' It had height, and a chancel of good depth.

Messrs Francis's reredos was of Caen stone, with columns of polished serpentine: the panels were filled with encaustic tiles. The pulpit was tall and thin and there was a carved prayer desk. The glass was by Wailes.

The church has had a large number of later embellishments. An alabaster pulpit of 1885. New vestry 1888 (faculty 27 August), and part of the previous vestry was opened into the church; new glass in the east window 1892. The clergy vestry was enlarged in 1895; and in the next year the 'vestry chapel' was extended northward, the gallery being removed, and it was fitted as a chapel. The sanctuary has been given an alabaster lining, with painted panels: ecclesiologists will be particularly interested in the first one on the north, which is to the memory of Benjamin Ferrey, who was churchwarden. The carving of Our Lord in glory, the pavement, and the rails, date from 1909. The parcloses, priest's desk, etc., are 1912.

There is glass by Powell: the west window by Wailes remains.

St Saviour's, Warwick Avenue

Begun in 1855, and consecrated on 12 April 1856. When it was first built, it stood on the very edge of the town, with fields beyond. Thomas Little was the architect, and the builders were Pollock and McLennan, of Osnaburgh Street. It is a very late example of its kind—'a big auditorium without aisles, but with a very flat roof, which', said the *Ecclesiologist,* 'we innocently thought had died out of London at all events ten years back'.

There is little to say about it; it is in fourteenth-century style, with a rather pretentious tower, and good, deep buttresses. The original chancel, though short, was 'as fine as polychrome and painted glass could make it'. The reredos—carved niches of Caen stone, with

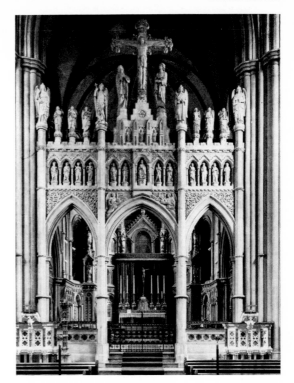

84 St Stephen's, Gloucester Road: G. F. Bodley's reredos, in the church designed by Joseph Peacock, 1866

85 St John the Baptist, Holland Road, by James Brooks, 1872 and later

86 St Augustine's, Queen's Gate, 1871 and 1876 by William Butterfield: altar piece, etc., by Martin Travers

87, 88 St Mary's, Paddington Green, rebuilt by John Plaw 1788–91.

89, 90 St Mary Magdalene's, Clarendon Crescent, by G. E. Street,
completed in stages and consecrated 1878. Exterior and north aisle

serpentine columns—the pulpit and the font, were executed by W. Farmer, of Westminster Bridge Road: the chancel glass and decorations were by Messrs Gibbs.

On 9 July Lady Burdett Coutts laid the foundation stone of a new chancel, which was consecrated in February 1884. The architect was Fairfax Wade-Palmer. Stone staircases were built under the tower at the same time. The chancel is large, with wall arcading containing life-sized figures of Apostles. The east window is by Clayton and Bell. The chancel arch was raised in 1887.

A window on the south of the nave, under the gallery, was erected by several residents as a memorial to the architect, Thomas Little, who died on 20 December 1859, aged 57.

St Stephen's, Westbourne Park

Built 1855–6 and consecrated on 21 April 1856. The architects were F. and H. Francis. The founder was the Rev Harvey William Brooks, who gave the money to complete it: he became the first vicar.

Of the usual Kentish rag and Bath stone, in late thirteenth-century style. The church must have looked rather old-fashioned in 1856: churches like this were being built ten years before. Nave and aisles, with west tower, from which the spire has been removed; transepts, and chancel with north organ chamber and south chapel. The font was a memorial to Brooks, who died in 1882. The chancel was altered in 1884, and the galleries in the aisles and transepts were taken down in 1888. In 1900 the apse was built, an apse at the end of the chancel aisle, a porch to the chapel, and a new choir vestry and lobby. The architect was W. Bassett Smith. The faculty (24 May) specifies that all the external masonry is to be of Doulting stone; a new altar table and reredos were provided. In 1911 a baptistery was formed.

There are windows by Gibbs, including one erected by the Francis brothers— Frederick and Horace—to the memory of their mother, who died in 1858. Several windows by Clayton and Bell were put up in this century. In the baptistery is a very large alabaster monument to Elizabeth Lindo, who died in 1889: she is bearing her cross, and approaching our Lord, to be crowned by Him.

St Michael's, Star Street

A brick church, 1860–1, designed by Rodhe Hawkins, to fill an almost square site, between two streets: it stands north and south. The most conspicuous feature is the tower, of

French appearance: 'that peculiar form of four-sided slate steeple, with unequal sides, which leads up to a ridge, and not to an apex.'

The church was bombed, and has remained derelict ever since.

St Mary Magdalene's, Clarendon Crescent (89, 90)

Some London churches are inseparably connected with their founders: this is one of them. Richard Temple West was curate of All Saints', Margaret Street, from 1860 to 1864. The congregation of All Saints' included some residents of Paddington, who wanted to have a church with similar services in their own district. A site was found, and a temporary chapel of St Ambrose was opened in February 1865. There was only one possible architect, G. E. Street, a member of All Saints' and a friend of West's; he was asked to make the design.

The site was extremely difficult: it was not level—because soil had been dumped there when the Canal was dug—and none of its sides were parallel; there was, too, a projection at the south-east. Street designed a crypt, vaulted with Dennett's patent concrete, in which he put the vestries. The projection of the ground suggested a south transept, and a thin octagonal tower and spire was placed between it and the chancel. The chancel ends in a three-sided apse, which follows the boundary-line. There is a full-sized aisle on the south; on the north there was no room for anything more than the narrowest of passage aisles. In High churches of the time the sexes were separated: the larger side was given to the women, as there were likely to be more of them. (The Bishop of Nassau, in West's biography, however, says that St Mary Magdalene's was attended largely by men.) West was very good at raising money and he was enthusuastically supported: when it was decided to make the church larger than had been intended, two ladies sold their houses and furniture to pay for it.

The nave and chancel, with a temporary roof, were opened on 21 October 1868: in 1870 the south aisle was thrown open to the nave. In 1872 the clerestory and roof were built, but before the roof was finished it was set on fire and destroyed. Rebuilding was begun at once, and the church was ready by the end of the year. It was consecrated in 1878.

The church dominates the rather out-of-the-way part of Paddington that lies between the Harrow Road and the Canal—which is now being completely rebuilt. The apse and tower rise sheer and unbuttressed from the pavements, and the spire soars above: contrast is provided by the horizontal bands of stone in the belfry stage. Street obviously enjoyed designing the church, and put his best into it. He was in full agreement with West and was specially pleased that he was allowed to build by stages: 'if that was the general rule', he wrote, 'we should have more fine churches, and architects would not complain that nothing grand or noble is possible.' He said that everything had been entirely his own design, drawn down to the smallest detail.

In the interior, he expressed the difference between the two sides by designing altogether dissimilar arcades. On the south are graceful clustered columns with thirteenth-century foliage: on the north, plain octagonal pillars, and the bays are divided into two by sub-arches: in the spandrels are medallions of the Stations of the Cross. But both are pulled together by the clerestory, which is the same on both sides. The nave has a painted cradle roof.

The chancel, which is well raised, is vaulted. The lower part of the walls is lined with marble, and above that is a diaper with mosaic panels. The reredos of the Crucifixion, with the Apostles under, was carved by Earp, who also executed the rest of the stone carving. The glass was designed by Henry Holiday, under Street. The whole interior is a most satisfactory nineteenth-century Anglo-Catholic ensemble, and it is so complete that practically nothing has had to be added to it.

In the crypt is the Chapel of St Sepulchre, fitted up by Comper, and finished in 1895. It is all complete: screens, altar with tester, wall-painting, glass, and a small organ with a pretty painted case.

St Augustine's, Kilburn Park Road (94)

This wonderful church owes as much to its founder, the Rev Richard Carr Kirkpatrick, as St Mary Magdalene's does to Richard Temple West.

Kirkpatrick was curate of St Mary's, Kilburn (see Hampstead), where a Catholic tradition was being established. In 1867 a new vicar was appointed, an extreme Low Churchman who determined to change things. Many of the congregation appealed to Kirkpatrick to try to build a mission church in the south end of Kilburn, where they could worship as they had been accustomed: Kirkpatrick said that he would not, if the vicar of St Mary's would provide an early celebration of Holy Communion on Sundays, and daily mattins and evensong. The vicar refused, and the Tractarians and Kirkpatrick walked out.

It was three years before the district was formed, and it was difficult to procure a site for the church: the site finally obtained was almost on the edge of the district. However, it was spacious, and J. L. Pearson made designs for a really large church. A temporary chapel was built in 1871, and a few months later the foundation stone of the church was laid. The contractors were Colls and Sons. The chancel was ready for use by June 1872, and the nave and aisles were completed in 1877. The consecration was on 24 February 1880. The tower and spire, 254 feet high, were built in 1897–8. These are of Pearson's usual proportions (though many of his towers and spires were never built): sheer and without buttresses, with tall pairs of windows in the belfry stage, and pinnacles at the base of the spire, set close to it. The basement forms a vaulted porch.

The church is an unbroken area, 58 feet in height, covered with a vault, with stone ribs and brick fillings. The buttresses are all inside, and are pierced with double aisles, and an upper gallery—each compartment vaulted—that runs all the way round the church, like the inner aisle below. There are transepts, with scarcely any projection at all. These are not visible from the nave, as the arcades and upper passages are carried past them. To the east of the south transept is the apsidal Lady chapel, which is treated, as usual in a Pearson church, as though it were a separate, smaller church.

Every part of the church is vaulted. The windows are all lancets, except for the large rose window at the west. At the four angles are square turrets, and there is a flèche at the crossing.

The chancel is divided from the nave by a stone screen of five arches, with a band of carving at the top of the same height as the front of the nave galleries. The galleries in the chancel have fronts of stone, with niches, filled with statues on the east wall; and all the walls below them have stone arcading. There is a stone reredos by Nicholls—who also did the rest of the stone carving. This is the least satisfactory part of the church. It is curious that Pearson never seems to have been able to design rich ornament—the carving in his churches is ordinary and overdone. The painting on the brickwork in other parts of the church by Clayton and Bell—now rather faded—is a more pleasing adornment. Clayton and Bell were responsible also for all the glass in the church, some of which is very good.

John Betjeman is right in saying that the way to see this church is to walk right round the inside, watching the vista that changes with every step. Paintings were given to the church by Lord Northcliffe: Christ and the Cross, by Crivelli; Virgin and Child, by Filippino Lippi; Adoration of the Infant, by Marco Palmezzano; Annunciation, by Titian.

St Peter's, Elgin Avenue

Built 1867–70, consecrated on 23 June 1870. Designed by Newman and Billing, and built by Dove Brothers of Kentish rag and Bath stone, with slated roofs; a rather wide nave, with aisles, and a south-west tower with a short, lead-covered spire; there are very wide transepts, a chancel with three-sided apse, a south organ chamber and a north vestry. It is one of those churches that combine French thirteenth-century features inside with four-teenth-century window tracery. There is some glass by Powell. The interior has been recently done up by Campbell, Smith and Co., under Macgregor and Partners.

St Matthew's, Moscow Road, Bayswater

This is partly on the site of Bayswater Chapel, designed by T. Cooper, and built in 1818. The new church was designed by J. Johnson (II), and built in 1881–2.

A large church, with walls of ragstone, dull in detail but quite interesting in plan. A very wide and lofty nave with passage aisles: gallery at the west, and a thin and lofty south-west tower and spire: an apsidal baptistery projects from one of the bays on the south. The vaulted sanctuary opens into the nave by a lofty arch: on each side is an arch opening into a transept. Each transept has a gallery: the vestries are beyond on the north.

Three east lancets, with a rose window above: the glass by Clayton and Bell, who also did the west window. ('East' and 'west' are used, to avoid confusion: the church in fact is not orientated.)

Emmanuel, Harrow Road

Foundation stone 27 June 1885, consecrated on 30 January 1886. By J. T. Lee. A large, plain brick church, old-fashioned for its date. A wide clerestoried nave with aisles, west porch, and a low south-west tower with brick spire. Slender marble pillars with foliated capitals. Most of the windows have coloured patterned glass, but there are two windows by Hardman. The reredos was erected in 1913.

St Simon's, Saltram Crescent

Built in 1898–9; J. S. Alder was the architect. The church is of red brick, in the Decorated-Perpendicular style, with a west porch and north-west turret. The east bay of the nave is the choir, and there is a three-sided apsidal sanctuary. The east bay of the south aisle is screened off as a chapel; the screen contains Hardman glass, no doubt from one of the two demolished churches, the parishes of which are now joined to St Simon's. These were St Luke's and St Jude's, both designed by J. T. Lee. The glass in the sanctuary is by Jones and Willis.

St Giles in the Fields

This was a very populous parish, with, at one time, some very bad slums in it. There were one or two short-lived chapels. The Victorians built Christchurch, Endell Street—a modest building, in which the Tractarian ideal of daily Mattins and Evensong was faithfully carried out. This has now gone.

St Giles in the Fields (63)

A petition to the Commons on 29 January 1718 said that the church was very old and ruinous. 'Very old' was the usual expression, not always to be taken literally: in fact, the church had been rebuilt in 1623–30. On 5 February a bill was brought in to make it one of the Fifty New Churches. The Commissioners objected, saying that it was their business to build new churches, not to rebuild old ones. But their objection was overridden. In 1729 £8,000 was appropriated for rebuilding St Giles's. Hawksmoor made a design, but the commission was given to Henry Flitcroft: the plans were ready in 1731, and it was agreed to finish the church by the end of 1733.

It is a good, sound church, of the type that Wren and Gibbs had developed: indeed, the influence of both these masters is so strong that it is not easy to see any personal contribution from Flitcroft. It is of Portland stone, with a rusticated basement. The steeple is almost the same as that of St Martin in the Fields, except that the octagonal stage has a balustrade, and the spire is banded.

The inside has galleries on square piers: the columns above are Ionic, and there is an elliptical barrel vault with plaster work. The east end is in two stages, like the rest of the church, with the entablatures returned round the east wall, and Ionic pilasters: the window has a pediment above. The altar piece, in the middle compartment, has a scrolled pediment, with an eagle standing in the middle. Moses and Aaron, at the sides, were painted by Francisco Vieria, court painter to the King of Portugal.

The beautiful inlaid pulpit was given by John Sharp, when he was rector: he became Archbishop of York in 1691. Flitcroft carefully specified that the old pulpit be used again.

In general, the fittings of the church were not much interfered with in the nineteenth century. The organ, built by Father Smith in 1671, keeps its case, and remains in the west gallery. There were rearrangements by Blomfield 1875, and Butterfield, 1896. All the Victorian glass was destroyed in the War, except for the east window.

In 1952–3 the church was restored, and very successfully redecorated (Gordon Jackson and Norman Haines). The wrought iron altar rails, which Butterfield had moved, were replaced. The font of 1810, which had been taken to West Street Chapel in 1875, was replaced; and a table from St Marylebone was put in the south chapel.

Monuments George Chapman, 1634, in the form of a Roman tombstone: it is said by Vertue to be by Inigo Jones. Lady Frances Kniveton, 1669, a figure in a shroud, by Joshua Marshall. Andrew Marvell, 1678: a monument erected in 1764. Sir Roger Lestrange, 1704. Luke Hansard, printer of the Commons Journals, 1828. The monument to John Flaxman, 1826, was erected by the R.A. in 1930.

Many famous people were buried in the churchyard. The Resurrection group in the churchyard gate dates from 1687: the carver was Love, who was paid £27.

St George's, Hart Street, Bloomsbury (95)

One of the Fifty New Churches, built in 1720–30, and consecrated in January 1731. Nicholas Hawksmoor was the architect: the masons were Edward Strong and Edward Tufnell, Christopher Cass and Andrews Jelfe: carpenters, James Grove and John Meard: carvers, John How and John Boson. The plasterer was Isaac Mansfield, and the joiner Thomas Phillips.

The Corinthian portico on the south is surely the finest in London. It is truly Roman: as Goodhart-Rendel wrote, it looks like one of the temples of Londinium preserved and adapted for Christian use.

The upper part of the tower at the west is intended to realise Pliny's description of the Mausoleum at Halicarnassus, remains of which are now in the British Museum not far away. Pliny is not very explicit, and no restoration has been quite satisfactory: Martial, anyhow, says that the upper portion of the Mausoleum was 'hanging in empty air'. But Hawksmoor made the attempt: that was the kind of thing that he liked to do. At the top is a statue of George I, who 'looks like the father of his people surveying his good city with complacency, and holding forth his protecting hand over it'. So wrote James Elmes, who defended the church against its critics. It is, he says, 'a bold, original, and striking composition, built in a masterly and scientific manner, and designed in a masculine style'.

The church is a square *atrium*, lit by a clerestory, with north and south aisles, divided from the square by pairs of columns supporting an entablature and a wide segmental arch: the north aisle has another, smaller one—now the sanctuary—leading out of it. At the east is an apse.

Early in the nineteenth century the altar piece from Montague House Chapel was brought here; and, as it was too large for the apse, it was placed in the north recess, and the furnishings were rearranged to face in that direction. The interior was refitted in 1871. The faculty (3 August) gave permission to demolish the galleries in the south and west aisles, construct a new gallery on the south, and reseat the church.

Christchurch, Woburn Square

Built in 1831–3 and designed by Lewis Vulliamy: of brick, with stone dressings. The plan is a cross within a square, with a flat roof. The tower and spire are in the front, with adjuncts on either side. East window by Goddard and Gibbs, 1955. The church is threatened with demolition.

Holy Trinity, Kingsway

The original church, in Little Queen Street, was designed by Francis Bedford, and built in 1829–31: the cost, £8,521, was all paid by the Commissioners. It was described at length by Carlos in the *Gentleman's Magazine* (1832, Part 1, pp 9–10).

The church was remodelled in the '80s, and rearranged with the altar at the other end. It became unsafe, owing to the making of the underground railway, and was taken down by a faculty dated 29 August 1909. The new church, in Kingsway, by J. Belcher and J. J. Joass, was built in 1909–11. The contractors were G. Godson and Sons. It is Renaissance, and was planned for a dome, and a tall tower designed to harmonise with those of St Mary le Strand and St Clement Danes. There is a curved front facing Kingsway.

St Luke's

The parish of St Luke's was formed in 1733 from that of St Giles's, Cripplegate. It was 'laid out in numerous streets and squares, covered with buildings in every direction, and has become one of the most extensive and populous parishes in the suburbs of the metropolis' (Lewis). There were several hospitals and other charitable institutions. It became overcrowded in the nineteenth century, and some new churches were built, which are no longer in existence.

St Luke's, Old Street

One of the Fifty New Churches, built in 1727–33. The minutes of the Commissioners refer to a design to be made jointly by the two surveyors, Hawksmoor and James. It is well known for its steeple in the form of an obelisk, which has been found fault with by almost all writers on London, as being incorrect and odd. The church was found to be in a dangerous condition in 1959, and has been closed, dismantled, and unroofed.

St Barnabas', King Square (97)

A Commissioners' church, designed by Thomas Hardwick, and built in 1822–6. It has a brick body, and an Ionic portico at the west, with a low tower and spike spire. The church was closed in 1940, and used for storing furniture from bomb-damaged churches. It became derelict, but was restored after the War as the parish church for the combined

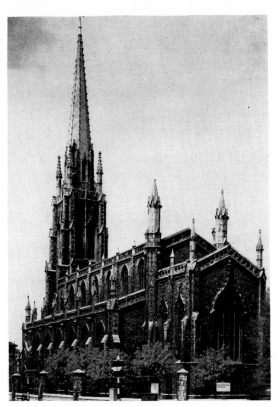

91 Holy Trinity, Bishop's Bridge Road, 1844–6 by Thomas Cundy

92 Christchurch, Lancaster Gate, 1854–55 by F. and H. Francis

93 St John's, Kensal Green, 1843–4 by H. E. Kendall

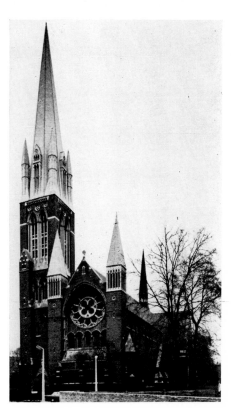

94 St Augustine's, Kilburn, by J. L. Pearson 1872–7; tower and spire 1897–8

95 St George's, Bloomsbury, 1720–30 by Nicholas Hawksmoor

96 St Marylebone Parish Church 1813–17 by Thomas Hardwick

97 St Barnabas', King Square, 1822–62

98 Christchurch, Cosway Street, 1822–4 by Philip Hardwick

99 All Souls', Langham Place, 1822–4: the tower and portico of John Nash's church

parishes of St Barnabas, St Matthew, and St Clement. St Matthew's, by Gilbert Scott, and St Clement's, by Butterfield, were both bombed, and it was decided to demolish them. The architects were Messrs Gordon Jackson and Partners. The galleries were demolished, and four Corinthian columns were introduced into the interior. A new organ gallery was erected at the west, and a ciborium over the altar. The pulpit was brought from Marylebone Chapel. The church was reopened on 11 June 1954.

St Marylebone

The St Marylebone vestry throughout the eighteenth century was mean, vacillating and incompetent in the matter of church building. The old church was rebuilt cheaply, but nothing else was done until the new church was begun in 1813. There was a considerable number of proprietary chapels, to make up for the lack of room in the church: but the parish ought to have done something for itself. Four large Commissioners' churches were built: St Mary's, Bryanston Square, All Souls', Langham Place, Christchurch, Cosway Street, and Holy Trinity, Marylebone Road. These all survive, though Holy Trinity is now the headquarters of S.P.C.K., and is no longer a parish church.

By 1851 there were 15 parish churches and nine chapels. The population then was 157,696: in 1861 it was 161,680. By 1951 it had fallen to about 76,000. Several churches have gone, and most of the chapels; but the best have been allowed to remain. St Andrew's, Wells Street, one of the best known of the Marylebone churches in the nineteenth century, has been rebuilt at Kingsbury, Middlesex.

St Marylebone Parish Church (96)

The old church of Marylebone was very small and out of repair. It was surveyed in 1740, but the vestry could not decide whether to enlarge or rebuild it. Gibbs made a design for a new church which was not adopted. Mr Lane's plan was accepted instead, and he built a small new church of brick: it was some time before his account was settled.

By 1753 the new church needed enlargement, and in 1754 the vestry was told that Gibbs had left £100 for the purpose. He had evidently left a plan as well, for in 1764 the vestry agreed that to execute it would take up great time and expense: all that they would consent to was the construction of some vaults.

In 1770 they agreed to petition Parliament for a Bill to convert the church into a parish chapel, and to build a new parish church. But from this time onward they seem to have been quite incapable of taking decisive action. They chose Sir William Chambers as their surveyor, and he made a design; but when they had obtained a piece of ground, they decided that they had not enough money to build the church, and used it only as a cemetery. In 1778 they failed to close with the offer of another site. When the Park was laid out, a church was included in the plan; but difficulties arose, and the site was lost.

Finally an Act of Parliament was obtained—in the session of 1810–11—and in 1813 a new chapel was begun from designs by Thomas Hardwick. The foundation stone was laid on 5 July. After it was begun, the committee decided that it was to be the parish church, and Hardwick had to alter the plan. Two columns were added to the portico, the Ionic order was changed to Corinthian, and a steeple was substituted for the turret. It was consecrated on 4 February 1817. The cost, including the fittings, was about £72,000.

An unusual feature of the plan is the two wings, set at an angle: these were family pews—two rooms to each wing—with fireplaces.

The interior of the church had two tiers of galleries, which stopped short of the wings. In 1815 an organ was erected on a level of the first gallery, over a room formed behind the altar: it was divided into two parts, with an arch between filled with a transparency, by Benjamin West, of the angel and the shepherds. The altar piece was a painting by West of the Virgin and Child. In 1826 the transparency was removed and the organ collected into one: the rooms in the wings were abolished, and the galleries were extended round to the organ.

In 1883 Thomas Harris, a churchwarden, made designs for enlarging and altering the church. Mrs Gladstone laid the foundation stone of the new chancel on 8 August 1884. A new priest's vestry was added. The upper gallery was removed, except at the west, and the iron columns were cased in wood. The body of the church was reseated and repaved. The marble-work was by Burke and Co and the glass by Campbell, Smith, and Campbell. A chapel to commemorate the centenary of the marriage of Robert Browning and Elizabeth Barrett in 1846 was designed by Michael Tapper. This was not built, but a chapel was fitted at the west of the church. The eighteenth-century church was taken down in 1949.

St Peter's, Vere Street

This is not a parish church, but it could hardly be left out.

It was formerly known as Oxford Chapel, and it was built as the place of worship for the Cavendish-Harley Estate. The owners of the property were Edward Harley, Earl of Oxford, and Henrietta, his wife: they built the Chapel, and James Gibbs, who supervised the architecture of the Estate, made the design.

The contract with Benjamin Timbrell and Thomas Phillips was made on 8 August 1721. The walls of the Chapel were to be of brick, with stone quoins: the windows and doorcases of the east and west ends and the portico were to be of stone. Pulpit and altar piece were to be made in accordance with Gibbs' directions, and the ceiling over the altar was to be 'distinguished with frettwork as the said James Gibbs shall direct'. It was to be finished by March 1723. The plaster work was by J. Bagutti.

Though outside it is very plain, the interior is most elegant: St Martin-in-the-Fields on a small scale. John Timbs wrote, 'It was once considered the most beautiful edifice of its class in the metropolis' (*Curiosities of London*). By the middle of the nineteenth century there were evidently reservations about it. In 1881 it was refitted by J. K. Colling, and the organ was moved: the side windows were given 'tinted church glass in agreeable geometrical patterns'. But the alterations were made more carefully than usual, and the church has not lost its atmosphere. There are windows by Burne-Jones, who also painted the altar piece.

When St Paul's church was built in Halifax, Nova Scotia, in 1750, it was modelled on St Peter's. The Rev William Tutty wrote to S.P.G., 'It is exactly the model of Mary'bone Chapel': and the Governor, writing to the Lords of Trade two days later, said, 'The plan is the same with that of Marybone Chapel.'

St John's Wood Chapel

Designed by Thomas Hardwick and begun in 1813, St John's was consecrated on 9 April 1814. It is a very attractive church, with an Ionic portico and turret. James Elmes, 1827, called it 'a substantial, unpretending chapel of the Ionic order ... a very useful and appropriate building, but of a fashion that is now gone by'.

In 1867 the pews were reduced to a uniform height.

The inside was badly treated in the nineteenth century, but it was restored after the War to its Georgian character, and redecorated in white and gold. The galleries have been cut off from the church.

Smith, in his *History of the Parish of St Marylebone*, mentions tablets 'by the most celebrated professors of the age; here may be seen the productions of Chantrey, Behnes, Wyatt, Hardenberg, Rouw, Austin, Blore, C. H. Smith, Lupton, Sams, etc'. In 1945 St Stephen's church was closed, and a new parish was proposed, of which St John's, in 1952, became the parish church.

All Souls', Langham Place (99)

This well-known Commissioners' church was designed by John Nash. and built by Robert Streather: the cost was £19,612, of which the Commissioners contributed £12,819. Foundation stone 18 November 1822: consecration 25 November 1824.

It stands at the top of Regent Street, at the point at which Langham Place turns to the north-west. If the church was to face the east, it would have looked very awkward with a conventional tower and portico at the west: so Nash provided a round tower with an encircling Ionic portico. This looks just right in its position, and successfully closes the view up Regent Street: the axis of the church is only noticed from close by. The capitals of the portico, which have the unusual addition of cherubs' heads, are of Coade ware. The spire, which is surrounded by a Corinthian peristyle, was criticised in Parliament, and a cartoon was published showing the architect impaled on top of the spire: but Nash did not much concern himself with correctness.

The body of the church is faced with Bath stone, and has a very respectable interior of the traditional eighteenth-century type. There is a Corinthian order above the galleries, which are returned at the east: the space between them forms the sanctuary. The ceiling has a coffered cove. The altar piece, by Westall, was a gift from George IV.

Very little remains of the original fittings, except for the organ case and the font: there was a refurnishing in 1876 by Blomfield. New seating 1890. H. S. Goodhart-Rendel made some improvements in 1928, and restored the church after War damage. It was rededicated in 1951.

Christchurch, Cosway Street (98)

A Commissioners' church, designed by Philip Hardwick, and built in 1822–4: the cost was £18,804, and the grant £13,804.

The front is to the east: an Ionic portico in front of the tower, the base of which is an octagonal, domed vestibule, with openings on each side to square vestibules containing the gallery stairs: they have doorways framed with pairs of Ionic columns.

The interior was rather gloomy, but has lately been done up to good effect. The church is of eight bays, with a Corinthian order: over the entablature is a clerestory: the windows cut into the low arched ceiling, which has ribs and oval panels, the ribs and the borders ornamented with scroll mouldings. The east wall has Corinthian pilasters, and painting by W. Cave Thomas, 1867. In 1885 a faculty was obtained (19 August) to remove the west gallery, construct a choir vestry at the south-west, reseat the area and the gallery in oak, substitute a light balustrade for the gallery fronts, and provide a new pulpit. The architect was Blomfield.

When Dr Davies visited this church in 1873, he noted a rumour that the bishop had refused to hold a confirmation in the church unless the vicar removed his beard, which some of the ladies considered to be a sign of Broad Churchmanship.

St Mary's, Bryanston Square (100)

A Commissioners' church, designed by Robert Smirke, begun in 1821, finished in 1823, and consecrated on 7 January 1824. The Commissioners granted £12,819 towards the total of £19,955.

The circular tower, almost identical with Smirke's earlier tower at St Anne's, Wandsworth, is in the middle of the south side, so as to close the view up Wyndham Place. The basement is embraced by a semi-circular portico, of the Ionic order that Smirke liked so much.

The body of the church is a large, unemotional rectangle, with a gallery-bay at the west, with a porch on each side; and a sanctuary at the east, flanked by vestries. The galleries have elongated Greek Doric columns above them, and there is a low segmental ceiling. The pulpit was originally in the centre, with the font in front of it. Sir Arthur Blomfield, who lived in the parish, 'improved and adorned' the interior in 1875: the usual things were done—reseating, and the formation of a choir. A faculty was given on 31 July 1900 to reconstruct the galleries, and remove the west gallery.

One window was brought here when St Paul's, Great Portland Street, was pulled down in 1906. There is not much other glass: the window near the font is by Gibbs, and there are other windows by Powell, and two by Horace Wilkinson.

Smirke's church of St Philip, Salford, is an almost exact duplicate of St Mary's.

Holy Trinity, Marylebone Road

1826–7, by Sir J. Soane: the builder was Daniel Sharp. The church is an improved version of the earlier St Peter's, Walworth. The chancel was added by Somers Clarke in 1876.

It is no longer a parish church: it has been adapted as the headquarters of the Society for Promoting Christian Knowledge.

St Paul's, Rossmore Road

A very inconspicuous church, sandwiched between other buildings. The date is 1838, and the architect seems to have been James W. Higgins. It is quite chancel-less, of five bays, with slim iron pillars and four-centred arches. The windows are all lancets. It has been poorly reseated, and the fronts of the galleries have been altered. The organ keeps its case, but it has been moved to the north-east corner of the gallery—which seems unnecessary in so small a church. The clerestory and the upper part of the aisle windows keep their original glazing: the glass in the aisles is by Curtis, Ward and Hughes.

The parish is joined with those of Emmanuel and St Matthew's, both the churches of which have been demolished.

All Saints', St John's Wood

Col Eyre gave the site, and £1,000 towards building the church. The architect was Thomas Little, and the builders were Burton and Sons. The estimate was £7,000. The church was begun in 1845, and consecrated on 9 July 1846.

The style is Perpendicular, and the outer walls are of Kentish rag, 'needlessly squared'. The *Ecclesiologist* commented on the scanty sacrarium, and an 'anti-chancel' at the west end to hold a gallery: there were galleries in the aisles, and the prayer desk faced west. The only features that could be praised were the pitch of the roof, and the temporary wooden belfry, which 'looked real'.

Glass by Clayton and Bell was put in the east window in 1880, and in the west window later. The tower and spire were completed by Christopher and White, and dedicated on 5 January 1890. D. Newman made plans for the interior: the galleries were taken down, and it was redecorated. From 1892 glass was put into the transepts (Clayton and Bell) and aisles (Bell and Beckham). Marble and alabaster pulpit 1894, chancel screen wall 1897.

St Mark's, Hamilton Terrace

The architects were Thomas Cundy, and Thomas Cundy junior, and the church was built in 1846–7. The tower and spire were completed later, in 1864.

The *Ecclesiologist* was disappointed: it had hoped that St Paul's, Knightsbridge, would be the last church to be built in the shape of a vast hall with galleries round three sides. But here was another.

Goodhart-Rendel called it 'a large broad Gothic riding school'. It is indeed large and broad, and it is Gothic—not particularly learned Middle-Pointed, with many pinnacles: but why a riding school?

The chancel, 1877–8, was designed by E. B. Ferrey. At the same time new porches and lobbies were erected towards the east of the nave, and the nave roof was covered with boarding. The panels of the reredos were painted by Edward Armitage, R.A. A faculty was given on 5 August 1886 to alter and embellish the chancel arch according to the plans of Messrs Underwood, and to open a window above it.

A baptistery was built in memory of Canon Duckworth, who died in 1911: the architect was Charles Stanley Peach.

During the War half of the spire was taken down after being damaged, and a good many windows were broken. The church was redecorated after the War: the nave was whitened, a piece of gallery was removed, the organ was moved back to the west gallery, and a chapel was furnished in what had been the organ chamber. The spire has been rebuilt (1955).

The chancel is full of good examples of Victorian craftsmanship. The glass is by Clayton and Bell. The best feature is the cradle roof, which is painted, above the sanctuary, with angels with musical instruments, and suns; and, over the west bay, with roses.

All Saints', Margaret Street (103, 104)

Margaret Chapel was built in about 1760, for some Deists under Dr Disney. It was taken over by a new group in 1776 for 'public worship on the Principles of Natural Religion apart from Revelation'. It did not succeed. It belonged for a time to the sect of Bereans (or Barclayites), and then became a proprietary chapel. William Dodsworth, afterwards of Christchurch, Albany Street, ministered there for some time until 1837. In 1839 it was taken by Frederick Oakeley, and became a centre of Tractarian worship. The altar was copied from Newman's at Littlemore, but this afterwards gave way to a more up-to-date ecclesiological altar. The music was famous.

Oakeley joined the Church of Rome in 1845, and was succeeded by Upton Richards, who stayed until his death in 1873.

He disliked the chapel, as Oakeley had done, and wanted to rebuild it. The Ecclesiological Society had the idea of building a model church; and in 1845 A. J. Beresford Hope, a leading ecclesiologist, suggested that the two schemes might be combined. This was agreed to: the Society would take charge of the architectural and ecclesiological side, and Sir Stephen Glynne and Beresford Hope were appointed executors. In fact, it was Hope who was mainly responsible, and he provided most of the money for the purchase of the site.

The designs were made by William Butterfield, and were ready in 1849. But after they had been made, it was decided to revise them, so as to include constructional polychrome. This of course increased the estimates, and the contract with the builder was not signed until September 1850. The last service in the Chapel had been held on Easter Monday, and the foundation stone of the new church was laid by Dr Pusey on All Saints' day. The general contractor was Kelk, the carving was done by Myers, the metal work was by Potter, and the tiles were made by Minton.

The church was not completed until 1859, and during the interval there were many disputes between Beresford Hope and Butterfield, who were both men of strong opinions. Butterfield wanted his own way, and Hope found his church turning out to be different from what he had intended—not in its main outlines, but in its details and decorations. These were not designed all at once: the patterns in the spandrels of the arcade were not settled until 1853, and the designs of most of the fittings were not made until 1856–8. Those who found differences between the various parts of the church were justified. It took a long time to complete, and during that time Butterfield was changing.

However, it was finished at last, and everyone agreed that the church was of great importance in the development of the Revival.

What ought a model church to be like? The ecclesiologists, ever since the Camden Society had first been founded in 1839, had been agreed about what they did not want. Classical architecture—Greek or Roman—was ruled out as pagan: a church must be Gothic. But most of the Gothic churches that had so far been built were nothing like the real thing: the architects were simply taking the ordinary type of eighteenth-century church, pews and galleries and all, and decking it out with pointed windows, and as many pinnacles, battlements, and grotesque carved heads, as the money would allow. But that was not building in a Gothic way: the essence of Gothic was honest construction. There must be solid stone walls, sufficient to sustain a high-pitched roof: the ornament was secondary. Everything must be real: plaster must not be made to look like stone, and window tracery must not be of cast iron.

And a church must be properly planned: what distinguished a church from a conventicle was not a tower or portico at the west end, but a chancel at the east end. Ornamental features could be dispensed with, but a chancel never could be.

Those were the ingredients of a model church. Its details would be those of the time at which Gothic reached its highest point—in the late thirteenth, or the fourteenth century: and it would be properly fitted with low seats, choir screen, and stalls, and suitably decorated.

But even if all this was attended to, it would not follow that the result would be satisfactory, especially in a town. It might be nothing more than a copy of a Northamptonshire village church. That was all very well as a beginning: but obviously the nineteenth century needed something more enterprising than that.

One thing that Beresford Hope was certain about was, that the needs of a nineteenth-century town would not be supplied by a church and a vicar: there must be several priests, living a common life, who would be able to keep up a round of services. So at All Saints' there was an ample clergy house, grouped together with the church and choir school. Butterfield had to pack everything into a very small site, so the buildings were grouped round a small court, with the church to the north, and the south side opening to the street through a gateway in a wall.

The church was to be, as Beresford Hope wrote, of a 'higher and more minster-like type' than had been attempted before: something more than an ordinary parish church. He did not think that Butterfield had quite succeeded in this; but the minster-like element was there. The church was necessarily small, but its proportions gave it very great dignity.

There was no longer any objection to the use of brick, and, for the constructional colouration, Butterfield used red and black brick and slates; and marble, granite, and alabaster inside.

When the church was complete, the ecclesiologists passed their verdict on it. There was nothing but admiration for the general force and power of the design. It was not pretty: it was like the work of the Preraphaelites, and had 'the germ of the same dread of beauty, not to say the same deliberate preference for ugliness': but that did not diminish admiration for the manly and austere design. Many artists could produce graceful and pleasing interiors, but Butterfield had approached the sublime.

The brickwork was masterly: Butterfield had been the first to show that brick was the best material for London, and that its use was compatible with the highest flights of architecture. The polychrome was successful, and on the whole moderate.

The best feature was the tower and spire: 'the dignified proportions of the former, the admirable treatement of the enriched belfry stage, and the striking outline of the spire, have secured a host of admirers and have outlived the hostile criticism which was at first provoked by their novelty'. (They may still be considered to be the finest in London.)

The interior was commended, with its Aberdeen granite and marble shafts, alabaster arcading in the chancel, glazed brick patterns in the nave, and, in places, ashlar filled with coloured mastic. The patterns in the nave, and over the chancel arch, were 'abrupt, disproportionate, and ungainly'. But as a whole the church was regarded as a great success.

Others agreed. Ruskin called it 'the first piece of architecture I have seen built in modern days, which is free from all signs of timidity and incapacity. . . . Having done this, we may do anything'. And G. E. Street wrote, 'This church is not only the most beautiful, but the most vigorous, thoughtful and original of all' the churches built since the Gothic revival began.

In one way Butterfield disregarded ecclesiological rules: he provided no chancel screen, only a low marble wall inlaid with colours. He preferred to keep his chancels open, and to design a well-raised and visible altar, surrounded by plenty of colour.

He would place his east window high up in the wall, so as to leave room for a reredos: but at All Saints' there could be no window, and the entire east wall is the background to the altar. This was an opportunity for painting, and the panels were painted by William Dyce in 1854–9. Dyce also coloured the parts of the chancel surrounding his pictures. (The paintings soon deteriorated, and were restored in 1864 by Edwin Armitage. In 1909 J. N. Comper executed a new set, which are fixed to panels in front of the old.)

133

The clerestory glass, of geometrical patterns, is by O'Connor. The rest was to have been by Henri Gérente, but he died, and it was entrusted to his brother Alfred, whose work was not considered to be successful. It remained in the baptistery, and at the end of the north aisle, but other windows were taken out and replaced by Gibbs: the west window, the Tree of Jesse, was altered and reconstructed in 1877. O'Connor did the east window of the south aisle. The baptistery window was damaged in the War, and clear glass, with some mediaeval medallions, was substituted.

The panels in the north aisle, which has no windows, are by Gibbs, 1873.

Comper was responsible for the reredos of the Lady chapel, 1911, the paintings north and south of the sanctuary, 1914, and the pyx, 1930.

The screen in the south aisle is by Laurence King, 1962.

St Mark's, Marylebone Road

A cheap church by Blomfield, begun in 1871, and consecrated on 29 June 1872. Of brick, with a tower which has Blomfield's usual pyramid top. The arcades have iron columns: there are no windows in the outer walls of the aisles.

Faculties: 12 November 1903, for various alterations, including a painting, and enlarging the reredos. (Certain articles had to be taken out.) 18 February 1904, for a painting of the Magi in the south chapel. 8 August 1913, to extend the floor of the chancel, and erect new choirstalls. The interior has been purified: the walls have been whitened, and the pillars painted black.

St Cyprian's, Clarence Gate

This church had a curious origin. The Rev Charles Gutch wanted to build a church in the parish of Christchurch, and rented two houses, backing on to each other, which were adapted to worship by G. E. Street: the first service was held on 29 March 1866. Lord Portman did not approve of Gutch's High churchmanship, and would not let him have a site for a permanent church. At last, after Gutch's death, in 1898, a site was promised in 1901, when the leases of some property would expire.

The new church was designed by J. N. Comper, and consecrated on 7 July 1903. It is on the lines of 'the last development of a purely English Parish Church', with fittings, screens, and glass designed by the architect. The screen was completed in 1924, font and cover 1930-32; the organ loft was built in 1931. Chapel of the Holy Name 1938; canopy over the high altar 1948. The church is beautifully spacious and delicate, and arranged on strictly *Parson's Handbook* lines: it is not surprising that, at the consecration, the floor was strewn with flowers and rushes. Liturgical fashion has now moved right away from this refined mediaevalism, and churches like this will never be built again. But as an expression of the best of Anglican Catholicism in the reign of Edward VII, St Cyprian's is unrivalled.

The Annunciation, Bryanston Street (101, 102)

This church is on the site of Quebec Chapel, which was built in 1787, and recast by Blomfield in the usual Romanesque style. A petition was made on 2 May 1911 for a faculty to demolish the Chapel. It was stated that the Chapel had originally been the riding school of the Portman Barracks: in 1894 it had been bought, and a parish had been assigned to it. The estimated cost of rebuilding was about £25,000. The faculty was issued on 23 August.

The chapel was taken down, and the new church was built in 1912–14: the architect was Walter Tapper.

It is of red brick, in the fourteenth-century style that Bodley liked. The south side, with its large buttresses, rises impressively above the pavement. There is an aisle on the north side only, and the windows on the south are those of the clerestory stage.

The interior is tall and cool: the whole church is vaulted. It has the fittings that a church of this kind ought to have: screen, rood loft, rood, and altar with painted triptych (by Bewsey).

There is some work by Bainbridge Reynolds.

The stations of the Cross, set up before and after the War of 1939–45, are by A. Beule of Ghent. There have been various additions to the furnishings in recent years.

Pictures A crucifixion, by Calvaert: *Ecce homo*, by an unknown Italian artist of the school of Guido Reni: and a copy (1680) of a picture of St Gregory by Annibali Carracci: the original, in the Bridgewater Collection, was destroyed in the War.

Monument A full-length brass in the chancel floor to the Rev Bernard Shaw, in whose incumbency the church was rebuilt.

St Pancras

Lewis's *Topographical Dictionary* (1840) says, 'This parish exhibits, in an extraordinary degree, the vast increase which within the last half century, and particularly within the last ten years, has taken place in the numerous districts bordering upon the metropolis. In the year 1765, it was a remote and isolated spot, consisting of a few scattered dwellings, and containing only 60 inhabitants; and its ancient church, of diminutive size, suited to the smallness of the population, formed a romantic feature in the landscape. Since that period, large tracts of meadow land have been covered with buildings, and it is now one of the most extensive and populous parishes in the vicinity of London, comprising Kentish-Town, Camden-Town, and Somers-Town. The streets are well paved, and lighted with gas. . . .'

In 1851 the population was 166,956 and in 1861, 198,788. The *Imperial Gazeteer of England and Wales* (1867) says that the increase of church accommodation had at least been 'proportionate to the increase of population'. There were, then, 21 Anglican parish churches, and five chapelries without districts.

St Pancras suffered badly from the coming of the railways. This always had a bad effect on property: the decent middle-class families fled into more remote suburbs, houses were subdivided, and less desirable tenants moved in: districts were sealed off by the railway lines, and roads became blind alleys. St Pancras has three termini: Euston, 1836–49, King's Cross, 1851, and St Pancras, 1868–74. Two churches were demolished to make room for railway works: one almost as soon as it was built, and the other before it was finished.

This was a parish in which the subdivision into new parishes was carried much too far. By the twentieth century, many of the new parishes were obviously ready for amalgamation with others, and some of the churches were ripe for demolition.

Old St Pancras, Pancras Road (105)

This very small old church was enlarged by A. D. Gough and R. L. Roumieu in 1847–8: the west tower was taken down and the nave prolonged westwards: a new tower was built on the south. The walls were thoroughly re-Normanised, and the general external appearance is early Victorian: but there is a piece of walling on the north of the nave which has traces of a doorway that may be eleventh-century. The doorway on the south of the chancel looks convincingly twelfth-century, but is mostly of cement, including Norman capitals found on the site. The chancel may have been rebuilt in the thirteenth century: there is a piscina of this date, and a sedile. Gough also added a north vestry. The remodelled church was reopened on 5 July 1848.

There was a further restoration in 1871, and another in 1888 by A. W. Blomfield. A faculty was given (17 January) to demolish the vestry and build a new and larger one; to move the organ; to remove the altar, pulpit, desk, and chancel seats, and provide new ones; to relay the chancel floor, and to shorten the side galleries.

In 1925 the timbers of the roof were exposed and the side galleries taken down: the half-timber top of the tower is presumably of this date. There has been post-War repair. The glazing is all clear: glass by Gibbs has disappeared.

The interior is extremely attractive: it looks much larger than one expects, and has a pleasant, old-fashioned atmosphere. The western addition is filled with a large gallery that includes some eighteenth-century panelling: the font cover is eighteenth-century. The roof is probably seventeenth-century. A light iron screen, and a painted reredos designed by Blomfield. A small early altar stone was discovered in 1848.

Monuments　There are a good many. In the nave, the canopy and background of a six-teenth-century tomb, with matrices of brasses: there is no inscription, but Weaver says that it was the tomb of Robert Eve and Lawrentia. A column to Richard Draper, 1756. Philadelphia Woolaston, who died in childbirth: seventeenth-century, but no date is given. John Waldron Wright, merchant, and magistrate in British Honduras, 1850, and Ann, 1843, by Beevers, Borough Road.

In the chancel, a brass of Mary, wife of John Beresford, 1588. A large monument, brought from the old Chapel of Highgate in 1833, restored at the cost of St John's College, Cambridge, but not in a particularly good condition now, of William Pratt, 1637, and Mary, 1687, with busts. John Offley, merchant, 1667, and Elizabeth, 1678: *W. Linton fecit*. Samuel Cowper, 1672, and Christina, 1693.

Many interesting people are buried in the churchyard, which is now a public park. The monument of Sir John Soane's wife, 1815, is obviously the design of Soane himself.

St James's, Hampstead Road

In 1789 an Act of Parliament was passed 'for providing an additional Burial Ground for the Parish of Saint James, Westminster, and erecting a Chapel adjoining thereto, and also a House for the Residence of a Clergyman to officiate in burying the Dead'. The rector and churchwardens had agreed with the Right Hon Lord Southampton for the purchase of a piece of ground in the parish of St Pancras. The Chapel was to be erected on the part of the ground that fronted the turnpike road.

On 13 August the trustees appointed Thomas Hardwick as surveyor, and George Malpas, bricklayer, to build the wall around the site. The burial ground was consecrated on 19 November 1789, and on 13 February 1790 it was agreed that the Chapel and houses should be built. On 25 June George Malpas was appointed to do the bricklayer's work, and Philip Peckham the carpenter's and joiner's. The Chapel was consecrated on 10 January 1793.

In 1864 the vestry of St James's agreed to sell the Chapel to the parish of St Pancras, and it acquired a parish. It is now surrounded by a hospital, and not used.

This is a simple, sober church, ornamented only on the front: the three middle bays project slightly and have a rusticated basement, pilasters and a pediment. A plain inside with a flat ceiling.

Monument Lord Southampton, 1810, by Nollekens.

Kentish Town Church (109)

Designed by James Wyatt, 1783: it had a Tuscan portico at the east, projections and porches north and south, and a shallow western apse. The walls of the western part remain, heightened and altered: the eastern end was greatly extended and completely transformed in the Norman style in 1843–5, by J. H. Hakewill. The additions were north and south aisles, with galleries, vestry and porch on the south, and the eastern parts: the sanctuary is flanked by two towers with spirelets—the bases of which open westward into aisles, which give a triple chancel arch effect: north and south of the towers are porches with much Norman ornament. This is all rather poor and crude, but the east end certainly catches, and holds, the eye from outside.

A faculty was given on 26 June 1889 to move the font, demolish the west gallery, put in a window on the south of the nave, remove the porch at the south-west corner, and alter the entrance: build a vestry and parish room, with porch and vestibule, in the south-west angle; and repair and reglaze. The interior was done up and lightened after the War, but no attempt was made to modernise it too much: it keeps its later Victorian *chorus cantorum*, its insignificant altar, and its numberless sittings. The bright glass is by Wailes.

Monuments A good many tablets—none of special importance, but looking very well, and recalling a Kentish Town somewhat different from what it is today.

St Pancras, Euston Road (106)

By an Act of Parliament of 31 May 1816 trustees were empowered to raise £40,000 and to build a church to take the place of the old St Pancras, which would become a parish chapel. A further Act was passed in 1821.

Early in 1818 there was a limited competition, and premiums were awarded to W. and H. W. Inwood, F. O. Bedford, and Thomas Rickman: the design of the Inwoods was accepted. William Inwood was a local surveyor, of ordinary capacities; Henry William, his son, had travelled in Greece and studied its architecture; the scholarly Greek detail of St Pancras, and of two other churches—Camden Town Chapel and St Peter's, Regent Square—was his contribution.

The new church was begun in 1819, and the foundation stone laid by the Duke of York on 1 July: the consecration was on 7 May 1822. Isaac Seabrook was the contractor: the terra cotta work was by John Charles Felix Rossi, and Messrs Brown and Young supplied the scagliola columns at the east end. The total cost was £76,679.

The west end of the church is arranged in the usual way, deriving originally from St Martin in the Fields: a vestibule with a tower above, chambers at the sides containing the gallery staircases, and a portico in front. The tower is a duplicated copy of the Tower of the Winds at Athens, an octagonal building, late in date, with an unusual kind of capital: the basement has a ring of short Doric columns on a frieze. The Ionic portico is derived from the Erechtheion at Athens, which was taken as a model for the rest of the exterior of the church. The Erechtheion is a combination of three small temples: the main building has two others projecting transeptally, the smaller of which has, instead of columns, a row of draped female figures (caryatides), one of which is now in the British Museum. Inwood adapted this, and provided the church with two almost-detached vestries, projecting beyond the east wall of the body of the church, as the other lesser temple projects beyond the Erechtheion: below them are vaults. The caryatides were modelled by Rossi in terra cotta around iron columns. The sanctuary is in the form of half a circular temple.

The interior is an undivided space, with a flat coffered ceiling, beautifully furnished with well made and carefully detailed pews, pulpit, and organ case. The organ gallery is supported by six Ionic columns: the other gallery columns must have been Inwood's own invention. The apse is most impressive, with its ring of six Ionic columns, of scagliola, standing away from the wall.

The walls were decorated by Messrs J. G. Crace in 1866, in what Bumpus calls 'a rich yet subdued, manner', and the windows were later filled with glass by Clayton and Bell. There was a big repair in 1951–3, after the church had been found to be in a dangerous state. The Victorian decoration has been removed, and the church is now much lighter than it was. But the glass has been kept, as it deserved to be: the windows behind the altar are particularly good.

St Mary's, Eversholt Street, Somers Town (107)

Built in 1822–4: the Commissioners paid the whole cost of £13,629. The architects were W. and H. W. Inwood: the builder was I. T. Seabrook.

The Inwoods here attempted Gothic, which they evidently knew nothing about. Most of the churches of this time received some perfunctory praise from someone, even if it was nothing more than the adjective 'neat'. But this—Seymour Street Chapel, or Mr Judkin's Chapel—has never been thought much of. The *Gentleman's Magazine* called it 'perhaps the completest specimen of Carpenter's Gothic ever witnessed'. Pugin illustrated it in his

Contrasts, as a foil to Skirlaw Chapel. And Sir John Summerson considers it to be 'one of the most pitiful bungles in the way of Gothic revivalism ever perpetrated'. It is unlikely that these verdicts will ever be seriously questioned. The church is of brick, with a thin tower, and a front with three very large doorways. Inside, there are slender iron pillars and plaster vaults.

A faculty was given on 20 June 1888 to enlarge and improve the chancel, to raise and reset the reredos in the new apse, provide a new and larger Communion table; to enlarge the vestries, remove the side galleries, and reconstruct the west gallery; to move the organ, and build a new parish room and lobby on the south of the church. The estimate was £1,550. Ewan Christian was the architect. The west gallery was taken down in 1890.

St Michael's, Highgate

The Grammar School was founded by Sir Roger Cholmeley, and the Chapel was rebuilt in 1576–8: it was also a chapel of ease to Hornsey, and the minister was to read prayers there on all Sundays except the first in the month, when the people were to go to the parish church. It was repaired and enlarged in 1616, 1628, 1720 and 1772.

The new church was designed by L. Vulliamy, and built by William and Lewis Cubitt: the foundation stone was laid on 4 March 1831, and the consecration was in November 1832. The cost was £8,171. It is of brick, Perpendicular in style, with a tower and spire like those of Christchurch, Woburn Square.

A faculty of 6 August 1878 gave permission to move the organ, reseat the nave and aisles, and extend the chancel to the east. The architect was C. H. M. Mileham. Before this, there was an eastern vestry.

In 1903 four figures of saints were erected and colour added to the reredos; in 1905, a screen on the south of the chancel. In 1906 a side chapel was furnished, the architect being Temple Moore.

The east window glass is by Evie Hone: some of the Kempe glass that was there before is in the east windows of the chancel aisles.

Monuments A few from the old Chapel, including Samuel Forster, 1752, and Mary, 1744; and Edward Gould (no date) who left the Chapel a legacy of £100.

Christchurch, Albany Street

This church was proposed by a group of laymen, and the building was helped by a grant of £1,000 from the Metropolis Churches Fund. The architect was Sir James Pennethorne, and it was consecrated on 13 July 1837. It is a rather ungainly church of brick: a large

100 St Mary's, Bryanston Square, the tower and portico of Robert Smirke's church 1821–30

101, 102 The Annunciation, Bryanston Street, 1912–14 by Walter Tapper. Exterior and chancel

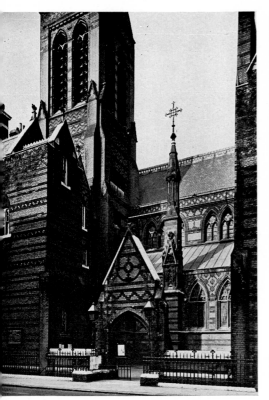

103, 104 All Saints', Margaret Street, 1850–9 by William Butterfield. The interior is from an old photograph to show the nineteenth-century arrangement of the sanctuary

105 Old St Pancras: ancient walls, but the visible detail is by Gough and Roumieu 1847–8

106 St Pancras, Euston Road, 1819–22 by W. and H. W. Inwood

107 St Mary's, Somers Town, 1822–4 by W. and H. W. Inwood

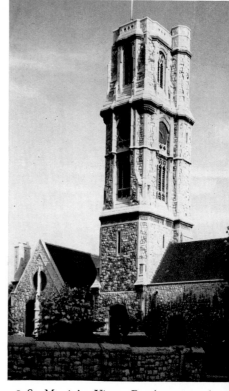

108 St Martin's, Vicars Road, 1864–5 by E. B. Lamb. The turret has lost its spirelet

rectangle, with slight projections at the angles, and a thin tower and spire. The organ was in a gallery over the altar.

The first vicar was the Rev William Dodsworth, from Margaret Chapel, a High Churchman, and a member of the Ecclesiological Society, which used to meet in the schoolroom. Most of the Tractarians officiated here, and the first Anglican religious community of the nineteenth century was established in the parish by Dr Pusey in 1847.

Dodsworth, of course, disliked the internal arrangements of the church, and as early as 1843 the organ gallery and the vestry under it were removed, and a small chancel was formed: a choir was arranged in 1849. R. C. Carpenter was the architect. The eagle lectern, 1849, was designed by Butterfield, from drawings made in Malta by Styleman Le Strange. A font was given by Lady Emma Pennant.

On the last day of 1850 Dodsworth joined the Roman Church, but his successor carried on the traditions of the parish. In 1853 Butterfield added the choir-stalls. A faculty was given on 8 August 1866 to remove the children's galleries and shorten the gallery at the east end on the north side; move the organ, reseat, alter the position of the pulpit, and decorate the walls. Two years later the font was cased in marble. The pulpit, carved by Earp, was erected in 1884. All these alterations were made by Butterfield. His colouring has been removed from the walls, but his dado of tiles has been allowed to remain.

The glass is nearly all by Clayton and Bell, but there is one small window designed by Rossetti and executed by William Morris. The picture over the altar, a copy of Raphael's Transfiguration, was painted by Thomas Brigstock: over the side altar is a Spanish painting of St Anthony of Padua by an unknown artist, given to the church in 1917.

Holy Trinity, Clarence Way, Haverstock Hill

The design was made by T. H. Wyatt and David Brandon and exhibited at the Royal Academy. The church was built in 1849–50, chiefly by the efforts of the Rev David Laing, who gave generously towards it. It is of Kentish rag in fourteenth-century style.

The design was adversely criticised by the *Ecclesiologist*, which objected to the two tiny aisles of the chancel: 'the *motif* of this vagary, we presume, was to produce a triple chancel-arch, after the fashion of Westwell church'. But this feature was admired by others: Timbs's *Curiosities of London* says the arches produce 'an elegant play of lines'. The side galleries were taken down in 1902.

The church was reduced in size after the War: the north aisle was converted into a hall, and the west gallery was taken down. East window 1951, by Goddard and Gibbs.

St Mary Magdalene's, Munster Square

In the 1840s Munster Square, then called York Square, had a bad reputation, and Edward Stuart, a young priest of private means on the staff of Christchurch, Albany Street, decided to build a church there. It was to be 'as nearly perfection as the handicraft of man, the skill of architects, and the experience and ingenuity of ecclesiastical art could make it', and it was to be free and open, without any rented seats. The first stone was laid in July 1849, and on 22 April 1852 the chancel, nave, and south aisle were consecrated. Stuart became the first vicar.

The contrast between Christchurch and St Mary Magdalene's is one of the best illustrations of the revolution in church building that the ecclesiologists accomplished: it is difficult to realise that hardly more than ten years separates the two. Christchurch had everything that the ecclesiologists detested: St Mary Magdalene's was, in every way, the kind of church that they dreamed of—correct Middle-Pointed in style, with a good-sized chancel, a properly vested altar, and low, open seats. The architect, R. C. Carpenter, had done well in his previous churches: this one, which was his last, was also his best. The *Ecclesiologist* called it 'the most artistically correct new church yet consecrated in London'; and Eastlake, writing 20 years later, when churches of this kind had become rather old-fashioned, praised it highly, and wrote of the simple grace of its proportions, and the modest reticence of its decorative features.

Stuart died in 1877, and the north aisle and north chancel chapel were added to his memory in 1883–4 by R. H. Carpenter, according to his father's plans. The tower and spire were never built.

St Mary Magdalene's has always had a Catholic tradition, and its arrangements, from the beginning, were ritually satisfactory. Additions and embellishments have been made from time to time, but they are, in general, such as the founder would have approved of: there are no baroque altars of the naughty twenties.

The altar, at first, was simply vested, and had two candlesticks: behind it was a dossal with gold diaper, and a large gilded cross. The arcading in the sanctuary had stencilled patterns. The glass in the east window was designed by Pugin and executed by Hardman.

In 1867 the paintings in the arcading on the east wall, and one on the north, were executed by Bell and Almond: the other panels were filled afterwards. The altar was lengthened in 1912: the reredos is by Sir Charles Nicholson, 1933.

The rood and beam, 1903, and the parcloses, 1906, were designed by J. T. Micklethwaite: a chancel screen was planned, but never materialised.

The west window, 1857, was by J. R. Clayton and Hardman: it was a memorial to Carpenter, and included a portrait of him. It was unfortunately destroyed in the War. The south aisle windows, made by Clayton and Bell under Butterfield, were also broken, and only fragments have been preserved. There are windows by Clayton and Bell and by Heaton, Butler and Bayne. The glass at the east of the south chapel, by A. K. Nicholson, 1935, took the place of a window by Hardman.

St Mark's, Prince Albert Road

Built in 1851–2, from designs by Thomas Little, who gave the site. The material is stock brick faced with Kentish rag and the style thirteenth-century—earlier and later. At the north-west is a tower and spire, with a single irrelevant spirelet at one angle. The *Ecclesiologist* did not like the design, and thought the west front pretentious, and the sides monotonous and clumsy. Faculties: 29 June 1889, to build a new choir vestry, move the pulpit, and form a baptistery under the west gallery. 19 July 1890, to extend the chancel, which was to correspond externally with the older work, and be faced internally with Bath stone ashlar: the other dressed stone to be Doulting. The east bay of the galleries, the west gallery and the children's gallery, were to be demolished. The architect of the chancel was Sir A. W. Blomfield.

1 August 1908, to remove the galleries from the aisles.

A large triptych, by Sir J. N. Comper, was completed in 1939, and wrecked, together with the rest of the church, in 1940: the east end was completely smashed. The church was rededicated in 1957, after reconstruction by A. B. Knapp-Fisher. A new reredos by Comper was dedicated on 17 January 1959. There is glass by him, and by Brian Thomas. The west window is by Goddard and Gibbs, 1956.

St Anne's, Brookfield

Founded by Anne Barnett in memory of Richard Barnett of Brookfield, the church was designed by Thomas Bellamy and built in 1852–3. It is ordinary late First-Pointed, with a west tower and a tall and quite graceful broach spire. There is a considerable assortment of Victorian glass. A Pre-Raphaelite window of the works of mercy in the south aisle. Faculties were given on 20 November 1878 to remove the pulpit and desk, and substitute stalls and a new pulpit; and to enlarge the vestry: and on 12 November 1903 to provide a new east window, and rearrange and enlarge the sanctuary.

St Matthew's, Oakley Square

Situated in what was known as Bedford New Town. The Duke of Bedford gave the site, and £1,000 toward the building of the church. The architect was John Johnson and the builder John Kelk: work was begun in 1852, and the consecration was on 23 December 1856.

The church, of Kentish rag and Bath stone dressings, is in an elaborate Middle-Pointed style: a clerestoried nave, and tower and spire on the south. A faculty was given on 1 December 1886 to move the organ and loft to an organ chamber. There was a considerable assortment of Victorian glass. The new post-War windows are by Goddard and Gibbs, 1952.

St Martin's, Vicars Road (108)

This church was built at the cost of J. D. Allcroft, of Stokesay Court, Salop, and consecrated on 3 December 1865. It was designed by E. B. Lamb—an architect who was the despair of the *Ecclesiologist*, which complained of his 'uncouth and grotesque combinations of incongruous *tours de force*', and of 'those eccentricities which render Mr Lamb the most affected and *outré*, and at the same time ineffective, of all our ecclesiastical architects'. The ordinary churchgoer regarded his work with mixed feelings: when his church at Englefield Green, Surrey, was opened, 'approbation, not unmixed with surprise, at the novelty of the design and the genius of the architect seemed to be the predominant feeling; but there were not wanting those who appeared to regard what they saw with a doubtful expression, if not with positive disapproval' (*Windsor and Eton Express*).

The liberties that Lamb took with Gothic—buttresses climbing up the middle of Perpendicular windows, and the improvisation of strange shapes—were similar to those taken by W. D. Caröe at the end of the nineteenth century, and the beginning of the twentieth. But he also took a delight in putting things in the wrong place, and using them for a purpose for which they were not meant. His planning was all his own, and his more ambitious churches are difficult to describe: they have in common rather low walls, and tremendous roofs.

St Martin's is in a sinister Perpendicular style, with a tall tower on the north: the base of this is an open porch, and at the south-west is a staircase turret, formerly with a spirelet. The western section of the nave is without aisles: then come three bays with aisles, and slightly projecting transepts of different shapes. There are square piers with strange shafts and brackets. The sanctuary is apsidal, with transomed windows under a heavy arcade with detached shafts. There is a hammer-beam roof of wonderful and original construction.

This is a church that it is not easy to describe: it must be seen.

St Luke's, Oseney Crescent (110)

The present church takes the place of St Luke's, King's Cross, which was demolished almost as soon as it was built to make room for the railway—and was rebuilt as a Congregational church at Wanstead.

J. Johnson, who had designed the first St Luke's, hoped to design the second also, but the commission was given to Basil Champneys, the son of the vicar of St Pancras. There may have been some unfairness about this; but the result was a much better church than Johnson would have designed.

The date is 1867–9. It is of red Suffolk brick with stone dressings, in thirteenth-century style. The aisles are carried past the chancel, over which is an impressive, simple, very tall, French-looking tower, with four gables. The base of it, and the apsidal sanctuary, are vaulted. There is a wheel window and three lancets at the west. The nave has a boarded ceiling, in need of repainting. The reredos, a flat marble slab, is a memorial to a vicar who was here from 1893 to 1932: the painting in the north aisle must be the original reredos. It is presumably by Heaton, Butler and Bayne, who did all the glass, except for two pairs of windows by Morris in the clerestory. There are some fittings from St Paul's, Camden Square, now demolished, including the lectern, 1882.

St Mary's, Dartmouth Park

The church was designed by Butterfield and the nave and aisles were opened in 1875: but there were 'unpleasantries', and Butterfield resigned: the chancel, 1881, was built by W. C. Street.

It is of yellow brick, banded with red, and (in the nave) patterned with red and black. The proportions are Butterfieldian. There is a tall clerestory, with four-light windows, very deeply splayed. The chancel arch is not as low as in some of Butterfield's churches: indeed, it is higher than the arcades—but the height of the clerestory gives it a good expanse of wall above, decorated with brick patterning, and two circular, traceried stone panels. The font and pulpit are Butterfield's. The rood beam and figures are 1913. The altar in the south aisle is by Comper.

St Michael's, Camden Road (111)

The district was formed in 1876, and services were begun in an empty shop: a temporary church was built in 1879. The foundation stone of the permanent church was laid on 6 June 1880: the site cost £2,470, and the building of the first part £9,704. The Ecclesiastical

Commissioners granted £5,300 from the proceeds of the sale of St Michael's, Queenhithe, in the City, which was pulled down in 1877. Bodley and Garner made the plans: it was their first church in London. The nave and aisles were completed in 1881 and consecrated on 29 September. The foundation stone of the chancel was laid on 24 June 1893: it was consecrated on 13 October 1894. The tower was never built.

St Michael's is of brick, with a long tiled roof covering nave and chancel. It is in the architects' favourite fourteenth-century style, which—as Bumpus says, though one is never sure whether his words are his own, or borrowed—'has been so intensely perceived and assimilated as to become a natural, almost intuitive expression'. It is curious that Bodley's refined, rather aristocratic style, which is entirely in place at Hoar Cross and Clumber, should not look incongruous in a busy London street: but it does not. The nave and chancel have pointed cradle roofs: the principals are formed by stone arches, supported by flying buttresses.

The original font came from the City church—but the present font is by Bodley, c. 1900.

The parishes of ALL SAINTS and ST THOMAS were united with that of St Michael in 1954.

St Barnabas', Kentish Town

Built in 1884–5 and consecrated on 18 July 1885. Ewan Christian was the architect. His usual thirteenth-century style, with an eastern apse, and one at the west of the north aisle. It was redecorated in 1900 to the designs of A. E. Nightingale. It was proposed to make this the parish church for the southern part of Kentish Town: a new vicarage was built after the War, and the church was renovated. But it was closed, and united to Holy Trinity, Clarence Way, in 1957. It was then let to the Greek Orthodox Church. The organ went to St Mary's, South Ruislip.

St Benet and All Saints', Lupton Street, Kentish Town (112)

This was a church designed by Joseph Peacock, begun in 1884, and consecrated on 1 November 1885. A tall chancel, in a simple Bodleian style, with north organ loft and vestries and south chapel, was added by Cecil G. Hare in 1908.

Peacock's church became unsafe, and a new nave was built in 1928, from Hare's designs, by a legacy from Jeanette Elizabeth Crossthwaite, and gifts from the faithful. It is of stock brick, aisleless, with west porches. The bays are alternately wide and narrow: the large bays have tall three-light windows under gables cutting into the concrete barrel vault. A tiny chapel at the north-east. Pulpit 1935, rails 1936.

Holy Cross, Cromer Street (now known as Holy Cross, with St Jude, with St Peter)

Built in 1887–8; Joseph Peacock. A brick church, quite small, simple, and, in its way, satisfactory. The nave has rather low aisles and tall clerestory, and a western annexe with baptistery and porches: the chancel is rather short, well raised, with small chapels arranged transeptally. There are none of the eccentricities of Peacock's earlier years.

The massive font was designed by J. L. Pearson, and the rood and other fittings by Sir Charles Nicholson, 1913. There are some fittings from St Jude's, Grays Inn Road, demolished in 1936. St Jude's was a church in which Peacock let himself go.

The organ loft is post-War.

St Peter's, Regent Square

A Commissioners' church (cost £16,450, all of which was paid by the Commissioners), designed by W. and H. W. Inwood, and built by I. T. Seabrook in 1822–4. It was bombed, and has remained a ruin since the War. The beautiful Ionic portico is based on remains that the younger Inwood found in Greece: this should be allowed to remain, whatever happens to the rest of the church.

All Saints', Camden Street

Another church by the Inwoods, also built in 1822–4, and also with Inwood's Ionic order in the portico—which, in this case, is semi-circular. The church is no longer needed by the Church of England, and is used by the Cypriots.

All Hallows', Gospel Oak (113)

The founder of this church was the Rev Charles Mackeson, the editor of the *Guide to the Churches of London and its Suburbs*, which handed on to the public all the information that the clergy were willing to give about the buildings, architects, organists, services, bells, endowments, etc.

A temporary church of the Good Shepherd was erected first, in 1885, and the Duchess of Teck laid the foundation stone of the permanent church on 23 July 1892. The consecration was on 23 June 1901—the year in which James Brooks, the architect, died. A grant was made from the proceeds of the sale of the site of Wren's All Hallows the Great, and the dedication recalls this.

The chancel was built to an altered design by Giles Gilbert Scott in 1913.

This is certainly Brooks's best church, and a most impressive example of the ambition of the later nineteenth-century church builders. The outside is of Kentish rag—a big, heavily buttressed mass, with two short turrets at the east. Nave and aisles are of the same height, with tall, cylindrical pillars without capitals: they carry the beginnings of a vault, which has never been completed. There are large lancets in the aisles, and a wheel at the west. The chancel, which has its vault, is of three bays: its north aisle is two-storied; the south is carried up without a floor.

St Silas', Prince of Wales Road, Kentish Town

A mission chapel was built in 1884. It became a recreation room after the building of the church in 1911–12 by E. C. Shearman. This is a tall, simple brick church, with capital-less brick arcades, passage aisles, an additional chapel on the south, an apsidal chancel, and a narrow ambulatory.

Goodhart-Rendel had decided opinions about this church: he found a 'sinister artiness' about it, with its odd internal use of Fletton bricks: 'everything seems to be deliberately unmeaning and odd'. But there is no need to agree with him.

Shoreditch

Lewis gives rather attractive descriptions of this borough. Shoreditch is 'well paved, lighted with gas, and amply supplied with water'. In Haggerston 'many new streets have been formed, consisting of neat ranges of houses of a moderate size: the parish is partially paved, and amply supplied with water'. Even in 1840 this must have been only part of the truth; and later in the century no one would have described the borough in such terms.

The Church Building Commissioners and the Metropolis Churches Fund provided new church accommodation at a time when the place was mostly as Lewis describes it. Later, when the district was poor and overcrowded, the Haggerston Church Scheme was responsible for building six new churches, including four by James Brooks, whose town churches, with their simple and rather austere interiors, culminating in a well raised sanctuary, are so admirably adapted for what was known as a ritualistic service.

109 Kentish Town Church:
J. H. Hakewill's extension
1843–5

110 St Luke's, Oseney Crescent,
1867–9 by Basil Champneys

111 St Michael's, Camden Road,
by Bodley and Garner, nave and
aisles 1880–1, chancel 1893–4

112 St Benet and All Saints, Kentish Town, by C. G. Hare,
chancel 1884–5, nave 1928

113 All Hallows', Gospel Oak, 1892 onward by
James Brooks, and Giles Gilbert Scott 1913

114, 115 St Leonard's, rebuilt by George Dance in 1736–40, exterior and interior

116 St Augustine's, Haggerston, 1866–7 by Henry Woodyer. Decoration has been removed leaving the reredos in an isolation that was never intended

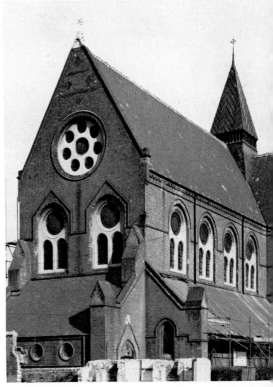

117 St Columba's, Haggerston, 1868–9 by James Brooks

118 St Chad's, Haggerston, 1868–9 by James Brook

Three of the earlier churches have gone, and two of those built by the Haggerston Church Scheme. Three of Brooks's churches, and one by Woodyer, fortunately still survive.

St Leonard's, High Street (114, 115)

One of the corners of the tower of the old church gave way on 23 December 1716, and 'the walls rent asunder, with a frightful sound, during divine service'. The church was patched up, but in 1733 it was decided that there must be a new building. An Act was passed in 1735, demolition began in 1736, and the new church was opened in 1740. The architect was George Dance, and the builders were William Goswell and Charles Dunn.

The body of the church is of brick, with stone dressings: the portico and steeple are of Portland stone. The steeple obviously recalls St Mary le Bow, but Dance has left the square tower without much connection with the octagonal stage above it, except for some brackets. He was not a very original architect: but St Leonard's is one of those eighteenth-century churches that suit London perfectly.

The inside is divided into nave and aisles by Doric columns on pedestals, with block entablatures and arches: there is a clerestory, and a flat panelled ceiling. The font and pulpit are contemporary. A faculty was given in 1734 to alter the pulpit, and to make the front of the west gallery uniform with the others. The side galleries were taken down in 1857, by T. E. Knightley, but the west gallery, with the organ, was left: there is a clock with a beautifully carved surround. The altar table is a scagliola slab with a mahogany frame. Blomfield made alterations to the interior in 1870.

The east window glass, 1634, was the gift of Thomas Austen, cloth-worker: it bore the signature of Baptista Sutton. It was destroyed in the War: the new east window, 1955, is by A. K. Nicholson Studios.

Monument   A remarkable one by Francis Bird, to Elizabeth Benson, 1710, depicting two skeletons tearing at a tree.

St John the Baptist, Pitfield Road, Hoxton

The cost of this church was entirely provided by the Commissioners. The design was first entrusted to H. H. Seward, but he was appointed surveyor general of H. M. Board of Works in December 1822, after which he gave up his surveyorship of Greenwich Hospital, and his general practice. He resigned in March 1823, and Francis Edwards took over. The church was begun in 1824, and consecrated on 26 June 1826. The cost, including the graveyard, was £16,444. It is large and rather dull, of seven bays, the east and west bays slightly projecting, with pilasters. The west end is a rather debased version of Soane, to whom Edwards was assistant: the tower is in the usual position, and there are two Ionic columns *in antis*.

There is a long catalogue of later alterations: 1840, stained glass in the east window, and the east end beautified: 1860, renovations, and glass in the east windows of the galleries: 1865, font: 1873, redecoration, the east end refurnished, organ repaired, and new east window: 1886, repainting, and the desk lowered: 1900, the body of the church re-seated: 1902, chancel floor raised, choir stalls, new pulpit (on rails), choir vestry built, and ceiling and walls painted. The wall paintings have gone, but the paintings of the Apocalypse on the ceiling remain: 1911, painting of the Disciples at Emmaus, as altar piece: 1914, organ moved to south gallery, and west wall redecorated.

The church suffered damage from bombs three times during the War, and on two occasions someone tried to burn it down. Then the ceiling was found to be ready to fall, and the church had to be closed for six months. But repairs were done in 1942, and there were further repairs in 1954–5. The organ was replaced at the west. East window, 1958, by Francis Stephens.

The list of later nineteenth, and early twentieth-century alterations might suggest that the interior has lost most of its character: but in fact it has not. The galleries remain, and small upper galleries on each side of the tower: and the modern woodwork is quite sober and restrained; the ensemble has considerable dignity.

Holy Trinity, Shepherdess Walk, Hoxton

Designed by William Railton, the architect of the Nelson column, and consecrated on 7 March 1848. The design was exhibited at the Royal Academy. Nave, aisles, tower and spire, and sanctuary: in Early English style.

A faculty was given on 25 July 1896 to convert a disused vestry into a chapel, and to make the base of the tower into a baptistery. The architect was Spencer W. Grant. The interior has been whitened, and a good deal cleared out. The reredos is by Martin Travers.

The pulpit came from St Mary Somerset, in the City—via St Mary's, Britannia Walk, which has been demolished. The organ is from Holy Trinity, Folkestone. The altar has stones from bombed churches.

All Saints', Haggerston Road,

Designed by P. C. Hardwick, and built in 1855–6. At first, it had aisles of two bays, and a piece of nave without any. The aisles had single-light windows. Arcades with square abaci and entirely unmoulded arches were considered by the *Ecclesiologist* to be too 'speluncar' for Haggerston. The east and west windows were, and are, Middle-Pointed. The aisles were afterwards extended to the west, rebuilt, and raised for galleries: the architect was T. E. Knightley. The organ was moved in 1879.

There was a certain amount of War damage: the glass in the east window is new.

St Paul's, Broke Road, Haggerston

A. W. Blomfield's first church, built in 1859–60. A rectangular nave, with the bays gabled outwards: iron pillars on Portland stone bases support beams to the walls. There are galleries; the chancel is apsidal. The walls are of stock bricks, relieved with red and black, the dressings of Bath stone. The font was the gift of the architect.

St Augustine's, Yorkton Road, Haggerston (116)

The church was begun in 1866, and consecrated on 25 April 1867. The architect was Henry Woodyer, and it is the only London church by this quiet, modest, and pious architect, who lived as a country gentlemen in Surrey, who belonged to no professional organisation, wrote nothing, and would not publish his designs. St Augustine's was designed for 'advanced ritual', and there is a wonderful Victorian picture of the singing of the gospel at a sung eucharist (*The Graphic*, 5 March 1881).

The reredos, with the Crucifixion and figures of saints, under a canopy, is very typical of Woodyer. It was executed by Nicholls, and coloured later by R. A. Briggs. There was restoration work done in 1914 by E. T. Dunn, and more in 1927 by J. H. Gibbons. The east window is by Shrigley and Hunt; the glass in the south aisle is by M. E. Rope.

St Michael's, Mark Street

James Brooks, besides remodelling St Mary's, Haggerston—now completely destroyed— designed four new churches in the borough of Shoreditch. They all had to be cheap, but because they were in poor districts, were required to be tall and conspicuous, to stand up above the houses, and to remind the whole neighbourhood of their existence. They were to be attractive and beautiful, but there would be an almost complete absence of ornament, since they were designed to save labour; they would also be solid and substantial, of a good size, and of a bold and severe dignity.

Such were the instructions that devoted Victorian churchmen gave to the architect when they planned churches for the poor.

St Michael's was the first to be built—begun in 1864, and consecrated on St Bartholomew's day, 1865. It is of a rather different character from most of Brooks's later churches: there are features that recall Woodyer, and others that almost suggest Butterfield. It is of yellow stock brick, with some bands of red, and occasional patterns in the chancel; and has low aisles, tall clerestory, and high-pitched slate roofs. At the west was a complex of buildings—clergy house, convent, and Hospital of St Mary of the Cross, which was completed by Sedding. Almost all of these were demolished in an untidy way, except for the clergy house: large pieces of Gothic wall were left standing. The church, which had outlived its usefulness, was closed in 1964 (31 January).

St Chad's, Nichols Square, Haggerston (118)

The foundation stone was laid on 2 February 1868, and the church was consecrated on 4 April 1869. It is—like the others—of brick: the architect, from now onwards, used red, and eschewed polychrome.

Nave and aisles, with west narthex, and transepts which do not project: and apsidal chancel, with south chapel, also with an apse. The aisles are low and windowless: the clerestory, with large plate-traceried windows, is tall. There are high-pitched slate roofs, and no buttresses. The north side towers above a narrow street: the south faces Nichols Square, which was designed by J. H. Taylor in 1841, and was very attractive, with small, semi-detached Tudor cottages, with which the church, and the vicarage to the south of it, were content to differ. The small houses have now all been swept away, and large blocks of new buildings are rising. There is a 12-storey block on the south of the vicarage.

The nave pillars are bulky, of stone, with uncarved capitals. The nave roof is ceiled and polygonal, with semi-circular ribs: the chancel is vaulted. There is a free-standing reredos, with Crucifixion, and other figures in niches. The reredos has recently been painted white, and other alterations made which have not improved the interior. The glass is by Clayton and Bell.

St Columba's, Kingsland Road, Haggerston (117)

Consecrated on 7 July 1869. Brooks planned this church to stand up above the surrounding buildings, and placed the windows high up to exclude noise. The nave, as at St Chad's, has low aisles without windows, and a tall clerestory. The entrance is through a north-west transept. There is the basement of a central tower, vaulted, with the choir under. The short transepts have barrel roofs, and there is a one-bay sanctuary with a vault. The columns were originally of brick, with stone shafts, but they showed signs of collapsing, and Brooks substituted stone. The mortuary chapel was an addition by the Rev Ernest Geldart.

The interior has been whitewashed: whether this has been an improvement or not must be a matter of opinion.

St Anne's, Hoxton Street

Built in 1868–9 and consecrated on 14 May 1870; the architect was Francis Chambers. Nave and aisles, transepts, and an apsidal chancel, with a vestry on the south and the base of a tower on the north. It is of brick, faced with ragstone where it can be seen, with gargoyles, etc. The style is Middle-Pointed, in some ways recalling A. D. Gough. The capitals of the arcades have been left uncarved. The reredos 1882, rood a 1914–18 memorial. There was some bomb damage: the east window of the apse has lost its tracery, and been given new glass, by Alfred L. Wilkinson, 1956.

The churches of ST ANDREW (1865, by C. A. Long), and ST SAVIOUR (1865–6, by Brooks), are demolished, and their parishes have been united with St Anne's.

Stepney

The seventeenth and eighteenth centuries made a good beginning of church extension in this very large parish. Chapels of ease were built at Wapping, 1617, Poplar, 1654, and Shadwell, 1656. St Mary's, Whitechapel, was rebuilt in 1673. Three of the Fifty New Churches were built here: St Anne's, Limehouse, 1712–24, St George's in the East, 1715–23, and Christchurch, Spitalfields, 1723–9. Bethnal Green church was built in 1743, and Wapping was rebuilt in 1756.

By the end of the eighteenth century the population was increasing very fast and in the early part of the nineteenth a great part of the district became slums. The Church Building Commissioners and the Metropolis Churches Fund erected several new churches; but their parishes were inhabited by people to whom ordinary Anglican worship made no appeal.

Everyone who reads the story of the Church revival in the nineteenth century knows the story of the riots at St George's in the East, where a mild attempt to introduce a choral service, coloured stoles, etc., met with a discouraging response; and of Father Lowder's work, which was more successful.

Churches were, as usual, multiplied. A good many were very High: St Mary's,

Whitechapel, was Evangelical; St George's, after its troubles were over, became Broad; and Canon Barnett's work at St Jude's, Whitechapel, was *sui generis*. Some of the churches were quite successful: others were not successful at all. Some parishes became almost entirely Jewish, and others were reduced by the clearing of slums. Several churches were weeded out before the second World War, and the district suffered from heavy bombing. Most of the damaged churches have not been rebuilt.

St Dunstan's, Stepney High Street (127)

The church stands among trees, in quiet surroundings.

There is thirteenth-century work in the chancel—e.g., in the sedilia; but the nave, aisles and tower were all rebuilt in the late fifteenth century, when the chancel arch was taken down, and the chancel reduced in length. The material is ragstone rubble. The vestry minutes record a good deal of work in the eighteenth century, which there is no room to specify in detail: it has, anyhow, all disappeared. The church was restored in 1847 by Benjamin Ferrey: the faculty (5 May) mentions the reconstruction of the seats, the repair of the interior and exterior, and the building of a south porch. Newman and Billing did work in 1872, and there was a restoration by Basil Champneys in 1885: a faculty 7 July, to clean and paint, move the organ, alter the levels of the chancel, provide a new pulpit, reredos, Communion table and seats; and remove the east ends of the north and south galleries. In 1889, under J. E. K. Cutts, the galleries were taken down, and the plaster was removed from the walls. In 1901 there was a fire in the roof, which was repaired afterwards.

There is a carved stone rood, perhaps early eleventh-century, and a fourteenth-century panel of the Annunciation. The glass was broken in the War. New east window by Hugh Easton, 1952: whether one likes it or not, it has to be looked at.

Monuments   Sir Henry Collett, 1510: a table tomb in a panelled recess. Sir Thomas Spert, erected in 1622. Lady Jane Detheck, wife of Alexander Neville, 1606. Robert Clarke, 1610, and Frances his daughter. Elizabeth widow of Richard Startute, 1620. (In 1756 the vestry was told that the Detheck monument and two others—Startute and Merrit—had partly fallen, and the remainder was soon likely to fall: Mr Chandler, mason, was to secure what part he could, and the rest was to be taken and laid by.) John Berry, 1689–90. Captain Nathaniel Owen, 1707–8, and two wives. Benjamin Kenton, 1800, by Westmacott junior.

St Anne's, Limehouse (121, 122)

One of the Fifty New Churches, built in 1712–24, and consecrated in 1730. Nicholas Hawksmoor was the architect, and there was the usual strong team of craftsmen: masons, Edward Strong and Edward Tufnell, Christopher Cass and Thomas Dunn: carpenters,

Robert Jelfe, James Grove, John James and John Meard: joiners, Thomas Holden and John Balshaw: carvers, Joseph Wade and Thomas Darby. The plasterer was Chrysostom Wilkins.

The tower still dominates the neighbourhood, and its effect has not been spoiled by out-of-scale buildings. Hawksmoor was obviously thinking of a fifteenth-century tower with a lantern on top, such as he tried to reproduce at All Souls', Oxford. Here it is translated into his own Roman style—though there is no Roman precedent for it.

The lower part of the tower is broadened by projecting buttresses to the north and south. At its base is a semicircular projection, with the main doorway: the vestibules at the side have an attic storey. The additional height of these, and the additional breadth of the tower, make the approach from the west tremendously impressive. The eastern angles have square turrets.

The interior is arranged as though the church were cruciform, with a large circle in the ceiling over the centre; a Greek cross, plus a western bay, and a projecting sanctuary.

There was a fire in 1850, and the rebuilding afterwards was done by Philip Hardwick and John Morris, who did it extremely well. The font and pulpit are theirs. There were further alterations by Blomfield in 1891.

The east window, with glass by Clutterbuck, forms the reredos. It looks very well, but the east end is less sumptuous than it was before the fire. Malcolm wrote: 'The space above represents a sky, glory, and cherubim withdrawing curtains. A real festooned curtain hangs in the window. Seven golden candlesticks are placed in the arch of the window, the cornices, and over the Decalogue, Creed, and Paternoster.'

Christchurch, Spitalfields (119)

Christchurch is another of the huge churches that Hawksmoor designed for the parish of Stepney. The design was accepted by the Commissioners for the Fifty New Churches in 1714. The taste of official bodies nowadays tends to mediocrity: but it was not so in the early eighteenth century. The foundation stone was laid in 1715, and the church was consecrated in 1729. The cost was £19,418. Mason, Thomas Dunn; carpenters James Grove and Samuel Worrall; plasterer Isaac Mansfield; carvers John Darby and Gervase Smith.

The tower is extremely strange. As at St Anne's, Hawksmoor extended the east and west walls, to give an appearance of great breadth; but here the extensions are flush with the walls. They continue for some way, and then come back to the square with curved ramps. Between them, on the north and south, are curved recesses, with windows under. Then comes a square stage, and then a small arcaded square with a tall octagonal spire, which is more of Gothic than of Classical origin. It had openings and crockets, but these were removed in the early nineteenth century, and the spire was smoothed out. The whole thing is the product of Hawksmoor's imagination; there is nothing like it anywhere else.

In front of the tower is a portico of four Tuscan columns, with a semicircular arch in the middle.

The church is the usual basilican plan, but on an exceptionally grand scale, with very tall Composite columns on pedestals. In 1866 Ewan Christian removed the galleries—which were, of course, part of the design; and, for some reason, chamfered the edges of the pedestals. The entablatures run to the aisle walls, and there are semicircular arches, and transverse barrel vaults in the aisles. There is a clerestory, and a flat coffered ceiling. The entablature is returned at the east end, with two extra columns, to form a screen: and at the west, where it is interrupted in the middle by the organ (by Bridge, 1730). Beyond the screen, at the east, are quadrant walls meeting the altar recess.

The altar was said, in the early nineteenth century, to have a majestic appearance: that could hardly be said now. The seats are by Ewan Christian.

The church was repaired in 1836, struck by lightning in 1841, and repaired again afterwards. There were alterations later in the nineteenth century, ending with Christian's meddlings. Of late years the fabric has deteriorated, and a great deal of money is needed for repairs. But it is unthinkable that the church should be allowed to decay, and repairs in fact have now been begun (1965).

Monuments　Edward Peck, 1736, by Thomas Dunn. Sir Robert Ladbroke, Lord Mayor, 1794, by Flaxman.

St George's in the East, Cannon Street Road (120)

Designed by Hawksmoor: built in 1715–23, and consecrated on 19 July 1729. Masons, Edward Strong and Edward Tufnell, and Christopher Cass: carpenters, James Grove and John Meard: plasterers, John and Chrysostom Wilkins: carvers, Joseph Wade and Thomas Darby. The total cost was £18,557.

The church was centrally planned, with an additional bay to the east and west, an eastern apse, and the western tower, with vestibules. The tower, which is slightly broadened by buttresses north and south, is crowned by an octagonal lantern—once again, a feature of Gothic origin—with buttresses which are carried up to support small round turrets. The gallery stairs are contained in four circular turrets.

The church was badly bombed in 1941, and suffered the usual drastic tidying up afterwards. The tower and the outer walls remained, and the apse with its plasterwork, and the font at the west end. Otherwise, everything went, and it was a moving experience to visit the church afterwards on a quiet afternoon, with no sign of a human being anywhere near. Though it was sad to see the church in its state of dereliction, there was no denying that Hawksmoor's walls made a magnificent ruin. (A Victorian pamphlet about spreading

119 Christchurch, Spitalfields, 1715–29 by Hawksmoor

120 St George's in the East, 1715–23 by Nicholas Hawksmoor

121, 122 St Anne's, Limehouse, 1712–24 by Nicholas Hawksmoor. The interior was restored after the fire in 1850

123 Holy Trinity, Mile End, 1836–9 by George Austin

124 St John's, Bethnal Green, 1826–8 by Sir John Soane. The windows have been remodelled

125 All Saints', Poplar, 1821–3 by Charles Hollis

126 St Paul's, Shadwell, 1817–20 by John Walters. The east end remodelled

Christianity among the working classes had somehow managed to survive, and was lying on the floor.)

Later, a temporary church was erected on the site of the nave. The demolition of the ruins was suggested; but fortunately the walls and tower have been kept, repaired and cleaned. The vaults were cleared of coffins—which were taken to Brookwood—and demolished, and a hall was built under a smaller church, which includes Hawksmoor's apse. A rectory, and flats for the curate, verger, and parish worker are also included within the walls. The work was begun in 1960, and dedicated on 26 April 1964. The architect was Arthur Bailey, and the main contractor was Fairweather.

St Paul's, Shadwell (126)

The church is in a secluded position, near the river, with trees round it. The first church was built c. 1656, and was given a parish in 1669. It was of brick, with a western tower: writers on London did not think much of it. The galleries were 'gaudily ornamented with gold'.

It was taken down, and a completely new church built in 1817–20 from designs by John Walters: the cost was £14,000. It is of brick, with a double row of rectangular windows: the front is stuccoed, with pilasters: the tower has a circular upper stage and spire. Galleries remain. The organ was originally in an eastern gallery: there was a door in the east wall, and the altar stood forward. Butterfield rearranged the interior in 1848. He removed the east gallery, and built a wall across the east end, with an arch in the middle, to the east of which a sanctuary was formed, with vestries on each side. An east window was opened, with glass by Ward and Nixon. The pulpit was moved, and the desk was cut down into clergy stalls. The font of the seventeenth-century church was rescued from the vaults, and replaced. A zinc reredos was afterwards set up.

Except for this operation on the east end—which was less drastic than it sounds—little has been done to the church, and it keeps its old-fashioned Anglican parish church atmosphere very well. The east window has recently been given glass by John Hayward.

Holy Trinity, Tredegar Road, Mile End (123)

Built 1836–9; the architect was George Austin, and it was built as a proprietary chapel: before it was finished it was bought from the lessee, and the freehold was given to Sir Charles Morgan of Tredegar. It is a satisfactory design in the Perpendicular style: seven bays, with aisles, and a west annexe like the base of a tower, with curved gables, and porches on each side. The aisles, lit by long two-light transomed windows, have lost their galleries. There are attractive panelled ceilings: the ceiling of the east part of the north aisle, which has been painted, is less attractive. The central part of the reredos has been placed here, and a substitute provided in the chancel.

St Peter's, Cephas Street

The church is in a quiet street behind Charrington's Brewery. To the east is the school, and to the west the vicarage; there are some trees. Built by the Metropolis Churches Fund in 1837–8: the architect was Edward Blore. A large rectangle, with a short sanctuary, of Suffolk brick, in a vaguely Norman style, with long two-light windows. On the south is a gable, which looks like a transept, but is not, facing down Cephas Avenue, with a turret on top and a doorway below. The church was damaged in the War, and has been well restored and entirely refitted (except for the Victorian Norman font) by J. Douglas Mathews and Partners. The altar has been brought out to the west of the sanctuary arch, and there are twin pulpits.

St Paul's, Dock Street, Whitechapel

Built as a seamen's church, in place of the Episcopal Floating Church (formerly the *Brazen* sloop-of-war). The Prince Consort laid the foundation stone on 11 May 1846, and the church was consecrated on 10 July 1847. The architect was Henry Roberts. It is ordinary Early English, with brick sides and a more ambitious front and tower and spire. The altar is in a shallow recess. Galleries were removed in 1901 when a chancel was formed.

St Mary's, Johnson Street

Built 1849–50: the architects were F. and H. Francis. It is cheap and very simple, of Kentish rag, in early Middle-Pointed style: a nave and aisles, and a sanctuary, with a thin tower and spire on the south.

St Peter's, London Docks (130)

The Rev C. F. Lowder went in 1856 as a mission priest in the parish of St George in the East, and was soon joined by others. An iron chapel of the Good Shepherd was built. In the next year, the seventeenth-century Danish Church in Wellclose Square became vacant, and Lowder rented it for services. Bishop Tait, as usual, made a fuss about ritual, and the church received some attention from the rioters in 1859.

On St Peter's day, 1865, after £4,000 had been given or promised, the foundation stone of St Peter's was laid: the church was consecrated on the same day a year later. The architect was F. H. Pownall. It is French Gothic, rather tall, of yellow stock brick outside, and red brick, with bands and patterns of black, inside. The pillars are of blue Pennant stone. Most of the carving has not been done.

The church was not completed at the west end: more was built later by Maurice B. Adams, and it was finished off in 1939. But the tower and spire, which were to have stood at the north-west, have never been built. The rood, to the memory of Lowder, dates from 1880, and the Lowder chapel from 1885. Two east windows, and four in the south chapel, are by M. E. A. Rope, 1952–4.

St Philip's New Road (129)

On the site of a Commissioners' church, designed by John Walters (but Francis Goodwin claimed to have made the design, and superintended the work). It was built in 1818–19, by John Trenchard, and cost £12,660, towards which the Commissioners granted £3,500.

The present church was the gift of the Rev Sidney Vacher, who inherited money and spent it freely: the cost was about £40,000. The foundation stone was laid on 18 July 1888, and the consecration was on 27 October 1892: the architect was Arthur Cawston, author of *A Comprehensive Scheme for London Street Improvements*—who shot himself accidentally in 1894. A faculty was given in May 1889 to pull down the western parts of the old church, and build the nave and aisles of the new: and, if funds permitted, to demolish the rest, and build the transepts, chancel, and chapel.

This is a very ambitious church, in a Pearsonic Early English style: all vaulted, with nave and double aisles of four bays, transepts, and an apsidal chancel, and Lady chapel, also apsidal, at the east. The porch at the west is the base of a tower that was never built.

St Paul's, Bow Common

William Cotton of Leytonstone, 1786–1866, was one of the great church-building laymen of the nineteenth century. He suggested the foundation of the Incorporated Church Building Society, and supported Bishop Blomfield's Metropolis Churches Fund. Bethnal Green was his special interest, and he lived to see the completion of all the new churches in that parish. In 1854 he was seriously ill, but recovered, and himself provided the church of St Paul, Bow Common, which was consecrated in 1858. Bishop Blomfield, on his deathbed, presented a gold Communion service, which had been made for Queen Adelaide. The architect of the church was Rodhe Hawkins, and the furniture and decoration of the sanctuary were by Street, 1869.

This church was bombed, and has been completely cleared away. The new church, designed by Robert Maguire, was begun in 1958, and consecrated in 1960: the cost was £44,000.

The planning is an attempt to realise the ideals of the Liturgical Movement—which are, in almost every respect, the opposite of those of the nineteenth-century ecclesiologists. The Church is the People of God, meeting around the Lord's Table: and all that is needed is the altar, and a space enclosed around it. What encloses the space is not of primary importance, and there is no need for the walls, etc., to be edifying.

So this church, of which the walls are brick (now being adorned with mosaics by Charles Lutyens), is a square, lit from the top by a glass lantern, under which stands a plain altar, with a ciborium over. There is an outer aisle all round. At the east is another holy table, where the Sacrament is reserved. There is practically nothing else in the building except for the font.

In the primitive Church, baptism—which was of nude adults—was certainly not public: the neophytes made their first appearance after the baptism. The Prayer Book gives several good reasons why baptisms (as now performed) should be done in the face of the congregation; and, in this respect, the Liturgical Movement follows the Prayer Book, and does not attempt to reproduce early custom.

Bethnal Green

Bethnal Green was originally part of the parish of Stepney. St Matthew's was built in 1743–6, and in 1826–8 Soane's St John's was built as a chapel of ease: it was afterwards given a parish.

This district was one of the chief spheres of Bishop Blomfield's church extension. Charles Booth, writing at the beginning of this century, said that there was 'wasted effort to such an extent that even now "remember Bethnal Green" is apt to be thrown in the teeth of those who try to inaugurate any great movement in the City on behalf of the Church'. Bethnal Green and Liverpool were the only places in England to have a set of churches dedicated to the twelve apostles—with St Paul and St Barnabas afterwards added. Towards the cost of the original Ten churches, the Church Building Commissioners gave £5,000. The rest of the money was provided by the Metropolis Churches Fund—except for St James the Great, which was built by a brother and sister of the bishop.

Of the original 14 churches, only seven are now in use: one, St Philip's, is a store for furniture. All the others have vanished.

St Matthew's, St Matthew's Row

The commissioners for building the Fifty New Churches bought 2½ acres in 1725, but nothing was done about building a church. On 10 January 1742, a petition was presented to the Commons for the building of a church, and forming of a parish. The church was designed by George Dance, and built in 1743–6. A good, sound, plain brick church: it was described, as usual, as neat and commodious. After a fire in 1859 it was restored by T. E. Knightley and reopened in 1861: the top was added to the tower. The chancel was refitted in this century by F. C. Eden.

The interior was destroyed in the Second World War: the reconstruction has been done by J. Antony Lewis, of Michael Tapper and Lewis. The altar now stands in the body of the church, and there are vestries where the sanctuary was. The Lady chapel is in a gallery at the east end: the murals were painted by Barry Robinson, and the panels in the screen by Peter Snow. Glass from St Philip's was put together in one window by Lawrence Lee, who also designed the other window in St Philip's chapel.

St John's, Bethnal Green (124)

A Commissioners' church, designed by Sir John Soane and built by Robert Streather in 1826–8. The front is divided into three bays by pilasters, with an attic in the centre on which the low tower stands. The best part of the interior is certainly the vestibule: the view across, through the arches that open to the basement of the tower, is very Soanian, and of great distinction. The church itself has little to recommend it: it was damaged by fire in 1870, and remodelled by W. Mundy. The windows are filled with the clumsiest tracery: the pillars above the galleries are of wood, supporting a hammer-beam roof. The chancel was extended in 1888 by G. F. Bodley—hardly the architect that one would expect. The altar piece is of marble, with a large Christ, after Thorwaldsen. The marble screen and side chapel were installed in 1903.

St Peter's, St Peter's Avenue

This and the next three churches are all that remain of the churches built by Bishop Blomfield. St Peter's was designed by Lewis Vulliamy, and built in 1840–1. The style is Norman. A large rectangular nave, with a west porch that becomes an octagonal tower; small sanctuary, and an eastern vestry. Like Vulliamy's church at Chingford, it has west windows stepped up towards the tower, and the brick partly faced with flint. The nave roof is of a most extraordinary design. Galleries have been removed, the nave has been re-seated, and the east bay has been divided off as a chancel. The faculty for the screen was given on 4 December 1911. The glass is by Heaton, Butler, and Bayne: some more was broken during the War. The church was restored and redecorated during the early '50s.

St Philip's, Swanfield Street

Built 1840–2 by T. L. Walker. Brick Norman; it is not now used for worship.

St James the Less, St James's Avenue

Another brick Norman church by Vulliamy, 1842. It was badly damaged in 1940, reconstructed by J. Antony Lewis, and reconsecrated in 1961. The organ came from the demolished church of St Matthias.

St James the Great, Bethnal Green Road (128)

Built 1842–3; the architect was Edward Blore. This is a cruciform church of red brick, Early English in style, with a turret in the angle between the nave and the south transept. A contributor to the *Ecclesiologist* visited the church before it was completed and noted the thin, octagonal brick piers, and the fact that the transepts were longer by one foot than the chancel. Why, he asked, must so many new churches have transepts? They are not suitable to Anglican worship; and if a church has to be cheap, why should expensive gable elevations be multiplied? Already there was a gallery, on cast iron Gothic pillars. The roof was being put on: it was of considerable height, but it did not, somehow or other, produce a good effect.

The church was reroofed, the gallery was removed, and a choir was formed, in 1897–8. The iron screen was erected in 1906.

The interior has been redecorated since the War.

St Bartholomews's, Coventry Street

Designed by William Railton, begun in 1843, and consecrated in May 1844. It is Early English, of brick, rather tall and thin, with aisled nave, and the stump of a tower at the south-west; lower transepts, and a chancel of the same height as the nave. Very simple, except for the eastern triplet, which has shafts and dogtooth, and glass of 1886. The west gallery remains: the upper gallery was taken down in 1868.

The church was repaired after War damage, and reopened on 14 September 1955: the interior is redecorated in blue and cream.

St Barnabas', Grove Road

Built as a nonconformist church; the foundation stone was laid on 15 May 1865. William Wigginton was the architect, and Thomas Ennor the builder. It was acquired by the Church of England some years later.

The outer walls remain, north-west tower and truncated spire, and arcade between the chancel and north aisle: it was otherwise destroyed by bombing in 1942, and rebuilt by J. Antony Lewis. The arcades have been suppressed, and the east end of the chancel has been cut off: there is a painted altar piece. Some odd, left-over bits of furnishing are not at all in accord with the prevailing modernity.

Bow

The parish of Stratford le Bow was separated from Stepney in 1730: it only became a considerable place in the nineteenth century. The population has greatly declined, and there was a good deal of War damage. There have been some casualties among the churches, but those that have gone were not very important.

St Mary's, Stratford le Bow

The church was built as a chapel of ease to Stepney, by a licence of Bishop Baldock in 1311. Most of the old work is fourteenth-century, but it has been so heavily restored at various times that it is not of much value. The aisles have remained unusually narrow. In the late fifteenth century the tower was built, and the nave and aisles were extended westward. The eighteenth century, as usual, did its part in repairing and adorning the church, Towards the end of it, in 1794, the south aisle was mostly rebuilt and refaced.

On 29 January 1829 the top of the tower fell, and William Ford surveyed the damage. He proposed to take down the whole of the church, except for the base of the tower, and build a new one. This was not acceptable, and all that he did was to rebuild the top of the tower.

Organ chamber 1870. In 1882 Sir A. W. Blomfield surveyed the church, and recommended that is should all be rebuilt, except for the tower. Once again, the church was saved, and certain repairs were done: but in 1896 part of the chancel roof subsided, and the proposal for demolition was renewed. The S.P.A.B. took notice, and the repairs were done, under the superintendence of the Society, in 1898–9, by A. W. Hills, of Bow.

There was heavy War damage, and repairs were done by Sir Albert Richardson, who rebuilt the top of the tower in brick. There are two Communion tables—one of about 1630, and the other early eighteenth-century; and two fonts—one fifteenth-century, and one eighteenth.

Monuments   Grace, wife of John Amcottes, 1551. Alice Coburne, 1689. Prisca Coburne, 1701. James Walker, 1712, and Dorothy, 1706.

St Mark's, Victoria Park

Built 1872–3; A. W. Blomfield. Practically all of brick: a wide nave, with west porch, transepts, chancel, and a north-east tower (St John's, Wilton Road, Westminster, on a small scale). The nave has plate-traceried windows, two to a bay: the roof springs from very low down. The fittings are poor and cheap. The organ came from St Philip's, Buckingham Palace Road.

St Paul's, Old Ford

Built 1878; Newman and Billing. A self-confident, rather ugly, townish church, well adapted for the worship of a congregation (though perhaps for a larger one than would be expected nowadays). Of yellow stock brick, with a slight admixture of red; French Gothic. There is a wide nave, lit by three-light windows under gables, with very narrow passage aisles; a north-west turret, and a west porch embracing a baptistery; an apse, with almost round-headed windows, and vestries. The interior was redecorated in 1954 by Gilbert H. Jenkins.

Poplar

Poplar was given a place of worship, St Matthias, in 1654, by the East India Company, but it was only a chapel of ease to Stepney. The parish was not formed until 1817, and the parish church of All Saints was built in 1821–3. The place was transformed by the construction of the West India Docks, the East India Docks, and various smaller docks; and

127 St Dunstan's, Stepney High Street,
fifteenth-century restored

128 St James the Great, Bethnal Green, 1842–3
by Edward Blore

129 St Philip's, Stepney, 1888–92 by Arthur Cawston

130 St Peter's, London Docks, 1865–6
by F. H. Pownall, completed later

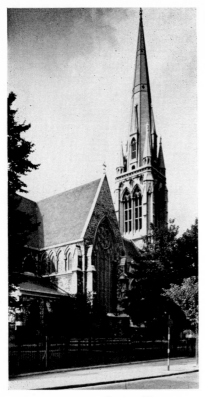

131 St Mary's, Stoke Newington, 1855–8 by George Gilbert Scott, tower and spire completed by J. O. Scott

132 St Mary's, Old Church, 1563 and 1829, restored after the last War

133 St Matthias', Wordsworth Road, 1851–3 by William Butterfield, restored after War damage

134 St John's, Brownswood Park, 1869 and lat by F. Wallen. The interior rearranged with t altar brought forward

it became a centre of ship-building, and of the manufacture of chain cables, wire rope, and other things connected with ships. Bromley St Leonard was a very small place until the nineteenth century: by 1861 the population had risen to 24,077.

St Matthias', Woodstock Street, Poplar

In 1642 the inhabitants of Blackwall petitioned the East India Company for a chapel, and a dwelling for the minister. The Company provided the site and 60 loads of stone. The foundation is said to have been laid in 1650. In 1652 the Company agreed to give £200: half when the walls were erected, and half when the roof was on. The first £100 was paid to the builder—John Tanner—in June of that year. The total cost was more than £2,000. The Chapel was largely rebuilt by the Company in 1776, when R. Jupp was their surveyor, and repaired and embellished in 1803.

In 1866 the Chapel was conveyed to the Ecclesiastical Commissioners, and a parish was formed. In 1868 the walls were faced with ragstone, and it was recast in an unattractive fashion, and given a rather gross turret. The architect was W. M. Teulon, and the contractors were Crabb and Vaughan. The chancel, designed by E. Evans Cronk, was consecrated on 21 December 1875: it was built by J. Kemp Coleman, of Poplar.

The church is extremely private-looking, behind the vicarage, and with only a small entrance from the road to the churchyard. The interior is more or less authentic, except for the windows and the fittings: no attempt has been made to recast the arcades or the roof. The plan is similar to that of St Martin's, Ludgate, Bermondsey, and Deptford: two bays; then a wider bay, roofed transept-wise; and then two more. Doric columns, some of wood, and a low barrel roof. The galleries were removed in 1868. There is some glass by Westlake.

Monument George Steevens, by Flaxman; he is shown 'earnestly contemplating a bust of our Great Dramatic Bard': the inscription is by Hayley.

All Saints', East India Dock Road (125)

Begun in 1821, and consecrated on 23 July 1823. The architect was Charles Hollis. It was an expensive church: the cost was £33,077. It might be expected to have been a Commissioners' church, but it was not.

It is a very handsome church, solidly built in Portland stone: the St Martin in the Fields formula, but translated into Greek. The portico is Ionic, and Ionic columns and entablatures adorn the north and south sides of the flanking porches—the south of which is now a chapel, and the north a vestry. The steeple is obviously copied from Gibbs, though it has been slightly grecianised. Altogether, the church looks more like 1720 than 1820.

Arthur Chandler, when he was vicar, 1891–1901, made some alterations of which he is said to have been his own architect. But in the 1950s the interior was entirely remodelled by Cecil Brown, architect: the contractor was R. W. Bowman. It has been given more dignity, and more of an eighteenth-century appearance than it had before. The west gallery, with royal arms and organ, is most imposing. The church was rededicated on 23 October 1953.

The chapel of St Frideswide recalls the church of that name which was bombed and since demolished.

Christchurch, Manchester Road, Isle of Dogs

William Cubitt developed Cubitt Town, and built this church for it in 1854–5. The architect was Frederick Johnstone. It is in a not very difficult Early English style, rather like Scott's in his Hanwell and Turnham Green period. Of brick, but uses some stone from old London Bridge; there is a nave, south tower and spire, wide transepts, and chancel. The painting over the chancel arch was the work of a former incumbent.

The chancel was redecorated in 1955: the scheme was devised by Alan Lindsey, and the architect was J. Morris. The eastern triplet was filled with hardboard, with figures of Christ, St John and St Luke, drawn, and enlarged by photography. The walls were covered with paper—red at the east, and pink on the side walls—made by Coles of Mortimer Street from a pattern a century old.

St Michael's, Bromley by Bow

A mission chapel, designed by J. W. Morris, was opened in 1861: the permanent church, also by Morris, was begun in 1864, and consecrated on 4 August 1865. A stalwart brick church, well suited to its surroundings: nave and aisles, wide double transepts, a short chancel, north chapel, and south tower. An eighteenth-century font, and a big, square muscular one of 1863. It was restored in 1901. The interior was purified in 1955: refloored, the woodwork pickled, and the walls whitened.

All Hallows', Devons Road, Bromley by Bow

One of the churches built with the money from the City church of All Hallows', Bread Street. Ewan Christian was the architect: foundation stone laid on 16 May 1873, consecration on 18 August 1874. It was a church of ordinary type: red brick Early English, with an apse. It was bombed on 18 September 1940, rebuilt in 1954–5, and reopened on 19 October 1955. The architect was A. P. Robinson, of Caröe and Partners, and the builders were Grace and Marsh of Croydon.

In the rebuilding, use has been made of most of what remained. The church has been somewhat reduced in size: the wall round the outside of the apse is the lower part of Christian's eastern vestries; and the south aisle has been dispensed with, except for two bays kept as a vestry. Christian's north arcade is built up in the wall, and a simple low arcade of round-headed arches has been built instead. A low tower has been added to the former organ chamber. The seats are original. For once, in these days, there is a chancel arranged in the usual way. The glass in the apse is by William Morris and Co. (F. W. Cole).

St Saviour's, Poplar

Built 1873–4; F. and H. Francis. The cost was about £7,000. Of yellow stock brick, with bands of red. The nave has stone pillars with simply moulded capitals: the capitals in the chancel have naturalistic foliage. The east window is by Heaton, Butler and Bayne: two windows in the aisles are by S. T. Clare. Father Dolling was vicar of this parish from 1898 to 1902: he enjoyed Poplar less than Portsmouth.

St Peter's, Garford Street

This church was built with the help of £8,000 from the sale of St Martin Outwich, in the City. The architect, Ewan Christian, reported that there were 16 feet of slush and water under the soil, and the foundations cost £2,977. The tender was £4,849 for the church and the total was £9,703. The builder was Nightingale of Lambeth. The foundations were laid in 1882–3 and the consecration was on 5 July 1884.

The church is hidden behind a high wall in a dreary approach to the Isle of Dogs. It is of brick and stone, and similar to St Stephen's, Upper Holloway. Early English style, with a wide nave and separately gabled aisles, and no proper chancel. The bell came from St Martin's. A chancel screen was erected in 1909, but has been removed. The interior was smashed by a vandal in August 1958, and was restored in 1961.

St Nicholas' and All Hallows', Aberfeldy Street

The original church was built from the proceeds of the sale of All Hallows', Bread Street, and was destroyed in the War. The foundation stone of the new church was laid on 10

October 1953, and it was consecrated on 2 October 1955. The architects were Seely and Paget. It is small and simple, with a north-west tower, with the organ in it. A hall on the north, which can be opened into the church. A painted ceiling by B. D. L. Thomas, with a dove in glory, angels, etc.; brick ambones.

St Nicholas', 1900, by W. Clarkson, was bombed, and has been demolished.

St Luke's, Millwall

Designed by E. L. Blackburne, and consecrated on 4 March 1870, it was refitted and restored by W. G. St J. Cogswell. It was bombed and subsequently demolished. A new, smaller church has been built—a chapel added to a hall: it is not a parish church.

Stoke Newington

There is little to be said about church extension in Stoke Newington that has not already been said under the heading of Hackney.

In 1848 Richard Foster joined with Robert Brett, and some other local churchmen, in setting on foot the building of St Matthias', which was consecrated in 1853. The small old church was superseded by a large new one (but fortunately not pulled down). St Matthias' was damaged in the War, but has been restored—though in a way that Butterfield would certainly not have approved. For some years after the War, St Faith's stood, an impressive bombed ruin. All Saints' lingered on, locked and disused, with litter accumulating round it, and grass growing in the gutters, until its time came, and the church-breakers descended on it.

St Mary's, Stoke Newington (132)

The old church was enlarged with a south aisle in 1563 by William Pater, lord of the manor: over one doorway is '1563 *Ab alto*', and over the other '*W. P. Prospice*'. A brick arcade with four-centred arches: the aisle is in two sections, the west part being a porch. North aisle 1716: chancel extended 1723. Sir Charles Barry added an extra north aisle, and the clerestory and roof, extended the chancel, and added the spire (1829).

The church was damaged in 1940, and restored in 1953. The north side is rebuilt, and there is no outer north aisle.

168

Box pews remain: the pulpit and iron rails are Barry's. The sixteenth-century glass in the east window was broken, though bits have been pieced together. The post-War glass is by H. Vernon Spreadbury.

Monuments John Dudley, 29 December 1580, and his widow Elizabeth, afterwards wife of Thomas Sutton, 1602. Joseph Hurlock 1793, and Sarah, 1766,—by Banks.

St Matthias', Wordsworth Road (now known as St Faith's with St Matthias') (133)

Robert Brett, 1808–74, proposed the building of this church. A committee was formed, which accepted plans by Butterfield in 1850. The *Ecclesiologist* approved the design, except for one or two features. E. A. Freeman, the historian and architectural critic, disliked everything about it: the saddleback tower was all wrong; the aisles ought not to be carried past the tower; the windows were ugly; the aisles were too low; the west front was a depraved copy of Dorchester and Wantage; and there should not be a west doorway. The *Ecclesiologist* replied that a saddleback was a very suitable termination for a tower that was also a chancel. It was true that they had objected to west doorways in smaller churches; but a large town church was 'quasi-collegiate'. Freeman must either admit the principle of development in modern town churches, or else 'boldly advocate the perpetuation of those small low structures which make the cities of England so inferior to those of Belgium or France'.

One thing that Butterfield did, in answer to criticisms, was to remove the pinnacles that he had designed for the angles of the tower: his supporters, as well as Freeman, had agreed that they would be out of place.

The foundation stone was laid on 29 July 1851, by Lord Nelson, and the church was consecrated on 13 June 1853. It is worth recording that Butterfield gave his services, and that the workmen worked overtime without pay. The *Ecclesiologist* praised the design even more enthusiastically when the church was built. It was a town church: the huge clerestory, high roof, and gabled tower stood out above the rows of houses. Inside, there was an effect of vast height, and the clerestory was especially imposing from within. The tower arches were somewhat low, and the sanctuary was vaulted. 'It would be difficult to speak too highly of the genius and power shown in the design of this fine church, and the admirable adaptation of its plan and arrangements to the proper performance of Divine Service is equally conspicuous.' There were faults: the woodwork was clumsy, and in the window tracery there was a 'general tendency to uncouth and cumbrous ornamentation'. It was natural to react from the prettiness and frippery of much modern design, but Butterfield went too far in the opposite direction. Still, it was an admirable church—and it was remarkable that it had all been built for £7,000.

The east window was by Wailes, from Butterfield's design. The font—though this was not mentioned—was by William Lowder, a pupil of Butterfield, who was afterwards ordained, and, as a priest, carried out various church restorations. E. C. Hakewill, the architect of St John of Jerusalem, Hackney, said, 'I would willingly surrender all claims to every work I have ever done, could I claim to be architect of St Matthias', Stoke Newington.'

The services were a great attraction in the early days. W. H. Monk, the musical editor of *Hymns Ancient and Modern*, was the organist: Helmore's plainsong psalter was used, and, on weekdays, the Ecclesiological Society's own *Hymnal Noted*. Butterfield would sometimes walk over on Sunday mornings from Adam Street, Strand, to join the queue: many people often had to be turned away.

There was a great deal of later adornment. The screen was designed by James Brooks, who was churchwarden from 1868 to 1879, and decorated by Westlake. Wall paintings by Daniel Bell were begun in 1896, and windows were inserted at different times (Wailes, O'Connor, Gibbs, and Clayton and Bell).

The church was damaged by blast in the raids, and in the first reorganisation scheme after the War it was proposed to pull it down, and also St Faith's, which was badly damaged —and build one new church to replace the two. Protests were made, and in the end St Faith's was demolished, and St Matthias' was restored. The chancel has been cut off, and the interior has been whitened. Butterfield would not have approved: but at any rate the church is still there.

St Mary's, Stoke Newington
(New Church) (131)

Begun in 1855, and consecrated on 25 June 1858. The architect was G. G. Scott, and the plan is similar to that of St Paul's Cathedral, Dundee, and St Andrew's, Ashley Place, Westminster, now demolished. A large, unclerestoried nave, with aisles gabled outwards. The arcades are lofty, with circular pillars and elaborate naturalistic capitals. There are transepts, with the arcades carried past them; a chancel with aisles, and an apse. At the west is a tower, of which only the lower part was completed by Scott himself: the upper part, with its very tall spire, was finished in 1890 by J. O. Scott. This is of Doulting stone: the older parts are of Kentish rag with Bath stone dressings. The font, with marble angels, was carved by the younger Westmacott. The church lost its glass during the War, and has been redecorated since. The new glass in the apse is by Francis Skeat, 1957–8.

St John's, Brownswood Park (134)

The foundation stone of the eastern parts was laid on 4 December 1869. Consecration 1874. The foundation stone of the west end was laid on 27 June 1877. The architect was F. Wallen.

An impressive church: big and lofty, in a purely Victorian style which it would be wide of the mark to call thirteenth-century. The central tower was never built. Dignified transepts, and an apsidal chancel with clerestory windows that echo those of the baptistery. The east end recalls that of Zanzibar Cathedral. The interior has been whitened, and a nave altar provided.

St Andrew's, Bethune Road

Built 1883–4; Sir A. W. Blomfield was the architect. Of ragstone, with slated roofs: a nave and aisles; the east bay is the choir, and is divided from the rest of the nave by an iron screen—as at St Mary's, Portsea. This bay has transepts: a spirelet is in the angle of the south transept. A sanctuary to the east. The style is late thirteenth-century: the church is imposing, but not very interesting. The glass by Heaton, Butler and Bayne. The east window is post-War.

St Michael's, Stoke Newington Common

The site was given by Amhurst Tyssen-Amhurst, M.P. The building committee first met on 5 April 1883, and J. E. K. Cutts was chosen as architect. The contractors were Holliday and Greenwood, of Loughborough Junction. Work was begun in 1884, and the consecration was on 2 May 1885. It is the usual tall, red brick, slate-roofed church. Messrs Lumley's cast concrete was extensively used, 'to the almost complete exclusion of stone'. The design included an enormous tower and spire, which were never built. The arch is blocked, and there is a small porch, an afterthought, at the bottom. This is at the west, so that there is not the usual three-arched baptistery. The walls inside are plastered—but in the arcades and clerestory only the spandrels. The pulpit was erected 1889, the dwarf wall and iron screen 1906. Glass by Heaton, Butler and Bayne.

St Olave's, Woodberry Down

Wren's church of St Olave, Old Jewry, was demolished in 1888–9, and this church was built from the proceeds in 1893–4: it was consecrated on 10 November 1894. It is one of

Ewan Christian's red brick Early English churches, with his usual apse: but it is unusual in that it has a very wide nave, and passage aisles. The font and pulpit are from the City church—both good. The pulpit stair has been given a brass rail, rather *art nouveau*-ish. The altar rails are similar: they were put up in the 1930s, but look a good deal earlier. All the glass is by Powell.

Westminster

The population of Westminster used to be very large. Lewis's *Topographical Dictionary*, 1840, gives the following figures for the different parishes: St Anne's, Soho, 15,600, St Clement's (including part of the parish that was in Holborn), 11,578, St George's, 58,209, St James's, Piccadilly, 37,053, St John's, 22,648, St Margaret's, 25,344, St Martin's, 23,732, St Mary le Strand, 2,052 (partly in Holborn), St Paul's, Covent Garden, 5,203. There were, of course, several chapels, proprietary and parochial, as well as the parish churches. The population was 241,611 in the 1851 census, and had grown to 254,623 ten years later.

The Church did its best to provide church accommodation. Cardinal Wiseman had a letter in *The Times* (20 November 1850) in which he contrasted the apathy of the Abbey with his own ardent desire to work among the poor in the slums. He was answered by a Westminster Layman—Mr Page Wood, M.P.—who said that the Abbey had no pastoral responsibility for the area, but that the Dean and Chapter had during the last ten years given nearly £8,000 a year towards the work of the Church in Westminster: they had also made a donation of £1,000 to the spiritual aid fund which one of the canons had begun, and for which he had raised nearly £20,000. Another canon was building a church which was expected to cost £6,000. Twenty years before, there were two parishes (St Margaret's and St John's: he was thinking of the immediate neighbourhood), and one chapel: now there were six churches, and there would soon be nine.

This is quoted by Canon Charles Smyth in his *Church and Parish* (pp 200–1). The chapter is called *The Prodigality and Carefulness of God*, and in it he discusses—though of course he cannot solve—the problem of why God allows things to disappear: not bad and unnecessary things, but institutions designed for His glory, which are not altogether failing to do their duty. He mentions several churches which, when he wrote, were ruined and awaiting demolition. 'Most, though not all, of these were among the new churches, to which in 1850 Mr Page Wood, M.P., in the character of "A Westminster Layman" had pointed with legitimate pride as a visible, not to say obvious, refutation of the strictures passed by Cardinal Wiseman on the alleged pastoral indifference of the Dean and Chapter' (*op cit*, p 209).

There are many other churches in London and the provinces where there was once a flourishing religious life, but which are now like wells that have dried up. Why does this

135 St Margaret's, fifteenth and sixteenth centuries, restored in the eighteenth and nineteenth centuries. Porch by J. L. Pearson

136 St Clement Danes, tower 1669–70, the church by Wren 1680–2, top of tower by Gibbs 1719–20

137 St James's, Piccadilly, by Sir Christopher Wren. Consecrated 1684, restored after the War

138 St Martin in the Fields, 1721–6 by James Gibbs

140 St George's, Hanover Square, by John James 1713–25

143 Christchurch, Down Street, 1864–5 by F. and H. Francis

139 St Paul's, Covent Garden, 1631–8, by Inigo Jones, restored after the fire in 1795, by Thomas Hardwick

142 St Mark's, North

141 St Peter's, Eaton Square, 1824–7

happen? and what becomes of the work? These are questions that arise again and again as one surveys the story of church building in London. But we are not concerned with theology or theodicy: all we need say is that some of the nineteenth-century churches of Westminster had done their work. The population had fallen, and the neighbourhood had changed: and when they were bombed, it was not thought necessary to rebuild them.

St Margaret's, Westminster (135)

This church, the parish church of the Houses of Parliament, was entirely rebuilt from about 1486 onward. The architect was Robert Stowell, the master mason of the Abbey, who died in 1505, the year after the nave was finished. He was succeeded by Thomas Redeman, and Redeman by his son Henry, who built the tower, which was begun in 1515: he died in 1528. The chancel was paid for by Abbot Islip, whose rebus is on the east wall. The church was consecrated on 9 April 1523.

The plan is the usual late Perpendicular rectangle, with no structural division between the nave and chancel: the tower is in an unusual position at the north-west. The church-wardens' accounts are very complete, and the alterations to the church in the reigns of Edward VI, Mary, and Elizabeth I are recorded in detail. In 1643 the church was purged, by order of the House of Commons, 'of all the scandalous pictures (that is to say all painted glasse) in the windowes, and of the *statua's* or images in the tombs and monuments'; and four months later the Solemn League and Covenant was accepted here by both Houses of Parliament and the Westminster Divines. In 1660 repairs were done, and the king's arms were set up again. On 26 February 1681/2 it was 'ordered that the 5th. and 6th. Seates in the fifth Rainge of the Church bee made into a seate for the Speakers of the House of Commons and other Persons of Quality'; and in 1691 it was 'left to the Churchwardens to beautifie and alter the High Chancell to the best of their power'.

The church was well looked after in the eighteenth century, and there are several pictures of its internal appearance. In 1734 the House of Commons granted £3,500 for repairs. The walls were cased with Portland stone, and the tower was raised 20 feet: the roof 'over the Grand or Middle Isle' was newly framed, and a ceiling was inserted underneath. The surveyor was John James, and the mason Samuel Tufnell. As usually happens, the repairs cost more than was expected, and on 14 February 1738 a petition was made to the House for further help, and an additional £2,000 was granted.

In subsequent years, repairs, alterations, and improvements were constantly being carried out. In 1758 the east end was 'wrought into a circular sweep, ending at the top in the form of a half cupola, wrought into squares of Gothic work: under the window, and round the sides of the altar, also variously ornamented in a similar Gothic stile'. This was a most sumptuous sanctuary, with an altar piece of the disciples at Emmaus, carved in wood by Seffrin Alken, under the direction of Kenton Couse, the architect: candlesticks for the altar were given in 1760.

£420 was paid for the glass in the east window, which was bought from John Conyers of Copt Hall, in Essex. The Bishop of Rochester, who was Dean of Westminster, objected to it, but the vestry firmly replied that 'they had no power, nor would it be safe to take down any part, or alter it in any way'. Though there was a lawsuit about it, it was allowed to remain.

The glass was probably made in the Netherlands, at the time of the marriage of Katherine of Aragon and Prince Arthur, whose kneeling figures are included. But Arthur died, and Katherine was married by his brother Henry, and the window was got rid of. It went first to Waltham Abbey, then to Boreham New Hall, Essex, and then to Copt Hall. The Crucifixion group is renaissance in character: what stands out is the vivid blue of the sky.

Parliament gave a grant for these works, and for various repairs and repewing that were done at the same time.

In 1799 a petition was made to the Commons for further help, and £6,721 was voted for a repair by S. P. Cockerell: in 1802 the vestry confessed that they had spent it all, and Parliament voted another £4,500. A further grant was made in 1813.

A great deal more was done than this, and it is not to be supposed that everything was done by Parliament: the parish did its share, and obviously had a great zeal for repairing and beautifying the church.

But by the middle of the nineteenth century the interior looked dirty and old-fashioned, and the pews and galleries were no longer thought handsome: they were regarded as encumbrances that needed to be removed as quickly as possible. In 1877 Sir Gilbert Scott was called in, and began the restoration, which was unfinished at the time of his death. All the eighteenth- and early nineteenth-century woodwork was removed, and the church was stripped down to the walls, which were cleaned and repaired. The window tracery was restored, a new roof was put on, and the interior was, of course, completely refitted. And so the church began the third stage of its existence: not as it had been in its few years before the Reformation, nor as it was after it, but restored for Anglican worship as it had developed in the nineteenth century.

The porches, at the west and south-east, were designed by J. L. Pearson. In 1905 the east end was extended. The triptych contains the Emmaus group from the eighteenth-century altar piece.

There was some War damage, and a good deal of the nineteenth-century glass has gone. The west window and north aisle west window are by Clayton and Bell, and there is a window each by Henry Holiday and Edward Frampton. The font is by Nicholas Stone, 1641.

Many well-known people are buried either in the church or in the churchyard—they include William Caxton, 1491, John Skelton, poet laureate, 1529, Nicholas Udall, school-master and dramatist, 1556, Sir Walter Raleigh, 1618, Admiral Blake, 1661, John Pym, parliamentarian, 1661, and Wenceslaus Hollar, engraver, 1677.

Monuments   There are many; e.g. Cornelius Vandan, 1577. Mary, Lady Dudley, 1600. Sir Thomas Seymour, 1600, and Esabel, 1619. Dorothy, wife of Sir William Stafford, 1604. Hugh Haughton, 1616, and Elizabeth his daughter, 1615. Sir Francis Egioke, 1622. Mrs Mary Brocas, 1654. James Palmer, B.D., 1660. Robert Stewart, 1714 (designed by Gibbs).

St Paul's, Covent Garden (139)

The 4th Earl of Bedford obtained a licence in 1630 to take down some old buildings, and erect new ones. He laid out Covent Garden, with houses to the north and east and the church to the west. Inigo Jones designed the church, which was begun in 1631, and conse-crated by Bishop Juxon on 7 September 1638. As a writer in the *Gentleman's Magazine* said in 1812, it created both in plan and in elevation a revolution in the established Christian mode of architecture. It was the first Classical church to be built in England—and the last for a good many years. It is very simple—'the handsomest barn in England'—with brick walls, and a portico at the east of the Tuscan order (the real thing, not the simplified Doric order that often passes as Tuscan). The ceiling was painted by Matthew Good-rich.

A faculty was given on 1 February 1703 for a new altar piece: this was 'adorned with eight fluted columns painted in imitation of porphyry, of the Corinthian order, and an entablature painted white, and veined'.

The fabric was kept in very good repair in the eighteenth century. In 1788 the vestry decided to recover the roof, and to case the walls in Portland stone: this was done under Thomas Hardwick.

The church was burned down in 1795, and various surveyors were called in to examine the ruins. On 5 October Thomas Hardwick made a report: the walls had suffered little injury: the portico ought to be taken down: the pilasters might be repaired. His estimate, given on 22nd, was £10,300. After reconstruction, the church was reopened on 1 August 1798. The new altar piece had angels, by Banks, reclining on the pediment: these have been removed. The pulpit and desk were in front of the altar. In 1872 Butterfield removed the side galleries, and used their columns to make screens enclosing a choir. The altar piece was raised, and the pews were made into open seats. The walls and roof were re-decorated, and a new pavement was laid down.

In 1888 a faculty was sought, and given on 23 March, to alter the seats, to restore the organ to its original position in the west gallery: to restore the Commandments, etc., to where they were before, and generally to repair and renew the church.

Monuments   There are two by Flaxman: John Bellamy, 1794, and Edward Hall, 1798.

St Clement Danes, Strand (136)

The tower was rebuilt in 1669–70 by Joshua Marshall; in 1679 the church was examined by surveyors, who decided that it must be rebuilt. It was taken down in 1680, except for the tower, and the new church was completed in 1682, 'Sir Christopher Wren, his Majesties Surveyor, freely and generously bestowing his great Care and Skill towards the Contriving and building of it'. The masons were John Shorthose and Edward Pierce: Henry Pierson and John Greene did the carpenters' work, and the plasterer was Powell. It is the only church by Wren (except for St Paul's) that has an apse: it is joined to the main body by a quadrant bay.

The vestry agreed in 1719 that the tower should be raised by 25 feet, '& over the bells an ornamental steeple not less than 50 ffoot'. Townesend was to be the mason, and the design was by James Gibbs. The work was finished in 1720. The steeple is in three stages— like Wren, but showing signs of Gibbs's Roman studies: the first stage Ionic, the second (concave) Corinthian, and the third Composite.

The interior was sumptuously fitted up. In 1720 the vestry agreed that the columns should be fluted and the capitals gilded. A glory over the altar was to be painted by Kent, James Richards executed carving at the altar, and Kent painted a picture for £63. This picture was taken down in 1725, by order of the Bishop, as it was alleged that it contained a portrait of the Pretender's wife (St Cecilia), and some of her family (angels). The altar was of porphyry, on a wrought iron frame.

'The roof of the interior is camerated, and supported with neat wood columns, of the Corinthian order; plentifully enriched with fret-work, but especially the choir, with cherubims, palm branches, shields, &c. and six pilasters, of the Corinthian order. Here are also the arms of England, in fret-work, painted. It is well wainscoted, and the pillars cased up to the galleries, which extend round the church, except at the west end. On the fronts of the south galleries are carved and painted the arms of the dukes of *Norfolk* and the earls of *Arundel* and *Salisbury*, formerly inhabitants of the parish.' (David Hughson, *A History and Description of London, Westminster and Southwark*.)

Little harm was done in the nineteenth century. There was a repair and redecoration by H. and P. Currey in 1897–8, when the pews were lowered.

The interior, with all its furnishings, was destroyed in 1941. It was rebuilt after the War as a central church for the R.A.F. The architect was W. A. S. Lloyd, of the firm of

W. Curtis Green, Sons, and Lloyd: the plaster work of the ceiling was by Clark and Fenn of Clapham. Glass by Carl Edwards. The church was reopened on 19 October 1958. This has been a very successful reconstruction.

St James's, Piccadilly (137)

This church was designed by Sir Christopher Wren for a rapidly developing neighbour-hood, and built at the expense of Henry Jermyn, afterwards Earl of St Albans, and the principal inhabitants of the district. Wren's letter, written in 1708, when he was appointed a commissioner for the Fifty New Churches, and printed in *Parentalia*, has often been quoted. He said that churches should be large, but not too large: 'The *Romanists*, indeed, may build larger Churches, it is enough if they hear the Murmur of the Mass, and see the Elevation of the Host, but ours are to be fitted for Auditories. I can hardly think it practic-able to make a single Room so capacious, with Pews and Galleries, as to hold above 2,000 Persons, and all to hear the Service, and both to hear distinctly, and see the Preacher. I endeavoured to effect this, in building the Parish Church of *St James's*, *Westminster*, which, I presume, is the most capacious, with these Qualifications, that hath yet been built; and yet at a solemn Time, when the Church was much crowded, I could not discern from a Gallery that 2,000 were present. In this Church I mention, though very broad, and the middle Nave arched up, yet as there are no Walls of a second Order, nor Lanterns, nor Buttresses, but the whole Roof rests upon the Pillars, as do also the Galleries; I think it may be found beautiful and convenient, and as such, the cheapest of any Form I could invent.'

It is indeed most skilfully constructed; and it is the complete working out of Wren's idea of a two-storied church—which became the model for the typical Anglican town church of the eighteenth century.

The church was consecrated on 13 July 1684, but the steeple was not finished for some years afterwards. Sir Christopher planned a domed top, but the vestry preferred Edward Willcox's design for a spire. The spire was built, but cracks appeared in the tower, and in February 1686/7 Willcox was ordered to take it down again, and keep it in his yard. Wren did not think that the cracks were dangerous—but the spire was not put back. In 1696 it was still lying about, and it was coveted by St Anne's, Soho. It was finally re-erected in 1699.

The outside is plain, with brick walls, and quoins, windows, and doorways of Portland stone. The inside is stately, elegant, and sumptuous. The galleries rest on square piers: above are Corinthian columns, bearing entablatures which run towards the walls, and sup-port tunnel vaults, which penetrate the arched ceiling over the church. The plaster work was accurately renewed in 1837, after a survey by Sir Robert Smirke.

This was the church of a large and wealthy parish, and the greatest care was taken over the fittings. The altar piece was carved by Grinling Gibbons. On 7 December 1684 John Evelyn paid a visit. 'I went to see the new church at St James's, elegantly built; the altar was especially adorn'd, the white marble inclosure curiously and richly carved, the flowers and garlands about the walls by Mr Gibbons in wood; a pelican with her young at her breast, just over the altar in the carv'd compartment and border, invironing the purple velvet fring'd with I H S richly embroider'd . . . There was no altar anywhere in England, nor has there been any abroad, more handsomely adorn'd.' Evelyn should have known: he was a great traveller.

The font, which was given by an unknown donor, was also carved by Gibbons: the shaft is the Tree of Life, with the serpent: Adam and Eve stand by. On the bowl are the Ark, the baptism of Christ, and the baptism of the Ethiopian. The organ, by Renatus Harris, was made for the Roman Catholic Chapel at Whitehall, and given by Queen Mary in 1691.

By the middle of the nineteenth century, admiration of the church had waned: it could only be called 'decidedly good (of its sort), considered merely as an Italian building and without reference to its object'. It would have to be improved. In 1846 the east window was filled with glass by Wailes; and other glass was inserted later, until all the seventeenth-century glazing had disappeared. The tables of the Commandments, etc., and the carving between them, were removed to make room for a painting of the Last Supper by Daniel Bell; and there were other alterations and well-meaning embellishments.

In 1937 the church was renovated by Sir Reginald Blomfield and Sir Albert Richardson, who tried to remove nineteenth-century enrichments, and restore it to what it had been. The glass was relieved of its borders, and releaded. The entrance to the church-yard was partly rebuilt, and Blomfield designed new gates of wrought iron. In 1940 the church was wrecked by bombing, but it was faithfully reconstructed by Sir Albert Richardson.

Monuments Henry Sidney, Earl of Rumney, etc., 1704, by W. Woodman. Lord Huntington, 1704, by Francis Bird. James Dodsley, 1797, by Flaxman.

St Anne's, Soho

In 1685, after the foundations had been laid, and the building had advanced above the ground, an Act was passed to enable the inhabitants to finish the church. It was conse-crated on 21 March 1685/6. The design was made by Wren. A steeple was added from designs by William Talman in 1714.

The church was bombed in 1940, and the remains were pulled down in 1953. All that was left was the tower. Talman's tower was taken down in 1801, and the new one was designed by S. P. Cockerell. It is well known for its unusual top, in the shape of two intersecting barrels, with the faces of the clock on the four sides. Plans for rebuilding have been made by Ahrends, Burton and Koralek.

St Mary Le Strand

The old church was pulled down in 1549 by Protector Somerset, who promised to remunerate the parish, but never did.

In 1711 the parishoners made an appeal to the Commons. Since the demolition of their church, they had been allowed to use the Savoy Chapel; but it was too small, and they were liable to be excluded. The Commissioners decided that a new church should be one of the Fifty.

James Gibbs was appointed surveyor to the Commissioners in 1713, and he made the plans for the church—the first that the Commissioners had erected, and the first building that Gibbs is known to have designed. It was decided that, instead of a steeple, a column with a statue of Queen Anne should stand in front of the church. Then the Queen died, and 'there was an end of the column, and everything belonging to it'. Gibbs designed a steeple instead, after the church had been begun. In 1715 he was dismissed from the surveyorship; as a Tory protégé, a Papist, and a Scotsman, he was not acceptable in the new reign.

The church was finished in 1717, and consecrated on 1 January 1723: the cost was £16,341. The masons were William and John Townesend: the carpenters were Robert Jelfe, John James, J. Grove and John Meard: the plasterers were Chrysostom and John Wilkins.

The church, being on an island site, and visible from all round, was designed with great care, and the Commissioners 'spared no cost to beautify it'. The apse, and the two-storied elevations, recall St Paul's, and the steeple derives from Wren's City churches: but the details show that Gibbs had been trained in Rome, as Wren had not. Taste soon changed: Baroque went out of fashion, and St Mary's was not approved of in the later eighteenth century.

As Gibbs wrote, 'it consists of two orders, in the upper of which the lights are placed: the wall of the lower being solid, to keep out the noises from the street, is adorned with niches'. The steeple, which had to be fitted in as an afterthought, is oblong instead of square. It must be one of the best-known steeples of London, both from its conspicuous position, and also from its appearance on the cover of the *Strand Magazine*.

The interior, of course, reproduces the two stages of the outside, with Corinthian pilasters on the side walls, and twin Corinthian columns at the sides of the chancel arch. This is surmounted by a pediment containing the Hanoverian arms: but, in spite of them, this is one of the least Anglican-looking of eighteenth-century churches. It is said to have been the only church in London without the Commandments over the altar.

The design of the ceiling, with its plasterwork, is derived from Roman examples. The pulpit, which had been on the south side, was removed to the east in 1795.

In 1871 there was a rearrangement by R. J. Withers, an architect who could not have had much sympathy with the church. But no great harm was done—though the seats are not worthy of the building; and some that was done has been put right.

St George's, Hanover Square (140)

One of the Fifty New Churches, begun in 1713, and consecrated on 18 March 1724/5. The architect was John James, who had not succeeded in getting himself appointed a surveyor to the Commissioners when the church was begun, but was chosen to succeed Gibbs in 1715. The masons were John Fletcher and Christopher Cass: the carpenter was John Meard, the plasterer Isaac Mansfield, and the carver John How.

James was a careful and conscientious architect, who attempted no high flights: he believed that 'the Beautys of Architecture may consist with the greatest plainness of the Structure'. St George's is a solid stone church, with a tower in the west bay: the vestibules have pediments to the north and south. The tower is of a Wren type, surmounted by a dome, and not carried up into a fanciful steeple. In front of the church is a Corinthian portico, the first portico in any London church: there was to have been a statue of George I on the top. Hanover Square—as its name, and the dedication of the church, suggest— was Whig in its politics, and presumably in its churchmanship.

The interior is of the St James's, Piccadilly, type, with a segmental ceiling: handsome and dignified, but without much originality. The altar piece has canted ends, with pairs of Corinthian columns: the painting is ascribed to Kent.

As soon as the church was consecrated, alterations were begun: in 1725 the vestry ordered Benjamin Timbrell to make a churchwarden's pew and a christening pew, and Timbrell and Phillips to make benches for the poor. The organ was rebuilt by Snetzler in 1760. There were repairs in 1801 and 1807.

The glass in the east window, a Tree of Jesse, came from Belgium, and is attributed to Arnold van Nijmegen. It was adapted and inserted by Thomas Willement about 1843.

In 1871 the interior was decorated by Benjamin Ferrey, who reduced the height of the pews and of the pulpit, removed the pulpit canopy, and cut down the desk. The lower windows were enlarged. There was further work by Sir A. W. Blomfield in 1894. Screens and stalls are by Sir Reginald Blomfield.

St John's, Smith Square

This church must be mentioned, though it will never again be used for worship.

It was one of the Fifty New Churches, consecrated on 20 June 1728. Thomas Archer was the architect, and it has one of the finest of baroque exteriors. The east and west porticoes have a pediment with a gap at the top, and the centre filled with an arch supporting a little pediment of its own. The angles of the cross are filled with four towers. The church was burned in 1742, and the interior was reconstructed by James Horne, without its pillars.

It was burned out in the raids on London, and left a shell. In the years after the War, several suggestions were made as to what might be done with it.

Its place has been taken by ST JOHN'S, CAUSTON ROAD, built in 1957–8 from the designs of Alban Caröe and Partners, a small church over a hall. Owing to lack of space, the font is opposite the pulpit, and its cover acts as a lectern. The figure of Christ on the east wall is by Harry Phillips. Cross and candlesticks came from the old St John's.

St Martin in the Fields (138)

The tower of the old church was rebuilt in 1663–8 'according to ye moddell & Estimate last brought in by Cap Ryder': the mason's work was surveyed by Edward Marshall in 1668. On 5 February 1717, the vestry agreed that a petition should be prepared to be presented to Parliament for the rebuilding of the church. On 5 January 1719 it was resolved that John James and James Gibbs should make plans for a new church.

The first meeting of the commissioners appointed under the Act of Parliament was on 23 June 1720: on 6 July they inspected plans and estimates, and on 17 August they visited several of Wren's churches. On 14 September Gibbs was appointed surveyor.

He first made two designs for a circular church: the plans were published in the *Book of Architecture*, 1728, which also has his alternative designs for the steeple. But the commissioners rejected these, on the ground of expense, and he made the present design, which was accepted on 23 May 1721. A model was to be made.

On 4 August Christopher Cass was chosen as mason. On 31 October it was agreed that 'the Windows Expressed on the South Side of the Modell being the Rusticated Windows on a plain Ground should be the Form of Window to be used for the Church'. The steeple was to be carried up higher. By the end of 1724 the church was ready for its interior decorations. The consecration was on 20 October 1726.

The total cost was £33,661, 'notwithstanding the great Oeconomy of the Commissioners'. Payments were made, among others, to Messrs Witt and Messrs Sledge, bricklayers, Messrs Courtney, smiths, Timbrell and Phillips, carpenters, Griffiths, joiner, Bagutti, fretworker, Bridgwater, carver, Wilkins, plasterer, and Goff, smith.

In 1758 temporary pews were put in the body of the church: it was decided in 1799 to erect permanent seating.

The usual alterations were made in the nineteenth century: a choir was formed, the pews were cut down, and the east end was redecorated. Alterations were made by Blomfield in 1887. Much stained glass was inserted: east window, 1867, by Clayton and Bell; most of the rest by Lavers and Westlake. This has now gone.

The church is simple in plan: a rectangle divided into nave and aisles by Corinthian columns. At the west is the tower, with vestibules on each side containing the gallery staircases: these are emphasised on the north and south by pairs of recessed columns. The side walls have Corinthian pilasters. At the west is the magnificent portico. West of the sanctuary, the walls are canted, and have closet pews: vestries and gallery staircases are on each side. The elliptical barrel vault is decorated with plaster work by Artari and Bagutti: the royal arms are over the sanctuary arch.

St Martin's, with modifications, became the model for many large town churches in the eighteenth century and early nineteenth, and it was very soon imitated in America, and even in India. Gibbs has often been criticised for combining the steeple and the portico in the way that he did; but it is untrue to say that the steeple sits on top of the portico: it stands behind it. No doubt it set a bad precedent, but, as Malton wrote, it is 'the most successful attempt to unite the light and picturesque beauty of the modern steeple, to the sober grandeur and square solidity of the Grecian temple'.

The interior is too well known to require any further description. The font is from the older church, 1689, and the bust of Gibbs is by Rysbrack.

When Dick Sheppard was appointed vicar in 1914 the church was of no importance in the religious life of London: he soon made it famous, and it has kept its position ever since.

St Peter's, Eaton Square (141)

There is a great deal about the building of this church in the vestry minutes of St George's, Hanover Square. A committee was appointed in 1819, and plans by various architects were examined. In 1820 the Commissioners were asked to defray one-third of the cost. The surveyor was Fisher, but he fell ill and resigned, and Henry Hakewill was appointed instead. He made several drawings, and finally a design and estimate, which the Commissioners, early in 1822, rejected. He then made a Gothic design, 'in Imitation of St Mary's Church at Oxford', and in May the committee agreed to submit it to the Commissioners: if they did not like it, there was also a Grecian plan for them to consider. The Grecian plan was accepted by them. The foundation stone was laid on 7 September 1824, and the church was consecrated on 20 July 1827. The builder was William Herbert. The cost was £22,427, of which the Commissioners paid £5,556. There was a fire in December 1836, after which the church was restored by J. H. Hakewill, according to his father's designs.

It is a big, solid church, with a spacious Ionic portico, and the usual tower, on an attic, above. The interior was 'chaste and simple': its chief ornament was the altar piece—a painting of Christ crowned with thorns, by William Hilton, which was given by the British Institution in 1826.

In 1870 G. H. Wilkinson—afterwards Bishop of Truro and of St Andrew's—was appointed vicar, and began an extraordinary ministry: the church, although it seated 1,650, was crowded out: some of the congregation sat on camp-stools, and others had to stand. In 1873 a chancel was added by Blomfield, and in 1875 his plans for altering the nave were adopted: the church was reopened on 27 November. Blomfield reseated the area, inserted an arcade, and built a clerestory—though he managed to keep the original roof. The new work is Romanesque: Bumpus once calls it Byzantine, and once 'a sort of Auvergnat Romanesque'. The galleries had to be kept, but they were made light and ornamental. (Wilkinson built the daughter church of St John, Wilton Road, designed by Blomfield, and purchased the lease of St Peter's Chapel, Buckingham Gate, which was used as a mission church. But nothing could prevent St Peter's from being full.)

After the reconstruction, Hilton's picture was sold for £1,000. On 27 September 1904 a faculty was given to erect a screen and pulpit of wrought iron, and to form a chapel on the south. The sanctuary has good glass by Clayton and Bell: that on the north of the chancel is by Powell. The post-War glass in the nave was designed by John Hayward.

St Mark's, North Audley Street (142)

On 27 February 1824 a committee of the vestry of St George's, Hanover Square, inspected plans for a new church, and chose six—those of Gandy, Donthorne, Inwood, Porden, Lloyd, and Thomas and Mead. On 12 April they made a short list of two—Donthorne and Gandy; and finally Gandy was chosen as architect. This was John Peter Gandy, a pupil of Wyatt, who on inheriting a property in 1828 took the name of Deering, and eventually gave up architecture altogether. The foundation stone was laid on 7 September 1825; the consecration was on 25 April 1828. The cost was £13,299, of which the Commissioners contributed £5,556.

The front of the church, which stands between houses, has a portico of two Erechtheion Ionic columns *in antis*, with a straight entablature, and a turret above. The doorway leads into a vestibule divided into aisles by four *antae* (if the word can be used of a detached pier: some writers allow it, and others do not). Gandy was an architect of considerable scholarship, and his Greek detail is good. Gilbert Scott said of the vestibule that it ought not to be touched—nor has it been. But the church, in 1878, underwent at the hands of Blomfield the same treatment as St Peter's, Eaton Square. New choirstalls were erected in 1914.

The east window is by Lavers, Barraud, and Westlake, who also painted the reredos. The east window of the un-reconstructed church was of lilac colour, with borders of honeysuckle.

St Paul's, Wilton Place, Knightsbridge

This very large church was built in 1840–3, from designs by Thomas Cundy, surveyor to Lord Grosvenor's estates. It is of brick, in the Perpendicular style: a 'vast be-galleried hall'. The gallery stairs are in the west bay, not in the usual chambers by the tower, which has an open basement. The tower originally had pinnacles: the parapet is by Bodley. There was a small chancel, with a reredos composed of niches. When the *Ecclesiologist* described the church, there was a 'long and narrow peninsula' projecting into the nave, with prayer desk and lectern. The church was 'a remarkable and gratifying *fact*, but at the same time quite unserviceable in all respects as a model for future church builders'.

It was gratifying to the ecclesiologists because the first vicar, W. J. E. Bennett, was a High Churchman, and there were lights and flowers on the altar, and a surpliced choir, and the prayers were intoned and the psalms were sung. Bennett resigned in 1851, tired out with rebukes by Bishop Blomfield, and went to Frome, where he restored the church, and created the Catholic tradition that remains to this day. At St Paul's, the choir was dispersed, and the credence, lectern, and candlesticks were removed. But after the agitations of the '50s, the church recovered itself, and continued in peace.

At the beginning, the windows were glazed with 'a sort of opaque golden coloured glass': a good many windows by Wailes were afterwards introduced. A faculty of 21 January 1858 confirmed the erection of ten windows, and authorised the erection of six more.

R. J. Withers took the church in hand in 1870. The faculty (21 August) specifies the work: to remove the organ, and the staircases of the west gallery; complete the tower arch, and open the tower to the church; build a new vestry, which would contain the organ; make a new window on the south of the chancel; place new chancel steps, floor, and choir seats; and replace part of the reredos in stone, alabaster, or mosaic. The lower part of the walls was decorated in the '70s.

A faculty of 25 November 1889 gave leave to take down the vestry and porch on the south side of the chancel, and build a chapel instead: also to reseat the church, and insert a new east window.

29 September 1891: a faculty to extend the chancel further to the east, and erect a new screen. For these two schemes, and for the new vestries, Bodley was the architect.

There is a good east window, of the Tree of Jesse, by Lavers and Westlake, who also did the glass in the south chapel. The sedilia and panelling are a memorial to Henry Montagu Villiers, priest, 1837–1908: there are paintings of Anglican divines, mostly nineteenth-century.

Monuments   A brass to Walter Sarel, 1873–1941, 'who did much to beautify this church as architect 1933–1940'.

St Michael's, Chester Square

The Marquis of Westminster laid the foundation stone on 20 May 1844, and largely contributed to the building. The church was consecrated on 2 April 1846. The architect was Thomas Cundy. The style is Middle-Pointed. An aisled nave of two bays only, and tower and spire beyond the north aisle; very wide transepts, and a short chancel. 'An attempt—but happily a most unsuccessful one—to find a 'protestant' development of the Christian styles' (*Ecclesiologist*). The exterior has a large number of rather aimless gables. The church was enlarged and improved in 1874: 'the spire was brought into better proportion with the rest of the structure than it had been before.'

A faculty was given on 19 February 1910 to erect a reredos of alabaster, and decorate the chancel walls; move the stalls westward; pave the chancel with marble, and renew the holy table.

In 1920–1 a War memorial chapel was added to the east of the north transept, from designs by Sir Giles Scott, in his characteristic Gothic style. A new reredos was installed in 1922. Two windows are by Morris, 1882: the west window is by Hugh Easton, 1951.

St Barnabas', Pimlico (145)

There was a bad patch in the parish of St Paul's, Knightsbridge, and Bennett appealed to his wealthy congregation for funds to build a church in the middle of it, with schools, and a house for a college of priests. The design was made by Thomas Cundy, with Bennett's suggestions, and with help, it is said, from Butterfield: certainly it was in a more correct Gothic than he had so far produced. The foundation stone of the schools was laid within a few weeks of the appeal, and the clergy house was begun in the autumn. The foundation stone of the church was laid on 11 June 1847, and it was consecrated on the same day in 1850.

The buildings are of ragstone, in First-Pointed style. The church has nave and chancel with aisles, a south porch, and a tower and spire at the west of the north aisle. The *Ecclesiologist* thought that it was too little like a town church, and that too much had been attempted at the west end: otherwise it was most satisfactory—'the most complete and sumptuous church dedicated since the revival'. The arrangements were all that they should be: there was a screen with a cross, a sanctuary rising on three steps of Purbeck marble, and the altar on a footpace, with silver cross and candlesticks. The glass was by Wailes: some of this has been superseded, which is a pity, as it exactly suits the church. Sir F. A. Gore Ouseley, the clerical musician, who was on the staff, gave the organ and paid for the choir: Mattins and Evensong were sung daily.

Bishop Blomfield—who was a well-meaning and energetic man, but an old-fashioned Churchman, who was not in sympathy with the new ideals of worship—found fault with the ceremonial. Unfortunately, 1850 was the year in which the Pope issued his bull establishing the Roman hierarchy in England. There was a general No-Popery scare, and the ritualists were considered to be in league with the Pope. There was a great outcry about ritualism, and Lord John Russell, the Prime Minister, wrote to the Bishop of Durham about the martyrs of the Reformation and the mummeries of superstition. There were riots at St Barnabas', and Lord Shaftesbury did not help matters by proclaiming that he 'would rather worship with Lydia on the banks of the river than with a hundred surpliced priests in the gorgeous temple of St Barnabas' (Acts xvi).

'Lydian worship' became a term of ecclesiastical slang for a while. Churchmen were much amused when someone remembered that Lord John Russell had written, some years before, a novel called *The Nun of Arrouca*, in which a young soldier, Edward Pembroke, visits a convent in Portugal, and falls in love with a novice, Miss Catherine. He makes off with her, and sits beside her—*close to a river*. 'Catherine leaned towards him, her soul seemed to melt at his voice; by an impulse of the moment he moved towards her, and their lips met.' The *Ecclesiologist* was much gratified: now, it said, we know what Lydian worship really means!

St Barnabas' was further adorned in the later nineteenth century, and the early twentieth. The large reredos is by Bodley and Garner, 1893, the Lady chapel by Comper, 1900, baptistery by Frederick Hunt, 1902, screen by Bodley, 1906, and new east window glass by Comper, 1953.

St Stephen's, Rochester Row (144)

The Baroness Burdett Coutts used her wealth generously, though not always very wisely, in good works; and this church was built and endowed by her as a memorial to her father. She laid the foundation stone in 1847, and the church was consecrated in 1850. Her architect was Benjamin Ferrey, whose churches, wherever they may be, are of much the same type: this was said at the time to have too much of the look of a country church. But it was highly praised for its correctness: it was a witness to true principles, the value of which it would be difficult to overestimate.

St Stephen's is built of Bargate ragstone from Godalming, with quoins and dressings of Morpeth sandstone: Caen stone is used inside. It is in the flowing Middle-Pointed style which, in the '40s, was regarded as the highest development of Gothic. Its details and furnishings were, in general, approved by the *Ecclesiologist*. The carving of the capitals was done by G. P. White, of Vauxhall Road, who afterwards worked at the cathedrals of Wells, Rochester, and Salisbury. The windows were filled with glass by Wailes, or with Powell's stamped quarries. Almost all the glass was lost in the War, but two windows by Wailes survive, and there is one by Burne-Jones.

The interior has had the usual post-War treatment.

By order in council, no one was to be buried in the church, except Miss Coutts and Mrs Brown, who were to be embedded in a layer of powdered charcoal, and entombed in brickwork well cemented. But William Brown, 1855, to whom there is a very large Gothic monument by G. G. Adams, was, as his epitaph says, buried in the chancel. The Baroness found a resting-place in the Abbey.

All Saints', Ennismore Gardens

Designed by Lewis Vulliamy, and built in 1848–9. It is a large Italianate church, somewhat of the Wilton type, but much plainer and cheaper, with very tall iron columns, and very plain aisle windows with ground glass. The original decorations were by Owen Jones. The tower was built afterwards, in the '70s.

Later in the century there was a large scheme of embellishment: decoration in sgraffitto work by Heywood Sumner, new vestries, the formation of a chancel, moving of the organ, new seating, and new west end. This was spread over a number of years: the west end, by C. Harrison Townsend, was 1892. In 1911 the apse was decorated by Derwent Wood, A.R.A. The organ case and screen, 1920, by Joubert, were completed in 1928.

When Canon Anthony Deane was vicar early in this century, he found that there were many distinguished parishioners, but that they all had country houses, and went away at week ends: most of the congregation came from outside. The attempt to keep the church going has now been given up, and it has been lent to the Russians.

St Matthew's, Great Peter Street

Designed by Scott, and built in 1849–51 in what used to be a bad slum. The foundation stone was laid on 8 November 1849, and the consecration was on 30 June 1851. The builder was George Myers.

The site was of so difficult a shape that it was thought that the church could not be orientated. However, Scott fitted it in, and the space to the south was used by adding an extra south aisle, and a tower serving as a porch. The church is Middle-Pointed, built of Kentish rag. The tower was never completed, but its massive base looks more impressive, probably, than the completed design would have done.

A faculty was given on 14 July 1869 to remodel the choir seats and remove the gallery.

The next faculty given for this church was dated 22 August 1891: to build a vestry on the south of the chancel, with a chapel over it; the chapel to be connected by a door to the new clergy house. Comper was the architect for this.

The ironwork screen, and rood and loft, are by Bodley, 1893. The south aisle altar by Martin Travers, 1928: the crucifix above the Trevelyan memorial altar carved by Alan Howes, 1951.

St Gabriel's, Warwick Square

The foundation stone was laid on 7 February 1852, and the consecration was on 12 May 1853. The architect was Thomas Cundy. The church both surprised and pleased the ecclesiologists, who had not expected much of a church designed by Cundy, and built by a committee: but it had—thanks to the incumbent—turned out to be a graceful Middle-Pointed structure, with a well-proportioned chancel, sufficient roofs, and a tower and spire. There were galleries, but also a pretty pulpit and a graceful font. The church was greatly enlarged in 1897 by Baker and Turrill, who added outer aisles and a west porch.

A faculty was given on 30 July 1889 for a new altar, with a painted front, on a plinth of marble. This was designed by J. F. Bentley.

Another faculty, 19 August 1897, gave leave to erect a reredos, and sides to the reredos of alabaster, with four figures in *opus sectile* and inlay; to line the walls of the chancel with alabaster, and relay the floor with marble; to erect oak sedilia; to transfer the existing reredos to the south chapel; and to erect a screen between the chancel and the south aisle. The mosaic, etc. is by Powell.

The east window, and the south window of the sanctuary, are by Kempe.

St James The Less, Thorndike Street, (formerly Garden Street) (146)

This church was built in 1860–1, at the cost of the Misses Monk, in memory of their father James Henry Monk, Bishop of Gloucester 1830, and of Gloucester and Bristol 1836–56.

144 St Stephen's, Rochester Row, 1847–50
by Benjamin Ferrey

145 St Barnabas', Pimlico, 1847–50
by Thomas Cundy

146 St James the Less, Thorndike Street, 1860–1
by G. E. Street

147 Holy Trinity, Prince Consort Road, 1902–3
by G. F. Bodley

148 St Mary's, Battersea Church Road, 1775–7
by Joseph Dixon

149 The Ascension, Lavender Hill, begun 1876
by James Brooks, completed by
J. T. Micklethwaite 1883

150 St Mark's, Battersea Rise, 1873–4
by William White

151 St Luke's, Ramsden Road, by F. W. Hunt,
begun 1883, completed 1899

It was G. E. Street's first work in London. Street had been travelling in Italy, and the design is influenced by Italian Gothic. But, as his son wrote: 'what is Italian has become so entirely absorbed in what belongs to the architect's own inspiration, that it is hard to put the finger on any actual features which recall Italian examples, the influence being traceable rather in the choice and management of materials, and the general massing of the block of buildings, than in any more specific points.' That is true: the church is not really a copy of anything: it is a nineteenth-century English church designed by Street.

Church and schools form a group together: at the east is a low wall with ironwork. The walls are of red and black brick, and the roofs of slate. The church consists of nave and aisles, and apsidal chancel with aisles treated as transepts. At the north-west is a detached tower, connected with the church by a cloister. The lowest stage is open on three sides: the fourth side has the tower staircase. The belfry stage has two large trefoil-headed windows on each side, with a central marble shaft and a canopy of brick: there is a projecting cornice, with a good deal of elaboration of brickwork, and a short spire with four spirelets at the angles—'a combination of Italian and Rhenish types'. Eastlake commented that if Street had never designed anything else, this tower would be sufficient to proclaim him an artist. 'In form, proportion of parts, decorative detail, and use of colour, it seems to leave little to be desired.'

The interior is extremely fine, and has fortunately not been touched by the reformers who whitewash brick walls and remove backgrounds from windows in order to let in light. The polychrome walls, polished granite pillars (with capitals carved with parables and miracles), glass by Clayton and Bell (and one clerestory window by Powell), the painting over the chancel arch—a 'modified Doom', by G. F. Watts; the paintings on the nave roof, by Clayton and Bell; the brick vaulting of the chancel and apse, the ironwork on the chancel wall, and the inlaid reredos . . . everything combines to make a wonderful ensemble, glowing with colour. I have never seen it early in the morning; but it looks lovely on a winter afternoon, at about the time that the children are coming out of school.

The *Ecclesiologist* very much approved of the church, but it criticised the 'barbaric bulk' of the pillars, and hoped that they would not be clumsily reproduced by other architects (as, of course, they were). The question had been raised whether it was necessary to have aisles at all: if pillars were to be made so low, and so stout, the opposition would be strengthened. 'Say what we will, the nineteenth is not the ninth or the eleventh century.'

That is a reasonable criticism, and Street himself realised that it was desirable that the congregation should be kept together, and able to see the altar: in some of his churches he provided a wide nave, and only passage aisles. But there are always some people who like to be hidden—whether they ought to like it or not. And an aisle of St James's would be a very good place to pray in.

St Saviour's, St George's Square

Another Middle-Pointed church by Thomas Cundy, of Kentish rag, with a rather weak tower and spire on the north. Foundation stone 20 June 1863, consecration 16 July 1864. The cost was £12,000.

The galleries were taken down in 1882, when a faculty (8 June) was given to erect a reredos, arcading round the chancel, and new steps; and to carve the capitals of the pillars, the label terminations of the arches, and the corbels supporting the roof of the nave. The altar in the side chapel is 1889; the pulpit and screen 1913.

The north vestry was added in 1913–14 by Nicholson and Corlette, who also designed the canopy of the altar in the chapel. The east window is by Clayton and Bell, as also are a few others elsewhere in the church.

Christchurch, Down Street, Mayfair (143)

Designed by F. and H. Francis, consecrated on 27 March 1865, and enlarged in 1868. It is Middle-Pointed, with brick inside walls: nave, no chancel, and a large transept: the site was provided by the demolition of two houses in streets standing at right angles. The church was much rebuilt after a fire in 1906, when the gallery was erected, the architect being R. L. Hesketh. There is an elaborate reredos to the memory of Thomas Henry Hope, of Deepdene: of Caen stone, with Devonshire marble shafts. Panels of the Acts of Mercy above the altar. It was executed by F. G. Anstey, who also carved the font.

All Saints', Grosvenor Road

A chapel of ease to St Saviour's, but of parish church dimensions. The church has new flats to the north of it, and the road and the river to the south, and looks rather lonely.

It was begun in 1869, and consecrated on 31 November 1871. The architect was Thomas Cundy III, the son of the Thomas who designed the other Westminster churches: he was born in 1820, and took over his father's practice, and the surveyorship of Lord Grosvenor's London estates. It was closed in 1940, damaged by bombs in 1941 and 1944, and rededicated after restoration on 31 October 1955. The church is of red brick, with bands of black: nave and aisles, with an almost-detached tower and spire at the south-west; apsidal chancel, south chapel, and north vestry. There are columns of polished granite with foliated capitals; the glass in the apse is by John Hayward, 1958.

St Mary's, Bourne Street

Built in 1873–4 as a chapel of ease to St Barnabas', Pimlico: it was afterwards given a parish. The architect was R. J. Withers, who, according to an obituary, built 'a good, cheap type of brick churches'. This is one of them. The cost was £4,500, and it is a good example of a nineteenth-century town church—like a small edition of one of Brooks's. It is of red brick, with a slated roof and flèche: a nave with low aisles and a round apse, the light coming from a tall clerestory which is continued round the east end. The extension on the north was designed by H. S. Goodhart-Rendel.

The church was fitted with altars, etc., at the time when baroque was regarded as the hall-mark of genuine Anglican Catholicism. The altar piece (by S. Gambier Parry) was remodelled, and other fittings were designed, by Martin Travers, about 1919.

Holy Trinity, Prince Consort Road (147)

This church preserves the dedication of Holy Trinity Chapel, Knightsbridge, an old chapel rebuilt in 1629, and again in 1699. In 1725 it was attached to St George's, Hanover Square, and in 1789 was enlarged; in 1861 it was rebuilt by Brandon and Eyton.

The new church, 1902–3, is on a different site. G. F. Bodley was the architect. It is of stone, and consists of a very lofty nave with aisles, and an additional aisle on the north to fit the site: the choir is in the east bay, with a chapel on the north and organ loft on the south. There is a projecting sanctuary, with vestries to the south and east.

The style is Bodley's fourteenth-century, with flowing tracery, and beautifully proportioned clustered columns. Everything fits in: the painted and gilded carved altar piece, coloured roofs, and Burlison and Grylls glass. Renovations were done in 1949.

CHURCHES SOUTH OF THE RIVER

Battersea

A pleasant riverside parish, which rebuilt its church in the eighteenth century. In the nineteenth, it was overrun with building, much of it of a cheap and poor kind. The population rose from 6,887 in 1851 to 24,615 in 1861.

John Erskine Clarke came to Battersea early in 1872, and remained vicar until 1909. He was an active parish priest, and has some claim to fame as being virtually the originator of parish magazines. He was an ardent believer in the erection of new churches and the subdivision of parishes. Four churches had already been built (or five, if St George's is counted, which was built before the main Victorian expansion). In Erskine Clarke's time, 12 more were added, and the parish church was restored. St George's, St John's, and St Andrew's have been demolished.

St Mary's, Battersea Church Road (148)

In 1771 the vestry agreed to build a new church. A report was made to the Commons on 15 March 1774: Richard Dixon said that the old church could not be repaired, and Joseph Dixon estimated the cost of rebuilding as £5,000. An Act was passed in May, and Joseph Dixon's plans were accepted: Richard was the builder. The first stone was laid on 10 July 1775, and the church was opened on 16 November 1777.

It is a plain, pleasant building of brick, with vaults beneath, and a low tower, with the copper spire that looks so well from the other side of the river. Work was done in 1876–8 by Blomfield—who described the church as 'well and solidly built, without show produced by false economy in essentials'. He formed a choir, provided new seating, etc.

The east window has seventeenth-century glass, preserved at the rebuilding: 'The Stone Work of the Gothic window with the painted glass in ditto that is now over the Communion Table in the Old Church is to be carefully taken down and re-set over the Communion Table of the New Church.' There is no record of its erection, but it is thought to have been given by Sir John St John, probably in 1631 or 1632, and the painter was perhaps Bernard van Linge. It contains the Stuart royal arms, and the arms of Oliver St John, Viscount Grandison and Baron Tregoze, and of Sir John St John. There are also portraits of Margaret Beauchamp, Henry VII, and Elizabeth I.

The glass in the round windows in the sanctuary—the Lamb and the Dove—was painted by James Pearson in 1796. The sanctuary once had painted crimson curtains, trimmed with amber, and held up by gold cord with heavy tassels.

Monuments   Sir Oliver St John, and Joan, 1630, by Nicholas Stone. Sir Edward Wynter, 1685/6, with a rhymed epitaph recording his feats: 'Alone, unarm'd a Tygre He oppress't:/And crushed to death yᵉ Monster of a Beast:/Thrice-twenty mounted Moors he overthrew', etc. Sir John Fleet, Lord Mayor, 1712. James Bull, 1713. Martha Hale, 1763, and Charles, 1739. Holles St John, 1738. Henry St John, Viscount Bolingbroke, 1751, and Mary Clara, 1750, by Roubiliac. John Camden, 1780, and his daughter Elizabeth Neild, 1791, by Coade.

St Paul's, St John's Hill

Built in 1868 for the Rev Dr Thompson, at a cost of about £6,300. The architect was H. E. Coe. It is much like his other churches. The walls are faced with Kentish rag. At the southwest is a tower, which turns octagonal, and is crowned by a spire. A wide nave, with aisles and transepts: there is no chancel, only an apsidal sanctuary. Polished granite pillars, with stiff-leaf capitals and square abaci: but, as so often in churches of this kind, the windows have Decorated tracery. The roof has hammer-beams and scissor-beams alternately.

The windows were broken on 17 June 1944. There are new west windows, and one in the south transept, by Carl J. Edwards, 1954. A window in the north transept by W. M. Geddes was made by C. F. Blakeman in 1956.

St Saviour's, Battersea Park Road

A roadside church, sited so that the front faces north, towards the road: behind it a whole area is being demolished and blocks of flats are being built. The ground was bought in 1868, and the architect was E. C. Robins—though Goodhart-Rendel says that the design was, in fact, made by G. Freeth Roper. The builders were Lathey Bros, of New Road. The foundation stone was laid on 4 January 1870, and the church was consecrated on 19 October 1871. The cost was £4,400.

A faculty was given 17 February 1896 to build a new vestry on the south of the chancel, and convert the old north vestry into an organ chamber; a new pulpit and stalls were also erected.

The church is of Kentish rag and Bath stone, with slated roofs and a spirelet: the style is French thirteenth-century. It is like many others, but has the advantage of being of a reasonable size. In 1930 there were repairs, and the choir stalls were removed from the very short chancel into the eastern bay of the nave.

The east window is by Ion Pace; two others are by Curtis, Ward and Hughes.

St Philip's, Queenstown Road

The site was given by Philip W. Flower; the design was made by J. T. Knowles, but a committee of six was consulted, including Street and Scott. Work was begun in 1869, and the church was consecrated on 13 July 1870. The cost was about £13,000. There was to have been a tall spire, but this was never built. The church is of Kentish rag, in early and later Middle-Pointed style: nave and aisles, with a low tower at what would be the south-west if the church was orientated. One of the transepts is an organ chamber, and the other a vestry; there is an apsidal chancel. The interior is almost exactly like Gilbert Scott's work, with its lavishly carved foliage, and apse with geometrical tracery. Many of the fittings were given by the Flower family. The glass was broken in the War: the east windows are 1954, by T. D. Randall of Faithcraft.

St Mark's, Battersea Rise (150)

A temporary church was built in 1868. The designs for the permanent building were made by William White: this was his first church in Battersea. He was an architect who did not waste money, and who obviously thought carefully about each church: he did not have, as some did, a stock design which he produced for all occasions.

St Mark's is built on clay, on a slope, and, for security, is of concrete, with a brick skin. The builder was T. Gregory of Battersea: the foundation stone was laid on 11 November 1873. The chancel is built over a large vaulted undercroft: this had, at first, only one central pillar, but the floor above it gave way, and it had to be constructed with more. The pillars in the nave were of brick, but before the centering was removed from the arches, it was decided that stone would be stronger and more dignified—so stone columns were carved and inserted. The consecration was on 30 September 1874, and the cost was only about £5,000, of which the I.C.B.S. gave £800.

The church consists of nave and aisles, with a west porch, and south-west tower with a wooden top and shingled spire: the clerestory is rather tall, with two-light windows. The chancel has a north aisle and south transept, and the sanctuary is apsidal, with an ambulatory round. This part of the church has short brick pillars, with naturalistic capitals.

The design of the tiles in the sanctuary was made by J. R. Clayton: there are similar tiles in Lichfield Cathedral. The pulpit came from the temporary church: the font, of Devonshire marble, with stones from the Jordan embedded in it, was given by the children.

W. H. Randoll Blacking proposed to whiten the whole church. This was fortunately not done; but he repaired it and designed the new altar (1928).

St Peter's, Plough Road

The temporary church, afterwards a school, was opened in 1874. George Cubitt promised £5,000 for a permanent building, and the foundation stone was laid on St Peter's day, 1875: the consecration was exactly a year later.

This is one of White's simple brick churches. The builder was Carter. A rather wide and short nave has aisles, and an apse at the west: there is only one window in the aisles, and the light comes from the clerestory, which is carried round the western apse as well. There is no chancel arch, and the chancel is of one bay only: on the south, organ chamber and vestry lead to an otherwise detached tower, with gabled spire—large in proportion to the rest of the church. This was completed in 1911.

The glass in the eastern triplet is by Heaton, Butler and Bayne; east of the north chapel, by Clayton and Bell; north of the chapel, by Tower.

The Ascension, Lavender Hill (149)

This big, brick church, impressively placed on the hill, was designed by James Brooks: the foundation stone was laid on 1 June 1876. The builder was Chessam of Shoreditch. Brooks's supervision was not thought to be satisfactory. The work was taken out of his hands, and the church was finished by J. T. Micklethwaite, and consecrated on 29 June 1883.

It is a simple and very impressive design: a tall nave and chancel, with a round apse, under one long, unbroken slate roof; and a low aisle, carried round the east end. A chapel to the north, and large vestries at the north-east, built on the slope of the hill. The tower, as usual, was never built.

The arcades are rather low, and there is a clerestory of lancets. The screen was erected in 1914, and the rood and loft by George Wallace in 1910. The glass is by Kempe and Tower.

All Saints', Prince of Wales Road

All Saints' is a large, dark red brick church, just south of Battersea Park. It has an unusually informative foundation stone. The church was built in memory of John Sutton Utterton, Suffragan Bishop of Guildford, who died while he was ministering at the altar, at All Saints', Ryde, on St Thomas's day, 1879. The stone was laid by his wife Eleanor on St Thomas's day, 1882, and the church was consecrated in 1883. The architect was F. W. Hunt.

It is in the Lancet style, with a rather unusual plan: nave and aisles, and transepts—the north of very slight projection, and the south of none—with the arcades carried past them. The tower is to the east of them, over the chancel, with a chapel to the north, and organ chamber and vestry to the south. The apsidal sanctuary has a reredos erected in 1911: its walls have been whitened, and there is post-War glass. The chapel reredos and screen are by W. Ellery Anderson, 1912.

St Michael's, Chatham Road

Built as a memorial to the Rev H. B. Verdon, curate of Battersea, who died in 1879; and to Philip Cazenove. The design was by White, and it was consecrated on 10 September 1881. A cheap church: the cost was £4,500, all given by the friends of Verdon and Cazenove.

The material is brick. The nave has wide aisles, under separate gables: the arcades are very light, with brick arches on pillars of granolith (granite chips and Portland cement). The nave and south aisle have dormer windows. The apsidal chancel, above an undercroft, has aisles. The roof principals are of planks bolted together, and plenty of iron is used. 'Everything very honest and thoughtful' (Goodhart-Rendel). A faculty for a chancel screen 1905, by Charles E. Howes.

There is some glass by Lavers, Barraud and Westlake. The sanctuary panelling dates from 1917.

St Mary le Park, Albert Bridge Road

A fragment of a most ambitious church, opened in May 1883. The scheme, proposed in 1881, was to make this the parish church, instead of the old St Mary's—but nothing came of this, and the new church was made a chapel of ease. It eventually gained a parish. White's design included a large tower and spire on the north of the chancel. What was actually built was the east end: apse with ambulatory, chancel, south chancel aisle (apsidal, used as a chapel); north chancel aisle, used as a vestry, and north transept (added in 1903 by J. S. Quilter): and two bays of the nave, with north aisle, and a makeshift aisle on the south.

Notwithstanding the general feeling of unsuccessful accomplishment, and the fact that the church is very poorly fitted, it is without doubt an impressive interior. The best part is the sanctuary: the pillars are circular and solid: rather unexpectedly, the capitals have naturalistic foliage. (Why have the arches been painted bright red?) The arch at the west is a good deal lower than the roof, and there is quite an effect of space; there are similar arcades north and south of the chancel. The screen is of iron.

St Luke's, Ramsden Road (151)

The iron building that had been the temporary St Mark's, Battersea Rise, was moved here in 1874, and became the temporary St Luke's. The designs for the permanent church were made by F. W. Hunt, and the foundation stone was laid on St Luke's day, 1883. The east end was built, and the temporary church served as a nave until 1889, when the rest was added. The tower followed in 1892, and the church was consecrated in that year, on All Saints' day. The baptistery was built in 1899. The contractors were Messrs W. Johnson and Co.

The church is an Italian basilica, except that the arcades have pointed arches. The walls are of brick, and the columns of Pennant stone, with bases of red, and capitals of white Mansfield stone. Alabaster and marble pulpit (1890), chancel wall (1894), and lectern (1901) were the work of Farmer and Brindley. The pulpit, like the other furnishings, was designed by W. White. Pulpit canopy, sedilia, stalls and bishop's throne by Harry Hems. In 1902 the Powell mosaic in the apse was begun—the framing, and the central panel. In 1906 C. J. Brookes, one of the founders of the church, gave orders for its completion, and it was dedicated on 4 February 1907. The glass throughout the church is also by Powell.

A really striking feature of the church is the electric light fittings, of 1903—a date when no one was apologetic about elaborate electroliers. They are imposing pieces of metalwork, and are also edifying: those in the chancel have Fra Angelico angels, and the component words of a text, hung above them; and those in the nave have the names of Christian virtues.

The south chapel was fitted by Martin Travers.

St Stephen's, Battersea Park Road

Another church by White: the foundation stone was laid on 15 May 1886, and it was consecrated in 1887. The material is the usual stock brick, laced with red. The style is fourteenth-century—later than that which White generally used: but in a church like this, style is not of much importance. The church has roads on three sides of it, and there is not much space to spare—so it is quite small, and has low, windowless aisles. The small tower, with a broach spire, is at the east of the north aisle. The clerestory stage has some dignity, and there is a substantial king-post roof. The apsidal chancel is raised on an undercroft: there is a small south chapel. A 1914–18 War memorial screen. The altar and rails are by Martin Travers, 1936.

St Barnabas', North Side, Clapham Common

This church owed its origin to the overcrowding of St Matthew's, Rush Hill—a church by White, now demolished. The Ecclesiastical Commissioners examined St Matthew's, and said that it was a temporary building, and could not be consecrated unless it was reconstructed—which would have cost too much. The plans of St Barnabas' were made by W. Bassett Smith, and the foundation stone was laid on 12 June 1879: the consecration was on 18 November 1898.

The church is internally of yellow brick with stripes of red, and externally faced with ragstone. There is a pinnacled tower at the west of the south aisle. The style is Bassett Smith's usual flowing Decorated.

The reredos, of stone and alabaster, was carved by Thomas Rudge of Clapham Common. There is a two-light window, by Clayton and Bell, to the memory of the architect, who died on 5 July 1910, aged 80.

St Bartholomew's, Wycliffe Road

Work in this dreary district was begun by the Rev T. L. Goslett, who held services in a shop, and in various small rooms, and eventually succeeded in getting the church built. The foundation stone was laid on 1 November 1900, and the consecration was in 1901. G. H. Fellowes Prynne was the architect, and the builder was W. H. Lorden, of Tooting.

The church stands between two roads, with a proper entrance from neither. It is of stock brick, varied with red, with a tall nave and chancel of the same height.

Christchurch, Battersea Park Road

The original church, which was consecrated on 27 July 1849, was a cruciform Middle-Pointed building with a spire, designed by C. Lee and T. T. Bury. It was demolished by a rocket in 1944, and has been completely cleared away.

The new church was designed by Thomas F. Ford, and consecrated in 1959: it stands on the site of the nave and transepts of the former church, and there is a hall where the chancel used to be. The carving on the west front is by Philip Bentham. There is the usual mural by Hans Feibusch. The grisaille painting above the Lady chapel altar is by Augustus Lunn: the glass in the chapel is by A. E. Buss. The candlesticks were a gift from the Liebfrauen Church, Bremen.

St George's with St Andrew's, Patmore Street

This church, in the new Patmore Estate, takes the place of two nineteenth-century churches, now demolished. ST GEORGE'S, 1827–8, was designed by Edward Blore, and enlarged with a chancel in 1874. The district became hopelessly dreary, and the church was not needed. ST ANDREW'S. The foundation stone—which has been kept—was laid on 1 May 1884. Henry Stone, architect, Macey and Sons, builders.

The new church was designed by Covell and Matthews, and the foundation stone was laid on 23 April 1955.

It has the usual concrete frame, and rather long windows. A tower-porch, with a copper-covered spire, at the north-west; and a sanctuary with a raised roof, lit from the top. The glass is by W. Carter Shapland. The seats and the organ came from St George's.

Bermondsey

Bermondsey was once a pleasant village, and had a spa in the latter part of the eighteenth century. It developed industries, and began to be slummy in the early nineteenth century: there were many old houses in a state of horrid disrepair. The *Imperial Gazeteer of England and Wales* says that 'the suburb is one of the filthiest seats of population connected with London'. There has, of course, been slum clearance and rebuilding.

Bermondsey has one of the best of the Commissioners' churches—St James's, by Savage. The other nineteenth-century churches are not specially interesting, except for the very ambitious St Augustine's, South Bermondsey, one of Richard Foster's churches.

St Mary Magdalene's, Bermondsey (155)

The decision to rebuild the church was taken on 2 February 1675/6. The rebuilding was done by Charley Stanton, who, on 6 May 1677, was to 'proceed to ffinish the worke of repaireing the Church fforthwith without delay'. The seating was begun in September. In April 1679 William Dowson the joiner was to be paid for his work done in the church.

The fabric was taken good care of in the eighteenth and early nineteenth centuries. In 1810 the tower, which had not been rebuilt in the seventeenth century, was giving trouble, and three reports by surveyors were read to the vestry in January 1811. That of Daniel Alexander said that the piers and arches were gradually being crushed under the load of the tower: he added that 'it was extremely ignorant and wrong to heighten the Tower (which appears to have been done about Forty or Fifty Years ago) upon such a substructure'. (There seems to be no record of this in the vestry minutes.) The upper part of the tower was taken down, and a temporary bell frame was erected. The west front, and the tower, were repaired and beautified, in an unlearned Gothic style, by George Porter of Bermondsey, in 1830.

There was a repair in 1852, and in 1883 the chancel was lengthened and re-roofed, and the north-east vestry was added.

The interior has Doric columns on high octagonal pedestals: the second bay of the nave is square, and the entablature is returned towards the aisles, giving a cruciform effect—though there is a projection only on the south. To the east of this are two unequal bays: the whole of the church is rather irregular. The nave has an elliptical, groin-vaulted ceiling, and the transepts have depressed vaults.

The galleries remain, with organ at the west: also pulpit, and altar piece (reconstructed). The font is of marble, on a stem of 1808. The candelabra are dated 1699 and 1703. There are three twelfth-century capitals from Bermondsey Abbey.

Monuments   William Casteil, of the merchant navy, 1681. William Steavens, 1712/13.

St James's, Thurland Road (152)

Foundation stone 21 February 1827, consecration 7 May 1829. This was the most expensive of the London Commissioners' churches, with the exception of St Luke's, Chelsea, and Holy Trinity, Marylebone Road. The cost was £22,990: the Commissioners gave £17,666. The architect was James Savage, helped by George Allen.

It is one of the best of the Grecian churches. E. J. Carlos wrote: 'upon the whole an excellent, as well as a very pleasing, specimen of the old school of church building; its arrangement is consistent with established rules, it has no features borrowed from either the theatre or the meeting-house, and in the division of nave and aisles the architect has shown a better taste than many of his brethren, who have deemed an assembly-room a fit model to copy.'

H. S. Goodhart-Rendel pointed out that 'every peculiar architectural difficulty of the type is solved in a design of great dignity and good sense'. The problem of combining a tower with a portico was solved by standing the steeple 'upon a mass which the portico only abuts, the nave overtopping the portico by the height of a clerestory. The solution is complete, but nobody seems to have thought of it before.'

The church, which is built of stock brick and Bath stone, stands on catacombs: the portico is Ionic. The interior is, as Carlos said, of the old school of church building: the galleries stand on square piers, and there are Ionic columns above, and a clerestory, and flat coffered ceiling. The organ remains at the west, in the base of the tower, over the vestibule. The sanctuary has an arched ceiling. There is a very large picture of the Ascension as an altar piece, painted by John Wood in 1844.

There was a redecoration in 1901 by A. H. Ryan Tenison: new pulpit, and reredos including backs of the pews. This fine church fell into disrepair, and was threatened with demolition in 1959: it was repaired in 1965.

Christchurch, Parker's Row

Built 1848, by George Allen: the designer was W. Bennett Hayes. The church is of brick, in Romanesque style, with what the *Ecclesiologist* called 'a knowing-looking clerestory thick set with windows', a south-west belfry, and a short sanctuary.

The church is now disused, and will almost certainly have disappeared before this book is in print.

St Anne's, Thorburn Square

Built 1869–70: the architect was J. Porter. It is of stock brick, varied with a little red: Victorian Gothic. A wide Evangelical nave, with aisles gabled outwards; a south-west tower with octagonal top and spire; and a very short chancel; iron columns with foliated capitals, and a clerestory of tiny quatrefoils. The east end has three lancets, and a wheel above: the glass is 1877, except for an inferior Good Shepherd of 1955 in the central lancet, by John Hall and Sons.

St Augustine's, Lynton Road (153)

One of Richard Foster's churches. The Victorians believed that poor districts should have fine churches; and this is one of them. It was begun in 1875, and the east end and part of the nave were consecrated on 20 July 1878. Foster laid a stone on 18 November 1882, to commemorate the beginning of the western part—which was completed in the next year. There was to have been a tall tower, with gables, and an octagon with a low spire; but this was never built. Vestries by Hesketh and Stokes, 1907.

The architects were Henry Jarvis and Son, who produced a most impressive church: nave and aisles, vaulted chancel with aisles and ambulatory, a north organ gallery and south chapel. The church stands on an undercroft with a concrete vault. The exterior is fairly austere thirteenth-century: the inside lets itself go. The pillars in the nave, of sandstone, are of an unusual plan: a figure of eight. The double lancets of the aisles have tracery on the inner plane, five openings to a bay: the plate-traceried windows of the clerestory have an inner arcade. At the east end of the chancel are three openings to the ambulatory: the one in the centre has a gable with crockets.

Various details are reminiscent of other architects: Jarvis and Son were certainly not among the leading architects of the nineteenth century. But the church as a whole is admirable.

St Crispin's, Southwark Park Road

The church built in 1879–80, designed by Coe and Robinson, was bombed in 1940, and has been demolished.

The new church, by Thomas F. Ford, was begun in 1958, and consecrated in July 1959. It has a square central space, with three shallow arms—organ gallery and transepts; and a larger sanctuary, with narrow aisles and a chapel on the left. There is a little Greek detail. The mural above the altar is by Hans Feibusch, 1959: the ceiling is painted with sky and clouds. The glass in the chapel is by M. C. Farrar Bell.

Camberwell

Camberwell was still mostly rural until the middle of the nineteenth century, with 'elegant villas, in a pleasing and appropriate style of building', at the Grove, Champion Hill, and Herne Hill. Dulwich was, and remained, very respectable. Peckham was still called 'a pleasant village' in 1840, but it was soon built up. Parts of Camberwell were filled with rather poor housing.

Most of the churches remain. The chief loss is Camden church, the one remaining eighteenth-century church, which had a curious and interesting history.

St Giles's, Camberwell Church Street (156)

The old church was too small for the growing population in the eighteenth century, and was repeatedly altered to fit in more and more sittings. In 1786 it was decided to add a new aisle on the south, 'to prevent the rising generation from assembling with Dissenting congregations': the surveyor was Robinson of Peckham. In 1818 the pulpit and desk were moved to make room for pews; and in 1825 there was an enlargement at the south-east by Francis Bedford. On 7 February 1841 the church was completely destroyed by fire.

There was a competition for the rebuilding, with Edward Blore as assessor. Carpenter was one of those who entered, but the design of Scott and Moffatt was chosen. They had planned a very ambitious church, vaulted in terra cotta, but this was thought by the parish to be too expensive, and the architects were commissioned to prepare a less costly design. The new church was begun in 1842. In the course of the work, Scott was converted 'to the exclusive use of real material', and insisted on the substitution of stone for work that was to have been executed in plaster. There was some trouble about this, but Scott thought that it was, all the same, a cheap building. It was consecrated on 21 November 1844.

'The best church by far which had then been erected', wrote Scott, who was not wont to underrate his own work. But in this case he was not far wrong, if 'best' is used in the ecclesiological sense. St Giles's—which is built of Sneaton and Caen stone—is late thirteenth-century in style, cruciform, with a central tower and lofty broach spire, and a long chancel. The *Ecclesiologist* called it 'one of the finest ecclesiastical structures of modern days'. There were faults, but they were chiefly in the fittings. Eastlake commented on the unnecessary regularity of the masonry: yet the church 'forms an excellent and well-composed group invested with a certain charm of artistic proportion'. That was high praise for work of 1840 when looked at from the more sophisticated point of view of 1870.

Inside, there remain the seats that the *Ecclesiologist* disliked, 'carved by Mr Pratt's newly invented machine'; the stalls, which were an unreality since they had canopies over an unbroken bench; and the reredos, which was considered heavy—but it has now been coloured by Comper. The galleries have gone.

This is a church that has really been improved by whitening. It used to be very gloomy, but since its treatment by Comper, after the War, it has gained greatly in beauty.

What stands out is the glass in the east window. Ward and Nixon offered a design, which was rejected, and the committee instructed two of its members—Ruskin, and his friend Edmund Oldfield—to prepare another. Ruskin was in France in 1844, studying thirteenth-century glass at Chartres and elsewhere, and he wrote to Oldfield giving suggestions about this window. Ward and Nixon executed the glass, which was put in at intervals. It is really good, and makes the two windows by Comper look amateurish by comparison. The west window, also by Ward and Nixon, includes some old glass given by the Rev J. G. Storie, the vicar at the time of the rebuilding. Glass by Lavers and Barraud, in the side windows of the chancel, has almost disappeared.

The sedilia and piscina from the old church have been replaced in the chancel. Several brasses are fixed to the backs of the stalls. As they are all together, and not difficult to read, it seems unnecessary to catalogue them. There are two palimpsests on the north side. Otherwise, there is a curious lack of monuments in the church.

St George's, Wells Way

A Grecian Commissioners' church in an out-of-the-way part of Camberwell. It stands on the south bank of the Grand Surrey Canal, for which the first Act of Parliament was passed in 1801: it leaves the Thames at Rotherhithe, and was meant to go as far as Mitcham, but got no further than Camberwell. Francis Octavius Bedford was the architect: the foundation stone was laid on 23 April 1822, and the Bishop of Winchester consecrated it on 24 March 1824. The cost was £16,700, towards which the Commissioners gave £5,000 (and a further £1,382 for repairs after the church was finished). Sharpe and Day were the contractors for the masonry, and Wells and Berriman for the bricklaying.

It is almost the same as Bedford's slightly later church of St John, Waterloo Road: a Doric portico with myrtle wreaths on the frieze, and a tower which is like the others that Bedford designed. The interior was described as 'naked and empty' soon after the church was built. The ceiling is flat and panelled, and there are galleries on Doric columns. The only ornament is the pilasters between the windows.

Repairs are recorded—as they ought to be—by inscriptions: 1862, William Berriman, surveyor, and 1880, T. V. Marsh surveyor. In 1893 an apse was added by Basil Champneys. In 1909 a graduate of Trinity College, Cambridge, gave the mosaic above the altar, the screens to the vestry and chapel, and the marble pavement in the chapel: the walls were 'newly decorated and embellished'. There was post-War work in 1954, by T. Carr. There is a number of wall tablets, none specially interesting.

Emmanuel, Camberwell Road

Built in 1841–2, after St Giles's had been burned down. The architect was Thomas Bellamy, and the cost was £4,899. It is brick Norman, with two low eastern towers flanking the sanctuary. The inside was done up by Frederick Etchells between the Wars. It became unsafe, and was closed. It was proposed at one time to use the Catholic Apostolic Church in Camberwell New Road (by J. and J. Belcher) as the parish church; but it has been taken over by the Greek Orthodox. The parish is now united with All Souls'.

St Paul's, Herne Hill

The building committee was formed in 1842. The foundation stone was laid on 4 August 1843, and the consecration took place on 21 December 1844. The architect was George

153 St Augustine's, Lynton Road, 1875–8 and 1882–3 by Messrs Jarvis

152 St James's, Thurland Road, 1827–29 by James Savage

154 St Katharine's, Rotherhithe, 1960–1 by Covell, Matthews and Partners

155 St Mary Magdalene, the west end: George Porter's repair and beautification, 1830. The tower was left when the church was rebuilt by Charley Stanton in 1677–9

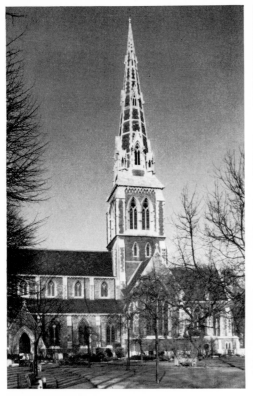

156 St Giles's, Camberwell, 1842–4 by Gilbert Scott

157 St John's, East Dulwich, 1863–5 by Charles Baily, reconstructed by J. B. S. Comper

158 St Anthony's, Nunhead, 1877–8 by Ewan Christian, reconstructed by Laurence King. Altar piece from St Antholin's, Watling Street

159 St Mary Magdalene, Peckham, 1961–2 by Potter and Hare

Alexander, of the firm of Stevens and Alexander: the builders were T. Howard and Son. A Perpendicular church with a tower and spire, elaborately adorned inside. The roofs, the spandrels of the arcades, and the panels of the pulpit, were painted, and every window was filled with stained glass by Ward and Nixon. The floors were laid with encaustic tiles, and the chancel steps with 'tasteful porcelain, by Copeland': the Commandments, etc., were written in illuminated characters on porcelain. The altar was of stone. Timbs calls it one of the earliest specimens of modern High Church embellishment, and no doubt it passed as such; but the ecclesiologists could hardly approve, on their principles, of a church in Third-Pointed style, with low-pitched roofs, and a rather short chancel.

On 13 March 1858 the church was burned down, and Street rebuilt it; the contractors were Holland and Hannen. The tower and spire survived the fire, and were kept: the outer walls also remained, and Street kept the former proportions: but he widened and lengthened the chancel, and added a chancel aisle. Indeed, the church was completely transformed in Street's own style, with a good deal of marble, carving by Earp, and glass by Hardman in all but three of the windows. Ruskin called St Paul's 'one of the loveliest churches of the kind in the country, and one that makes the fire a matter of rejoicing'. The *Ecclesiologist* made a sensible comment: that 'not a little of the excellence of the external effect is due to the fact that Mr Street is not afraid of blank wall, than which in due proportion nothing gives more character to a design'.

The rood screen is a 1914–18 memorial: it was dedicated on 21 March 1921. Bombing destroyed nearly all the glass, and only two complete windows remain: west of the south aisle (St Peter), and west of the north aisle (St John). The east window now has glass by Lilian J. Pocock, 1949. The interior was redecorated in 1965.

St John's, East Dulwich Road (157)

The predecessor of this church was East Dulwich Chapel, founded in 1827 by Thomas Baily, who died in 1833 aged 92. The church was designed by Charles Baily, the son of Thomas: the builder was J. W. Sawyer. The foundation stone was laid on 18 June 1863, and later in the year Wailes's designs for the east windows were accepted. The church was opened on 30 August 1864, and consecrated on 16 May 1865. It is in French early thirteenth-century style, with walls of Kentish rag, in small pieces, tiled roofs, and a tower and broach spire on the south. Vestries were added in 1883 by A. Burt, and a new choir vestry in 1914, by H. S. Rogers.

It was badly damaged by bombing in 1940, reconstructed by J. B. S. Comper, and re-dedicated on 5 May 1951. The aisles were rebuilt on a smaller scale (with an additional chapel on the north), and a clerestory and concrete vault were added to the nave. A west gallery was erected, and a ciborium was put over the altar—both decorated with gold and colour. Some Comper glass (only one window, by Kempe, remains of what was there be-fore), and the usual Comper lighting. The walls have been whitened. It has been made into a very attractive church.

Christchurch, Old Kent Road

The original church was designed by Samuel Angell: the foundation stone was laid on 17 August 1837, and it was consecrated in 1838. The site was wanted by the gas works, and the new church, on the other side of the road, was begun in 1867, and consecrated on 1 July 1868. The architect was E. Bassett Keeling. It is of stock brick, with some red and black, in Keeling's usual style, which was called 'early French Gothic freely treated'. The tower, to the south of the chancel, is quite a feature of the Old Kent Road. There is a broad nave, and a south aisle: the arcade has columns of cast iron.

The church was burned out by fire bombs in October 1940, and restored after the War by T. F. Ford. The aisle, and the west end of the nave, have been cut off, and turned into rooms for parish purposes, and the church has been cut down to a reasonable size: it used to be a particularly dreary interior. The nave has been reroofed, and the walls have been whitened. East window by Alfred L. Wilkinson, 1958. The organ came from Corpus Christi Mission.

St Stephen's, College Road, Dulwich

Begun in 1867, and consecrated on 23 November 1868. The architects were Banks and Barry, and the builders Messrs Perry of Stratford. The church was completed in 1875. There was a window to the memory of Henry Andrewes Palmer, J. P., who largely pro-moted the building and ornamentation of the church. The building is of Kentish rag and Bath stone, with a rather thin tower and tall slated spire at the (ritual) north-west. The clerestory windows are gabled, and there is a roof of variegated slate. Inside, the orna-mentation is rather overdone. The circular pillars, with naturalistic capitals, have quatre-foil abaci, above which are carved angels, spreading their wings to fill the spandrels, with shafts rising from them.

In the arch on the south of the chancel is a painting of the trial and stoning of St Stephen, by Sir E. Poynter, 1872. The glass, mostly by Hardman, has gone: all that re-mains from before the War is the east window of the apse, by the Kempe firm. The new west window 1952, is by Moira Forsyth.

All Saints', Blenheim Grove

Begun in 1870, and consecrated on 21 July 1872. The architect was H. E. Coe. A rather wide nave, with a hammer-beam roof: aisles, and the basement of a tower, acting as a porch, at the north-west: chancel, and a semi-circular apse. It has an unaltered Evangelical interior: even some gas-lights remain in the aisles. An open bible is propped up behind the holy table.

St Augustine's, Honor Oak Park

In a good position, on One Tree Hill, with grass and trees round it. The site and £750 were given by Edwin Clarke. The foundation stone was laid on 3 October 1872, and the church was consecrated on 26 May 1873. William Oakley was the architect, and Messrs Roberts were the builders. It is said that Gothic was chosen 'as being in harmony with the surrounding residences'. This does not sound very likely: Gothic was the natural style for a church in 1872, and it stands away from houses. The style is rather crude thirteenth-century: the walls are of Kentish rag.

As first built, the church consisted of nave, with incomplete tower on the south, the aisle to the east of it, and transept; and the apsidal chancel with south vestry. The tower was to have had a spire: it was completed, without a spire, in 1888. The reredos, 1889, is by Vincent John Grose, the north vestry 1894. The north aisle, which had been added previously, was enlarged in 1900: the architect was Grose. The chancel wall was erected in 1903. Most of the glass was lost during the War: the south aisle windows were by Warrington. The west window, and one on the south, survive: these are by Heaton, Butler and Bayne. The church was repaired, and rededicated on 21 November 1953.

St Peter's, Lordship Lane, Dulwich

The site was the gift of Dulwich College, and the foundation stone was laid on 1 May 1873. The architect was Charles Barry, junior, and the builder W. Downs of Southwark. The church was opened in 1874, but the nave was left incomplete. The tower and spire were completed in 1885, at the cost of F. H. Horniman. The foundation stone of the extension of the nave was laid on 16 July 1885. The vestry was enlarged in 1893.

Of Kentish rag outside, and brick inside: the walls of yellow stocks with bands of red, and the arches of red and black, with Bath stone hood-moulds. The clerestory windows have marble shafts. The pulpit, of Caen stone, was carved by Messrs Brindley.

Bumpus had a particular affection for this church, as he saw it being built when he was a schoolboy, and became a member of the choir. He considers it to be a decidedly meritorious, if not a great work: the architect tried to do what was right. But money was wasted on external sculpture, and the spire is of very poor and commonplace outline. But he admires the clerestory, the brickwork, the foliaged ornament, the delicate diapering of the apse walls, the tiled pavement of the chancel, and the glass by Hardman in the central window of the apse.

Emmanuel, Clive Road, West Dulwich

Francis Peek laid the foundation stone on 8 July 1876, and the first part of the church was consecrated on 8 September 1877. The architect was E. C. Robins, but the design is said to have been made by G. F. Roper: the contractors were T. H. Adamson and Sons. The two west bays, baptistery and porches, were added in 1893 by E. T. Hall, who lived at Dulwich, and was a governor of the College. The church is in thirteenth-century style; white brick inside, and Kentish rag outside. Cruciform, with the basement of a tower that was never completed at the north-east.

St Anthony's, Nunhead (158)

There was a temporary church, dedicated to St Michael, built at the cost of the Rev A. W. Drew.

Wren's church of St Antholin, Watling Street was demolished—a sad loss—in 1875. This was the successor-church, begun in 1877, and consecrated on 11 May 1878. Ewan Christian was the architect. It was a large red brick church, with an additional passage aisle on the south, and a triple chancel arch. Two bells from the City church, and the altar piece, were brought here.

In 1938 Martin Travers made a scheme for the improvement of the east end, and the restoration of the altar piece, which lost its upper part at the removal. The work was done in 1939, but at the end of 1940 the church was gutted by fire bombs. It was reconstructed after the War by Laurence King, and reopened and rededicated on 12 October 1957. The nave was reduced to two bays, and the outer south aisle was suppressed: the new roof is of lower pitch. The inside walls have been plastered. The altar piece fortunately remains: panelling was added at the sides, there are new rails, and the sanctuary has been enlarged. The church was known as St Antholin's, but now calls itself St Anthony's: 'Antholin' was a picturesque corruption.

St Mark's, Cobourg Road

By R. Norman Shaw, begun in 1879, and consecrated on 6 June 1880; the part of the church facing the road was not completed until 1932. It is Gothic, with some 'Queen Anne' detail; octagonal red brick pillars, and wooden vaulting: there is a stone screen. There was some War damage, and the church is out of use.

St Saviour's, Copleston Road

Built by Francis Peek, and designed by Weeks and Hughes: begun in 1880, and consecrated on 22 February 1881. St Saviour's is a large brick church, with only its rather pretentious west end appearing between the houses. It has a nave and aisles; arcades, with circular stone columns with moulded capitals: a chancel arch with marble shafts: all rather heavy and uninspired. The screen was erected in 1907, by Harold S. Rogers, and south chapel 1911, by the same architect.

St Bartholomew's, Barkworth Road

One of the churches promoted by Richard Foster. The architect was E. Tapnell Allen. The foundation stone was laid on 15 June 1886, and the church consecrated on 25 June 1887. Work was done in 1911 by G. H. Fellowes Prynne.

Early English style, of brick—red outside, and yellow and red within. It has a nave and aisles of four bays, and a short west bay; a lofty chancel, with organ in the base of an unbuilt tower on the north, and a chapel on the south. Some of the details look Butterfieldian. There are four windows by Heaton, Butler and Bayne in the north aisle; and one by G. Cooper Abbs in the chapel.

St Barnabas', Calton Avenue, Dulwich

A building committee was appointed in 1891, and plans were made by W. H. Wood, of the firm of Oliver, Leeson and Wood, of Newcastle. The first builder was Richardson, of Brixton, who failed to complete the contract: Dove Bros succeeded. The foundation stone was laid on 27 July 1892, and the consecration was on St Barnabas' day, 1895. The tower was built in 1908, by J. W. Bowman. St Barnabas' is a large church, Perpendicular in style, with a continuous clerestory: there are prosperous suburban churches like this all over the North. The materials are red brick from Cranleigh, red Mansfield stone and Bath stone. From the time of the consecration onwards, a succession of wood-carvers under F. E. Day worked on the fittings, e.g. the stalls, 1895, screen to south chapel, 1929, organ case, 1931, reredos, 1934. The east window is by E. B. Powell, 1922.

St Silas', Ivydale Road, Nunhead

A large stone church in fifteenth-century style by J. E. K. and J. P. Cutts: it was begun in 1902, and consecrated in the next year. The foundation stone at the west end is dated 25 October 1913. J. E. K. Cutts left England in 1912, and the completion of the church was done by P. C. Boddy, his chief assistant. The baptistery opens into the nave with the usual Cutts triple arch. There is nothing worth noting in the way of fittings or glass.

St Faith's, Sunray Avenue, Herne Hill

Built by Greenaway and Newberry in 1907: it was destined to become the hall of a larger church, that was never built. It was a chapel of ease to St Paul's, but has now become a parish church.

St Luke's, Rosemary Road

The original church was built in 1876–7, from designs by J. E. K. Cutts. It was bombed, and there is nothing of it left. Its predecessor, a school-chapel of 1874, survives. The foundation stone of the new church was laid on 28 March 1953, and the consecration was in 1954. The architect was Arthur C. Martin, who died before the church was completed: it was finished under Milner and Craze.

The design belongs more to the '30s than the '50s: it is brick Byzantine, and very substantial for the post-War years. There is a square central space, carried up as a tower, with a short nave, and aisled chancel, with an apse. The transepts are so arranged that an altar placed at the bottom of the chancel would be visible from everywhere—but the altar was, in fact, placed in the apse.

The glass in the east windows by D. Marion Grant, 1956, and in the south chapel by Robert Hendra, 1962.

St Clement's, Barry Road, East Dulwich

Francis Peek promised in 1881 to build a new church at his own cost, on a site to be chosen by Bishop Thorold, if the people of South London would build nine others. The money for the others was raised, and this is the church that he built. It was begun in 1884, and consecrated on 31 May 1885. The architect was William B. Hughes.

This large, red brick church was destroyed on 17 October 1940. After the War, plans for a smaller new building were made by L. Keir Hett and J. C. H. Odam: Princess Alexandra laid the foundation stone on 20 October 1956. It is a simple church, built on reinforced concrete ribs, with a pantiled roof. The statue of St Clement is by Joseph Cribb, and the glass in the Lady chapel by J. Francis Lowe.

St Mary Magdalene's, St Mary's Road, Peckham (159)

The original church was built in 1839–41: the architect was Robert Palmer Browne. The cost was £4,309: the Commissioners (second grant) gave £1,000. The baptistery and apse were added in 1910 by A. Heron Ryan Tenison.

It was bombed in 1940, and has been demolished. The new church was designed by Potter and Hare, and built by Trollope and Colls: the foundation stone was laid on 21 October 1961, and the church was consecrated on 3 November 1962. It is cruciform, with the four ends filled with glass, and glass in the ridges of the roof: the low walls are faced with brick. It is planned with the altar in the middle, with seats on three sides, choir and organ at the east end, and pulpit-with-desk behind the altar facing west: all the furniture, including the font, is movable.

The motive of this arrangement is obvious: 'the people of God comprise the Church, and the building is only of secondary significance:' there is no attempt to achieve what the ecclesiologists called 'sacramentality' in the building itself. One thing that is questionable in a church like this is the quantity of glass: the whole of the interior can be seen from the outside. In primitive times, when Christians may have worshipped round a central table, there was a separation between the Church and the world: those who were in, were in, and took part in the holy mysteries: those who were outside were excluded. Ought what goes on inside the church to be visible to those who are outside?

St Philip's, Avondale Square

The original church, consecrated in 1875, was designed by Coe and Robinson. It was damaged by bombing in 1940, and has been completely cleared away. The neighbourhood has been rebuilt with enormous blocks of flats, and the new building is on a modest scale, and does not try to compete with them. It cost £33,000, and was designed by N. F. Cachemaille-Day, and built by Pitchers Ltd. The consecration was on 2 February 1963.

It is faced with handmade bricks, and has a copper roof and an aluminium turret. The lower part is square, the upper part octagonal, with four clerestory windows: there is a projecting Lady chapel, and a passage to the hall, which survived the War. The ceiling has paintings on canvas by John Hayward, who also painted the crucifix behind the altar. The window above the altar is by Christopher Webb. This is rather a pleasant little church.

St Jude's, Meeting House Lane, Peckham

The church built to Blomfield's designs in 1875–6 was bombed, and has been demolished. The parish was united in 1961 with that of ST CHRYSOSTOM, an attractive church, built as a proprietary chapel in 1813. It was restored in 1961, but demolished two years later, when it was found to be infested with dry rot. A new church for the united parish is to be built on the site of St Jude's. The architect is David Bush. The foundation stone for this was laid on 22 July 1965.

Charlton

Charlton is a village, recognisably surviving, with Charlton House, 1607–12, to the south of the church. The population increased in the nineteenth century, largely with people moving out of Woolwich. First the parish church was enlarged: then a church was built at New Charlton, and then another at Old Charlton. Blackheath, which has its own character, is mostly in Greenwich and Lewisham, but Charlton included part of it.

St Luke's, Church Lane

In 1630 Sir Adam Newton left money to rebuild this small village church. It is probable that some, at any rate, of the old walls remain, and were simply cased in brick. The porch was added, and probably the north chapel. The north aisle was added in 1693 by bequest of Sir William Newton.

It is attractive Gothic survival, with no new ideas, except for the porch with its Dutch gable. The south window of the chancel is probably Perpendicular, anyhow. The tower has clasping buttresses, which are carried up as turrets, and is embattled: it may be later than *c.* 1630. The arcade has square piers with shafts worked on the angles: it looks almost like a reminiscence of a twelfth-century arcade.

An additional chancel, and north organ chamber, were built in 1840, on the site of a charity school and vestry, built in 1713. The north aisle was restored, an organ chamber added, and the vestry enlarged, in 1873. At the same time, the organ gallery was taken down, and the pulpit and desk moved. The architect was Ernest Turner.

The old chancel roof is seventeenth-century: that of the nave was reconstructed in this century. Font and pulpit are seventeenth-century: the canopy of the pulpit is, for some reason, fixed to the ceiling under the tower. The glass in the east window, though a good deal restored, was of the time of the rebuilding: this has gone, and there is new glass by C. F. Blakeman. There is heraldic glass in the aisle. Arms of Queen Anne.

Monuments   These contribute a great deal to the interior. They include Edward Wilkinson, 1568, and Clare. Katherine, wife of Sir Adam Newton, and Sir Adam, 1630, by Nicholas Stone. Elizabeth, wife of James Craggs, 1712. Grace, wife of Patrick, Earl of Ardmagh and of Sir William Langhorn, 1700, and Sir William, 1715. The Hon Michael Richards, surveyor general of the Ordnance, 1721: a statue in armour. Elizabeth Thompson, 1759. General George Morrison, 1799, by Regnart. Spencer Perceval, Prime Minister, 1812: a bust by Chantrey. Sir Thomas Hislop, 1834, by Westmacott.

St Thomas's, Maryon Road, Charlton (160)

Designed by Joseph Gwilt: the foundation stone was laid on 4 October 1849, and the consecration took place on 31 July 1850. The cost was £5,169. It is a late example of its kind: Romanesque, of red and white brick, with pilaster buttresses. There are constructional galleries, of brick: the upper arches are of wood. It is an impressive interior. The small windows in the eastern apse have glass of Christ and the Evangelists. There was renovation by Ewan Christian in 1892–3: he altered the chancel, and designed new choir stalls.

St James's, Kidbrooke Park Road

A large church by Newman and Billing, begun in 1866, and consecrated on 3 July 1867. The tower, between the east end of the north aisle and the chancel, had a spire 160 feet high, which has gone. Rather tall arcades, with naturalistic foliage; and some exuberant carving in the base of the tower. The baptistery, at the south-west, was formed in 1926: this is now a chapel. The church was bombed, and has been reroofed, and much brightened up inside. The post-War glass is by Carl J. Edwards, 1955.

Holy Trinity, Woolwich Road, North Charlton

Foundation stone laid 5 August 1893, consecration on 9 April 1894. It is of red brick and stone, in lancet style. The architect was John Rowland, who lived at Charlton. The screen is 1910, by Greenaway and Newberry.

Clapham

Clapham Common was 'redeemed from a morass', and planted, in the eighteenth century. Around it, many decent eighteenth-century houses were built, some of which remain. Clapham Park was laid out from 1824 by Thomas Cubitt, who built several streets of large detached houses. The Cedars estate, on the opposite side of the Common, was the work of James Knowles. Thorne, who does not sound very enthusiastic, says that it is 'spotted over with large and costly residences of the latest model'. Knowles's church of St Saviour, Cedars Road, was bombed, and has been demolished. There was also the usual undistinguished Victorian suburban development, and churches were provided for the new inhabitants in the usual proportions.

Holy Trinity, North Side, Clapham Common (161)

The old church of Clapham, dedicated to St Mary, was enlarged several times in the second half of the seventeenth century, and in the eighteenth. In 1753 the vestry decided not to repair it any more, but to build an entirely new church. Nothing came of this for the time being, and it was not until 1768 that it was decided to apply to the patroness and the rector to obtain their consent to pulling down the old building; to prepare a petition to Parliament, and to get plans and estimates.

In 1773 it was agreed that the north aisle should be kept. Mr Couse the surveyor was to make plans and estimates for 'a strong neat Church large enough to contain 800 Persons'.

On 26 January 1774 Kenton Couse gave evidence before the Commons, and a Bill was brought in for vesting a piece of waste ground in trustees, and enabling them to build a new church on it. The Bill was passed on 14 February. A contract was made with John Hanscomb. The site turned out to be very wet, and additional work had to be done on the foundations. The church was consecrated on 9 June 1776.

In 1812 a new west porch was built, designed by Francis Hurlbatt. J. B. Papworth designed extra accommodation for the children in 1842: he also exhibited at the R.A. in

1845 a suggested 'ornamental casing in Italian'. In fact, nothing much was done to the church, except that the pews were cut down in 1865.

The chancel was added by A. Beresford Pite in 1902: this took the place of a shallow apse, rather sumptuously decorated, with a painted window. The galleries remain: the pulpit, now reduced in height, used to stand in the middle: it was of uncommon elevation, with a canopy, supported by two pillars, above it. A repair, under Thomas F. Ford, was carried out in 1925–8. Damage was done by a rocket in 1945: the church was repaired under Ford, and reopened in 1952.

The Evangelical Clapham Sect, who worshipped here, are commemorated—including Zachary Macaulay, Granville Sharp, Henry and John Thornton, John Venn, and William Wilberforce.

St Paul's, Rectory Grove

This church, consecrated in 1815, was built in the churchyard of old St Mary's, the remains of which were removed. The architect was Christopher Edmonds. It is a very plain brick building, now whitened inside, with the north and south galleries taken down. The transepts and chancel, in Romanesque style, were added by Blomfield in 1879. The new pulpit and stalls were erected in 1905, by T. E. Lidiard James.

Monuments   Those from the old church were badly treated when the new church was built: of the Clerke monument, 1589, only one figure remains. The Atkins monument was buried in the family vault, and rescued in 1886: there are five life-sized figures, of Sir Richard, 1689, Dame Rebecca, and three children. These are of very good quality, and ascribed to William Stanton.

Also Martin Lister, doctor of physic, 1711/12, and Hannah, 1695. William Hewer, clerk and partner of Samuel Pepys, 1715.

Of later date, there is J. B. Wilson, 1835.

St John's, Clapham Road

Built by subscription in 1840–2: the architect was T. Marsh Nelson, 7 Charles Street, St James's; this is a very late example of this kind of church. At the east, facing the road, is a hexastyle Ionic portico: behind it are three doorways. The body of the church, of white brick with square-headed windows, is a plain rectangle, with galleries on Ionic columns. To begin with, the galleries extended round the east end, where there were the organ and the children's seats. A vestry was underneath, and the altar stood to the west of this, between two pilasters. The interior was decorated in 1870, by A. C. Morton. In 1883 everything was cleared away from the east end and a choir was formed: the ground floor of the church was reseated. The architect was T. J. Bailey, of Battersea.

The remodelling was not very well done, and the original arrangements would be preferable. The font, old-fashioned for its date, was given in 1900. About 1914, the west wall was rebuilt, further alterations were made at the east end, and the original pulpit was sold. The church was repaired after bomb damage, and reopened in July 1949.

All Saints', New Park Road

The money was raised by a committee of local gentlemen and the church was opened in June 1858, and consecrated on 19 January 1859. The architects were T. Talbot Bury and Hering: the builder was George Myers. It is the usual Talbot Bury design: Middle-Pointed with a tower and spire at the (ritual) north-west: cruciform, with a rather short chancel. There are Kentish rag walls, with Bath stone dressings and slate roofs. The front rises from the pavement, and there are trees and grass on the left. Tall arcades, with naturalistic capitals; there are galleries at the west and in the transepts.

Christchurch, Union Grove

Designed by Benjamin Ferrey, begun in 1861, and consecrated on 6 May 1862. It is of Kentish rag, in early Middle-Pointed style, with rather wide aisles under separate gables. A faculty was given in 1906 for a screen to the north chapel, by Norman and Wheeler, of Orchard Street. All the glass has gone, except for a little in the tracery, and one small window in the sanctuary: this is by Clayton and Bell, as was most of the vanished glass. The new east window, 1950, is by William Morris and Co. This was the first church in London in which the use of the eucharistic vestments was revived in the nineteenth century.

St Stephen's, Weir Road, Clapham Park

The story is that the daughter of Sir James Knowles wanted to marry the Rev George Eastman. Her father would not allow her to, so she did the next best thing, and built him a church to her father's designs. She also left her fortune to him. A number of Evangelicals left St Mary's, Balham, where the preaching was not to their liking, and built an iron church in Elmfield Road. When they heard that Eastman was retiring, they bought St Stephen's, and placed the patronage in the hands of suitable trustees.

216

The building—which was consecrated on 22 June 1867—was completed early in this century. The faculty was given in 1909. L. W. Simpson, of Carlton Chambers, Regent Street, completed the north aisle, of which only the west wall had been built. It is one of those Victorian churches of which the outside does not match the inside. The exterior, with the window tracery, is English fourteenth-century: the arcades are French thirteenth-century, with square abaci and stiff leaf foliage. The nave has a rather thin hammer-beam roof.

The stone reredos, with a relief of the Last Supper, and Commandments, etc., is a 1939–45 War memorial—very old-fashioned for its date.

There was slight War damage: the church was restored and redecorated in 1954. The east window is a replacement, by Alfred L. Wilkinson. Other glass has disappeared, except for three windows in the north aisle: Ward and Hughes, Lobin of Tours (damaged), and Mayer.

St Peter's, Clapham Manor Road (192)

Built in 1878, this is an early work of J. E. K. Cutts, and quite a good example of a town church of the time; of stock brick, relieved with bands and diapers of red, and with red brick arches. It has a wide and lofty interior: the aisles, chancel, and north chapel have been whitened. There is an iron screen; the font and pulpit, by C. E. Kempe, were dedicated in February 1914: the big, carved triptych is a 1914–18 memorial. The east window, and east window of the chapel are by Kempe. The glass in the small aisle windows is a mixture.

The Holy Spirit, Narbonne Avenue (162)

Built in memory of Canon Green, vicar of Clapham, who obtained the site. The foundation stone was laid on 27 April 1912, and the consecration was in January 1913. The architect was H. P. Burke Downing. This is a very simple, nicely proportioned Gothic church: nave and chancel under one roof, and a north aisle with organ loft and vestry at the east. Nave and chancel have a pointed cradle roof with plasterwork ornaments. The interior is all very white and austere: there is no stained glass.

St James's, Park Hill (163)

The original church 'a spacious and elegant structure', designed by Lewis Vulliamy, was consecrated on 17 November 1829. It was enlarged with transepts, chancel, and tower, in

1870–1, by Messrs Francis. The reredos, 1884, was by A. R. G. Fenning. This church was destroyed in 1940, and nothing remains of it.

The new church was designed by N. F. Cachemaille-Day, and built by J. Longley and Co. Foundation stone laid 1 June 1957, consecration 13 September 1958.

The concrete frame has been given an arched form, suggesting a vault—as at the architect's church of St Barnabas, Tuffley, Gloucester: and here, as there, concrete piers divide the eastern part into choir and aisles. There are small, round windows in the roof. The walls are faced with brick. At the east end is a slight projection: the lower part is filled with stained glass, forming a background to the altar: the organ is above, on a concrete beam, with a wrought iron grille in front, by Hurst, Franklin and Co. The furniture was executed by J. Wippell and Co, and the glass is also their work: the scheme for the windows was devised by the architect, and the designs were made by A. F. Erridge. The font came from Fellowes Prynne's church of St Saviour, Ealing, which was damaged by bombs, and has been demolished.

Deptford

The old parish church of Deptford was taken down in 1696, and rebuilt. The commissioners for the Fifty New Churches decided that this was a suitable place for a new church, and St Paul's was begun in 1712, and consecrated in 1730. During the nineteenth century the riverside part was much built up, and suffered the usual decline. The inland parts became respectably suburban. The Victorian churches were all built in the second half of the century: none are, or were, particularly interesting.

St Nicholas', Deptford Green (164)

On 1 July 1696 the parish was ordered to repair the church, and on 10th a rate was agreed to. The body of the church was taken down and rebuilt by Charley Stanton: it was ready for seating by the middle of 1697. There was some disagreement between Stanton and the vestry about payments, and on 6 July 1699 it was agreed that no more money be paid for extra work. On 22 February 1701 the vestry agreed to erect 'a White Marble Stone well Ornamented' to commemorate 'all such Subscriptions and free gifts as Isaac Loader Esqr hath bestowed upon the new building & Beautifying of the Church and Erecting the Charnell House'. This has survived the bombing.

On 25 February 1710/11, the vestry agreed on a petition to the Commons: the old steeple had been left when the church was rebuilt, but was now dangerous. A new church was needed, and they hoped for £6,000, or other such sum as they should think fit, for rebuilding the steeple and building another church. The petition was presented on 6 April, and Thomas Lucas, bricklayer, testified to the weakness of the steeple: to rebuild it in brick would cost above £2,000. The rebuilding was not done, but in 1713 it was agreed to lay out £17 on repairing and amending it. A stone on the south side says that the church was supported and strapped with iron in 1716. On 8 August 1791 it was decided that the church, chancel, and organ should be repaired, whitewashed, and decently ornamented.

The church had little done to it in the nineteenth century. In 1901 the upper part of the tower was destroyed in a gale: it was restored in 1903–4 by George Parker. It was bombed, but fortunately the altar-piece, pulpit, etc. had been stored. The restoration was done by Thomas F. Ford and Partners, and the church was reopened on 14 February 1958. The east bay and the sanctuary were cut off, and converted into hall, etc., making the church a square.

The church shelters behind high walls, and cowers beneath the forbidding bulk of a power-station. The tower, c. 1500, with reconstructed top, is of ragstone. The body of the church is of brick—a builder's version of some of Wren's. The second bay is treated transept-wise: now that the church is a square this looks more logical than it did before.

The best feature of the interior is the altar piece, Corinthian, with a curved pediment, and panels with the usual writings and Moses and Aaron. The organ case has gone, and the new organ is tucked away in the cut-off part to the east, with an opening into the church. The pulpit is seventeenth-century, of earlier date than the church. The portrait of Queen Anne, by Kneller, has been cleaned and replaced: at the time of the restoration, the Evangelical church council passed a resolution that no other pictures should be admitted into the church. The wood carving of Ezekiel and the bones has also been preserved: it is ascribed to Grinling Gibbons.

Monuments   A few have survived: Roger Boyle, 1615, of alabaster, with a relief of him kneeling, and a cherub drawing back a curtain to reveal a skull: and Edward Fenton, 1603. William Boulter, 1714, and Richard Wilkinson, 1725. Katherine wife of Captain Francis Wivell, 1713, and others. Ann, wife of Thomas South, 1732, and Ann, daughter of Ann, 1748. There are a few fragments of others.

St Paul's, Deptford High Street (165)

The vestry's appeal to the Commons in 1710/11 stated that the parish church could not possibly accommodate the parishioners, and they hoped that the Commissioners' 'pious and charitable zeal for the glory of God, the good of souls, and the honour of the Established Church', would show itself by a grant for rebuilding the steeple of St Nicholas', and for the building of another church.

The vestry minutes contain an account of the choice of a site for St Paul's, and there are one or two mentions of the progress of the work, which was begun in 1712, and progressed slowly. By 1717 it was so far advanced that the plastering, glazing, and other works and materials, might suffer if they were not looked after, and a man was paid to 'watch and take care'. But the church was not consecrated until 30 June 1730.

The architect was Thomas Archer, one of the Commissioners; and the craftsmen included Edward Strong and Edward Tufnell, Christopher Cass and John Strong, masons; James Grove and John Meard, plasterers; and James Ellis and James Hands, joiners. John Gilliam of Greenwich was paid £200 for making the altar piece, pulpit, and desks.

Archer was one of the few English architects to design in the style of the Roman Baroque, the buildings of which he had seen for himself. Baroque soon became out of date in England, and buildings like St Paul's were regarded as heavy and incorrect. The Victorians thought them pagan and pompous. This church has never been scoffed at in the same way as Archer's other church in London—St John's, Smith Square: it is less easy to find, and it has not the obvious oddities of St John's. But it was not a church that people thought of admiring. Now, of course, its value is realised.

It is a most imposing church, and is made more so by the stone platform on which it stands. It is almost square—though it is, in fact, planned as a nave and aisles. At the four corners are the usual vestibules and vestries, two-storied, with canted walls within the church. The two sides have slight projections of three bays, with pediments: the walls are adorned by pilasters with intermittent rustications.

The tower is circular, with windows, like those of the towers of St John's, Smith Square, and a spire: the basement is surrounded by a semi-circular portico. At the east is an apse, with a Venetian window which follows the curve. The order inside is Corinthian. The ceiling has admirable plaster work.

There were Victorian repairs in 1856 (John Whichcord) and 1883 (Thomas Dinwiddy), and a sympathetic restoration in the 1930s by Eden and Marchant. The Victorian Norman font came from Rochester Cathedral: the original font was sent to a mission church abroad.

Monuments　Matthew Ffinch, 1745, and Maria, the same date. Admiral James Sayer, 1776, by Nollekens. The Rev Charles Burney, 1817.

St James's, St James's Road, Hatcham

A building committee was formed in 1844, and a temporary church was built in 1846. A site was bought from the governors of Christ's Hospital. The design was made by W. L. B. Granville, and shown at the Royal Academy in 1849. The *Ecclesiologist* found fault with

160 St Thomas's, Charlton, 1849–50 by Joseph Gwilt

161 Holy Trinity, Clapham, 1774–6
by Kenton Couse, porch
by Francis Hurlbatt

162 The Holy Spirit, Clapham,
1912 by H. P. Burke Downing

163 St James's, Clapham Park, 1957–8 by N. F. Cachemaille-Day

164 St Nicholas', 1696–7 by Charley Stanton, reduced in size after the War

165 St Paul's, 1712 onwards by Thomas Archer

166 St Luke's, 1870–2 by T. H. Watson

the design: 'This promises to be one of the worst specimens of modern Pointed which the last few years have produced . . . We were in hopes that this particular form of architectural enormity had died away.'

The foundation stone was laid on 18 June 1853, and the church was consecrated on 17 October 1854. The cost was £4,695. From the ecclesiological point of view, there is a good deal of fault to find. The details were old-fashioned at the time that the church was built, and the plan is pretentious: why should a parish church of this size have transepts with both eastern and western aisles?

The Rev A. H. B. Granville resigned in 1863, and was succeeded by the Rev Arthur Tooth—a person of no special importance in himself, but who is remembered as one of the confessors of the ritualistic movement. In his time there were several alterations to the church, by F. Rogers. An unusual operation was performed on the north transept: the aisles were extended by apses, and one was made into a sacristy, and the other into a baptistery. He also erected a screen, a Lady chapel altar, and several windows. An altar stone was inserted into the wooden holy table—and afterwards removed. Tooth was imprisoned in Horsemonger Gaol in 1877, under the Public Worship Regulation Act.

A new vestry was built in 1897, designed by W. Gilbee Scott.

The inside has been redecorated, and there is post-War glass by Francis H. Spear.

St John's, Lewisham Way

St John's is a large and handsome church, by P. C. Hardwick, built in 1854–5; it is early Middle-Pointed, with walls of Kentish rag: a tower and spire at the west of the south aisle. A gallery in the west bay, and poor galleries in the aisles: it is 'well adapted for hearing, this having been made an important point in the commission'. A large east window of seven lights, with glass restored in 1951 after War damage: a west window of six lights, with glass by Ward and Hughes.

Monuments   A pretty, sentimental monument to John Allan, 1865, and Judith, 1866, with an angel holding a cross—by M. Noble, 1868.

St Peter's, Wickham Road, Brockley

The foundation stone was laid on 25 May 1866, and the church consecrated on 13 August 1870. The architect was Frederick Marrable, superintendent architect of the Metropolitan Board of Works. The tower was completed by A. W. Blomfield: a faculty was given in 1890.

This is a very striking church, with an unusual plan. The base of the tower is engaged with two large gabled vestibules, lit at the west by Teulon-like windows: these, and the tower, open into the nave by arches of equal height. There is a gallery. The nave is wide, with low passage aisles through the buttresses. There are large transepts with galleries, and a vaulted chancel with aisles and an eastern apse. This sounds rather auditorium-like; but it is expensively carried out, with marble shafts and a good deal of decoration, and looks impressive. The glass is nearly all by Clayton and Bell.

All Saints', New Cross Road

The foundation stone was laid by the Earl of Shaftesbury on 8 May 1869: the church was opened in December of that year, and consecrated on 1 November 1871. The cost was £5,629: the Haberdashers' Company gave the freehold of the site, and £1,500. Newman and Billing were the architects, and Dove Bros the builders. It is of Kentish rag, 'in the decorated style of Foreign Gothic': nave, aisles, transepts, and chancel with three-sided apse. A tower at the north-west has not been built. A large circular traceried window is at the west end; the east windows have glass of 1954 by Goddard and Gibbs (A. E. Buss).

St Luke's, Evelyn Street (166)

In March 1867 the old Bethel Independent Chapel was secured for services. The site for the church was given by W. J. Evelyn, who laid the foundation stone on 19 July 1870: the church was consecrated on 30 July 1872. The architect was T. H. Watson. Nave and aisles, a central tower, and apsidal chancel. Most of the light comes from the large windows in the west wall. Windows in the apse by Carl J. Edwards were inserted in 1954.

St Catherine's, Pepys Road, Hatcham

Built in 1893–4; this is a large Early English church, brick inside, and faced with rag, designed by Henry Stock, the surveyor to the Haberdashers' Company. His style recalls G. G. Scott (west end), and J. O. Scott (arcades, etc.). The church was burned by suffragettes in 1913, and restored by Stock, Page and Stock.

It was damaged in 1940. The nave has been reroofed, and the high altar has been placed at the west of the chancel, with bishop's throne behind. The east window is 1953, by William Morris and Co.

Eltham

Eltham was celebrated for its royal Palace, the decline and fall of which dates from the seventeenth century: Evelyn 'went to see his Majesty's House at Eltham, both palace and chapel in miserable ruins, the noble wood and park destroyed by Rich the rebel'. Little but the Great Hall now survives.

Thorne, in the '70s, says that the village 'wears an air of old-fashioned respectability, and some of the old houses are worth looking at'. But there has been much demolition and redevelopment, and the district is mainly suburban.

St John Baptist's, High Street

The church stands in a large churchyard that has a good many eighteenth-century stones, and has not been too much tidied up. The arcade of the old church fell when a vault was being made for Sir John Shaw in 1667, and there was rebuilding afterwards. There was a Doric colonnade: the Shaw chapel on the north was seventeenth-century Gothic.

This church has been entirely demolished, and its place taken by a much larger Early English church of Kentish rag designed by Sir A. W. Blomfield: a faculty was given 9 July 1872. The low tower and spire at the south-west, which do not add much to the dignity of the church, were built later.

It is so like other churches by Blomfield that there is very little to be said about it. The inside has been whitened. The iron screens at the sides of the chancel have been allowed to remain, but that at the west—which suited the church very well—has been taken down: a part of it is in the arch by the font. There are a good many tablets from the old church, but none that deserve particular mention. Some north aisle glass is by Burlison and Grylls: the east window is by Comper.

Holy Trinity, Southend Crescent

Built by G. E. Street in 1868–9; not very interesting, and not specially characteristic; in thirteenth-century style, unclerestoried, with a kingpost roof. There used to be a lead spirelet. An organ chamber was added in 1872.

A faculty was given in 1909 for a new east window, and another, later in the year, gave leave to add two bays to the nave, and build a narthex; to add a south chapel; to raise the floor of the sanctuary, and extend the choir into the nave; to erect a wall, with a low iron screen, at the entrance to the chancel; etc. Architects, Sir A. Blomfield and Sons. The reredos was completed by W. D. Caröe. Other alterations were carried out. In 1913: organ case, figures in canopies on the east wall, painted panels, oak cornice to the chancel roof, oak altar rails—by C. E. Kempe. In 1916: beam and rood, panelling and reredos in south chapel—Kempe, again. The chapel was made, after the first World War, a memorial to the 29th Division. There is glass by Tower and by Powell.

St Andrew's, Court Road, Mottingham

A red brick church, designed by E. F. C. Clarke and built in 1878–9. It has an aisleless nave, with double transepts towards the east: one bay on the south has never been built. The chancel and porch were added in 1912, by E. J. Gosling. There was some damage early in 1944, and repairs afterwards.

All Saints', Bercta Road, New Eltham

This is the successor of an iron church in Footscray Road, opened in 1884. It was built in 1898, by Peter Dollar, and is of red brick, with lancet windows. The Perpendicular chancel dates from 1930. The west end was completed in 1937.

St Luke's, Westmount Park Road

Temple Moore was appointed architect in 1905, and the tender of Messrs Goddard Bros, of Dorking, was accepted on 5 May 1906: the nave, chancel, and north aisle were to be built for £4,315. The foundation stone was laid on 14 July 1906, and the consecration was on 6 July 1907.

This is one of Temple Moore's simple, and very attractive, churches. The nave and chancel are under one roof with plain rectangular piers: waggon roofs.

The screen, by Hedley and Pollock, of Baker Street, was dedicated on 28 June 1915. A window in the north aisle is by C. J. Woodward, 1922. The south aisle, chapel, and vestries were added in 1933: the architect was J. B. S. Tolhurst.

St Barnabas', Rochester Way

A temporary church was built in 1916 by the War Office. In 1932 an offer was made of the Dockyard Chapel at Woolwich. This was built from plans by Scott in 1859. It had to contain galleries, and was planned with this in view. There were iron pillars, and arches of wood: the bays were gabled transversely, and the rafters underceiling the gables were arched to match the arcades. A timber-framed clerestory, and an eastern apse lit by lancets. The Chapel was taken down and rebuilt at Eltham by Thomas F. Ford: the builder was W. E. Ismay.

It was bombed, restored in 1956–7, and rededicated on 22 June 1957. Architects, Thomas F. Ford and Partners, with Alan Ford in charge: the builder was Ismay. The outer walls survive: the interior has been remodelled in neo-Regency style. The aisles are screened off: there is a barrel ceiling: the aisle walls are painted pink. The semidome of the apse is painted by Hans Feibusch. The pews, stalls, font and organ came from St Michael's, Lant Street, Southwark.

St Saviour's, Middle Park Road, Eltham

Built in 1932–3; the architects were Welch, Cachemaille-Day and Lander. This church made a great sensation when it was first built: it has worn better than some Modern churches of the '30s. It is of concrete and brick, with a concrete roof: nave with passage aisles, and a sanctuary carried up as a low tower. All the windows are tall and narrow: those in the sanctuary have blue glass. The pulpit and desk are of brick. A concrete reredos with the figure of Christ is by Donald Hastings.

Greenwich

This is the parish which has the credit of having suggested the Fifty New Churches scheme in the reign of Queen Anne. The parish church was sumptuously rebuilt from plans by Hawksmoor: the Victorian view of it is expressed by the *Imperial Gazeteer*, which calls it 'a large edifice, in poor, mixed, Grecian style'.

A great deal of extra church accommodation was provided by the building of two Commissioners' churches—St Mary's, and Holy Trinity, Blackheath Hill, which held respectively 1,700 and 1,200. Both of these have gone.

Greenwich churchmanship in the nineteenth century was Evangelical, under Canon J. C. Miller, the originator of Hospital Sunday, who was vicar from 1866 to 1880: he urged Bishop Thorold to take strong measures against the Ritualists, and if possible drive them from the Church. Afterwards, under Brooke Lambert, St Alphege offered 'a good parochial service and the broadest of Broad Church doctrine'.

So there are no churches by Pearson, or Brooks, or Bodley, with sanctuary lamps, Lady chapels, etc. S. S. Teulon built two—not his best—of which one has been demolished.

St Alphege, High Street (167)

On 6 April 1711 a petition was presented to Parliament. The steeple—so the petitioners said, but it seems to have been the roof—of Greenwich church had fallen on the night of 28 November, and the church would have to be rebuilt: the estimate was £6,260, which was more than the parish could raise. As the parishioners had, for 40 years past, contributed to the building of St Paul's, and other churches, by a duty on coals, and as St Paul's was nearly finished, could not a sum of £6,000 be assigned for the rebuilding of the church of Greenwich?

A committee was appointed to consider this, and also to examine the whole question of church building in London, Westminster, and the suburbs. The result was the Fifty New Churches Act of 1711.

Greenwich was the first of the new churches to be finished. It was taken down, except for the tower, in 1711, finished by 1714, and consecrated in September 1718. Hawksmoor was the architect: masons, Edward Strong and Edward Tufnell; plasterers, James Ellis and James Hands. John Smallwell, joiner, supplied the pulpit and desks. Payments for carving were made to Grinling Gibbons, and also to Richard Jones, Joseph Wade, John Boson and Thomas Darby. The painting about the altar was done by Sir James Thornhill.

The plan of the church is not very exciting: a rectangle, with north and south projections: at the west, a vestibule and vestries: at the east a shallow internal apse. The external walls have Doric pilasters. The main front is towards the east: at the angles are small vestibules: between them is a Doric portico with an open arch in the middle.

Hawksmoor made a design for a tower, but this was not executed. The rather ordinary steeple, built on the lower part of the old tower, was added in 1730 from plans by John James: the masons were Christopher Cass and Andrews Jelfe. The steeple was rebuilt in 1813.

The interior had noteworthy furnishings, but it was wrecked in the War. Sir Albert Richardson did the reconstruction, and the church was rededicated on 18 April 1953. The pews and stalls are by Dove Brothers: the pulpit, a replica of the original, by White of Bedford. Thornhill's paintings were thought to have been destroyed, but they were restored by Glyn Jones. The east window glass, 1953, is by Francis H. Spear, who also designed other windows, 1956.

St Michael's, Blackheath Park (168)

The estate was bought in 1784 by John Cator. His son John developed it and built the church at a cost of £4,000 in 1828–9: he laid the foundation stone on 20 December 1828. The architect was George Smith, the builder W. B. Moore. The church is of white brick, in the usual Perpendicular style, tall and slim. The feature which it is worth coming a long way to see is the eastern tower, which is low, pinnacled, and with an east window the tracery of which is Smith's own invention—on top of which is a slim octagonal stage, with an open parapet and pinnacles, and the most slender and needle-like spire that ever was. A vestry at the north-east was added in 1879.

The interior is more ordinary, though more than usually thin and pinched-up. The foliated corbels are of plaster. The east end has another Smith-Gothic window, with borrowed light, and a large stone altar-piece. The church has been reseated, and the galleries have been altered: in 1920 a War memorial pulpit of stone was erected, and the east end adapted for a surpliced choir. But the organ remains in the gallery at the west.

Christchurch, Trafalgar Road

Built 1847–9 from designs by John Brown and Robert Kerr, of Norwich, who won a competition. The cost was £7,741.

The *Ecclesiologist* did not criticise this church: if it had done so, it would certainly have had a good deal to say. The plan would have been found fault with: a wide, galleried, aisleless nave, with a south-west tower (designed for a spire that was never built): a projection on the south, a north vestry, and an eastern apse. The style is Perpendicular, with ragstone walls and brick quoins. There are two-light windows and a larger window at the west, which looks quite well. The galleries have been removed, except at the west, and a small projection on each side. The new vestry was designed in 1887 by Thomas Dinwiddy, of Greenwich. The elaborate font and pulpit are later than the church: the carved sanctuary chairs are no doubt original.

St John's, St John's Park, Blackheath (169)

Designed by Arthur Ashpitel: the foundation stone was laid 9 July 1852, and the church was consecrated on 10 August 1853. The cost was £6,500. A dignified and scholarly Perpendicular church, with a western tower and spire, which stands effectively in the middle of the tree-lined St John's Park. Churches in this style were rare in the '50s and when architects used Perpendicular they were apt to try to improve on it: but this is quite straightforward, and the interior is like that of a decent suburban church of 30 years later—especially as it has been given a screen and reredos and panelling in the sanctuary by H. S. Rogers, and glass by Powell and by Heaton, Butler and Bayne.

St Paul's, Devonshire Drive

Built in 1865–6, designed by S. S. Teulon. Of Kentish rag, in French thirteenth-century style. Restored after War damage, in 1950.

St George's, Kirkside Road, Westcombe Park

Built in 1890–1: the architects, Newman and Newman, builders, Balaam Bros. It is an ordinary red brick church. The best thing about it is the site: it stands on a steep hill, sloping from south to north, and there is a lower storey on the north side. The chancel was not built: a small sanctuary was added later.

SS Andrew' and Michael', Tunnel Avenue (170)

Designed by Basil Champneys, and built in 1900–2. The church was partly built with the money from the demolition and sale of St Michael's, Wood Street, in the City, the font of which was brought here.

It is an attractive design, carried out in stock brick, with pantiled roofs. Passage aisles run through the buttresses: the arcades have octagonal piers opposite the buttresses, and the bays are subdivided by smaller arches. A clerestory and barrel roof: there are no aisle windows. At the west is a narthex, with flying buttresses above: the window is, as usual, large. Two octagonal turrets. The chancel is much raised, with rooms below.

But the church is quite out of place. The district was expected to develop into a pleasant suburb, but it never did: there is only a thin line of small houses, stretched out beside the road to Blackwall Tunnel, along which lorries continuously thunder. The church is overshadowed by enormous gasworks, and surrounded by a high fence of concrete posts and wire, with locked gates: in spite of the height of the fence, the local inhabitants have succeeded in depositing an extraordinary quantity of rubbish in the precinct.

Lambeth

The old church of Lambeth is by the river, next door to the Palace. But the parish extended for several miles inland. A chapel of ease was built at Stockwell in the eighteenth century, and there were a few proprietary chapels. But the first large-scale building was done in the 1820s, when the four massive Commissioners' churches, dedicated to the four evangelists, were erected at Brixton, Kennington, Norwood, and Waterloo Road. St

167 St Alphege, Greenwich, 1711–18 by Nicholas Hawksmoor, tower by John James 1730

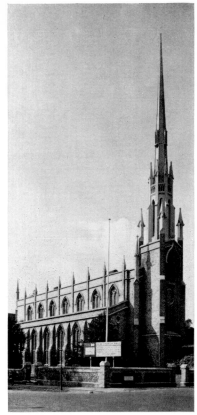

168 St Michael's, Blackheath Park, 1828–9 by George Smith

169 St John's, Blackheath, 1852–3 by Arthur Ashpitel

170 SS Andrew and Michael, North Greenwich, 1900–2 by Basil Champneys

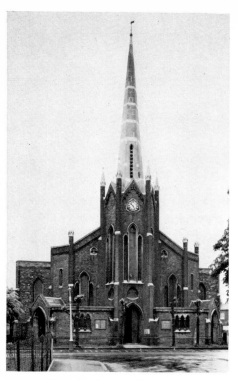

171 St Michael's, Stockwell, 1840–1
by William Rogers

172 All Saints', West Dulwich, 1888–91
by G. H. Fellowe Prynne

173 St Peter's, Streatham, the front added by G. H.
Fellowes Prynne 1886–7, to the church by R. W. Drew

174 St Margaret's, Lee, 1839–41 by John Brown,
restored by James Brooks 1876

Mary the Less, Lambeth, was also a Commissioners' church. Holy Trinity was built by the Metropolis Churches Fund and the diocesan society.

The *Imperial Gazeteer* describes Lambeth itself in the '60s as consisting of 'narrow streets and disagreeable thoroughfares, with mean houses or malodorous factories'. It had also some really bad patches, such as are described in Michael Sadleir's *Forlorn Sunset*. Church work was not easy here, nor was there much response in the better working class areas.

The outer parts were quite different: they contained 'a vast aggregation of fine new thoroughfares and places with a character in striking contrast to that of Lambeth proper'. This character remained in some parts, and still does, but there was a social decline in most of it, and the open spaces were filled up with a good deal of mean building.

Church extension went on as usual during the second half of the century. Most of the churches are still there—indeed, all, except for a few mission chapels—in the outer areas. Those that have gone are in the parts nearer the river.

St Mary's, Lambeth Palace Road

The church was newly built in 1377, and the parishioners were told to rebuild the tower: the tower—repaired in 1834-5—is all that remains: the church was entirely rebuilt by P. C. Hardwick, in fourteenth-century style, in 1851-2. At first the old pews were used, there were galleries in the aisles, and the organ was in a gallery: the *Ecclesiologist* looked forward to a further stage of the restoration—which duly came to pass. Glass was inserted: the east window was by O'Connor. A new font was given in 1852, and the old font, given in 1615, went to Holy Trinity (a church by Edward Blore, now demolished). New seating by J. O. Scott, was installed in 1885. The reredos, 1888, by J. O. Scott, had panels of terra cotta by Tinworth: this was damaged in the War, but a portion remains. The total immersion font, 1904, by J. Arthur Reeve, was a memorial to Archbishop Benson. The pulpit, from St James's, Kennington Park, was set up in 1924: the rails, from the Archbishop's Palace at Addington, probably came from All Saints', Maidstone: a part of them has been put up at the entrance to the baptistery. The faculty for the organ was given on 8 November 1699.

Post-War repairs were undertaken by Godfrey Allen. The new east and west windows and the 'Pedlar' window are by Francis Stephens.

Monuments   Table tombs of Hugh Peyntwyn, Doctor of Laws, 1504: and John Mompesson, 1524 (or, it may be, Henry, 1509). A bust of Robert Scott, 1631. Samuel Goodbehere, 1820, by Henry Westmacott. Thomas Lett, 1830, by Chantrey. Brasses: Katherine Broughton, wife of Lord William Howard, 1535. Thomas Clere, 1545.

Several Archbishops of Canterbury are buried here.

St Andrew's, Stockwell

In 1711 the inhabitants of Lambeth petitioned the Commissioners for the Fifty New Churches that an additional church might be built in the Parish. Sir John Thornycroft, lord of Stockwell Manor, offered a site, and the Commissioners agreed that a church should be built. But nothing was done. In 1767 a piece of land was obtained, and a chapel was built. The east end was extended in 1810. In 1867 it was remodelled in Romanesque by H. E. Coe; the nave was extended westward, a tower was built on the south, and the galleries were reconstructed. It was consecrated on 11 June 1868. Vestries 1891; side chapel 1894, by Alfred J. Pilkington; reredos 1914, by H. Hems. The galleries were removed in 1924.

St Anne's, South Lambeth Road

In 1793 several gentlemen agreed to erect a chapel at their joint expense, at a cost not exceeding £3,000. The builder was Thomas Wapshott, of Tufton Street. The Chapel was damaged by fire in 1856. It was consecrated as a parish church on 3 February 1869.

A faculty was given in 1874 to build a new wall across the church at the east, leaving three openings, and to build a new chancel, with a vestry on the south, and a tower at the north-east over an organ chamber, which was to be completed as high as the belfry floor, and covered with a temporary roof. Also to demolish the galleries, and build a new gallery at the west, and to make new entrances; to erect a new open timber roof of deal; to unite the windows previously divided by the galleries; and to reseat.

The architect was R. Parkinson. These alterations were in a Romanesque style: nothing but the walls was left of the eighteenth-century church.

Percy Dearmer, as curate in 1891, made his first attempt at church improvement: 'We are to have a Morris tapestry baldachino and some delicately simple Morris frontals; the whole to be under the direction of Selwyn Image.'

In 1927 the interior was redecorated, and an attempt was made to restore some eighteenth-century character. It was damaged by bombing, and repaired after the War.

The four churches in the old parish of Lambeth, dedicated to the Evangelists, are generally called the Waterloo Churches. I was told this, by some older person, when I lived in South London as a boy: and no doubt the story is still passed on—that these churches are, in some special way, a memorial to Waterloo.

It was indeed proposed in Parliament that a church, or churches, should be built as a War memorial; but nothing was done about it, and there is no reason to suppose that the Lambeth churches were specially built for the purpose. The origin of the legend seems to be that St John's, being in the Waterloo Road, was referred to as 'the Waterloo Church'; and people seem to have supposed that, if it was a Waterloo Church, then the others were as well.

St Matthew's, Brixton

This fine church was designed by Charles Ferdinand Porden, the nephew of the better-known William Porden. The foundation stone was laid on 1 July 1822 and the church was consecrated on 21 June 1824. The contractor who began the work was Mercer of Millbank: it was completed by Thomas Want, John Richardson, and J. and H. Lee. The contract was for £15,192, though it cost more: the Commissioners' grant was £7,917.

The church is a rectangle, with a tremendous Greek Doric portico at the west. The architect did not attempt to combine it with a tower, but put his tower at the other end. This is the usual combination of Greek elements: it has its points, but without doubt the west end is more impressive without it.

The interior has been little altered: the galleries and the box pews remain, and the organ is in its proper place at the west. The central pulpit was not removed until 1910. The altar recess has two Doric columns, and a window to the base of the tower. The rails are of ironwork. There used to be some Victorian painting, but this has been obliterated. The church was reopened after repair on 21 December 1954.

Monuments   At the north end of the churchyard is a striking monument to Richard Budd, 1824, by R. Day. Almost all the other monuments have been removed.

St Mark's, Kennington

The architect was D. R. Roper, a well-known London surveyor, but the design was in fact made by A. B. Clayton. The foundation stone was laid on 1 July 1822 and the consecration was on 30 June 1824. The contractors were Moore, Grimsdell and Davis: the cost was £16,093, of which the Commissioners contributed £7,651, and the parish of Lambeth the balance.

The body of the church is unimpressive: rectangular, with splayed angles. It has 'stone pilasters attached to the piers between the windows, which are in the dwelling house style, and utterly at variance with the Grecian portico'. This is Doric, *in antis*, with a pediment. The tower behind it has an octagonal vestibule in the basement, and a circular Ionic temple above, with a cupola and cross. The gallery staircases are in chambers at the sides. The altar is in a very dignified recess, with two pairs of Ionic columns on each side of the east window.

The interior was restored by S. S. Teulon in 1873–6: choir stalls were introduced, and the organ was moved. In 1898 the pulpit from St Michael's, Wood Street, in the City, was brought here. There was repair and redecoration in 1901–02, by Basil Champneys: altar rails 1905. Work was done in 1931 by R. W. K. Goddard, who was partner with Basil Champneys from 1899–1906: the contractors were J. Dorey and Co.

In 1937 considerable restoration was done, at a cost of £7,500, including a glass dome over the centre: a south chapel was formed.

The church was damaged in September 1940, opened and rededicated after partial restoration in 1949, and finally reopened on 12 March 1960. The architects were Thomas F. Ford and Partners. The galleries have been divided off. The interior is now extremely attractive.

St Luke's, West Norwood

Francis Bedford's plans were chosen, and the church was begun in 1822: it was consecrated on 15 July 1825. The contractor was Elizabeth Broomfield. The Commissioners gave £6,449 towards the total of £12,947.

The church stands on an imposing site, where the ground rises at the north of Norwood Road, and the road divides into Norwood Street and Knights Hill. It stands north and south: it could hardly do anything else. But the Commissioners decided that the altar should be at the east, with the pews facing it. There was to have been a gallery only on the west side, but in 1824 it was decided to add others at the north and south ends. After the building was finished, the west gallery was enlarged, and another gallery was built over the altar.

The portico is of six Corinthian columns: above it is Bedford's usual tower.

In 1870 G. E. Street began a complete remodelling of the inside. It was divided into nave and aisles—running north and south—by arcades in Italian Romanesque style; and a chancel was formed. The windows were divided by stonework in a T shape. The paintings in the blind windows above the altar were done in 1885 by W. Christian Symons, from designs by J. F. Bentley. The reredos was erected 1886 by A. Bickerdike. A faculty was given 5 February 1936 to enable Sir Charles Nicholson to redecorate the interior: some of the fittings are his.

St John's, Waterloo Road

Another of Francis Bedford's churches. The foundation stone was laid on 30 June 1823: and the consecration took place on 3 November 1824. The cost was £18,034: the Commissioners' grant was £9,976. The church was built on a basement, which extends westwards under the terrace in front, as the road had been considerably raised to meet the level of Waterloo Bridge. The chief feature is the Greek Doric portico, with chaplets of myrtle on the frieze. The tower rises above it.

The plain interior terminated in an altar piece with a pediment on antae of white marble, with the Commandments, etc., on black marble tablets. This was removed later in the nineteenth century. The white marble font, which survived the bombing, is eighteenth-century Italian: it was given by the Rev Dr Barrett, the first incumbent. Between the Wars, Sir J. N. Comper erected a free-standing altar under a ciborium.

A bomb fell on 12 December 1940 and wrecked the inside: the walls and the portico stood firm. The church was reconstructed by T. F. Ford for the Festival of Britain in 1951. The galleries were taken down, except at the west: the west gallery was reconstructed in steel and concrete. The sanctuary was moved back to the east wall, and the breadth was reduced by enclosures on the north and south. New pulpit and desk were erected. The roof was replaced in steel, with a fibrous plaster ceiling. Remains of the original altar piece were found, and it was restored, with a painting by Hans Feibusch in the central panel: another is in the east window. The colour scheme is pale fawn: the plaster ornaments are partly gilt, on a ground of green and terra cotta.

St Mary the Less, Black Prince Road

A Gothic church by Francis Bedford, begun in 1827, and consecrated on 26 August 1828: the builder was William Woods. The church is standing at the present moment, but is due to be demolished.

St Michael's, Stockwell Park Crescent (171)

The site was given to the Church Building Commissioners in 1839, and William Rogers's design was accepted in 1840. The church was begun in that year, and consecrated on 18 November 1841. The builder was John Jay.

The style is Early English. The main front is towards the east, where there is a low, hexagonal tower with a thin spire. On either side are lobbies added in 1844. The ground plan is unusual, as there are outer aisles, under the galleries. There are very tall and thin iron columns.

In 1880 the interior was reconstructed, the altar was put at the west end, and the furniture was turned round: the architect was Thomas Dashwood, of 30 Hatherley Grove,

Bayswater. The organ has been moved, but keeps its case. The pinnacles were renewed, and the tower and exterior were repaired, in 1896: the builders were Maxwell Bros. A. R. Powys renovated the interior in 1920: the builder was F. R. Logan. The church was restored after War damage by Thomas F. Ford, and reopened in 1952.

The interior is dark and sombre, and has not been much decorated. On the north side is a window that was made in 1924 by John Trinick, and remade by him in 1953. The glass in the lancets in the apse is predominantly blue, with tall, thin figures, and panels of roses on a blue ground.

St Barnabas', Guildford Road, Kennington

The site was given by the Dean and Chapter of Canterbury. The Duke of Cambridge laid the foundation stone on 27 July 1848, and the church was consecrated in 1850. The cost was about £4,800, and the architects were Isaac Clarke and James Humphrys. It is of Kentish rag, with Bath stone dressings, Early English in style, with nave and aisles and a small aisleless part at the west, which once had a gallery; there are tall arcades, a small clerestory, and a hammer beam roof. The sanctuary is apsidal: a half-hearted attempt has been made to give an impression of vaulting at the east end: but there is really only a flat ceiling.

A faculty was given in 1884 to repair the church, and to remove the west gallery, and the western parts of the side galleries. Architect, Charles Moore, of 33 Lansdowne Gardens, S.W. The galleries were completely removed in 1888, by J. Moir Kennard.

The church was repaired in 1948. The organ came from All Saints', Lambeth, and the pulpit from St Augustine's, Clapham Road.

St John's, Angell Town, Brixton

Begun in 1852, and consecrated on 30 August 1853; it was built at the cost of William Stone, of The Casino, Herne Hill. The builders were H. and R. Holland. The architect was Benjamin Ferrey—most of whose London churches have been demolished: they were built at a time when church extension was being done in districts that have since become run-down or depopulated. This is a simple and decent Perpendicular church, of Kentish rag with Bath stone dressings, with a pinnacled tower. Perpendicular churches of this date are rare, but Ferrey did design one or two. A faculty was given on 10 August 1876 to clean and repair the church, build a north transept, move the organ, etc.

The east window glass, by Hudson, was too violent in colour for the taste of the between-War years; but the parishioners did not want it removed. So a curtain was placed in front of it, which could be pulled or drawn back. There was a fire in 1947, and a restoration afterwards by Thomas F. Ford. The altar has been brought forward, and the chancel is used for other purposes.

Holy Trinity, Trinity Rise, Tulse Hill

Begun in 1855, and consecrated on 6 February 1856. The architect was T. D. Barry of Liverpool. His churches are all much alike: in a rather decadent fourteenth-century style, with squeezed-up windows, and too much naturalistic foliage. He liked tall, thin spires, and rather small belfry windows. The condition laid down for the design of Holy Trinity was that there should be no internal supports. It is cruciform, with an aisleless nave, short chancel and apse, and tower and spire, with a porch at the bottom, on the north side.

The windows in the apse are by Clare Dawson, 1951–3, replacing glass broken in the War.

St Stephen's, St Stephen's Terrace (176)

Built at the cost of the Rev Charles Kemble, vicar of Bath, in 1860–1: the architect was John Barnett, and the builder George Myers. Of Kentish rag and Bath stone, with flowing-traceried windows. An auditorium plan, like that of many nonconformist chapels: a wide, unaisled nave, transepts, and a very short chancel. A tower and spire at the north-west. The nave has gabled windows at the sides, and there are circular traceried windows at the east and at the west.

St Philip's, Kennington Road

A fund was opened at the end of 1849 as a thanksgiving for preservation in the cholera epidemic; but the church was not begun until 1862. It was consecrated on 2 June 1863. The cost was £8,500. The architect was H. E. Coe. It is rag-faced, with slate roofs, in fourteenth-century style. It has a low south-west tower, with an octagonal top stage: the spire was replaced by a copper roof in 1960.

A faculty was given on 20 June 1913 for a choir vestry, south chapel, oak screen between chancel and chapel, and new pulpit. The architect was H. S. Rogers.

The interior was whitened in the '20s, roofs and all.

St Peter's, Kennington Park Road, Vauxhall (177, 178)

J. L. Pearson was the architect; it was built in 1863–4, and consecrated on 28 June 1864. The design was exhibited at the Royal Academy in 1861: the *Ecclesiologist* commented: 'We have seldom had a more important design—or one more thoroughly satisfactory— than this before us.' The church was to have been more ambitious, with a very tall tower and spire: this was left out, and the west front was simplified.

It was said at the time that this was what a town church ought to be. It should depend for its exterior effect on breadth of composition, height above the surrounding houses, and solidity of construction: the interior should be spacious and imposing, and sufficiently rich in decoration, of the kind that would look well in the imperfect light of a London church, and would bear some years of its atmosphere.

That is well said: it would be difficult to find a better church of its kind. It was the first of Pearson's large town churches, and is in many ways the best. In his later churches there is a good deal of obvious thirteenth-century detail: here, there is practically no detail at all, and everything is simple, solid, and, as the ecclesiologists would have said, real.

It is of stock brick, with a little red, and vaulted throughout: nave and aisles, with a west porch and south-west baptistery: apsidal chancel, with a two-storied sacristy on the north, and a transeptal organ chamber on the south. A north chapel of two bays lies along-side both nave and chancel. There is no chancel arch, and nave and chancel are of the same height.

The west front is most impressive, with the low porch between the buttresses, opening straight on to the pavement: there is a large plate-traceried, French-looking window on each side of the central buttress, and a circular window above.

Inside, the pillars are solid and cylindrical: the next stage has panels, divided by the vaulting shafts; and there are plate-traceried clerestory windows. In the apse, the triforium stage has open arcading, with small windows behind: the glass in these windows, and the panels below, are by Clayton and Bell: the upper lancets have glass by Lavers, Barraud and Westlake. A pedimented reredos with mosaics: iron parcloses, and ironwork on the screen wall at the west of the chancel.

The interior has been carefully preserved: it is free from well-meaning later embellishments and has never been whitewashed. There is no other Anglo-Catholic church in London in which the austere and dignified sanctuary arrangements of the 1860's have been allowed to remain.

Christchurch, Gipsy Hill

A large ragstone church, with slated roofs, French thirteenth-century in style, with polished granite pillars and foliated capitals. The architect was John Giles, of Giles, Gough and Trollope, and the church was consecrated on 7 June 1867. The tower, at the north-east, was completed in 1889, and vestry and porch were added in the same year.

St Saviour's, Herne Hill Road

A Romanesque church designed by A. D. Gough: foundation stone laid on 29 June 1866, and the consecration 25 June 1867. Of Kentish rag and Bath stone, in the Norman and Transitional styles. The chancel and south transept were added in 1870, from designs by W. Gibbs Bartleet.

St Jude's, Dulwich Road, Brixton

The site for this church was given by Joshua Blackburn in 1862. There was a competition for the design which was won by E. C. Robins. The foundation stone was laid on 3 August 1867, and the church was consecrated on 28 October 1868. The builder was John Kirk of Woolwich. The cost was £7,900. It is a large and rather dreary church, of Kentish rag and Bath stone; cruciform, with a very low tower and spire in the angle of the transept, facing the road. The chancel was damaged by fire in 1923, and restored by G. H. Fellowes Prynne.

The church was damaged by bombing in 1940. On 24 May 1952 the south aisle was rededicated for use as a church: the rest was brought back into use later.

St James's, Knatchbull Road

In quite a pleasant position, opposite to Myatts Fields. The church was the gift of J. L. Minet, the owner of the estate, who gave the site, paid for the building (about £8,000), and provided an endowment. The foundation stone was laid on 19 June 1869, and the consecration took place on 27 June 1870. The architect was George Low, and the builders were Dove Bros.

It is a large church, in a rather Gilbert Scott-ish late thirteenth-century style: the walls are faced with Kentish rag, with Bath stone dressings; it has nave and aisles, with a tower and spire at the north-west, low transepts, and an apsidal chancel. The clerestory is a row of foiled circular windows.

The inside is quite simple, without the carved foliage that might be expected. The aisles and transepts have glass by Ward and Hughes. The windows in the apse, and the west window of the nave, are by Clayton and Bell.

St John the Divine, Vassall Road, Kennington (175)

The foundation stone of a temporary church in Elliot Road was laid on 22 October 1869: the architect was Gould. An appeal for funds to build the permanent church was made at Easter 1871. The plans were made by G. E. Street. It would be an extremely fine church, and it was not proposed to try to build it all at once: there would be three stages—first the chancel, then the nave and aisles, and then the tower and spire.

The foundation stone was laid on 4 July 1871, and the eastern parts were completed by September 1873. Then a gift of £10,000 from 'Anon'—who was, in fact, Canon Brooke—made it possible to undertake the nave and aisles. A new builder was engaged, and the church was consecrated on 14 November 1874.

It is very large, and simple in plan: a wide, unclerestoried nave, with an aisleless bay at the west, and the rest with aisles: the arcades are tall, with clustered shafts, and capitals carved by Earp. The last bay is canted inward to connect with the narrower chancel. The nave has a waggon roof. The noble tower and spire were built in 1888–9, after Street's death, by his son A. E. Street.

In 1890 Bodley set to work to decorate the church. The nave roof was painted first, and then, in 1892, that of the chancel. The sanctuary floor was relaid with marble, and a very large reredos (carved by Farmer and Brindley) was erected. The earlier reredos, a triptych by Clayton and Bell—which was certainly more suitable to the church—was moved to the chapel. Later, the walls of the aisles were panelled. The Blessed Sacrament Chapel was designed by Sir Charles Nicholson.

The church was burned by a fire bomb in 1940, and there was further damage in 1941. Repairs were done in 1955–8 by H. S. Goodhart-Rendel and H. Lewis Curtis: the builders were Ward and Patterson, the cost was £140,000. Street's drawings had been kept, and this was a church that deserved to be reinstated properly: Goodhart-Rendel did this, and refrained from whitening the red brick walls. But the altar has been brought forward to the west of the chancel. The new glass is by W. T. Carter Shapland.

St Saviour's, Lambert Road, Brixton

The foundation stone was laid by James Watney on 15 July 1874, and the church was consecrated on 29 September 1875. The architect was E. C. Robins. St Saviour's is a large church of Kentish rag, in French thirteenth-century style. A tower is at the west end of the north aisle, pinnacled, with an octagonal, slate-covered cap. The nave is of six bays, with low, rather wide aisles, and a clerestory of plate traceried windows. The chancel is rather short.

Glass in the east window by Heaton, Butler and Bayne, 1875: in the nave and aisles, Powell.

St Paul's, Santley Street, Brixton

An eloquent Irishman, the Rev G. Blake Concannon, began to minister in an iron church, and then transferred to a larger one: he then decided to build a permanent church. St Paul's was erected, at a cost of £16,000, to provide a greater number of sittings than any other church in the neighbourhood. The architects were W. G. Habershon and E. Fawckner; the builder was James of Gloucester. It was consecrated on 29 July 1881. Of yellow brick, banded with red: large and unattractive. The nave has a hammer-beam roof; there were galleries, but they have been taken down.

All Saints', Rosendale Road, West Dulwich (172)

One of the most impressive examples of ambition in suburban church building. The church was proposed in 1887, and the College gave the site: the foundation stone was laid on 31 October 1888, and the completed portion was opened on the same day in 1891. The consecration was on 13 November 1897. The cost was about £16,000.

The architect was G. H. Fellowes Prynne, who was a comparatively young man at the time: he was born in 1853. The style is ordinary: lancets in the nave, and fourteenth-century in the eastern parts. But the plan is, for a parish church, most unusual. A wide nave with aisles is joined to the chancel by a narrow canted bay, with openings to the chancel aisles below, and, above, to the organ loft and minstrels' gallery. The chancel is apsidal, with long, thin, rather German-looking windows. There is an ambulatory round the apse. The Lady chapel, on the north, also has its apse and ambulatory. The church is built on a steep slope from west to east, and stands on a lower storey, with classrooms and vestries: there is an open arcade round the east end, and a covered way, through the buttresses and under the ambulatories.

The church was never completed, and never will be: the western bays of the nave and aisles were not built; nor was the tower, or the tall flèche at the junction of the nave and chancel. The fittings were mostly temporary. The marble font, with its tall cover, was erected in 1917, and the pulpit some years afterwards.

At the entrance to the chancel is a traceried stone screen, filling the whole of the opening: the first example of a feature that Fellowes Prynne repeated later. The glass in the aisles is by Burlison and Grylls: of the windows that Kempe designed for the apse, only one was put in.

The church was damaged in 1944, and restored in 1952 by J. B. S. Comper, who erected a small tower in the place where Fellowes Prynne's tall tower would have been.

St Matthias', Upper Tulse Hill

The Raleigh Park and Elm Park estates were sold, and quickly built up. An old skating rink was first used as a place of worship for the district.

The site was bought in 1881. The foundation stone was laid on 2 June 1894; the church was opened in December 1894, but not consecrated until 1899. The architects were J. T. Newman and William Jacques. This is a red brick church in the lancet style, about which it would be difficult to find much to say.

Christchurch, Brixton Road

On the site of Holland Chapel, which was built for the Independents. In 1835 it had to be sold, to meet the demands of the mortgagees, and the friends of the minister, the Rev John Styles, built Claylands Chapel in 1836. Holland Chapel became episcopal, and was consecrated as Christchurch in 1855.

It became unsafe, and Professor Beresford Pite made plans for a new church. Princess Christian laid the foundation stone in 1898. The old building was taken down in 1899, and the new one was consecrated on 3 November 1907.

The church is, and always has been, conservative Evangelical, and the new Christchurch was planned so that a congregation of 1,300 could see and hear the minister. It has an aisleless nave, and very wide transepts, with porches: the holy table is free-standing, in an apse, with a passage round.

The style is Byzantine Romanesque, with an octagonal tower over the vestibule at the front, and a low dome over the crossing: the material is brick, with stone dressings on the front towards the Brixton Road.

St Anselm's, Kennington Cross

In 1911 plans were made by S. D. Adshead and S. C. Ramsey for a cruciform, Italianate church with a central dome: the design was exhibited at the Royal Academy in 1913. The Prince of Wales laid the foundation stone on 13 July 1914, but work was stopped by the War, and a temporary church was used. In November 1932 work was resumed, and a much plainer church was built—'a simple early Christian basilica'. It was consecrated on 16 September 1933. The capitals of the arcade were carved by A. H. Gerrard, and the font by Derrick Frith.

St Andrew's with St Thomas's, Short Street

The double dedication recalls two demolished churches, both designed by S. S. Teulon. St Andrew's had a gabled, German-looking tower and slated spire, which was quite a feature of the South Bank. It was bombed, and stood as an empty shell for some years. It has now been cleared away. Of St Thomas's very little was left after the War: the nave had disappeared, and the east wall had a gaping rent where the window once was. The south aisle remained, with its coloured brickwork looking pathetic.

The new church, 1960, by David Nye and Partners, is ordinary. A concrete frame, with aisles on each side of it, and an apse: at the other end, a hall, and between the two a vestibule, with tower-porch towards the street. It is arranged on conventional lines, with choir stalls in the usual place.

Lee

Thorne, as usual, describes the place vividly: 'its convenient distance, the pleasantness of the neighbourhood, and the proximity of Blackheath, have made it a favourite place of residence with City merchants and men of business, for whose accommodation every available piece of ground has been appropriated. Parks . . . in which the houses are not too closely packed, mingling with the terraces of detached and semi-detached villas and genteel cottages, and a sprinkling of older houses in good-sized grounds, secure the place from the cheerless monotony of some suburban districts, but leave little to interest a visitor.'

St Margaret's, Lee Terrace (174)

The old church was taken down, except for the tower, and rebuilt by Joseph Gwilt in 1813–14. It soon became unsafe, and it was decided to build a new church on the other side of the road. The plans of John Brown of Norwich were accepted, and the foundation stone was laid on 17 July 1839. The church, and the new churchyard, were consecrated on 11 March 1841. Gwilt's church was taken down, but the lower part of the tower—which had had a wooden top—was left. The old churchyard has a good collection of monuments.

John Brown's church is Early English, with nave and aisles of equal height, and tall, slender arcades: the side walls have tall coupled lancets, such as he was fond of, and used, e.g. at St Michael's, Stamford, and St John's, Bridgwater. The tower has a square lower stage, gabled and pinnacled: but its inside is octagonal, and supports an octagonal upper stage with a spire.

In 1876 the church was remodelled by James Brooks, who added a two-bay vaulted chancel and aisles, keeping close to Brown's style. The rest of the church was given wooden vaults, and there was a general refitting. North and south porches were added. The nineteenth-century glass is all by Clayton and Bell, and as good as usual: that on the north side is post-War. The crypt chapel was formed in 1940, and has furniture and memorials from the demolished churches of Christchurch and Holy Trinity.

Monuments   Brasses of Elizabeth Couhyll, 1513, Isabel Annesley, 1582, (a palimpsest), and Nicholas Ansley, 1593. Scraps of the monument of Bryan Anslye, 1604, and Awdry, 1591.

St Mildred's, St Mildred's Road

Built in 1878–9 from designs by H. Elliot; it is of brick inside, and Kentish rag outside, in the late thirteenth-century style. It has a restless interior, with notched bricks in the arcades and the heads of the aisle windows. The apse to the south transept was added in 1910, by Sir A. Blomfield and Sons.

   The apsidal chancel has five two-light windows, which were filled in 1953 with glass by William Morris and Co.

The Good Shepherd, Handen Road

The church by Ernest Newton, 1881, was bombed in 1940, and has completely disappeared. An unenterprising new church was built in 1956–7 from designs by T. F. Ford.

   St Peter's, Courtlands Avenue, 1870–1, by Newman and Billing, was damaged, and has been taken down: the seats and font are in The Good Shepherd.

   A new St Peter's has been built as a chapel of ease (1960).

Lewisham

Booth's Survey of the various parts of this borough mentions a rapid increase in building everywhere. The rich were disappearing, and their place was being taken by clerks and respectable artisans. There were a few pockets of poor streets. There was a good number of churches, and he mentions one curiosity: St Paul's, Forest Hill, which had an accommodation greater than the number of parishioners: the church was seated for a thousand, but the population of the parish was only 678. Churches were well attended. Some were crowded, and only one is mentioned as being empty. Church tended to be more successful than Chapel. Rather more churches than one would have expected have been pulled down.

St Mary's, High Street (179)

The tower was in course of erection in 1471. In 1773 the vestry discussed whether they should repair their parish church, or rebuild it. They appointed a surveyor, who reported that it was in a very bad condition. In January 1774 they decided to rebuild, and an Act of Parliament was obtained in that year. The old church was taken down, except for the tower, which was given a new top stage; and rebuilt in 1775–7: the architect was George Gibson, and the contractor Oliver Burton. The walls are of ragstone, with dressed stone quoins: on the south is a small portico. There was a fire in 1830, a few years after the church had been redecorated: it was repaired afterwards.

In 1881–2 Blomfield added a chancel in Romanesque style instead of Gibson's apse, refitted the nave, and divided it up with very tall and thin wooden posts, carrying light wooden arches. The altar has now been removed from the east end into the nave. There is some post-War glass, in place of what was broken.

Monuments   Thomas Wilkieson, 1786, and Charles, 1795. Anne Petrie, 1787, by Vanpook of Brussels. Margaret Petrie, 1791, by Banks. Mary Lushington, 1797, by Flaxman, with epitaph by Hayley. John Thackeray, 1851, by Baily. Sir Henry Watson Parker, 1881, by R. Belt.

The Ascension, Dartmouth Row, Blackheath

A chapel, founded by Mrs Susannah Graham before 1695. The apse remains, and a short bay to the west of it. The rest was rebuilt by Lord Dartmouth in 1834. At the entrance to the apse are two Corinthian columns, and a round-headed arch: an entablature is carried over two openings at the sides. It was made a parish church in 1883. Vestries were added in 1905.

The church was restored after the War by Robert Potter. The north and south galleries were removed, and the west gallery was cut back; the nave was given a new ceiling, and the east end was redecorated. The contractors were Messrs Hudson Bros, of Clapham. There is heraldic glass by Francis Skeat in two windows.

St Bartholomew's, Westwood Hill, Sydenham

Built at a cost of £9,485, almost all of which was given by the Commissioners (second grant). The architect was Lewis Vulliamy. The builder was William Woods: the church was begun in 1827, but work was suspended because of a dispute between the Commissioners and the parish about the site for a second church. When it was begun again, a new contract was made with Thomas Smith. The consecration was in 1832. It is a large church, of Suffolk brick and stone dressings, with a tower: the style is Perpendicular. The apsidal chancel was added in 1858 from designs by Edwin Nash. In 1883 Nash widened the north aisle, and added a vestry at the east of it; and took down the west gallery. The altar was installed in 1901, and panelling and carving in the sanctuary (very good) 1905. The west window is by Clayton and Bell; two in the north aisle by Burlison and Grylls. The post-War glass is by Francis H. Spear.

Christchurch, Forest Hill

The church was proposed at the same time as St Bartholomew's, Sydenham, but, as there was the difference of opinion about the site, nothing was done for several years.

The design was made by Ewan Christian, and the foundation stone was laid on 21 May 1852. The nave, chancel, and south aisle were built first, and consecrated on 16 May 1854. The north aisle and vestry were then added, and the church was reopened on 4 June 1862. The spire was built in 1885. In 1893, a new reredos, panelling and choir stalls were erected.

It is a straightforward Middle-Pointed church, in a good position on top of a hill, with trees around. Its appearance is greatly improved, in comparison with many such churches, by the fact that the tower is at the west end, and is therefore of good size. The glass was repaired after the War by Alfred L. Wilkinson. Several windows were destroyed, but some remain, e.g. three by Powell and one by Comper.

All Saints', Blackheath (183)

The foundation stone was laid on 26 October 1857, and the church was consecrated on 1 November 1858, the architect being Benjamin Ferrey. It stands on the edge of the heath, all by itself, and makes no attempt to be part of the surrounding buildings. Ferrey was influenced by the fashion of the time sufficiently to give it square abaci, and a certain amount of plate tracery, but otherwise it is still the kind of church that he had designed in the '40s: modest, simple, and in no way out of the ordinary. The tower and spire are at the southwest. The west porch was erected in 1893.

All the interior has been whitened, with a little colour in the roof, and the sanctuary roof coloured brightly. Practically all the glass was destroyed in the War. The east window, 1949, is by A. L. Wilkinson.

175 St John the Divine, Kennington, 1871 by G. E. Street, the tower and spire built under A. E. Street, 1888–9

176 St Stephen's, South Lambeth, 1860–1 by John Barnett

177, 178 St Peter's, Vauxhall, 1863–4 by J. L. Pearson. The west front

The interior, still as Pearson left it

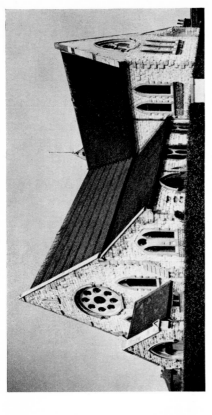

180 St Philip's, Sydenham, 1864–7 by Edwin Nash and J. Round

179 St Mary's, Lewisham, rebuilt 1775–7 by George Gibson: chancel by A. W. Blomfield, 1881–2

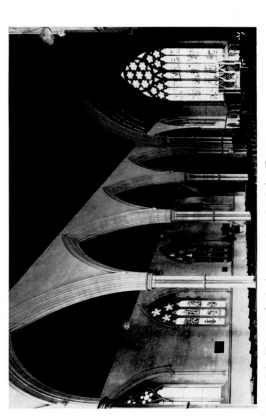

St Stephen's, Lewisham High Street

The Rev S. R. Davies, assistant priest of Lee, inherited money and decided to build a church: Scott was chosen as architect, and he was unlimited as to cost: £16,500 was spent. The church was begun in 1863, and consecrated on Easter eve, 1865. It was meant to have a tower and spire, but these were never built, owing to the nature of the site.

The walls are of Kentish rag, with Bath stone dressings: the detached shafts are of Mansfield stone. The style is Scott's thirteenth-century, with some French details—'eclecticism of a chastened kind, and the union in some degree of the merits of the different styles'. The glass, all by Clayton and Bell, was mostly destroyed in the War. The reredos, by Charles Buckeridge, Scott's young and trusted assistant, was carved by Redfern and decorated by Bell (1873). A faculty was given on 11 September 1875 for a chancel screen by James Brooks, and a south chapel, to which the reredos, removed from the chancel, was to be taken. A further faculty, 20 June 1899, gave leave for a new marble credence, and iron gates to the chapel: the architect was P. A. Robson.

The organ gallery was erected by Sir Charles Nicholson just before the War. In 1952–3 the sanctuary was remodelled, and the reredos cleaned and painted. The east window, and windows of the south chapel, are by J. E. Nuttgens, 1954.

St Philip's, Taylors Lane, Sydenham (180)

Sydenham Wells were discovered in 1640, and were very popular for a time: the waters were supposed to cure almost everything. But their popularity waned, and the Wells were closed. This church is built on the site.

The foundation stone was laid on 1 November 1864, and the consecration was on 17 December 1867. The architect was Edwin Nash with J. Round, and the cost was about £6,350. A faculty of 29 September 1874 gave leave for the erection of a vestry and organ chamber. Chapel in the south transept 1896, by C. H. M. Mileham.

The church is of Reigate stone, in a thirteenth-century style, without mouldings. The plan is unusual, but not ineffective: a rather short nave, with aisles; transepts with eastern aisles, and a round-apsed chancel. The inside has been whitewashed. There is hardly any detail, except for a good deal of stiff-leaf foliage on the capitals of the crossing. Two south aisle windows, and the west window, are by Powell, and there is some post-War glass.

St Saviour's, Brockley Rise

Begun in 1865, and consecrated on 8 May 1866; the architect was W. Smith. The church was left incomplete. A faculty was given on 17 August 1875 for an organ chamber and choir vestry, and a lobby at the west of each aisle: the architect was A. E. Hennell, of Bedford Row. The church was finished in 1928 by T. F. Ford. It was damaged by bombing in 1940, and restored at a cost of £28,000, again by T. F. Ford, and reopened in 1952. The chancel was shortened by two-thirds of its length, and the south aisle was walled off, and converted into vestries and meeting-rooms.

Holy Trinity, Sydenham Park (181)

The site was given by Robert Harrild, and the church was designed by John Emmett. The foundation stone was laid on 27 May 1865, and the consecration took place on 13 December 1866. The cost, with the endowment, was £15,000. This is an enormous church, of ashlar inside and out, strictly in the Geometrical style, without any Victorian embellishments or improvisations. It has a nave and aisles, with tall clustered columns; chancel with south chapel, and north organ chamber and vestry; a west window of six lights, and east window of seven. The stone reredos by J. O. Scott, 1906, was erected in memory of Henry Stevens, the founder and first vicar, who died in 1901: an open bible stands in the middle of it.

The east window had glass by Lavers, Barraud and Westlake, 1871: this has gone, though there are three other surviving windows by the firm. The north aisle has one by Heaton, Butler and Bayne, and another by William Morris and Co. The east window, the two other windows in the sanctuary, and one in the south aisle, now have glass by Alfred L. Wilkinson.

St Mark's, Clarendon Rise, Lewisham

Built in 1870 from the designs of W. C. Banks. This church is now closed.

St George's, Perry Hill, Catford (182)

The site was given by R. J. Chaplin, and an iron church was erected in 1871.

The permanent church was built at the cost of George Parker, J.P., of Lewisham House: the foundation stone was laid by Louisa Parker on 23 November 1878, and the consecration was on 17 January 1880. The design was made by W. C. Banks, who lived at Lewisham.

It is a large ragstone-faced church, with a pretentious west front: a baptistery, with Teulonic windows, and narthex with a porch at each end, projecting beyond the aisle walls. The west end of the nave has a large rose window. Unlike most suburban churches,

St George's had its tower completed, so that it remains in the memory rather more easily than some other churches: it stands on the north of the chancel, and has three pinnacles of moderate height, and a large one on top of the staircase turret. Parker thought that it was not tall enough, and had it heightened in 1887. There is a wide nave, with aisles (the arches have unexpectedly slender pillars), and a broad and low apsidal chancel. It is a change, in these days, to find an un-modernised altar and sanctuary, with six candles and hanging lamps. The glass in the rose window is by Henry Holiday, 1900. The rest of the windows of the nave and aisles (with one exception) are by Percy Bacon and Rupert Corbould, of Hemming and Co, who also did the mural decoration. The low chancel screen, 1914, is by Hart, Peard and Co.

St Augustine's, Baring Road, Grove Park

The chancel and transepts were built in 1885–6, from designs by Charles Bell: they are early French Gothic, of Kentish rag lined with white brick. There is a five-sided apse. The reredos, 1907, is by Wispelaere, of Bruges.

A nave and aisles were added in 1912: the architect was Percy Leeds. This part is also of rag, lined with brick, but in Perpendicular style. The aisles are vaulted with brick.

St Lawence's, Catford Road

A large church of Bracknell brick and Corsham stone, by H. R. Gough, built in 1886–7. As originally designed, it had nave, aisles, and chancel: then transepts were added, and a central tower with a slated pyramid spire. The cost was £8,450. The pillars are of Bath stone, the arches of brick. The chancel screen by W. D. Caröe was erected in 1908; the two west windows, in 1951, by Mrs R. M. de Montmorency. In 1965 it was proposed to demolish the church, sell the site to the Lewisham Borough Council, and build a new church, youth centre, community centre, hall, flats, a vicarage, and a playground.

The architect is Reginald Covell, of Messrs Covell, Matthews, and Partners.

St Swithun's, Hither Green Lane (185)

The nave and aisles were built in 1892–3. The architect was Ernest Newton, whose practice was almost entirely domestic: Goodhart-Rendel says that this church was detailed by by W. R. Lethaby. The chancel was consecrated in 1904. It is more ordinary than one would expect: a tall church of red brick, in fourteenth-century style, with large east and west windows: inside, plastered walls and barrel ceilings.

The reredos was carved in Belgium by Wispelaere of Bruges, and put up in 1911: the figures of saints were inserted later. The church was damaged in 1940, and repaired in 1946.

All Saints', Trewsbury Road, Sydenham

The foundation stone was laid on 2 November 1901, and the consecration was in 1903. The architect was G. H. Fellowes Prynne, and the builders were Goddard and Sons.

Only three bays of the nave and aisles were completed. There are tall octagonal brick piers, without capitals, banded with stone; and brick and stone arches. A barrel roof. The entrance to the chancel is filled with one of Fellowes Prynne's stone traceried screens. The chancel has an organ loft on the north, and an aisle under it leading to the vestry. A permanent nave altar has recently been erected.

Church halls do not usually deserve a mention, but that of All Saints' does. A Chapel was built about 1760 for a nonconformist cause begun by John Quicke in the seventeenth century, and continued by his widow, who died in 1708. In 1794 the lease expired, and it was licensed by the Bishop of Rochester. When the Rev Henry Stevens retired in 1866, the Chapel was put up for sale, and bought by Edward Covell, who leased it to Samuel Marsh, a nonconformist. In 1873 Marsh joined the Church of England, and became curate to the vicar of St Bartholomew's, who took the lease of the Chapel: it was known as Christchurch. It later became a chapel of ease to St Michael's, and finally the hall of All Saints'.

It is disappointing that there is not more to see. The Chapel seems to have been entirely rebuilt, presumably after 1866. It has a high-pitched roof, and is divided into nave and aisles by slender iron columns.

St Andrew's, Sandhurst Road, Catford

The relatives of the Rev J. C. Pedley promised to build the eastern parts in his memory, if the rest of the church were built at the same time. The money was raised with the help of the Lewisham Deanery Church Extension fund. The foundation stone was laid on 23 June 1904, and the Bishop of Rochester consecrated the church on 28 October. The architect was P. A. Robson, who was chiefly employed in building schools and houses, and did not do much church work. His chapel at St Gabriel's College, Kennington, is another example of it in South London, in a similar Edwardian Gothic style.

St Andrew's is of brick, with large buttresses. The heads of those of the aisles push up through the roof, and the flying buttresses are inside. The flying buttresses of the chancel are outside. The tall, octagonal brick pillars are without capitals, and are panelled at the base.

The chancel is of the same width as the nave, but the choir and sanctuary are so arranged as to leave a passage all round. They are enclosed by woodwork and ironwork with *art nouveau* details, all of which look like illustrations in the *Studio*. There is later glass by Martin Travers.

St Hilda's, Stondon Park

Built in 1907 and designed by F. H. Greenaway and J. E. Newberry. This was their first church: they repeated the plan, but were not quite as Art-and-Craft-y as this afterwards. The window tracery is without cusps, and the buttresses batter: the windows in the east gable are pushed up as high as they will go: the tower, to the south of the chancel, with vestries in the basement, is very low.

The inside is very simple, with whitewashed brick walls. The chancel, which has a chapel under it, is well raised. There is not much in the way of furniture. All the windows are clear, except for those at the east, which have glass of 1912. But the north transept window has three saints nicely outlined in the leading.

The church of ST CYPRIAN, 1900, by Sir A. W. Blomfield and Sons, was bombed and has been demolished: the parish has been joined to St Hilda's.

St John's, Bromley Road, Southend (184)

The Chapel of Ease was built and endowed by John Forster in 1824. This is now a parish hall. An enormous new estate was built here by the L.C.C. in the '20s: the new parish church was designed by Sir Charles Nicholson, and built in 1926–7: it has not yet been completed. It is traditional, sound, and pleasing.

The monuments, and some glass, from the chapel were brought here. There is a War memorial figure by Cecil Thomas, 1923.

The daughter churches of St Dunstan, Bellingham (1925), St Barnabas' (1928–9), and St Luke (1937–8) are also by Nicholson.

St Michael's, Champion Crescent, Sydenham

1863–4, designed by J. T. Knowles.

This church was bombed on 10 September 1940, and nothing now remains of it. The new church was consecrated on 26 July 1958. It stands on the same site, but faces south, not east. The architects were David Nye and Partners. It has a reinforced concrete frame, with narrow aisles, and windows in the space above them, between the piers; a west organ gallery, and north chapel; and a cheerful colour scheme inside, chiefly blue. The seats are from the former church.

St Paul's, Taymount Rise, Forest Hill

The original church in Waldenshaw Road—the one that was seated for more than the total population of the parish—was designed by Appleton and Mountford, and built in 1882–3. It was bombed, and has been entirely demolished. The church in Taymount Rise was built as a Congregational church in 1863: the architects were J. Hine of Plymouth, and T. Roger Smith. It afterwards became Spiritualist (St Luke's Church of the Spiritual Evangel). It was bought as the new St Paul's, adapted, and consecrated on 24 January 1965. It is an ugly, rather pleasant little building, with an open porch, French thirteenth-century, in the front, and a small tower beside it. The inside is divided into nave and aisles by iron columns bearing round arches: the galleries have been taken down. Font, pulpit, and lectern are from the old St Paul's: the priest's stalls came from a Baptist chapel at Reigate. The wheel window over the altar has glass by Alan Younger. This is a far more attractive church than its ambitious predecessor.

Newington

Newington, as a distinct place, does not exist. The parish was small, and consisted mostly of fields and market gardens: from the late eighteenth century onwards, houses were being built, and it became simply a part of South London. The *Imperial Gazeteer*, 1866, refers to 'very numerous streets, some of them spacious, many well edificed, and most running in straight lines, chiefly at right angles to one another, or with such angular connexions as comport well with convenience'. The development came early enough for the parish to get two large Commissioners' churches; and the later nineteenth century provided all the church accommodation that was likely to be needed.

St Mary's, Kennington Park Road, Newington

In 1719 the parish tried, unsuccessfully, to get the church included among the Fifty. It was rebuilt, except for the tower, and reopened on 26 March 1721. In 1792 a faculty was given to take down the roof, most of the walls, and the tower, and to rebuild the church in brick and stone, extending it to the west. The architect of the rebuilding was F. Hurlbatt.

A new church was built, on the present site, from designs by J. Fowler of Louth, and consecrated on 1 May 1876: the eighteenth-century building was removed to widen the road. St Gabriel's was built, on the other side of the old churchyard, as a mission church; but it was never of very much use, and was taken down in the 1930s.

Fowler's St Mary's was a large, rather frigid church in thirteenth-century style. It was destroyed in the War, and only a fragment remains—part of the west front, and base of the tower. A small church was built on the site in 1957–8, at a cost of £53,000: the architect was A. Llewellyn-Smith.

St Peter's, Liverpool Grove, Walworth

This is a Commissioner's church: £9,354 was granted towards the cost of £18,592. Sir John Soane's designs were accepted: the foundation stone was laid on 2 June 1823, and the church was consecrated 28 February 1825.

The church is similar to Soane's later church of Holy Trinity, Marylebone Road. It is rectangular, built above catacombs, with gallery-stair compartments in the west angles, and vestries in the east. In the middle of the west front, four Ionic columns are recessed: the cornice is carried across, and the tower stands behind. The tower is slim, with a square lower stage, a circular stage with a peristyle of eight Composite columns, and a dome.

The galleries stand on solid Doric pillars, and above are thin octagonal pillars carrying semi-circular arches. The east end was altered by Ewan Christian in 1888.

There was bomb damage: the church was restored by Thomas F. Ford, and reopened in 1953. The new glass in the east windows is by Clare Dawson.

Holy Trinity, Trinity Square (188)

A Commissioners' church, designed by Francis Bedford: the Commissioners granted £8,960 towards the cost of £16,259. The first stone was laid on 2 June 1823, and the consecration was on 16 December 1824. The brickwork was by Elizabeth Broomfield, and the masons' work by William Chadwick. It was seated for 2,008, 'but a far greater number can always be accommodated without inconvenience'.

The Corinthian portico is on the south, with the steeple above. The interior is a large unbroken area, with galleries on Greek Doric columns. The font is of Croggan and Co's artificial stone. There were alterations by Henry Jarvis and Son in 1898.

In 1930 Martin Travers erected the altar and canopy, adornments round the east window, and glass in it. The church was damaged in the War.

St John's, Larcom Street, Walworth

Henry Jarvis was the architect: the foundation stone was laid on 30 March 1859 and the consecration was on 28 June 1860. The cost was £5,283. It is Early English, rag-faced, with a saddleback tower at the west of the south aisle. There are slender pairs of iron pillars, with foliated capitals, on tall stone bases: a clerestory of circular windows under steep gables. New vestry 1912, by Greenaway and Newberry. The reredos of alabaster and tiles has been superseded by Comper hangings: the new altar, rails and lighting were installed in 1928, the rood in 1938, also by Comper. The rood in the chapel came from the chapel of the Priory of St Austin, in the New Kent Road—the headquarters of the Rev George Nugée and his Order of St Augustine. Nugée died in 1892, and his Order soon faded out. Lady chapel altar 1960.

St Andrew's, Glengall Road

The church was built mainly through the efforts of the Rev Daniel Moore, of Camden Church. The foundation stone was laid on 17 December 1864: the consecration was on 23 October 1865. The architect was E. Bassett Keeling, who has kept himself fairly well in check. The church is ragstone faced, and shows its west front toward the street: a low north-west tower, with a porch at the bottom, and a narthex with a door at the south end. The style is early French Gothic. The spire has been taken down.

There is a north aisle, and a north transept, which is balanced on the south by a narrow aisle of two bays. Apsidal chancel. The windows, except on the north, have a coarse kind of plate tracery. The arcades have foliated capitals. The windows in the apse are by Alfred L. Wilkinson, 1955.

The parish of ALL SAINTS' is now joined with St Andrew's. All Saints' church, 1893, by Walter Planck, was a large, unwanted church, which was badly damaged during the War. Some of the materials were afterwards used for building a church at Biggin Hill.

St Matthew's, New Kent Road

Begun in 1866 and consecrated on 7 December 1867. The architect was Henry Jarvis. It is a cheap church, with brick sides and a ragstone front: at the right of the front—the church does not face east—is a porch, carried up with an octagonal stage and low spire. There are iron columns, and an apse. It was completely remodelled in 1926–7 by Martin Travers, who cased the iron pillars with wooden Tuscan columns, and built a wall in front of the apse, with his usual altar and altar piece in front of it. The lighting was also his usual design. I saw this work being done, and admired it at the time: after nearly 40 years, it does not look as enterprising as it did. There is a little glass by Martin Travers.

All Souls', Grosvenor Park (now known as St Michael, with All Souls', with Emmanuel)

All Souls' is a very large and lofty church, built in 1870–1, by H. Jarvis and Son, of stock brick, cruciform, with a central tower which stands well up above the houses: as yet there are no blocks of flats near enough to humble its pride.

The inside is spacious (two bays of the nave are screened off at the west), and not unimpressive. It was redecorated in 1925, and after the War. There is very little to take notes on, except perhaps the paintings of Old and New Testament worthies in the spandrels of the arcade.

St Agnes', Kennington Park

This beautiful church was designed by G. G. Scott, junior, and built in 1875–7: it was completed by Temple Moore, who designed some of the furniture. It was tall and simple, with nave and chancel under one roof, in a style rather like Bodley's—late fourteenth-century, with unnecessary features eliminated, but richly fitted, with screen, rood loft, rood, altar piece, etc.: an ideal setting for sung eucharists and processions.

It was bombed in 1941, and its place has been taken by a small new church, 1956, by Ralph Covell, in which some fittings were replaced: others went to the church of the Holy Spirit, Southampton. The glass is by T. Shapland.

Lady Margaret Church, Chatham Street

The church was founded by St John's College, Cambridge, and named after their founder, the Countess of Richmond. The foundation stone was laid on 18 June 1888, and the church was consecrated in June 1889. The architect was Ewan Christian, and this is one of the most successful of his simple brick Early English churches. It has a rather wide nave, with brick arcades opening into low and narrow aisles, without windows. Very shallow transepts—the site being constricted—and a round apse. A solid cradle roof, with tie-beams and king-posts. The glass in the apse is by Clayton and Bell. There is a bust of Lady Margaret, erected in 1920. This simple and quiet church has quite an atmosphere.

St Paul's, Lorrimore Square

The original church, designed by Henry Jarvis, was begun in 1854, and consecrated on Christmas Eve 1856. Under its second vicar, it became a centre of ritualistic worship. Bishop Thorold, when he first became Bishop of Rochester, was determined to stamp out ritualism, and the vicar, fearing for the future, helped to found St Agnes', Kennington—to which, when the Bishop appointed a vicar who would alter things, the congregation migrated. But St Paul's afterwards reverted to its former ways.

The church was extensively repaired in 1909–14. It was destroyed by incendiary bombs on 10 May 1941, except for the tower and spire: nothing remains of it now.

The plans for the new church were made by H. G. Coulter, of Woodroffe, Buchanan and Coulter, and recommended by Milner White, the Dean of York. The foundation stone was laid on 6 May 1955 and the consecration took place on 12 December 1956.

The church stands above a ground floor with a hall, coffee bar, etc., and a covered way round three sides. The framework is of reinforced concrete: the walls are of concrete blocks, with small windows between. The roof has wedge-shaped panels of boarding, and is covered with copper: there are pointed dormer windows. The small flèche is covered with copper. The porch at the south-west, with stone-faced steps up to it, has inward-sloping concrete columns supporting a canopy, with a triangular-shaped belfry above. The Lady chapel at the east projects over the covered way. The carving of the risen Christ over the altar is by Freda Skinner.

All Saints', Surrey Square.

The original church, built 1864–5, was designed by R. Parris and S. Field. It was bombed and has been cleared away. Its place has been taken by a simple church, consecrated in 1959, of a concrete frame and brick facing. The altar is under a ciborium: to the east is an apse, with vestry below, and Lady chapel above. The architect was N. F. Cachemaille-Day. The reredos, a calvary with a background of gold leaf, is by Christopher Webb. The colour scheme is yellow and blue, 'intended to appeal to the youth of the district'. The parish is united with that of St Stephen's, Walworth Common—a church by Messrs Jarvis, bombed and demolished.

Plumstead

Plumstead was quite a small place which developed in the nineteenth century in the direction of Woolwich. The Burrage Town estate was built up with workmen's houses and small villas, and given its own place of worship. Elsewhere there were large and genteel houses. The population was 8,373 in 1851, and 24,502 ten years later. The old church, on the edge of the Marsh, was rather remote, and the new St Margaret's was made the parish church in 1865. Several new churches were built later in the century.

St Nicholas', High Street (197)

The south wall was built in the twelfth century, and has two small windows of that date. The small transept was added in the thirteenth. The north aisle was built in the fifteenth century.

The church was in decay in the seventeenth century, and was repaired, 'after above 20 years lying waste and ruinous', by the 'care and industry' of John Gossage, who died 1672, aged 50. The work was begun in 1662, and finished two years later. The tower is of brick, in a belated Gothic style, with clasping buttresses carried up as turrets, and finished off with battlements. It looks very old fashioned for c. 1660, and it bears an obvious resemblance to the tower of Charlton, which is generally ascribed to c. 1630. Still, it is not impossible for a date after the Restoration; and the tower of Charlton may itself be later than the body of the church.

The chancel was curtailed, and the north aisle afterwards fell into ruin: the north arcade was walled up in 1780. In 1818 the aisle was rebuilt, and there was a restoration in 1867–8 by Charles H. Cooke. In 1907–8 a new nave and chancel and aisle were added on the north, and an apsidal chapel was built on the site of the old chancel. The architects were Greenaway and Newberry.

The church was badly damaged by bombing in 1945. It was well repaired by Thomas F. Ford and Partners, with Holliday and Green as the builders, and reopened on 2 June 1959. The south chapel was reduced in size. There are three altars by Stephen Dykes Bower. The reredos of the high altar was painted by Donald Towner.

St James's, Burrage Road

A proprietary chapel, built in 1855. The name of the architect has not so far been discovered. It is an unusual little building, of brick, with pairs of long, thin windows. I described the style as engine-house Italian: Dr Pevsner calls it slightly Italianate, of the type of King's Cross Station—which amounts to the same thing. It was consecrated in 1878. Two rather useless little aisles were added, and a small Gothic chancel.

St Margaret's, St Margaret's Grove

Built in 1858–9, designed by William Rickwood, of Plumstead. It has ragstone walls, and a tiled roof, with a pinnacled tower: the style is early Perpendicular, with rather tall octagonal pillars, and small twin two-light clerestory windows.

The foundation stone of the chancel was laid on 4 February 1899: the architect was R. J. Lovell. The east window—Decorated, with a large wheel in the head—fills the entire east wall above the altar: the glass is by Hardman.

The south aisle windows are also by Hardman. One window in the north aisle by the Warham Guild: west of north aisle, Jones and Willis.

St Paul's, Hector Street

A large church, hidden away down a side street. The architect was W. Bassett Smith. The first portion—the chancel, and two bays of the nave and aisles, which had cost £4,150—was consecrated in November 1901. The rest was built in 1908. The church is of red brick, with Bath stone dressings, and slate-covered roofs of pitch pine, in fourteenth-century style.

The Ascension, Timbercroft Lane

The architect was A. E. Habershon. The foundation stone was laid on 24 October 1903: the consecration was in 1904. It was left in a very incomplete state, and a faculty was given in 1911 to build the west bay of the nave, and the narthex; the south aisle, the east end of the chancel, and new vestries. It was a very old-fashioned church for 1903; in the lancet style, of stock brick, with red arches, diapers, and stripes inside, and terra-cotta window-heads, etc., outside. The chancel and south chapel have been whitened. The hanging rood was installed in 1920. The east window is by Jones and Willis, the south chapel window by Clayton and Bell.

St Mark's, Old Mill Lane

The church stands on the edge of the Common. The architect was C. H. M. Mileham: the foundation stone was laid on 16 October 1901, and the church was consecrated in 1902. It is Romanesque, with two small towers at the west end: the walls are roughcast. It is divided into nave and aisles (there is no structural chancel) by solid arcades. Only one capital has been carved. The nave has a concrete barrel vault, and the aisles have cross vaults. The architect designed a screen (not Romanesque) to run right across the church. The low wooden screen that has been erected west of the choir is to the memory of John Cox Leeke, the first vicar, and the first Bishop of Woolwich.

All Saints', Ripon Road, Shooter's Hill

The first church, designed by Habershon and Pite, was begun in 1873, and the nave and aisles were consecrated on 6 July 1875. The tower was completed in 1881, and the chancel in 1889.

It was bombed, and a completely new church was built, on a different site, after the War: the foundation stone was laid on 18 February 1956. The architect was Thomas F. Ford, and it was built by Thomas Edge Ltd, of Woolwich. The style is 'the Greek Classic of the early nineteenth century, modified and adapted to suit modern materials and requirements'. The usual Feibusch mural is on the east wall.

Putney

Putney was a riverside village, with the church, as usual, by the river. The Heath is to the south, and to the west of the Heath is Roehampton, which had, from the seventeenth century onwards, large houses belonging to the nobility and gentry. A good many large and respectable villas were built in the neighbourhood in Victorian times, and church accommodation was provided as usual. When Roehampton new church was built, far more money was subscribed than had been asked for.

St Mary's, Putney High Street

The tower is fifteenth-century, much restored. The chantry chapel north of the chancel (originally on the south, but moved when the church was rebuilt) was built by Nicholas West, a native of the place, who was bishop of Ely from 1515 to 1533. It is of two bays, with a fan vault, on which are the bishop's arms and initials. The chapel was restored in 1878.

The church was rebuilt by Edward Lapidge in 1836–7: the builder was John Young. It is of brick in a fairly correct, rather lifeless Perpendicular, with flat roofs and a shallow sanctuary. The galleries remain, and have escaped reseating. The rest of the church has been restored and redecorated several times. A faculty was given in August 1876 to alter the east end, and to move the organ from the gallery into an organ chamber. The reredos was erected in 1904, and the east window is by Henry Bryans. The chancel was extended in 1913, the reredos and window being replaced: new sedilia, low chancel screen, and pulpit.

Monuments   (John) Welbeck, 1478, and Agnes (brasses in the West Chapel). Katherine, wife of Sir Anthony Palmer, 1613. Margaret, his second wife, 1619. Richard Lusher, 1615. Mary, wife of Richard Lusher and of Thomas Knyvett, 1623. James Martin, 1651. Edward Martyn, 1655. Sir Thomas Dawes, 1655, and Judith, 1657. Robert Gales, 1669. Sir Robert Wymondesolde, 1697. Daniel Belt, 1697. Thomas Payne, 1698. Andrew Welch, 1704. Mary Cary, 1738.

Two out of the four other churches in Putney are chapels of ease to St Mary's: but they are of sufficient size and importance to be mentioned.

St John's, St John's Avenue

Built chiefly at the cost of J. L. Leader, M.P. for Westminster. The foundation stone was laid on 26 May 1858, consecration was on 21 July 1859: the architect was Charles Lee. Its details and proportions are old-fashioned, and suggest the '40s rather than the '50s. It is plain later thirteenth-century in style, and rather tall and thin. The transepts do not project. The slender tower and spire at the north-west were completed in 1865.

In 1888 the church was enlarged, with a new chancel and aisles: the architects were Lee Brothers and Pain—actually, it is said, Charles Lee and his second son Sydney Williams Lee. A vestry was added on the north in 1898. In 1910 a faculty was given to remove the vestries on the south of the chancel, and open arches into a new chapel: a porch was to be added on the south. Architects, Lee and Pain-Clarke, of South Square, Gray's Inn. The north chancel aisle was fitted as a chapel in 1934.

The pre-War glass was broken—including windows to the memory of the architects. Post-War glass by Francis H. Spear.

All Saints', Putney Common

Begun in 1873, and consecrated on 25 April 1874. The architect was G. E. Street. It is of stock brick externally, and internally red brick, varied with a little black—more in the chancel than the nave. There are waggon roofs to the nave and chancel, and flat roofs to the aisles, all nicely painted. Large circular panels in the spandrels of the nave arcade: this part of the church has a curious resemblance to the work of J. O. Scott. The vaulted baptistery, at the west of the north aisle, is enclosed with iron screens, and there is an iron screen to the chancel. The chancel, for a church by Street, is rather unimpressive.

All the glass is by Morris, of various dates, but all of a piece. At the west is a painting of St John, angels, and landscape: it is no doubt the reredos, banished to make room for the present curtains.

Holy Trinity, Roehampton

A Chapel in the house of the Earl of Portland was consecrated by Laud, then Bishop of London, on 26 May 1632. It was pulled down in 1777 by Thomas Parker, who built a new Chapel about 100 yards from the house.

This was superseded in 1842 by a new church designed by Benjamin Ferrey. It was Early English with a stone altar, and an eastern triplet with glass by Wailes. It was, on the whole, very much approved of by the ecclesiologists: later, it came to be regarded in much the same way as Newman's Chapel at Littlemore was—well intentioned, and the real thing, as far as it went, but soon made out-of-date by the progress of ecclesiology. It was altered and enlarged in 1862. This building stood for many years after it had been disused for worship, but was pulled down in 1928.

The foundation stone of a new church, designed by G. H. Fellowes Prynne, was laid on 18 April 1896, and the consecration was on 19 February 1898.

It is of Corsham stone externally, and brick within: very large, with a tower and spire at the north-west. There is a traceried stone screen, as at All Saints', West Dulwich. The panels of the altar were painted by E. A. Fellowes Prynne.

St Margaret's, Putney Park Lane

Built for the Baptists in the late '50s, and used from 1878 by the Presbyterians, until they built their church in Briar Walk. From 1897 it stood derelict. In 1912 it was given to the parish, as a chapel of ease, by Seth Taylor, the owner of Granard House, in the grounds of which it stood. Alterations were made by A. G. Humphry, architect: the lobby wall was taken down, a new floor made, etc. The builders were Adamson and Sons. The Chapel was consecrated on 5 October.

In 1923 it became a parish church. An eastern part, with aisles of two bays, an apsidal chancel, chapel, and vestries, was added in 1925 from designs by Forsyth and Maule: the builder was F. G. Minter.

The original chapel is of Kentish rag, Gothic, with apsidal transepts. The new parts, Gothic also, are of brick.

Rotherhithe

Rotherhithe, with its docks and wharves, has its own character, and there is still a distinctive, seafaring atmosphere about the place. The parish church is in a rather secluded part: its steeple can best be seen by those who are sailing on the river.

St Mary's, Marychurch Street (186)

The old church was repaired in 1687, but by 1705 the vestry had decided that it needed to be rebuilt. An Act of Parliament was obtained, and a brief was issued: but progress was very slow, and the faculty was not applied for until 1714. By 7 June 1715 the new church was 'near Finish'd and Pew'd'. But the parish found difficulty in paying the bills, and an Act was obtained in 1716 to enable them to raise money. There was a further Act in 1737, to finish the church. The tower was presumably begun after this, and the sanctuary is supposed to be of the same date: but it was not until 1746 that the vestry agreed to complete the tower. On 5 March 1754 they passed a resolution that Mr Dowbiggin should be told firmly that he must send in his bill 'for rebuilding the Steeple and making other alterations relating to our said Parish Church, which hitherto he has neglected to do'. This was presumably Launcelot Dowbiggin, whose steeple at St Mary's, Islington, bears a slight resemblance to this. In 1782 George Dance reported on the steeple, which was repaired as he suggested.

The spire was rebuilt in 1861, and a restoration under Butterfield was completed in 1876. It involved the usual things: new seating, north and south galleries taken down, the pulpit lowered, a choir formed, etc.

A pleasant, simple brick church, with stone quoins: the spire rises from a circular open stage with Corinthian columns. Inside, the order is a not very elegant Ionic, and there is a segmental ceiling with panelled ribs. The altar piece remains, with panelling on the north and south walls of the sanctuary, and some other eighteenth-century woodwork: the organ—which keeps its case, and has not been moved—was erected in 1764. There is a brass chandelier, and a seventeenth-century painting of King Charles, kneeling, and holding a crown of thorns.

183 All Saints', Blackheath,
1857–8 by Benjamin Ferrey

84 St John's, Southend, 1926–7
y Sir Charles A. Nicholson

185 St Swithun's, Hither Green,
by Ernest Newton 1892–3

186 St Mary's, Rotherhithe, 1715 and later, steeple completed 1746 onward

187 St George's, Southwark, 1734–6 by John Price

188 Holy Trinity, Newington, 1823–4 by Francis Bedford

189 All Saints', Wandsworth, tower 1630, altered 1841 and post-War. South side of church 1779

Monuments   A brass of Peter Hills, mariner, 1614. Captain Anthony Wood, 1625, with a carved panel of a ship. Joseph Wade, King's Carver in His Majesty's Yards, 1743: very pretty. In the churchyard is buried Prince Lee Boo, of the Pelew Islands, 1784.

Christchurch, Jamaica Road

Built 1838–9, by Lewis Vulliamy. This church still stands, but it was closed in 1958, and is used as a store for parts of organs. The parish is united with that of St Crispin, Bermondsey.

St Barnabas', Plough Way

Built in 1870–2, by Butterfield, but now closed: the parish is united with St Katharine's.

St Katharine's, Eugenia Road (154)

One of the churches that was built with the help of Richard Foster. The architect was W. O. Milne, and the foundation stone was laid on 3 May 1884, by the Rev F. H. Murray, one of the original proprietors of *Hymns Ancient and Modern*, and rector of Chislehurst for 50 years.

This rather ordinary red-brick church was badly bombed. The remains were eventually cleared away, and the new church was built on the site. The architects were Covell, Matthews, and Partners: Gordon R. Myatt was the assistant in charge. Main contractors, Leslie A. Keats and Partners. The foundation stone was laid on 22 July 1960.

The bell and the furnishings of the high altar came from the previous church. Seats, organ and font were brought from St Barnabas', and its high altar was placed in the chapel of St Barnabas. The glass is by W. T. Carter Shapland.

Holy Trinity, Bryan Road

Built in 1837–8, designed by Sampson Kempthorne, and built by Thomas Sneezum: the cost was £4,149: the Commissioners (Second Parliamentary grant) gave £1,161 towards the cost. The new church, by Thomas F. Ford, was consecrated in 1960; there is a mural by Hans Feibusch.

Southwark

Southwark was well supplied with church accommodation in the eighteenth century, and the nineteenth built more churches than were really needed.

Booth gives a dismal picture of the borough as it was at the end of the last century. The rich had gone, the fairly comfortable people were leaving: the poor remained, and would stay until they were evicted. The churches were doing their best, but none of them was very successful: the people were apathetic, and most of them were only on the look out for doles. His picture of Newington and of Walworth is not much brighter.

The population has, as usual, declined a good deal in recent years.

Christchurch, Blackfriars Road

The church was founded and endowed by John Marshall, of Southwark, and consecrated on 17 December 1671: the tower and spire were completed in 1695. It soon became unsafe, and in 1737 Marshall's trustees applied to Parliament for authority to rebuild it, with £2,500 that had accumulated in the trust. A new church was built in 1738–41, almost certainly designed by James Horne. In 1802 it was closed as dangerous, and in the next year the vestry agreed to rebuild it. They applied to Parliament, but a committee of the Commons decided that rebuilding was unnecessary. In 1811 the vestry agreed to repair the church (Robinson, surveyor) and erect north and south galleries. S. S. Teulon added an apse in 1870–1, and in 1890–1 C. R. Baker King remodelled the interior and built a Romanesque chancel.

The church was damaged in 1941, and the tower and most of the nave disappeared. A smaller church has been built at the east of the site, by R. Paxton Watson and Barry Costin: the contractors were Dove Bros. It was opened on 24 February 1960. There is glass by Frederick Cole.

St Thomas's was rebuilt in 1702: the master mason was Thomas Cartwright. It was threatened with demolition, but was adapted by A. E. Bartlett as the Chapter House for Southwark Cathedral.

St George's, Borough High Street (187)

The House of Commons considered a petition from the parish on 16 February 1732: William Lessaw and John Townsend gave evidence that the church was in a bad state, and the Bill for rebuilding passed the Commons on 12 March. The Commissioners for the Fifty New Churches made a grant of £6,000. The design was made by John Price, and the contractor was James Porter.

The first stone was laid on St George's day 1734, and the fabric was completed in the next year. A rate had to be levied to supplement the Commissioners' grant, when it came to furnishing. The church was opened in 1736. In 1742 the east end was beautified and adorned, iron rails were placed, and the galleries were altered: Spiers made the design, and Johnson executed the work.

On 2 August 1806, the vestry considered Cockerell's report on the state of the church. Extensive repairs were done (faculty 1808) under James Hedger: William Harland repaired the paintings at the east end.

A new ceiling, adorned with cherubim, was put up by Basil Champneys in 1897. The church was repaired by Frederick Etchells in 1938, and by Thomas F. Ford, after War damage, in 1951–2.

The body of the church is built of pleasant red brick, with Portland stone quoins. The Portland stone tower has diminishing octagonal upper stages, and a spire. The central bay of the west end has two engaged Ionic columns supporting a curved pediment. The church fills its island site admirably. There are not a great many details to take notes on; but it is, outside and in, a good, decent, sober Georgian parish church.

St Stephen's, Manciple Street

Built 1849–50, by S. S. Teulon. I wrote a full account of this simple little church, for which I had a genuine admiration: it was unusual, and had a rather ingenious plan. At the last moment, I heard that it had been demolished. So what I had written was crossed out: but I felt that I should like to give it a few lines, to preserve its memory.

St Michael's, Lant Street

By A. E. Newman. Built in 1866–7; it is now used as a hall.

All Hallows', Pepper Street

This was a lovely church, designed by G. G. Scott, junior, and built in 1879–80: very tall, of red brick, with large buttresses and passage aisles. Even the reporter for the *Record*, who had come to report on illegal ceremonial, admired it, and admitted that it was a very beautiful building, and that its interior had an impressive appearance. Churchmen in the late nineteenth century thought that the poorest districts deserved the best churches. Unfortunately, All Hallows' was bombed, and has not been rebuilt. A small portion (the north aisle) has been restored, but that is all.

St Alphege, Lancaster Street

Built in 1880–2 and designed by R. Willey. A very simple brick church, aisleless, with no chancel arch, and a somewhat raised sanctuary. There are many objects of piety of a counter-reformation kind. This church was constantly denounced by Protestants for its romanising tendencies.

St Jude's, St George's Road

This church stands on the site of the Chapel of the Philanthropic Society, which was opened in November 1806: 'a neat structure of brick, in Carpenters' Gothic style'. It was said to have been well attended, and indeed a picture of its interior shows an enormous congregation listening attentively to the sermon. It was consecrated in 1850.

In 1871 a faculty was given for building a new vestry and classrooms, inserting new windows, and other alterations: the architect was Robert Parris. In 1888 it was decided to build a new church, and there was a competition: Aston Webb adjudicated, and chose the plans of Walter John Hopkins Leverton, of 10 Lancaster Place, Strand.

The building committee first met in November 1897, when it was agreed to raise the church on a crypt, with a floor of concrete. The builder chosen was J. N. Try, who began to take down the old church on 27 June 1898. The new church—simple Early English, of red brick—was finished in 1899. The organ was transferred from the old church: the rest of the furniture was disposed of. Most of the new fittings were by Jones and Willis.

Streatham

Streatham was, from the eighteenth century, 'a favourite place of abode for opulent citizens'. Dr Johnson spent much of his time at Streatham Place, with the Thrales: after Henry's death, he prayed 'that he might with humble and sincere thankfulness remember the comforts and conveniences that he had enjoyed there'. Benjamin Hoadley was rector here while he was Bishop of Bangor (1716–21) and of Salisbury (1723–34): it was a good living, and he saw no reason for giving it up. There has been the usual nineteenth-century development, and twentieth-century rebuilding; but parts of Streatham keep the old atmosphere. It has been well supplied with churches: one—St Anselm's, by R. J. Withers —has gone.

St Leonard's, Streatham High Road

The base of the tower is all that remains of the old church. The vestry in 1773 agreed to a drastic recasting: Oliver Burton testified that it could be done without endangering the church, and that it would be a great improvement to it. It involved the removal of all pillars and arches; the raising of the north wall; the rebuilding of the south wall, and extending it to the east end; reroofing; and new galleries, etc. The rebuilding was done in brick, and the windows had wooden mullions: there was a new porch on the south. The top of the tower, and the spire, were rebuilt at this time.

The whole church was rebuilt, except for the tower, in 1830–1, by J. T. Parkinson: the builders were Hayes, Skinner and Borsley. The work was not well done, and there were disputes between the parish, the architect, and the contractors.

The spire was struck by lightning in 1841, and the top of the tower and the spire were rebuilt by John Thompson of Camberwell. In 1843 Cubitt was called in to make the church secure. The chancel, 1862, was designed by William Dyce and carried out by Benjamin Ferrey. There were further alterations, including a new roof, by B. E. Ferrey in 1877. The screen was erected in 1915, the reredos in 1920 (by Harold C. King), and the rood figures in 1925.

The font is fifteenth-century, restored in 1893, and the pulpit seventeenth-century, on a modern base.

Glass by Clayton and Bell (south chapel and west window), Curtis, Ward and Hughes, and A. L. and C. E. Moore; many of the windows were broken in the War. There is post-War glass by Lawrence Lee (Lady chapel and east window), and F. W. Cole (north chapel).

Monuments There are many, e.g., defaced figure of a knight, fourteenth-century, thought to be John Ward. William Mowfurth, rector, 1513 (a brass). Robert Livesaye, 1608, and Anne, 1617. Edmund Tylney, 1610. Thomas Hobbes, 1632. John Massingberde, 1653, and Cecilia. Cecilia Lee, 1664. John Howland, 1686, probably by John Nost, the best in the church. Walter Howland, 1692, and John, 1674. Mrs Hester Lynch Salusbury, 1773 (inscription by Johnson). Henry Thrale, 1781, probably by Wilton (inscription by Johnson). Peter Brown, 1800, by R. Westmacott. Major Frederick Howard, 1815, by Westmacott. Elizabeth Steward Laing, 1816, by Peter Rouw. Thomas Brown, 1822, by Henry Westmacott. Sophia Hoare, 1824, by Flaxman. Jane Brown, 1829, by Westmacott junior. William Dyce, 1865 (a brass).

St Mary's, Balham High Road (194)

This was a proprietary chapel, built by the inhabitants in about 1806, under the management of a committee of twelve. It was enlarged in 1824 by James Arding and Son, Dorset Street, who added the two wings. Benjamin Harrison gave it 'to God and the inhabitants', and it was consecrated on 24 May 1855. There is a monument to Harrison by J. Towne, Guy's Hospital. A petition was made on 16 November 1881 for a faculty to add a chancel, from designs by Arthur Cawston. The south chapel and vestries were not to be built yet.

On 21 March 1891 a petition was made to build new galleries in the transepts, to cut back the west gallery, and to remove those on the north and south. Architect, W. Newton Dunn, 152 Bucklersbury.

There used to be a simple Tuscan portico: a faculty was given in 1904 to extend the church one bay to the west, and build west front, tower and baptistery. Also to take down the galleries in the transepts, and to add porches. W. Newton Dunn was the architect.

The chapel in the south transept, by Robert Potter, was dedicated on 6 July 1952. There is glass by Clayton and Bell (sanctuary), and Heaton, Butler and Bayne (baptistery). Also a terra-cotta panel of the Entombment, the gift of Louisa, widow of Edward Browning, F.R.I.B.A., 1886.

Christchurch, Christchurch Road (191)

The residents of Streatham Hill first worshipped in a United Church, 1829, from which the Anglicans withdrew in 1837. The Rev Henry Blunt, curate of Streatham, offered to raise the money for building a church, on condition that he should be the first incumbent. Subscriptions amounted to about £6,340, and there were various gifts. In addition, the Church Building Commissioners gave £300, the I.C.B.S. £500, and the Winchester Diocesan Church Accommodation Society £500.

John William Wild was chosen as architect, on the recommendation of the Bishop of Winchester, who praised both his powers of design and the accuracy of his estimates. There are several letters from Wild among the parish records. In one of them (10 February 1840) he says what he thinks a church ought to be like: 'It appears absolutely necessary that a church should have the appearance of solemnity & that the only means of attaining this attribute is by severe simplicity in design and by avoiding all appearance of having attempted more than could be accomplished.' He made the design, and the foundation stone was laid on 11 August 1840. John Thompson was the builder, and M. Wilson Foster the clerk of the works. The consecration was on 19 November 1841.

It is a very striking church, admired by Ruskin when it was first built, and by Good-hart-Rendel in recent years—'unrivalled in its excellence as a specimen of a modern basilica designed with spirit and grace'. The *Ecclesiologist*, of course, did not approve: 'Why were our own ecclesiastical styles deserted for forms which are at best imperfectly developed?' It was felt to be rather exotic—but there has been a curious variety in the words that have been used to describe it: 'Romanesque of the South of Europe' (*Ecclesiologist*), 'Byzantine' (Mackeson), 'Lombardic' (Thorne), 'Italian Gothic' (Bumpus), 'Neo-Romanesque' or 'eclectic Romanesque' (Goodhart-Rendel), and '*Rundbogenstil*' (Pevsner). It is certainly Italian, but it is not really Romanesque: it has pointed arches. Perhaps it can be called Italian with some Saracenic influence. But, whatever it is, Wild's source must have been illustrated travel-books. He did indeed travel in the Mediterranean: he studied mosques, and the houses of the Arabs, and he designed an Anglican church for Alexandria in the Islamic style. But his travels did not begin until 1842.

He explained that he was placing the tower as in an early Italian church. He thought of the church as Byzantine, but did not consider Byzantine to be a fully developed style. On 10 November 1840 he wrote to say that he agreed that the cornice was too Egyptian, and too massive. Byzantine cornices were 'rather pretty than noble' (here he gives a sketch) 'and although they might be admired—yet they contradict the quiet severity of the style at which I aim.' The cornice would be taken down and done again. So he admitted that he was being eclectic.

Christchurch is a basilica of brick, with yellow and red window-heads: at the east is an apse, and at the south-east a tall campanile, with its windows recessed in very long and thin brick niches, three to a side. The arcades are tall: each bay is subdivided by two lesser arches that carry the gallery.

There was decoration by Owen Jones. In 1925–33 the whole church was elaborately redecorated by Arthur Henderson, an architect and archaeologist, who did work in connection with the Temple of Diana at Ephesus, and St Sophia, Constantinople. This has now gone, and the church has been whitened—which is a pity: it needs plenty of colour. Most of the pre-War glass (Willement, O'Connor, and Lavers and Barraud) has also gone. The best of what remains is the two windows by Walter Crane, 1891.

Holy Trinity, Trinity Road, Upper Tooting

The site was given by Henry Browse. The architect was Anthony Salvin, who was asked to design a church like his St Stephen's, Shepherd's Bush. The builder was Samuel Nowell, of Grosvenor Wharf, Pimlico. The church was begun in 1854, and consecrated on 26 June 1855. It was of brick, faced with Kentish rag, with Bath stone dressings, in Middle-Pointed style, and consisted of nave, aisles, and chancel. In 1860 the tower was added by Benjamin Ferrey: this is earlier in style than the rest. The west window, with its bright glass, is one of the best features of the church.

There were subsequent enlargements by his son, B. E. Ferrey (builders, W. H. Lorden and Son), which have caused the church to outgrow its strength. In 1889 the north aisle was widened, and the transept built; in 1891, vestries were added; in 1893 the south aisle was widened. The south-west porch was built in 1904. A faculty was given, 1906, for a chancel screen by West and Collier. There is post-War glass in the east window by H. Warren Wilson, 1951. Redecoration has been done by Campbell, Smith and Co (1955).

Immanuel, Streatham High Road

Founded by Andrew and Frances Eliza Hamilton. A small church was built in 1854, from designs by Alexander Ross.

It was practically rebuilt, and much enlarged, in 1864–5, and consecrated on 17 June 1865. The architect was Benjamin Ferrey, and the builder was Mason. The spirelet that was on the gable of the nave was replaced at one side of the front to the street.

The walls are of Kentish rag, and the style is late thirteenth-century. It was built for galleries, and has two rows of windows in the aisles—which is most unusual for an Anglican church of this date. But the plan is otherwise ecclesiological: nave with aisles, and a tower at what should be the north-west (but the church is not orientated): and a good-sized chancel.

The priest's vestry was added in 1891. The galleries were taken down in 1928.

There is a good altar window of 1867, by Clayton and Bell. The interior has been redecorated since the War.

St Peter's, Leigham Court Road (173)

The architect was R. W. Drew, a nephew of Butterfield, and the church, of yellow brick patterned with red, might almost be one of Butterfield's: the chancel is particularly characteristic. At first, only three bays of the nave and aisles, and the chancel and vestry, were built: they were consecrated on 2 July 1870. The western parts, and the baptistery, were added in 1886–7, from plans by G. H. Fellowes Prynne. As the church stands on a steep hillside, there is a lower storey under the baptistery, and a flight of steps up to the porch. A faculty 7 July 1915 for dormers (Fellowes Prynne), rood (Aylmer Vallance), and iron screen between chancel and chapel (Blunt and Wray).

The inside has been much lightened by the destruction of the glass in the War: only fragments remain, by Ward and Hughes, and others. And the chancel has been whitewashed—though the reredos, sedilia and piscina have been allowed to keep their colour. The font is by Fellowes Prynne; the pulpit is by F. E. Howard, 1930.

268

St John The Divine, Bedford Hill, Balham

An appeal for funds was made in 1880. The design was made by R. J. Withers, and the foundation stone of the chancel was laid on 10 November 1883. The temporary nave remained, and the debt was not paid off until 1897.

Plans were then made for the completion of the nave and aisles, and those of E. H. Elphick, a member of the congregation, were chosen: work was begun in 1899, and the consecration was on 16 October 1900. It is an unremarkable church, built of the usual stock brick, relieved with red: the chancel has been whitened. Some glass in the south aisle was designed by the Rev Ernest Geldart, and executed by Curtis, Ward and Hughes. The rood and beam are by Caröe and Passmore, 1915.

The Ascension, Malwood Road, Balham

The architect was Arthur Cawston, whose father was a member of the building committee, and gave the site. The builders were J. and C. Bowyer. The foundation stone was laid on 3 May 1883, and the church was consecrated on 22 May 1884. The south transept was not completed at the time of the consecration. The reredos was erected in 1886. In 1889 it was decided to complete the church: the new parts were consecrated on 26 January 1890. The porch and tower were not built.

It is a brick church, now all whitened inside. The architect has tried very hard to be original. The arcades have very slender octagonal pillars, without capitals, and the arches are obtusely pointed, with pierced spandrels. The clerestory windows are triplets in a wall arcade. There are large double transepts: the western one on the north is the base of the unbuilt tower. There is no chancel arch. Three arches in the east wall open into a very narrow eastern aisle, which is put there simply for effect: there is no way into it. The east wall of this aisle has tile mosaic of 1888. The baptistery and north transept windows are by Lavers and Westlake: the east triplet by Clayton and Bell.

St Alban's Fayland Avenue

Begun in 1884, the church was consecrated on 2 April 1887, and finished in 1893. The architect was E. H. Martineau. The tower was never built. It is of red brick, in Byzantine style, with an apse and ambulatory.

The first vicar, the Rev S. M. Ransome, who was a brother-in-law of the architect, decided to fill the windows with Morris glass. They were the work of J. H. Dearle, d. 1932, who worked for the firm, and went to live at Streatham so as to be near the Morris works at Merton. It is said that the upper windows in the chancel were from designs by Burne-Jones, and that most of the rest were by Dearle. The roof was destroyed in the War, and most of the glass was broken.

The church was burned on 29 December 1947: a temporary roof was put up, and it was reopened on 22 June 1949. The restoration was done by J. B. S. Comper, who erected an aluminium vault over the nave: there is the usual Comper lighting. The church was rededicated on 11 September 1954. Windows in the apse by Sir J. N. Comper, and west window by H. B. Powell, were dedicated on 24 June 1956.

St Andrew's, Guildersfield Road

The foundation stone was laid on 3 June 1886 and the consecration was on 18 May 1887. The architects were Ernest George and Peto. The church is of brick and terra cotta, Perpendicular in style. The aisles are cross-gabled. The arcades are Norman Shaw-like with octagonal, capital-less pillars. A tall clerestory: north-east turret. The chancel screen dates from 1913 and is by Jones and Willis. The iron font cover, by Wippell, was erected in 1907.

St Margaret's, Barcombe Avenue

Charles Booth, or one of his colleagues, who had the pleasure of exploring the suburbs in about 1900, reported that St Margaret's had just 'shuffled off its iron casing and reached the dignity of a properly built church'. It was only a small part of what was projected, but it was opened free from debt, and with great hopes.

The foundation stone was laid in 1899, and the church was consecrated on 1 December 1900. It was completed in 1907. Architects, Rowland Plumbe and Harvey. A big, red brick building, the parish church of several streets of uniform red brick and terra cotta houses. Cruciform, with a spirelet at the crossing: at the west end, two turrets, five lancets under an arch, and a baptistery. A spacious and not undignified interior: a carved wooden reredos by W. D. Caröe, 1908, illustrating the early history of the church in Britain, and an east window by Burlison and Grylls. It is probable that churches of this kind that have not been modernised—as this has not—will some day come back again into favour.

St Thomas's, Telford Avenue

A temporary church was built in 1885. The permanent church was begun in 1898, opened in 1901, and consecrated in 1903. The foundation stone was laid by the Lord Mayor on

11 May 1901 : it records that the architects were Sidney R. J. Smith and Spencer W. Grant, and that the builder was F. G. Minter, of Westminster. The aisles and the baptistery were added later. It has a 'very tolerable plain uninspired nave and aisles', of red brick outside, and stocks within, with red stone columns. The chancel and transepts, in Perpendicular style, were added in 1927.

St James's, Mitcham Lane

The building committee was formed in 1906, after a committee of Immanuel, the mother parish, had accepted a design by Newman and Newman. In 1907 another design was obtained, from P. K. Allen of Tunbridge Wells. Nothing more was heard of this, but Arthur Newman was asked to make fresh plans, which were accepted. Tenders were asked for in 1908, but in January 1909 the committee decided that they were all too high, and that other plans would have to be obtained.

Newman was paid off, and in February E. H. Lingen Barker made designs for a cheap church, of brick, lined with adamant plaster, with tracery, arcades, and other dressings, of terra cotta. B. E. Nightingale's tender was accepted, the foundations were laid, and the foundation stone was duly placed in position on 9 October. On 3 November the committee was told that the architect had contravened the directions of I.C.B.S.: they drew up a list of 16 awkward questions, and on 20 December Lingen Barker resigned. He would not let them have the plans.

On 1 January 1910, Frank Peck was appointed in his place, but there were difficulties with him, and with the contractors, who stopped work for a time. Peck said that he did not wish to resign, and the nave and aisles were consecrated on 30 March 1912.

For the completion of the church, W. S. Weatherley was chosen as architect, and the contractor was John Garrett of Balham Hill. The chancel was built in 1914–15, and the spirelet at the west was added from Weatherley's design.

The architect has rather strained after effect, with flying buttresses at the west end, and, inside, acutely pointed arches rising right up to plain circular clerestory windows.

The original electric light fittings have recently been cleaned up, and used over again : they are quite a feature of the interior.

St Paul's, Welham Road

Plans were made by Greenaway and Newberry in 1914, but the War delayed the building of the church. The congregation worshipped in the Seely Hall. After the War, the designs were modified.

The foundation stone was laid on 5 June 1925, and the church consecrated in 1927. The walls are of Fletton brick, faced with brown Crowborough brick, with tiled roofs. The architects' usual plan, but carried out in a cheap-looking way, with lancet windows. The inside almost looks like a church of 1840, de-galleried, reseated, and redecorated. The font was designed by Sir Aston Webb, and came from the chapel of the Seely family at Sherwood Lodge, Nottingham. The glass in the east triplet is by Martin Travers.

Holy Redeemer, Churchmore Road

One of the Bishop of Southwark's Twenty-Five New Churches. It was built as a memorial to the Clapham Sect; begun in 1931, and consecrated on 5 March 1932. The architects were Martin Travers and T. F. W. Grant: the design was shown at the Royal Academy in 1933. It is in a modified Perpendicular style, with a renaissance cupola. It was said at the time that 'the windows have just enough tracing to give the suggestion of a church of the characteristically English trend'. It is of multi-coloured stock bricks, with pre-cast stone tracery: the roof of steel construction, covered with copper, with a plaster ceiling inside. The planning is straightforward: nave and aisles, no structural chancel, and a sanctuary.

Tooting

There is not much to be said about this parish. 'The atmosphere', says Lewis, 'is considered very salubrious, and the environs are studded with elegant cottages and villas.' The population was under 3,000 in the '70s. At the end of the nineteenth century, a few poor streets were built: then the L.C.C. bought land for an estate of its own. Booth said that it had suddenly become predominantly a working-class district. Upper Tooting was in the parish of Streatham.

St Nicholas', Church Lane

The old church had a round tower. The chancel was enlarged under a faculty of 12 April 1710, by Sir James Bateman, who was desirous to bring within the church a vault that he had made in the churchyard. There were repairs in 1763. A new church was built in 1833, by subscription, by the sale of part of Tooting Common, and by a grant of £350 from the I.C.B.S. The architect was T. W. Atkinson, and the builder was Hicks, junior, of Tooting: the cost was £6,247. It is of brick, with a pinnacled tower, with the usual proportions of a Gothic church of the time.

The desk pulpit, and lectern were designed by E. Swinfen Harris in 1868. The chancel, vestry and organ chamber were added in 1873–5 by J. P. St Aubyn, and transepts in 1889. The new seating was installed in 1884, new reredos in 1906. There was a repair in 1939. The glass in the windows of the apse is by A. L. Wilkinson, 1954.

Monuments   Elizabeth Fitzwilliam, 1582, and William, 1597. Sir John Hepdon, 1670. Esther, wife of Sir Thomas Bateman, 1709, ascribed to Francis Bird.

All Saints', Brudenell Road (196)

This very fine church was built by a bequest from Lady Charles Brudenell-Bruce, in memory of her husband: it was begun in 1904 (foundation stone 22 October), and consecrated on 7 July 1906. Temple Moore was the architect. It is of stock brick, in fourteenth-century style, simple in its details, and beautifully proportioned: a nave with double aisles, north tower, aisled chancel, and an eastern Lady chapel, opening into the chancel by three arches, as at Moore's St Wilfrid's, Harrogate. Columns of Forest of Dean and Quarella stone: the wooden vaults are painted white.

The renaissance fittings of the chancel were collected by the vicar, Canon Stephens, on the Continent, and adapted by Sir Walter Tapper. The altar piece came from Bologna, the candlesticks from Florence, and the stalls, etc., from a church near Como. They look extremely well. The painting in the altar piece is a copy of the Crucifixion by Velasquez in the Museo de Prado, Madrid. The altar piece in the Lady chapel is French sixteenth-century. The lectern is a copy of one from Italy, which Stephens gave to Blankney church, Lincs.

The glass in the chancel east windows is by Victor Milner. The marble font and cover, the pulpit and organ case, are by Sir Walter Tapper. There was a vicarage of a size commensurate with the church, but it was pulled down in 1960.

St Augustine's, Broadwater Road

An iron room was built in 1884, and an iron church in 1890. The permanent church was designed by H. P. Burke Downing: the plans were shown in the Royal Academy in 1929. The foundation stone was laid on 30 November 1929, the consecration took place in 1931. The builders were Messrs Dorey and Co. The church has an aisled nave and chancel, under one long roof; a south chapel and north vestries: the style is fourteenth-century. This is not as successful as the architect's earlier churches.

Wandsworth

Wandsworth became industrial at an early date, though the neighbourhood of the Common, and East and West Hills were residential. The population in the early nineteenth century was large enough for a Commissioners' church to be built. Several large institutions were built here later in the nineteenth century.

All Saints', Wandsworth (189)

The tower was built in 1630: it was refaced and raised in 1841. The parish records of the late seventeenth century, and the first part of the eighteenth, contain many references to work on the church. In 1716 the vicar, at his own cost, built a new aisle on the north side of the nave and chancel. In 1726 the steeple was reported to be in danger, and an estimate was obtained for rebuilding it: in the next year Mr Price surveyed it, and it was repaired. Repairs to the church were done in 1750.

A committee was appointed in 1779 to alter the church, and the congregation migrated to the French Chapel: on 17 November a faculty confirmed the work that had been done. The committee had rebuilt the whole of the south wall and part of the east wall, refaced and raised the north wall, and reroofed the whole church. The surveyor was William Jupp, and the main contractors were Parker and Langton. An organ was bought in 1781, and there were many repairs to the church in this year and the next.

The church was painted and ornamented in 1828, and altered and improved in 1841. Further alterations were made in 1859. In 1899–1900 E. W. Mountford added the chancel and reroofed the church.

The interior has Adam-like Doric columns of wood, painted as marble, with a frieze and enriched cornice. The galleries have not been removed, and the pulpit, small marble font, and the churchwarden's pew, remain. Parts of the altar piece are on the front of the west gallery. The Transfiguration window of 1859, now in the south aisle, was over the altar. The upper part of the tower was destroyed in 1941: post-War repairs were completed in 1955.

Monuments A damaged brass to Nicholas Maudyt, serjeant at arms to Henry V, 1420. Susannah Powell, 1630, and Alderman Henry Smith, 1627.

Holy Trinity, West Hill

A chapel of ease, consecrated on 6 June 1863. The architect was J. M. K. Hähn, who lived at Wandsworth, and designed the parish school. The spire was added in 1888, by G. Patrick.

St Anne's, St Anne's Hill (190)

A Commissioners' church, begun in 1820, and consecrated on 1 May 1824. The cost was £14,511, all of which was paid by the Commissioners. The architect was Sir Robert Smirke, who never deserted his usual type. The portico is of his favourite Ionic order, and there is a two-staged circular tower on a square base. The body of the church is of stock brick with stone dressings. The galleries are on square piers, with slender Doric columns above.

There were alterations by William White in 1891, and the chancel was added by E. W. Mountford in 1896.

The church was reopened in 1946 after War damage had been put right, but the roof was destroyed by fire in 1950. Restoration was done by Caröe and Partners, and the church was reopened in 1951.

St Stephen's, Manfred Road

The foundation stone was laid on 1 November 1881: the consecration was on the same day a year later. The architects were Lee Bros and Pain. St Stephen's is an ordinary brick suburban church. The interior, rather old-fashioned for 1881, has stock brick walls striped and diapered with red, and French thirteenth-century pillars, with stiff-leaf capitals and square abaci. The chancel ends in an apsidal sanctuary. Here is glass by Heaton, Butler and Bayne. The glass in the aisle lancets, and in the west window, is by Jones and Willis, who were also responsible for the screen and reredos, in 1906.

St Michael's, Wimbledon Park Road

The foundation stone was laid by the Duchess of Teck on 10 April 1897: another stone was laid on 24 June 1905, when the eastern parts were being added. The architect was E. W. Mountford.

This is one of those large and handsome late Victorian churches that rose so grandly above the roofs of newly built suburbs, and were planned to be even more impressive: this one, in the architect's drawing, had a large tower on the north. It has instead a lead-covered spirelet at the junction between nave and chancel.

It is of red brick, with a somewhat Caröe-ish west window. The pillars are without capitals: the lower part of them is panelled. The renaissance altar piece and panelling, 1923, are not a satisfactory termination eastward: there should be a large triptych, painted and gilded. Still less are the choirstalls, lectern, and pulpit satisfactory: they were put up in 1958, and aim at being contemporary. There is glass by Burlison and Grylls.

St Faith's, Ebner Street

This very large church is hidden away down a side street, and stands rather uncomfortably on the edge of a hill. It was designed by J. E. K. Cutts. The estimate was £7,500 for the whole church, but only £2,500 was to be spent at first. It was begun in November 1882; the foundation stone was laid on 2 February 1883, and the church was consecrated on 1 November of the same year. It is of brick, in Early English style, with low aisles and a rather tall clerestory. Goodhart-Rendel called it 'typical *early* Cutts, not very happy, but fairly strong'. The west end has a porch, and, at one corner of it, a tower which was once gabled, and surmounted by a flèche, but is now truncated. In 1925 the interior was white-washed, and the sanctuary was altered.

St Mary Magdalene's, Wandsworth Common

St Mary's is sandwiched between houses: the west end has to be viewed from one street, and the east from another. The foundation stone was laid 1 November 1887, the church consecrated in 1888. The architect was B. E. Ferrey. The chancel was not built, and the Rev H. Cottrell Evans, vicar from 1895, worked to complete the church: the chancel was added in 1900; the north aisle in 1906, by Cole A. Adams, of Victoria Street: porch 1907. The church is in the usual thirteenth-century style, and the usual stock brick, varied with red. The aisles have no windows: the light comes from the west end and the clerestory.

The inside looks larger than one expects. It has been adorned with a pulpit, 1902, a carved stone reredos, with marble shafts and a good deal of alabaster, 1916—extremely old-fashioned for its date—by W. J. Wilson, of Old Bond Street; and a screen which is a memorial of the 1914–18 War. It might be worth mentioning that a faculty was given in 1909 for a reredos in the south chapel from the Army and Navy Stores. The glass at the north-west, 1954, is by Mrs R. M. de Montmorency.

St Paul's, Augustus Road, Wimbledon Park (195)

A temporary church was built in 1877: the site was given by the Earl of Beauchamp. Micklethwaite and Somers Clarke designed the permanent church. The chancel was built in 1888 at a cost of about £2,000, with the temporary church remaining as a nave. The Rev

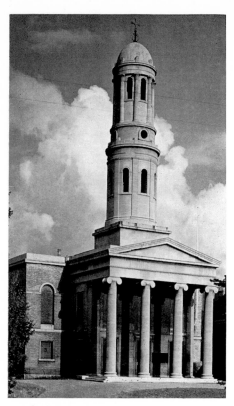

190 St Anne's, Wandsworth, 1820–4
by Sir Robert Smirke

191 Christchurch, Streatham Hill, 1840–1 by J. W. Wild

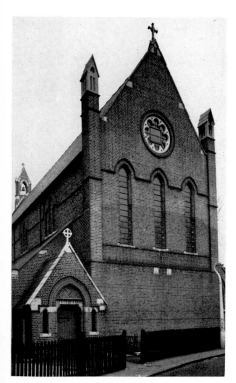

192 St Peter's, Clapham, 1878
by J. E. K. Cutts

193 St Andrew's, Wandsworth, 1889–90 and 1901–2
by E. W. Mountford

195 St Paul's, Wimbledon Park, 1888 and 1896, by J. T. Micklethwaite and Somers Clarke

197 St Nicholas', Plumstead, twelfth-century and later, with seventeenth-century tower

194 St Mary's, Balham, the chancel added by Arthur Cawston to the body of c. 1806

196 All Saints', Tooting, 1904–6 by Temple Moore

E. C. Brace left a legacy of £2,000, which was spent on the carved wooden reredos (C. E. Kempe and Co.), panelling, screen (a memorial to two Liddons, 1893 and 1894), the painting of the roof, and the glass by Kempe. The nave was begun in 1896: the contractors were Messrs Adamson. The pulpit was the gift of Canon Henry Scott Holland. The tower was never built.

This is the late Victorian suburban church at its best. Nave and chancel under one roof, with a copper-covered flèche between them. The only unsatisfactory thing about the interior is the heavy, art-and-crafty seating in the nave, dating from between the Wars.

St Andrew's, Garratt Lane (193)

This large church, designed by E. W. Mountford, was begun in 1889, and the chancel, south chapel, and three bays of the nave were consecrated on 8 February 1890. The builder was William Johnson. The two west bays, and the north and south porches, were consecrated on 1 March 1902.

The nave and chancel are of the same height, under one long tiled roof. The clerestory is tall in proportion to the aisles, and looks quite Pearsonic. There are transepts of the slightest projection. At the west are two turrets, with an arch between, and a porch at the bottom of it: this front stands up well above the winding, rather dismal street, and a projecting clock, a memorial to Edward VII, adds to the effect. The outside is of red brick, the inside of stocks, with red arches and diapers. There is no chancel arch. The screen and lectern are by J. Starkie Gardner: the font was designed by Tinworth, and executed by Doulton.

The three windows in the east wall have glass by Heaton, Butler and Bayne (which goes well with brick walls). The west window of the south aisle is by Martin Travers.

St Mary's, Keble Road, Summerstown

The original Summerstown Chapel was built by Joshua Stanger in 1835-6: the architect was William Moseley. It was consecrated in 1845: an apse was added in 1861, and an aisle in 1870. It became dangerous, and was taken down in 1894. An iron church was used for some years.

Godfrey Pinkerton made plans for a church to hold 800 and to cost £8,000. It was built in 1903, on the site of the school, and consecrated on 30 April 1904. The builders were Messrs Johnson and Co. of Wandsworth Common.

This is rather a good church—of brick and stone, Byzantine in style with invented traceried windows. Alternate bays of the aisles are arranged transeptally, with barrel roofs and large windows. The lower bays have double arches opening to the nave, with granite columns: the blind arches above are filled with paintings. The chancel has an incomplete south tower containing the organ loft: and, on the north, a projection similar to, though somewhat deeper than, the transeptally arranged bays of the aisles. The carving, including the font and cover, was by Laurence A. Turner. The east window is by Morris, 1928.

St Barnabas', Lavenham Road

Built 1906–8, architect C. Ford Whitcombe. Another handsome church of the big suburban type. Nave and chancel, with aisles, are continuous, and there is a small projecting sanctuary. The chancel is raised over an undercroft. There was to have been a tower on the north, but it has never materialised. The material is red brick, the style Perpendicular. A pierced stonework parapet has only been put on one bay. Inside, only one pier has been carved. The glass is of different shades of green, and yellow in the clerestory.

St John the Divine, Garratt Lane

A temporary building by Greenaway and Newberry, built in 1921.

Woolwich

Woolwich is a place that may easily be overlooked, as just another part of South London, like all the rest, and not worth visiting. But it is, in fact, a place with a character of its own. The old town, with its rather stodgy eighteenth-century church, is down by the river, with its dockyard and arsenal; on the high ground there remain pleasant commons, dotted with military establishments—the R.M.C., barracks, etc.

St Mary Magdalene's, St Mary's Street

£1,141-odd was collected by brief in the reign of Queen Anne; but the old church was found to be beyond repair, and a petition was presented to the Commons on 22 December 1718. A new church must be built, of which the cost would be £5,069, and the parish wanted to be included in the scheme for the Fifty New Churches. The petition was granted.

On 3 August 1727 it was agreed that since £1,550 had been collected, Matthew Spray of Deptford, bricklayer, should begin digging the foundations, and that he and the other workmen should carry them up as far as the surface of the ground. By 1731 money had run short, and an appeal was made to the Commons: Spray, and other workmen, said that the church could not be built for less than £5,069. It was ordered that leave be given to bring in a bill.

On 25 February 1738 the vestry signed another petition: the £3,000 given by Act of Parliament had been spent, and the total, with sums that had been collected, was £5,328:16:11: the body of the church, and the steeple, had been built, but £1,000 more was needed to finish the work.

The church was finally completed in 1739, and consecrated in 1740.

It is not known who made the design. It is of brick, plain, substantial, and rather heavy: the least inviting of the Fifty New Churches. The body is of five bays: the galleries rest on octagonal columns, which may be regarded as elongated bases of the Ionic columns above. A segmental arched roof to the nave, and flat ceilings in the aisles, with plaster roses. It has been reseated, and the galleries have been removed from the eastern bay: the rest of the galleries has recently been shut off from the church. The chancel, organ chamber and vestry were added by J. O. Scott in 1894, in an unobjectionable Classical style. Wrought iron rails remain: the Ionic altar piece has been removed to the south chapel. Here are also collected a few tablets—not particularly interesting.

Christchurch, Shooter's Hill

The congregation first met in the assembly rooms of the 'Bull Inn'. The Board of Ordnance gave the site, on condition that £2,500 should be raised by subscription within a year.

The church was built in 1855–6: the architects were Tress and Chambers. It is in the Early English style: small, cruciform, with a bellcote. It was opened on 21 December 1856, but not consecrated until 19 June 1865. In that year, the chancel was lengthened and an organ chamber—forming the base of a tower—was added.

In 1900 there were decorations by Temple Moore, including the screen.

St Michael's, Borgard Road

The foundation stone of the chancel was laid on 15 July 1875. This is of brick, solid Early English, vaulted, with a south chapel. J. W. Walter was the architect. The nave was opened in 1888: this is by Butterfield. One would naturally assume that it is earlier than the chancel: but Butterfield never altered his style. It was planned as three aisled bays, with the usual western transept, but neither the aisles nor the transept were built.

The walls have been whitewashed, but a band of tiles under the clerestory has been left, and, fortunately, the painted ceiling. The seats are low, as usual, and there is the usual marble font (and a small eighteenth-century font, not used).

In 1955 a narrow and unambitious aisle, and a south-west transept, not open to the church, were added by Thomas F. Ford and partners. A reredos was designed by the Rev Ernest Geldart, but the description of the design does not correspond to what was erected: this is of Bath stone and Devonshire marble, carved by Harry Hems: a painting of our Lord and the 24 elders in the middle, and carved angels at the sides.

In 1944 the glass in the south chapel was destroyed by enemy action: it has been replaced by unremarkable new glass.

St Michael's, Abbey Wood

Consecrated on 11 April 1908; a routine production of the firm of Blomfield and Sons, of red brick with stone dressings, and the usual suburban plan. Like most of such churches, it has too many doors, including some that are never opened, and never need to be. The east window, and east of north chapel, are by Tower.

NOTES ON
SOME ARCHITECTS

No attempt has been made to include in this list everyone who designed a church in London: it is simply a few notes on some of the more obvious men, and on a few of the others.

ARCHER, Thomas, c. 1668–1743
  Travelled abroad for four years, and in 1705 was appointed Groom Porter. One of the Commissioners for the Fifty New Churches. He introduced into his designs baroque elements derived from Italian architects.

ASHPITEL, Arthur, 1807–1869
  A pupil of his father: he retired early, and his churches are few.

ATKINSON, Thomas Witlam, c. 1799–1861
  A north-countryman, who also worked in London. Author of *Gothic Ornaments selected from the different Cathedrals and Churches in England*, 1829.

BAKER, Arthur, 1841–1896
  A pupil of Scott, and associated with him for a time. He was partner with J. F. Wadmore, 1822–1903.

BARKER, Edwin Henry Lingen, 1838–1917
  Restored a large number of churches, especially in Wales. Architect to ten school boards.

BARRY, Sir Charles, 1795–1860
  Travelled abroad, after serving his articles. He realised that Greek architecture was on the way out in England, and that Gothic and Italian 'had the mastery of the field'. He used Italian for his clubs, and remodelling of classical houses, and Gothic for churches (except for St Andrew's, Hove). In 1836 he was awarded the first premium for rebuilding the Houses of Parliament, and this became his life's work. He was knighted in 1852.

BARRY, Charles, 1823–1906
  Son of Sir Charles Barry. In 1847 he entered into partnership with Robert Richardson Banks, who died in 1872 aged 59.

BARRY, Edward Middleton, 1830–1880
  Another son of Sir Charles, and worked with him.

BASEVI, George, 1794—1845
  A pupil of Sir John Soane. He built Belgrave Square, 1825–40, and streets in Chelsea. Architect of the Fitzwilliam Museum, Cambridge. He died as the result of a fall from Ely Cathedral.

BEDFORD, Francis Octavius, 1784–1858
  Travelled in Greece, and was a careful student of Greek architecture.

BELCHER, John, 1841–1913

Son of John Belcher, architect, and his partner for some years from 1865. His work 'is the striking outcome of a traditional education in classical architecture stimulated to revolt by the Gothic revival, and producing an eclecticism which opened the way for new alliances with sculptors and painters untrammelled by convention' (*D.N.B.*).

BILLING, Arthur, 1824–1895

In the offices of Ferrey and Hardwick. He was partner with A. S. Newman 1860–73, with A. E. Billing from 1890, and J. W. Rowley from 1893.

BLACKBURNE, Edward Lushington, 1803–1888

Author of *History of the Decorative Painting of the Middle Ages*. His churches are in the French Gothic style.

BLOMFIELD, Sir Arthur William, 1829–1899

Son of Bishop Blomfield of London. Trained by P. C. Hardwick. He was mainly a church architect, and those buildings that were not churches had some useful purpose—e.g. several schools, Sion College Library, and Church House, Westminster. He followed the fashion: first a French thirteenth-century style, and then Early English and Perpendicular.

His sons Charles James and Arthur were also architects (Sir Arthur Blomfield and Sons).

BLORE, Edward, 1787–1879

A clever draughtsman, and interested in mediaeval architecture. 'Special architect' to William IV, and to Victoria in the early years of her reign: he worked at Windsor Castle, and completed Buckingham Palace. Surveyor to Westminster Abbey 1827–49. Designer of many houses and churches: none of his designs are very interesting.

BODLEY, George Frederick, 1829–1907

A pupil of Scott: as a young man he designed some strongly French Gothic churches—e.g. St Michael's, Brighton, St Martin's, Scarborough, and Selsley, Glos., which have pre-Raphaelite decoration. In All Saints', Cambridge, and St John's, Tuebrook, Liverpool, designed in the 60s, he came back to an English fourteenth-century style. He took Thomas Garner (1839–1906) into partnership, which lasted until 1898. Having found his style, Bodley kept it to the end: all his churches are in a delicate and refined Decorated—earlier or later—which manages to be so personal that even the smallest works have the unmistakable Bodleian character. He took care of all the furnishing and decoration of his churches, which, when complete, have screens and rood, carved and painted reredos, and painted walls and ceiling. His favourite colours were olive green, dull red, white, and gold.

BRANDON, David, 1813–1896

Articled to George Smith: partner with T. H. Wyatt 1838–51. His practice included a good deal of church work.

BROCK, Edward Philip Loftus, 1833–1895

A pupil of W. G. and E. Habershon. He was afterwards partner with the latter.

BROOKS, James, 1825–1901

A pupil of Lewis Stride, and attended the classes of Professor Donaldson. A convinced High Churchman (churchwarden of St Matthias', Stoke Newington). He designed large, simple, and solid churches, generally of brick, which are suitable to the town surroundings in which they stand.

BROWN, John, 1805–1876

County surveyor of Norfolk, and surveyor to Norwich Cathedral, which he repaired in 1851.

BURY, Thomas Talbot, 1811–1877

Pupil of the elder Pugin, and began practice in 1830. He helped to prepare the designs of the Houses of Parliament, with Pugin, under Barry. Author of *Remains of Ecclesiastical Woodwork*, and of *History and Description of the Styles of Architecture of Various Countries*. He was partner for a time with Charles Lee, who had been with Thomas Cubitt, in the office of Nash, and a partner with Henry Duesbury.

BUTTERFIELD, William, 1814–1900

Associated with the Cambridge Camden Society, and the Ecclesiological Society, and made drawings for the *Instrumenta Ecclesiastica*. His most important early work was the building of St Augustine's College, Canterbury. No architect expressed better in his works the uncompromising and entirely unromantic spirit of nineteenth-century High churchmen. Like most of them, he had a strong personality, and could be very difficult: he had no desire to placate clients, or to please the general public. He got on best with churchmen like Butler of Wantage, with whom he must have had much in common.

His three great London churches—All Saints', Margaret Street, St Matthias', Stoke Newington, and St Albans', Holborn—are his best: later, he tended to repeat himself. But there is such an individuality about his work that it can always be recognised—even if it is no more than a few fittings in a cheaply restored church.

His constructional colouration was found amusing in the nineteenth century; and even now a certain type of churchman can never see it without wanting to whitewash it. Butterfield regarded it as essential, and did not want pictures of his buildings to be published unless the colour was shown.

CARÖE, William Douglas, 1857–1928

A pupil of J. L. Pearson, and was responsible for a great deal of the detailing of Truro Cathedral. Architect to the Ecclesiastical Commissioners (with Herbert Passmore), to the Charity Commissioners, and to various cathedrals. 'A faithful representative of what may be called the closing phase of the Gothic revival.'

CARPENTER, Richard Cromwell, 1812–1855

Articled to John Blyth, and practised in London. No architect produced churches that more nearly fulfilled the ideals of the ecclesiologists: Carpenter's are correct, simple, and well-proportioned, and have a sincerity about them that is often missing from later Gothic revival work. Their fittings matched their architecture.

Carpenter designed the earliest of the Woodard Schools—Lancing and Hurstpierpoint; and carefully restored churches in Sussex and Kent.

CARPENTER, Richard Herbert, 1841–1893
Son of R. C. Carpenter: partner with William Slater 1865–70, and with Benjamin Ingelow 1878–93. Architect to the Woodard Schools.

CHAMPNEYS, Basil, 1842–1935
A pupil of John Prichard. Architect of many school and college buildings, and of some churches.

CHRISTIAN, Ewan, 1814–1895
A pupil of Matthew Habershon, and afterwards with John Brown of Norwich, and William Railton. He was architect to the Ecclesiastical Commissioners from 1852, and built or restored very many churches. His new churches are simple and undistinguished, and he did not aim at effect. He is said to have designed about 200 parsonage houses.

CLARKE, Thomas Chatfield, 1829–1895
Architect and surveyor in London. President of the Surveyors' Institute 1894.

CLARKE, Somers, 1841–1926
In Scott's office with J. T. Micklethwaite, with whom he collaborated. Surveyor to St Paul's Cathedral 1897.

COMPER, Sir John Ninian, 1864–1960
In the office of C. E. Kempe, and articled to Bodley and Garner. His earliest work was done in Scotland, where he was born. He began by using late Gothic, and then moved on to 'unity by inclusion'. 'The purpose of a church is not to express the age in which it was built or the individuality of its designer: its purpose is to move to worship.' The note of a church should be 'not that of novelty, but of eternity'. Comper designed everything in his churches, and set a new fashion in stained glass—which has been continued by imitators who have not his genius.

COUSE, Kenton, 1721–1790
Trained under Flitcroft, who in 1762 appointed him as his clerk. He was afterwards clerk of the works at Whitehall, Westminster, and St James's; and held other positions. Surveyor to the Goldsmiths' Company.

CUNDY, Thomas, 1790–1867
Son of Thomas Cundy, senior, surveyor to Lord Grosvenor's estates: he worked in his father's office, and succeeded to his appointment.

CUTTS, John Edward Knight, 1847–1938
In the office of Ewan Christian. He and his brother John Priston Cutts (1854–1935) designed a large number of big suburban churches, all more or less alike.

DANCE, George, d. 1768
Clerk of the City Works, 1735; architect of the Mansion House, 1739–52.

DANCE, George, junior, 1741–1825
Studied in Italy, and succeeded his father as clerk of the City Works. Architect of Newgate Prison, St Luke's Hospital, Old Street, and several other London buildings.

DAUKES, Samuel Whitfield, 1811–1880
Articled to Pritchett of York, and set up business in Gloucester and Cheltenham. An architect with wide interests, which included railways as well as churches.

DOLLMAN, Francis Thomas, 1812–1900
A pupil of the elder Pugin. He was employed by George Basevi 1838–45, and in practice in London 1845–95. Author of *Examples of Ancient Pulpits*, and *Examples of Ancient Domestic Architecture*. 'The last of a good old school'.

DONALDSON, Thomas Leverton, 1795–1885
Professor of Architecture at University College, London.

DOWNING, Henry Philip Burke, 1865–1947
Chief assistant to Joseph Clarke: began independent practice in 1889. Consulting architect to I.C.B.S. and to London Diocesan Fund: diocesan architect to Chichester.

FERREY, Benjamin, 1810–1880
A pupil of the elder Pugin, and afterwards with William Wilkins. Diocesan architect to Bath and Wells, and restored Wells Cathedral. His *Recollections* of A. W. N. Pugin were published in 1861. The architect of a large number of churches, mostly rather ordinary: he was 'rather a close adherent of precedent than a bold originator'.

FLITCROFT, Henry, 1697–1769
Assistant to Lord Burlington; clerk of the works at Whitehall, Westminster, and St James's, 1726: Comptroller of the Works 1758.

FOWLER, Charles, 1791–1867
Articled at Exeter, and came to London in 1814: with David Laing, and then began independent practice. Architect of the markets at Gravesend and Exeter, and of Covent Garden and Hungerford Markets.

FOWLER, Charles Hodgson, 1840–1910
Articled to Scott, and helped with his restoration of Durham Cathedral. He designed many good churches, mostly in the North, and was a careful restorer. Architect to the cathedrals of York, Durham, Rochester and Lincoln.

FRANCIS, Frederick John, 1818–1896
In partnership with his brother Horace.

FRANCIS, Horace, 1821–1894
In partnership with his brother Frederick John.

GEORGE, Sir Ernest, 1839–1922
Partner first with Thomas Vaughan, and afterwards with Harold Peto, 1828–97. He 'cast off his early allegiance' to Street, and favoured an Anglo-Dutch style, using brick and terra cotta. The architect of many houses.

GIBBS, James, 1682–1752

Studied in Rome, and came to England in 1709. One of the surveyors for the Fifty New Churches, but dismissed in 1715. Patronised by Edward Harley, Earl of Oxford, and other Tories. Architect of the Senate House, and of new buildings at King's College, Cambridge; of the Radcliffe Library at Oxford; and of many houses.

GODWIN, George, 1815–1888

Son of George Godwin, architect, of Brompton. Editor of *The Builder* 1844–83. His brother Henry was also an architect.

GOUGH, Alexander Dick, 1804–1871

Articled to Benjamin Wyatt. Began practice in 1836 with R. L. Roumieu, and worked independently from 1848. Surveyor to several small railways.

GOUGH, Hugh Roumieu, 1843–1904

Son of A. D. Gough; began practice in 1870.

GWILT, George, 1746–1807

Surveyor to the County of Surrey, district surveyor for St George's, Southwark, etc.

GWILT, George, junior, 1775–1856

Son of George Gwilt. He restored the eastern chapels of Southwark Cathedral.

GWILT, Joseph, 1784–1863

Son of the elder George Gwilt: chiefly known as a writer on architectural subjects.

HAKEWILL, Henry, 1771–1830

Architect to Rugby School, which he rebuilt. His church at Wolverton, Bucks., is an early example of Norman revival.

HAKEWILL, John Henry, 1811–1880

Articled to his father Henry Hakewill.

HAKEWILL, Edward Charles, 1812–1872

Another son of Henry Hakewill. Articled to Philip Hardwick. Surveyor to St Clement Danes and St Mary le Strand. Moved to Suffolk, where he did a good deal of church restoration.

HARDWICK, Thomas, 1752–1829

A pupil of Sir William Chambers: architect to St Bartholomew's Hospital 1808, and clerk of the works at Hampton Court, 1810.

HARDWICK, Philip, 1792–1870

Son of Thomas Hardwick. He held a number of official appointments. Best known for the Doric entrance to Euston Station, now demolished. His health broke down in 1847, and his son Philip Charles Hardwick took over his work.

HARDWICK, Philip Charles, 1822–1892

Son of Philip Hardwick, and took over his practice. Architect of the new Charterhouse School. His churches are apt to look rather like those of Gilbert Scott—e.g. the beautiful little church at Newland, Worcs., which is an unusually complete example of mid-nineteenth-century furnishing and decoration.

HARRIS, Thomas, 1830–1900
Author of a booklet which advocated a National Architecture, adapted to the wants of the nineteenth century. He is said to have been the first to use the adjective 'Victorian'.

HAWKSMOOR, Nicholas, 1661–1736
'Domestic clerk' to Sir Christopher Wren; clerk of the works at Kensington Palace, etc. Worked with Sir John Vanbrugh. One of the surveyors for the Fifty New Churches: succeeded Wren as surveyor to Westminster Abbey in 1723, and designed the west towers.

HORNE, James
A London architect. Surveyor to the Foundling Hospital 1742, and to Westminster Abbey 1746.

I'ANSON, Edward, 1812–1888
Largely employed as a surveyor to estates in London and Southwark.

INWOOD, Henry William, 1794–1843
Son and pupil of William Inwood, architect. He travelled in Greece, and was an authority on Greek architecture. He helped his father with the churches in St Pancras parish.

INWOOD, Charles Frederick, 1798–1840
The second son of William Inwood, whom he assisted.

JACKSON, Sir Thomas Graham, 1835–1924
A pupil of Scott. Many works at Oxford, mostly renaissance. His biography—*Recollections of Thomas Graham Jackson, 1835–1924*—was edited by Basil H. Jackson.

JAMES, John, c. 1672–1746
Joint clerk of the works with Hawksmoor at Greenwich, and his successor in 1736: master carpenter to St Paul's, 1711, and assistant surveyor 1715. In that year he was appointed assistant surveyor for the Fifty New Churches. Surveyor to the Dean and Chapter of Westminster 1725, and to the fabric of the Abbey 1736.

JOHNSON, Thomas, 1794–1865
With Potter of Lichfield, and the elder John Shaw. Designed several churches in Staffordshire.

JOHNSON, John, 1808–1879
Studied in Italy 1836–40. *Reliques of Ancient English Architecture* is a collection of admirable drawings of churches: there is no letterpress. His churches are, of course, Gothic, but he designed in other styles: he was architect, with Meeson, of the Alexandra Palace.

KEELING, E. Bassett, 1836–1886
A pupil of Draper of Leeds. He 'cultivated the Victorian style'.

KENDALL, Henry Edward, 1805–1885
Son of the architect of the same name, and his pupil.

KNOWLES, Sir James Thomas, 1831–1908
Knighted 1903. In the office of his father, J. T. Knowles, and studied in Italy. He said that he had built 'many hundreds of houses, besides several churches, hospitals, clubs, warehouses, stores, roads and bridges'. Founder and editor of the *Nineteenth Century*. He gave up architecture in 1883.

LAMB, Edward Buckton, 1806–1869
Articled to L. N. Cottingham. The son of a water-colour painter, he made attractive sketches of old churches. He knew what they looked like, and his few restorations were quite moderate. But his new churches are determinedly original: even the small nave-and-chancel designs have something odd about them, and his larger churches are unlike those of any other architect of the time.

LAPIDGE, Edward, 1793–1860
Surveyor to the County of Surrey, and architect of Kingston Bridge.

LITTLE, Thomas, 1802–1859
A pupil of Robert Abraham: practised as an architect and surveyor in London.

MARRABLE, Frederick, 1818–1872
A pupil of Blore: superintendent architect of the Metropolitan Board of Works.

MICKLETHWAITE, John Thomas, 1843–1906
A pupil of Scott, and a learned ecclesiologist and antiquary. His churches, in much the same style as Bodley's, are all very good.

MOORE, Temple Lushington, 1856–1920
A pupil of G. G. Scott, junior, with whom he was associated. When Scott gave up practice, he developed his own style of simple, reticent Gothic.

MOUNTFORD, Ernest William, 1855–1908
Articled to Habershon and Pite. Church work in Wandsworth: but his chief works were town halls, schools, etc. His best known building is the Central Criminal Court, Old Bailey.

NASH, John, 1752–1835
Favourite architect of the Prince Regent: laid out Regent Street and Regent's Park, and designed Buckingham Palace. (See Sir John Summerson, *John Nash*.)

NASH, Edwin, 1814–1884
A pupil of James Field. He was assistant to Gilbert Scott. His son, Walter Hilton Nash, 1850–1927, was in partnership with him, and helped with some of his church building and restorations.

NEWBERRY, John Ernest, 1862–1950
Assistant to J. L. Pearson: partner with Francis Hugh Greenaway, who was a pupil of Sir Aston Webb.

NEWTON, Ernest, 1856–1922
Articled to Norman Shaw. His practice was almost entirely domestic.

NICHOLSON, Sir Charles Archibald, 1867–1949
  Articled to J. D. Sedding, and was afterwards with H. Wilson: he began independent practice in 1893. Partner at first with H. C. Corlette, and with T. J. Rushton from 1927. Consulting architect to seven cathedrals. The architect of many admirable, simple churches.

PARKINSON, Joseph T., 1783–1855
  Laid out the Portman estate, and designed some of the houses.

PEACOCK, Joseph, 1821–1893
  His earlier churches were rather wildly original: his later designs were more ordinary.

PEARSON, John Loughborough, 1817–1897
  In the office of Ignatius Bonomi, and then worked with Salvin and Philip Hardwick. He began independent practice in 1843.
  His earliest churches are in a simple fourteenth-century style: then he had an early French Gothic period: and he ended by using a thirteenth-century style, which owed something to France and something to the great thirteenth-century churches of the North, but is really all his own. The details are not the strongest point: Pearson's large churches are distinguished for their planning and for their construction: most of them are vaulted, and there was no nineteenth-century architect who understood vaulting better, and constructed it with more ingenuity.
  In 1878 he was chosen as the architect for the new Cathedral at Truro, and he was also consulting architect to some of the older cathedrals.
  Pearson was a dedicated architect, completely absorbed in his work.

PENNETHORNE, Sir James, 1801–1871
  In Nash's office, and assisted him. In the Office of Works. Architect of the west front of Somerset House, and of the Record Office. Knighted in 1870.

PITE, Arthur Beresford, 1861–1934
  President of the Architectural Association 1896, Professor of Architecture at Royal College of Art, South Kensington, 1900–23, Architectural director of L.C.C. School of Building, 1905–28.

PLAW, John, c. 1745–1820
  Architect and master-builder at Westminster, and afterwards at Southampton. Author of Rural Architecture, Ferme ornée or Rural Improvements, and Sketches for Country Houses. He emigrated to Canada.

PLUMBE, Rowland, d. 1919 aged 80
  Articled to N. J. Cottingham. He practised in the City: his churches are few.

PORDEN, Charles Ferdinand, 1790–1863
  Articled to his uncle, William Porden, and in the office of G. Wyatt. For ten years with Sir William Tite, and helped in the building of the Royal Exchange.

PRYNNE, George Halford Fellowes, 1855–1927
  A pupil of Windeyer of Toronto, and of Street. His practice was almost entirely ecclesiastical, and he specialised in large suburban churches.

RAILTON, William, 1801–1877

A pupil of William Inwood, and travelled abroad. Architect to the Ecclesiastical Commissioners 1838–40. He made a design for the Houses of Parliament, and erected the Nelson column.

REILLY, Sir Charles Herbert, 1874–1948

Articled to his father: assistant to John Belcher: partner with C. S. Peach.

RICHARDSON, Sir Albert Edward, 1880–1964

At one time Professor of Architecture in London University, and P.R.A. An authority on eighteenth-century architecture.

ROBERTS, Henry, 1803–1876

A pupil of Charles Fowler, and in the office of Sir Robert Smirke. Architect to Lord Shaftesbury's Society for Improving the Conditions of the Labouring Classes.

ROBINS, Edward Cookworthy, 1834–1918

An architect with a wide general practice.

ROBSON, Philip Appleby, 1871–1951

Son of E. R. Robson, architect to the London School Board: he was articled to J. L. Pearson. He was chiefly a designer of schools and houses.

ST AUBYN, James Piers, 1815–1895

A pupil of Thomas Fulljames of Gloucester. Surveyor to the Middle Temple, and restored the Temple Church. He designed and restored many churches, particularly in the West Country, from which his family came.

SALVIN, Anthony, 1799–1881

A pupil of John Nash. He restored many castles—on which he was an authority—and restored and built many large houses. His churches are careful and correct Gothic.

SAVAGE, James, 1779–1852

Articled to D. A. Alexander. He was interested in bridge building. Architect to the Middle Temple, and began the restoration of the Temple Church in 1840.

SCOTT, Sir George Gilbert, 1811–1878

The best known of the great Victorian architects. Knighted after the erection of the Albert Memorial. He gives an account of his rise to eminence in his *Personal and Professional Recollections*—which mentions some of his works, particularly his restoration of cathedrals. He designed buildings of every sort, including a very large number of churches. Much of his work was done by other people, but his staff 'were able to produce work which, curiously enough, did fall into something of a consistent style that passed for Gilbert Scott's, and which one can always recognise wherever one meets with it as coming from that office'. (Sir T. G. Jackson)

Scott's most characteristic churches are in a thirteenth-century style, with a great deal of carved foliage.

He considered himself to be an interpreter of the Gothic revival to the ordinary man: his success showed that he could provide people, from the Queen downward, with what they wanted.

SCOTT, George Gilbert, 1839–1897

Eldest son of Sir Gilbert Scott. He had a distinguished career at Cambridge. Author of *Essays on the History of English Church Architecture*. His few churches are very good, but he had a breakdown and withdrew from practice.

SCOTT, John Oldrid, 1842–1913

Second son of Sir Gilbert, and his pupil: he helped with many of his works—e.g. the erection of St Mary's Cathedral, Edinburgh, and the restoration of six cathedrals. He designed many churches, and restored many more. Consulting architect to the dioceses of Oxford, Ripon, and Wakefield, and to I.C.B.S.

SEDDING, John Dando, 1839–1891

In Street's office. In 1865 he joined his brother Edmund at Penzance. Edmund died in 1868, and John went to Bristol: he came to London in 1875. He was interested in all kinds of Arts and Crafts, and wanted the best in everything. His churches are generally in an eclectic late-Gothic style, but he sometimes used renaissance.

SEDDON, John Pollard, 1827–1906

Articled to Professor Donaldson. Author of *Progress in Architecture*, 1852. From 1852 to 1862 he was partner with John Prichard, and built and restored many churches in Wales. He worked on Llandaff Cathedral, and it was owing to him that Rossetti painted the altar piece. His style was influenced by foreign Gothic. He designed stained glass, and he liked to adorn his churches with painted chancel roofs and elaborate tiles.

SHAW, John, 1776–1832

A pupil of the elder George Gwilt. Architect to Christ's Hospital, and designed new buildings for it, including the Hall. Architect to the trustees of Ramsgate Harbour.

SHAW, John, junior, 1803–1870

Son of the elder John Shaw. Surveyor to Eton College, and architect of the Royal Naval School, Deptford, and of Wellington College.

SHEARMAN, Ernest Charles, 1859–1939

Articled to Charles Barry, junior, and his assistant for nine years. He concentrated mostly on church work: an obituary said that his churches have 'a simplicity and dignity all too uncommon'.

SMIRKE, Sir Robert, 1781–1867

Travelled abroad. In 1813 appointed one of the three official architects to the Boad of Works: knighted 1832. An extremely popular and prolific architect. Many public buildings in London, including the British Museum, and King's College.

SLATER, William, 1819–1872

With R. C. Carpenter, and completed some of his churches after his death. He took R. H. Carpenter into partnership.

SMITH, George, 1783–1869
Articled to R. F. Brettingham, and clerk to James Wyatt, D. A. Alexander, and C. Beazley. District surveyor to the Southern division of the City, surveyor to the Mercers' Company. etc.

SMITH, William Bassett, 1830–1901
He restored many churches, particularly in the Midlands. His new churches are not particularly original in design.

SOANE, Sir John, 1753–1837
Articled to George Dance, junior. Travelled in Italy. Architect of the Bank of England, and held several government appointments. Professor of Architecture at R.A., 1806. 'The most original British architect since Vanbrugh.' He developed a strongly personal style, using some classical elements, but was not bound by Palladian rules. (See Sir John Summerson, *Sir John Soane*.)

STREET, George Edmund, 1824–1881
Served his articles with Owen Carter at Winchester, and then went into the office of Scott and Moffatt. He became a member of the Ecclesiological Society, and in 1850 was appointed diocesan architect of Oxford. In 1855 his *Brick and Marble Architecture of North Italy* was published, and in 1856 he moved to Oxford. Street was much influenced in the 1850s by foreign Gothic; but he did not copy: he assimilated what he admired, and it contributed to his own distinctive style. His architecture was certainly inspired by his religion. He accepted wholeheartedly the Tractarian belief in the catholic nature of the Church of England; and the revived Anglican worship of the mid-nineteenth-century was entirely congenial to him. He planned his churches for this, and they suit it perfectly.

Perhaps he was at his best in small country churches: he could be simple in a way that seemed to elude some of his contemporaries.

His later churches, though extremely able, are less interesting and for many years he was kept far too busy with the Law Courts.

He was extremely careful about detail, and himself designed as much as possible. In his earlier days, he believed that an architect should work with his hands, and adorn his own buildings: he tried his hand at wall-painting. He soon realised that he had not the time for this; but he superintended everything with great care.

His son Arthur Edmund Street wrote his life, and completed some of his buildings after his death.

STREET, William Charles, 1835–1913
Practised at Walbrook: architect of various buildings in the City of London.

TAPPER, Sir Walter John, 1861–1935
Chief assistant to Bodley and Garner for many years. Architect to York Minster, and surveyor to Westminster Abbey. P.R.I.B.A. 1927–8.

TEULON, Samuel Saunders, 1812–1873
Pupil of George Legg and of George Potter. He could design churches in a perfectly orthodox style; but he liked to experiment with new kinds of Gothic that he invented for himself. He was

much in demand for recasting eighteenth-century churches in what was called a byzantinising style.

TRAVERS, Martin, 1886–1948
Trained by J. N. Comper. He specialised in baroque fittings of gilded and painted wood: an accomplished designer of glass: he was given the Grand Prix de Paris in 1925, and was instructor in stained glass at the Royal College of Art.

TRUEFITT, George, 1824–1902
Author of *Designs for Country Churches*, 1850, in which he stated his architectural creed: copyism must give way to original design: he had attempted to think in Gothic, and to forget precedent.

VULLIAMY, Lewis, 1791–1871
Articled to Sir Robert Smirke. A very prolific architect, who designed buildings in any style that was required.

WALTERS, John, 1782–1821
A London architect, who was also interested in naval architecture.

WATERHOUSE, Alfred, 1803–1905
Articled to Richard Lane, in Manchester, where he began practice. Architect of Manchester Town Hall; and then of a succession of large buildings, municipal, commercial, and educational—all well planned, and adorned with hard detail; he made great use of terra cotta. His churches were comparatively few.

WEBB, Sir Aston, 1849–1930
A pupil of Banks and Barry. Architect of the Naval College, Dartmouth, the Admiralty Arch, new front to Buckingham Palace, etc. Not primarily a church architect.

WHITE, William, 1825–1900
He studied at Leamington, then came to London, and worked with Scott: he was a friend of Street and Bodley. In practice first at Truro. Some years before his death, he was said to have built, or restored, nearly 250 churches. He was interested in correct planning and arrangement, and tried to design churches that would be both cheap and good.

WILD, James William, 1814–1892
Articled to Basevi. He travelled abroad, and studied the architecture of the Arabs.

WITHERS, Robert Jewell, 1823–1894
A pupil of T. Hellyer. He designed, or restored, nearly 100 churches, many of them in Wales. He built 'a good, cheap type of brick church'.

WOODYER, Henry, 1816–1896
A pupil of Butterfield. All his work was ecclesiastical or domestic. He lived as a country gentleman in Surrey, belonged to no societies, wrote nothing, and would not allow his designs to be published. His Gothic style is as personal as Butterfield's—though he had a very different personality; and only very occasionally—e.g. St John's, Hafod, Swansea—did he design anything that is not immediately recognisable as his.

WYATT, Thomas Henry, 1807–1880

In the office of Philip Hardwick. In partnership for a time with David Brandon. Architect of the Exchange Buildings, Liverpool, the Adelphi Theatre, the Guards' Barracks, Hyde Park, etc. A large number of churches: Wyatt was diocesan architect of Salisbury, and many of his new churches, and restorations, are in that diocese.

BIBLIOGRAPHY

General

There are so many books on London that it is difficult to make a selection. All the general surveys naturally mention the churches—e.g. J. P. Malcolm, *Londinium Redivivum*, Nichols, 1807; David Hughson, *A History and Description of London, Westminster and Southwark* (4 vols), James Robins, no date; and Thomas Allen, *The History and Antiquities of London, Westminster and Southwark, and parts adjacent*, George Virtue, 1830. *The Topographical Dictionary of England*, by Samuel Lewis, S. Lewis and Co., 1840, is useful, as for the rest of the country, so for London. John Timbs, *Curiosities of London*, Virtue and Co., 1855, contains a great deal of miscellaneous information, including 115 pages on the Anglican churches and chapels.

James Thorne's *Handbook to the Environs of London* (2 vols), John Murray, 1876, is admirable for the outlying parts. The various volumes of the *Royal Commission on Historical Monuments* are full of information, but the limitation of date is a drawback. The more recent volumes of the L.C.C. *Survey of London* have no such limitation, and mention the churches of all periods. The two London volumes of Dr N. Pevsner in the Penguin *Buildings of England* series—*London, except the Cities of London and Westminster*, 1952, and *London, the Cities of London and Westminster*, 1957—include all the important churches, and some of the others. For the Georgian period there is Sir J. Summerson, *Georgian London*, Pleiades Books, 1945.

Churches

James Paterson, *Pietas Londiniensis*, Downing and Taylor, 1714, gives an interesting picture of churches and of church life at the beginning of the eighteenth century. The title of *Ecclesiastical Topography. A Collection of One Hundred views of Churches in the Environs of London*, William Miller, 1811, sufficiently describes the book. It does not include the City, and it illustrates a good many churches that are outside the London boundaries. There are short descriptions. G. Godwin, *The Churches of London* (2 vols), C. Tilt, 1838–9, is extremely useful.

A Guide to the Churches of London and its Suburbs, by Charles Mackeson, came out annually from 1866: it contains a large amount of information, sometimes enlivened by misprints—e.g. in 1867 the surname of A. D. Gough is transmuted into Gouyn, and Basevi becomes Bagster.

I have often referred to T. Francis Bumpus, *London Churches Ancient and Modern*. This was originally published by James Pott and Co. in 1881–2; the more recent edition, by T. Werner Laurie, 1908, is in two parts: *Ancient Churches* and *Classical and Modern*.

The pre-nineteenth century churches are dealt with in G. H. Birch, *London Churches of the 17th and 18th Centuries*, B. T. Batsford, 1896; G. Cobb, *The Old Churches of London*, B. T. Batsford, 1941: and Wayland and Elizabeth Young, *Old London Churches*, Faber, 1956. M. H. Port, *Six Hundred New Churches*, S.P.C.K., 1961, gives an account of the work of the Church Building commissioners, 1818–56, and has a useful list of churches, their architects and their cost. A large number of them were naturally in London.

For the 19th century it is impossible to do without C. L. Eastlake, *A History of the Gothic Revival*, Longmans Green and Co., 1872. He too has a useful list of churches.

Architects

H. M. Colvin, *A Biographical Dictionary of English Architects 1660–1840*, John Murray, 1954, is invaluable.

Lives of particular architects that might be mentioned are, J. Elmes, *Memoirs of the life and works of Sir Christopher Wren*, Priestley and Weale, 1823; Sir John Summerson, *Sir Christopher Wren*, Collins, 1953; H. S. Goodhart-Rendel, *Nicholas Hawksmoor*, Ernest Benn, 1924; Bryan Little, *The Life and Works of James Gibbs 1682–1754*, B. T. Batsford, 1955; A. Barry, *The Life and Works of Sir Charles Barry*, John Murray, 1867; Sir G. G. Scott (ed. G. G. Scott), *Personal and Professional Recollections*, Sampson Low, 1879; and A. E. Street, *Memoir of George Edmund Street, R.A., 1824–81*, John Murray, 1888.

Histories of Particular Churches and Parishes

These are innumerable, and it is only possible to mention one or two. C. Symth, *Church and Parish*, S.P.C.K., 1955, is an admirable account of St Margaret's, Westminster, by a Church historian who sees the great issues in Church and State reflected in the life of a particular parish. St Martin in the Fields has been dealt with in several books—e.g. John McMaster, *A Short History of the Royal Parish of St. Martin-in-the-Fields*, G. Holder, 1916; and Katharine A. Esdaile, *St. Martin in the Fields New and Old*, S.P.C.K., 1944.

Judith G. Guillum Scott, *The Story of St. Mary Abbots, Kensington*, S.P.C.K., 1942, is both scholarly and readable. Bumpus dealt with his favourite St Matthias', Stoke Newington, in *An Historical London Church*, 1913. Perhaps the most thorough account of any of the parish churches is J. G. Taylor, *Our Lady of Batersey*, George White, 1925.

There are also very many smaller books. Many churches have been described in brochures and year-books which were mainly intended for the people in the parish; some are of little interest to those outside. But others contain exactly what a visitor would want to know; and the worst of them are better than nothing. The small books are often difficult to get hold of: they disappeared from the church after a year or two, and the vicar, though he is sure that he had a copy, cannot lay his hands on it. Many are to be found—if they are to be found at all—only in the reference room of the local library.

Two books which do not fit in elsewhere, might be mentioned at the end.

The third series of Charles Booth's *Life and Labour of the People in London* dealt with *Religious Influences*: the seven volumes were published by Macmillan in 1902. Booth is more interested in the Social Gospel than in the religious side of Church life, and he does not seem to see much point in worship, except as a means of improving the Working Class. But he is useful as giving a picture of the Church in its environment, at a time when the parishes were full of people, when slums were really slums, and when the suburbs were delightfully suburban.

C. Maurice Davies, *Orthodox London*, Tinsley Brothers, 1876, is a most entertaining book. Davies was a Broad churchman of wide sympathies, and also an admirable reporter: he describes his experiences in various churches, High and Low, vividly and humorously. He dressed himself— or so he says—to suit the churchmanship of the church to which he was going, and almost always enjoyed himself. His best piece of reporting is his account of a sumptuous sung eucharist at St Matthias', Earls Court, which will arouse nostalgia in elderly churchgoers: that type of service has disappeared almost as completely as the particular church in which Davies witnessed it.

INDEX OF ARCHITECTS, BUILDERS, CRAFTSMEN AND ARTISTS

303

INDEX OF CHURCHES

If a church is generally known by the name of the street in which it stands, this is given first – e.g., All Saints', Margaret Street, St Marylebone: not All Saints', St Marylebone. Churches shown *in italics* have been demolished. The numerals in **Bold Type** refer to the figure numbers of the illustrations.

GENERAL INDEX